Visionary Poetics

Visionary Poetics

MILTON'S TRADITION AND HIS LEGACY

By JOSEPH ANTHONY WITTREICH, JR.

Huntington Library

Copyright © 1979
Henry E. Huntington Library and Art Gallery
San Marino, California
Library of Congress Card Number 78–52569
ISBN 0–87328–101–2
Printed in the United States of America by Kingsport Press
Designed by Ward Ritchie

for Stuart Curran
and Kathleen Williams

Nature could no further go . . .

. . . the great Prophet may sit in heav'n rejoicing to see that memorable and glorious wish
of his fulfill'd, when not only our sev'nty Elders,
but all the Lords people are become Prophets.
—John Milton, *Areopagitica*

I will not cease from Mental Fight,
Nor shall my Sword sleep in my hand:
Till we have built Jerusalem,
In Englands green & pleasant Land.

Would to God that all the Lords people were
Prophets.

—William Blake, *Milton*

Contents

Illustrations

Preface

Poetic Genius . . . is every where call'd the Spirit of
Prophecy.
> —William Blake

. . . the real relation to a predecessor is the common
relation of both to the archetypal vision.
> —Northrop Frye

Having already explained that "it was Milton's function to
create the form of Christian vision for an English public" and
that "any attempt to continue his tradition will involve a renewed
study of his archetype, the Bible," Northrop Frye quips: "Milton
wished for nothing more than to steal as much as possible from
the Bible." And Miltonists have taken heed: a succession of books
(by James H. Sims, Michael Fixler, John M. Evans, Barbara K.
Lewalski, Christopher Hill, Austin C. Dobbins, and William
Kerrigan) has moved us beyond the tabulation of biblical echoes
in Milton's poetry to the study of individual books (Genesis, Job,
and Revelation) as they relate especially to Milton's last poems.
These studies have begun to challenge the notion that Milton's
poems are all classical in form; and those by Fixler, Hill, Dobbins and Kerrigan have demonstrated the extent to which the
·Book of Revelation shaped the concerns and even the content of
Milton's poetic visions.

It is right that these critics have turned our attention to the
Apocalypse; for if the prophetic books of the Bible, rather than

the historical or didactic ones, have sculpted Milton's vision, then the Book of Revelation, throughout the Renaissance regarded as the most perfect example of prophecy, merits special attention. Since it represents the culmination of scriptural prophecy and is the vision not just of a prophet but of the prince of prophets, the Apocalypse—the purest and highest example of prophetic poetry—was thought to contain the great code of Christian art—to be the source book, as it were, for a Christian poetics. That poetics, it appears, was appropriated by Spenser, perfected by Milton, and then delivered by them to future generations of poets. For many post-Miltonic poets, the tradition of prophecy was synonymous with a Christian poetics; and both were inextricably involved in what came to be regarded as the Milton tradition.

"Tradition," according to Harold Bloom, "is influence that extends past one generation, a carrying-over of influence." An influence on late seventeenth-century poetry, Milton by the middle of the eighteenth century had come to represent a tradition of experiment with which pre-Romantic and Romantic poets were quick to align themselves. By the end of that century, Thomas Warton observes, "the whole of Milton's poetical works" had come to participate "in one common interest, jointly and reciprocally cooperat[ing] in diffusing and forming ideas of a more perfect species of poetry. A visible revolution succeeded in the general cast and character of the national composition." Milton was undeniably the great formative influence on the Romantic poets, who were to become the conduit through which his influence would extend into the modern world. The Milton tradition—the tradition of prophecy and the whole aesthetic system it implies (what I have here called "Visionary Poetics")—is Milton's legacy, his gift to later poets, both English and American.

This is an obvious conclusion, but such conclusions sometimes require painstaking investigation and detailed proof. That is the case here, where my thesis is expounded in two monograph-length chapters: the first is an essay in criticism, taking as its subject the great tradition of English poetry, which is also the tradition of Spenser and Milton; the second is a critical essay, focusing upon Milton's first great poem, but glancing from it toward Milton's last poems, which are themselves the constituent parts of a "harmonious vision." Mindful of James Muilenburg's insistence that "the study of forms must not be isolated from the historical and theological contexts in which they exist," I have, in Chapter I, charted the trajectory of an idea, of prophecy, and thus have written the history of both a genre and an aesthetic that in Chapter II are related to *Lycidas* and to Milton's final poems. Other poems by Milton, as well as his prose works, invite attention and interpretation in the light of prophetic tradition; but these poems serve the purposes of my study best, for better than any others they incarnate this tradition, condensing and codifying it as a system, and so, as Claudio Guillén might say, these poems "symbolize other poems."

For this reason especially, I had once expected these two chapters to be accompanied by a third that would be an excursion into literary history—that would, in a systematic way, explore Milton's tradition as it impinges upon Romantic poetry. But as the present book grew in complexity and length, and as the Romantic poets' ties with this tradition became more evident, more fascinating, and came to seem more all-embracing of their poetry, it became clear that this projected chapter would have to be another quite separate book. That book, which explores prophecy as the ur-genre of Romantic poetry, is now underway; and it enables me, in the present study, to concentrate more fully on the poet who, with the assistance of Spenser, created a new literary norm, a tradition, to which the Romantic poets would be the self-appointed heirs.

The orientation of my book is historical: it is both a response to Rosemond Tuve's appeal for further study of poetry in "historical context" and a reflection of A. S. P. Woodhouse's belief that the office of historical criticism is "to recover . . . forgotten assumptions and expectations," both aesthetic and intellectual. Implicit in these chapters, moreover, is the assumption that our understanding of the historical backgrounds for Milton's poetry and of those for the Romantics' requires revision, if not rewriting. Though Rosemond Tuve issued her manifesto to Miltonists in 1957, the situation then plaguing literary criticism persists today: "the prestige of historical studies" is still "at a low ebb, and the discipline required for them unpopular"; still, it is fashionable to "cast arrows at the aridities of scholarship, and criticism without footnotes is an idol." This situation is unfortunate for various reasons, but especially because those who have broken away from the historical method have done so, in part, because they believe it has already accomplished its goals. Acquiescing in that assumption, moreover, those who regard themselves as practitioners of the historical method seem to prefer retracking the old, rather than breaking new ground. The historical critic who has seemed the spiritual enemy of the New Critic is all too eager to adopt the words of his adversary: "The work has been done, the reorientation effected."

In consequence, a major *topos* of Milton criticism at the beginning of the century persists today: Harry Beers' contention (1910) that Milton is classical in the severe sense of having abandoned Renaissance forms in order to model his last poems "on the antique, applying Hellenic forms to Hebraic material," is matched by Woodhouse's belief (1972) that, despite Milton's "theoretical conviction that the Bible will yield forms and models at least comparable with the classics," his poetry belongs to "the European classical tradition." Even those who assume that Milton excels in everything he did often exhibit a very restricted sense of what Milton was doing; for invariably they argue, as Lafcadio Hearn once did, that "the scope of . . . Milton's work was limited to classic form. There is nothing Romantic about Milton," says Hearn, thereby revealing how much we need a new literary history that will show more clearly the extent to which what Christopher Caudwell calls "Miltonic Romanticism" is one of the main sources of post-Miltonic poetry. The eighteenth century recognized that Milton made "noble use" of Scripture—that, as John Douglas claims, Milton's poetry is indebted for "the Groundwork of [its] Plan . . . to the Bible." The eighteenth century realized, too, that Milton's biblical debt, in the main, was owed to the prophets: it was reminded by Pierre Bayle in his dictionary that Milton had Isaiah read to him. This one element of what was later to be associated with Romanticism, the eighteenth century discovered, and at times coveted, in Milton's poetry. That century was as aware as the nineteenth would be that "To give the history of the bible as a *book*" (I am quoting from Coleridge's *Biographia Literaria*) "would be little less than to relate the origin or first excitement of all literature and science, that we now possess." It would be, most emphatically, to investigate the wellsprings of Milton's poetry and of its own.

"History has to be rewritten in every generation," says Christopher Hill, because "each generation . . . finds new areas of sympathy as it relives different aspects of the experience of its predecessors." A new history may not uncover what was never perceived before, but it is apt to place accents where they had never been positioned before. That, for example, is what William Kerrigan is doing when he claims "the prophetic Milton" as his own discovery. As I would do, Kerrigan is writing the history of an idea by way of developing new contexts for criticism. Yet Kerrigan also overstates, as I shall try not to do, the uniqueness of his proposition: he has not in any real sense *discovered,* though he does further substantiate and thereby accentuate, Milton's indebtedness to the Bible, especially its prophetic books. My own book was in process when Kerrigan's appeared, and the availability of his study proved a considerable advantage in writing this one. Perhaps the greatest advantage was that *The Prophetic Milton* enabled me to refocus my own work. His book, as Kerrigan explains, is a "history of prophets rather than of prophecy." My book, in contrast, presents the history of prophecy, seizing upon the historical moment when prophecy established itself as a genre; but it also peers beyond that moment, looking at another moment in history when prophecy gripped the poet's imagination and became the informing influence on his art.

Over one hundred and thirty years separate Milton from Blake's great celebration of him as England's prophet. Yet during those intervening years, Joseph Addison pointed repeatedly to Milton's use of the prophets—even to his use of the Book of Revelation; and lest the prophetic Milton seem Addison's invention, it should be remembered that, in a widely known poem, Andrew Marvell apostrophizes Milton, saying God "Rewards with *Prophesie* thy loss of sight." The very century that ferreted out Milton's classicism recognized that it nourished, and was nourished by, the biblical character of his poetry. Philip Neve was to explain, for example, that Milton is often most biblical, most Christian, "where he is thought most to follow a classic original." In eighteenth-century America, as in eighteenth-century England, Milton is placed, as George Sensabaugh demonstrates, "in the hallowed circle of singers and prophets"—Milton and the scriptural authors are regarded as peers. It is the English Romantic poets, though, who bring the prophetic Milton into sharp focus: the "blind prophet," as Wordsworth calls Milton, was said to feed on the writings of other prophets, thereby keeping "converse with God." Leigh Hunt calls Milton "the new Elijah." In Byron's view, Milton "took his text from the Old and New Testaments" and then proceeded to freeze "the blood of monarchs with his *prophecies*"; and Shelley, of course, holds a similar view of the poet. Identifying Milton as one of "England's prophets," Shelley later says that this poet "shook / All human things built in contempt of man." The prophetic—the Romantics'—Milton may recede into the background during the Victorian period; but even then, James Nelson has shown, Milton is frequently cited to exemplify the poet in his role as *vates*. Our own century, clearly, cannot be credited with discovering the prophetic Milton, but it is now in process of recovering him.

My book, then, provides an alternative perspective to a criticism that pursues Milton's classicism while ignoring his romanticism; and its perspective should serve as a corrective to those critics who, even with their historical bias and despite their vast learning, presume with Murray Roston that Milton represents a "tradition of biblical subject-matter in classical form," always turning to classical forms by way of expressing the inferiority of biblical forms and style to sublime content. Not only Roston's, but also Sir Maurice Bowra's presumption should be checked, that the Romantics were the first to combine the two roles of poet and prophet in a single art. It is evident, René Wellek observes, that admiration for the Bible as poetry "presages a new conception of poetry and . . . a new gospel"; yet such admiration does not belong to the eighteenth century alone, nor is Saint-Martin's description of "prophetic poetry [as] the only genuine poetry" a judgment peculiar to the Romantic period. Milton, for example, could give accolades to prophetic poetry because of the admiration his age bestowed upon the Bible; and he could easily subscribe to the claim made a century later by Johann Georg Hamann, that genius finds its greatest manifestations in the prophets and that "the Bible is not only the Word of God but also the highest poetry"—a poetry that instead of observing the rules rejects them. In *The Reason of Church-Government,* Milton advances his position plainly: "in them that know art, and use judgement" the abandonment of rules "is no transgression, but an inriching of art." This proposition the Romantic poets would easily comprehend.

What Bowra says of Blake—that in England he was "the first great exponent" of prophecy—is a claim that Blake (and indeed all the Romantic poets) would first make for Milton. And rightly so, for Milton and Spenser, among the Renaissance poets, best confirm Barbara Lewalski's insistence that "sixteenth- and seventeenth-century Protestant theory regarding the literary elements of scripture affected contemporary English poetry and poetics," both of which ought to discourage "the idea that Protestantism is inherently anti-literary." To be sure, Renaissance poetics is conditioned by classicism; yet that classicism is modified by a tradition of biblical aesthetics that would turn poets to prophecy, encouraging them, as it did Milton, to pattern a sacred poetry, as well as a visionary poetics, upon it.

Not all Renaissance poets follow a single theory of art, but most do combine classical and Christian elements: "Without inconsistency," John Steadman explains, the poet may turn to either or both of these sources, and he often does so even if he is un-aware of a theory that would justify his practice. Moreover, while a poet may borrow his subjects, as well as his imagery, from Scripture, he also finds there certain models. That he should prefer the biblical to the classical model, says Steadman, can be explained by the fact that the Reformation and Counter-Reformation "heightened the tension between classical and Christian traditions," which existed together as "incompatible but indispensable marital partners." Within the "quarrelsome wedlock," Steadman concludes, there is "little doubt as to where the sovereignty resided; it belonged to . . . the Scriptures." That, in any case, is true for Spenser and doubly true for Milton, both of whom turned to the prophetic books of the Bible, not just for subject matter and imagery but for artistic models as well.

What the Bible was to Milton, Milton was to the Romantic poets: they took from him what he took from it, the biblical aesthetic to which he had accommodated his poetry. Turning to Milton, Blake and the other Romantics isolated his "prophetic, apocalyptic strain—and developed it," says Lorna Sage, "until Milton begins to merge with Jesus and the Old Testament prophets of the Millennium. This is Milton in his 'eternal lineaments' " —the Romantics' Milton who is "an embodiment of the perennial revolutionary, provoking always new visions, overturning even his own certainties." It is poetic justice that the great myth maker among England's poets should himself become a myth in the Romantic period.

It may be "new," as Alastair Fowler observes, "for literary history to be branded as a system preserving the social order, a structure subserving bourgeois oppression"; but such an attitude toward literary history, if finally inexcusable, is at least understandable. The attitudes of two historical critics, Brian Vickers and Rudolf Gottfried, toward two (in their opinion) *un*historical critics, Stanley Fish and Angus Fletcher, illustrates the point. Vickers faults Fish's notions of reader harassment and of the self-consuming artifact as belonging to "a peculiar phase in twentieth-century aesthetics, . . . wholly inappropriate to seventeenth-century writers"; and Gottfried, leveling a similar charge at Fletcher, suggests that "historical scholarship . . . supplies a kind of elaborate packaging rather than real substance" for Fletcher's books, concluding, with specific reference to *The Prophetic Moment,* that it "is hollow . . . at the center of its argument"—that, in calling *The Faerie Queene* a prophecy, Fletcher distorts "the poet's meaning almost beyond recognition." Countering Fletcher's argument that *The Faerie Queene* is a prophecy, yet displaying no awareness of what a prophecy is, Gottfried suggests that only one stanza in the entire poem justifies labeling it a prophecy (III.iii.42), and then asks the question that stands behind my own book: "How well . . . does it [prophecy] account for the content and the structure of *The Faerie Queene?*" Extending that question to Milton, I shall argue that in Spenser's poetry, as in Milton's, prophecy accounts very well for both; and likewise, prophecy accounts for those aesthetic features which, focused by Stanley Fish, are so often pushed aside as new-fangled, non-historical conceptions. What the so-called unhistorical critic like Fish or Fletcher shows us through his omissions is the need for a constant interplay between history and criticism created by an analogous interplay between history and the artifact. On the other hand, avowed historical critics like Vickers and Gottfried reveal that historical and contextual studies have lagged behind interpretation which is so dependent upon both; together these scholars through their various limitations remind us of what Alastair Fowler has been recently telling us: that much of literary history has yet to be written for the first time.

Visionary Poetics, which in part is about influence, is itself a manifestation of influences. Questions raised both by Fish and Fletcher and by their critics stand behind the theoretical concerns of my own study. In it, the antithetical influence of Harold Bloom will be evident to many readers, along with the more genial influence of Northrop Frye and Christopher Hill, and of the late Kathleen Williams, whose lot it was to inspire a work she would not be burdened with reading—a work that would have been even more difficult to write were it not for her Spenser books, a gift from John B. Vickery, which are now in my library. Professor Williams read a woefully inadequate version of my first chapter, though of course she could not read the finished manuscript; and Stuart Curran, as he has done with all my others, read this book in manuscript—a particular generosity inasmuch as he had already listened patiently and repeatedly to all its arguments and unwittingly had helped to shape some of them. This book is dedicated to Stuart Curran and to Kathleen Williams; it is a gift of reciprocity to a mental prince and to a woman who was truly a queen.

In the course of writing this work, I have incurred many other debts. In our too infrequent but always intense conversations, both Ted Tayler and Joan Webber have helped to fashion many an insight that has gone into this book. My friend and colleague Raymond B. Waddington contributed so much to my intellectual life and, through conversation, so much to this book, both of his learning and critical acumen, that I was loathe to ask him, as I did others, to read it in manuscript. Carol Barthel and Andrew Weiner read and commented on my first chapter; and Richard Ide, a colleague with uncommon perception, read this study in its entirety, saving me from some lapses and saving it from many infelicities of style. During the time when the final version of this book was being written, I was fortunate in having the use of Vincent Newton's typewriter, which has produced its second Huntington Library manuscript, and in having access to Joseph Holland's impressive library. These Californian friends were a constant source of inspiration and, with James Maaske, a regular source of encouragement. When the manuscript was finally completed, I gave it to Noelle Jackson who read it attentively and typed it expertly. Julie Tonkin came to my aid once this manuscript was revised, and with comparable care typed many of its pages anew. The keen eyes of George Pitts and Neil Fraistat were strenuously exercised in reading galleys and page proof.

My research for this book has been generously supported by the Newberry Library, the Folger Shakespeare Library, the National Endowment for the Humanities, the University of Wisconsin Graduate School, the University of Wisconsin's Institute for

Research in the Humanities, and the Henry E. Huntington Library and Art Gallery. While conducting my research, I also benefited from the resources of the British Library, the New York Public Library, the Library of Congress, the Alverthorpe Gallery, and the William Andrews Clark Memorial Library. The greatest of these debts, however, is to the Director, his staff, and the fellows of the Huntington Library—James Thorpe; Virginia Renner and Mary Wright; the late Claude Simpson, Hallett Smith, and John Steadman. They all buoyed my confidence, opened my mind, enlivened my days, were generous with their learning and patient with the lapses in my own. Finally, I wish to acknowledge that in Chapter II of this book, with the kind permission of their original publishers, I have borrowed freely from two essays: "Milton's 'Destined Urn': The Art of *Lycidas*," *PMLA*, 84 (1969), 60–70; and " 'A Poet Amongst Poets': Milton and the Tradition of Prophecy," in *Milton and the Line of Vision*, ed. Joseph Anthony Wittreich, Jr. (Madison: University of Wisconsin Press, 1975), esp. pp. 111–42. Here I should also mention that in the course of revising this book, which involved considerable condensation of some sections, I have lifted materials from Chapter II, the section entitled "The Genres of *Lycidas*," incorporating them within another essay, "From Pastoral to Prophecy: The Genres of *Lycidas*," to be published in 1979 by *Milton Studies*. Readers of my book will find supplementary material in that essay.

I have left until last the acknowledgment of two people who, more appropriately, might have been mentioned first: Jane Evans and Betty Leigh Merrell. They are two of three graces presiding with Debbie Smith over the upper regions of the Huntington Library. They read this manuscript in its various states, always with wonderful sensitivity and impressive insight. Whenever this manuscript missed the mark, they adjusted my aim; wherever the manuscript was without grace, they supplied it.

JAW

The Huntington Library
San Marino, California
19 May 1977

Citations

All citations from Spenser and Milton, given parenthetically within the text, unless otherwise indicated are from *The Works of Edmund Spenser: A Variorum Edition,* ed. Edwin Greenlaw *et al.* (10 vols.; Baltimore: Johns Hopkins Press, 1943–57); *The Works of John Milton,* ed. Frank Allen Patterson (18 vols.; New York: Columbia Univ. Press, 1931–38)—I have used this edition (hereafter cited as *Columbia Milton*) for Milton's poetry and, occasionally, for his prose; and *Complete Prose Works of John Milton,* ed. Don M. Wolfe *et al.* (8 vols.; New Haven: Yale Univ. Press, and London: Oxford Univ. Press, 1953–   )—whenever possible, I have used this edition (hereafter cited as *Yale Milton*) for Milton's prose. Quotations from the Bible, unless I document them otherwise, accord with the King James version.

Visionary Poetics

Chapter I

Revelation's "New" Form:
The Recovery of Prophecy by Spenser
and Milton

New Wine requires new Bottles.

—Johann A. Bengel

The genius of the prophetic poetry is to be explored
by a due attention to the nature and design of prophecy itself.

—Robert Lowth

Prophecy is one of those bonds that unites the Middle Ages
and the early Renaissance; but thereafter, says Marjorie Reeves,
it ceases "to be of importance, except on the fringes of modern
civilization." For Reeves, as for Austin Farrer, prophecy, because
it reaches its apogee in the Apocalypse, is synonymous with that
scriptural book, though that book, both critics argue, is without
influence in the modern world.[1] Others, like D. H. Lawrence,
have thought differently. "The least attractive" and "most de-
testable" of all the scriptural books, the Book of Revelation "has
had, and perhaps still has more influence than the Gospels or the
great Epistles"—an influence that Lawrence regards as pernicious.
"The work of a second-rate mind," he concludes, the Apocalypse
"has had a greater effect on second-rate people throughout the
Christian ages, than any other book in the Bible."[2]

What Lawrence does not say, but what recent criticism has
begun to show us, is that the Book of Revelation has had an

equally great effect (and not at all a debasing one) on first-rate minds and talents—Michelangelo and Albrecht Dürer; Langland, Spenser, and Milton; Henry Fuseli and John Martin; Blake and Wordsworth; Coleridge, Byron, and Shelley.[3] From the Apocalypse, artists have derived both subjects and an iconography for representing them. So too have poets. But in addition poets have taken from John's Apocalypse the code for their art—a whole aesthetic system, together with those supports, structural and ideological, that any formally recognized genre lends to a poet. The story of the alliance between prophecy and literature does not begin in the Renaissance (it has a preludium that looks backward to Homer and Virgil, to Dante and Langland); yet its first main chapter necessarily focuses on Spenser and especially Milton, the poets who twinned epic and prophecy, and on the age that gave formal recognition to prophecy as a literary form. That recognition was accompanied by an understanding of the Revelation prophecy, of its inner workings, that persisted into the middle of the nineteenth century, both in England and America, and that through its transmitters came to exert a profound influence upon the arts. Henry Fuseli may be thought to speak for poets and painters alike when, singling out the Book of Revelation as the model for Christian art, he praises John's method there as the proper medium of art for all those committed to purveying the truths of the spirit. In such art the veil of eternity is rent— the sky is split open by revelation.

This is the kind of artistic commitment and the sort of poetic experience that the Romantic poets found here and there in Spenser's poetry and everywhere in Milton's; and thus it is in Milton, the perfecter of prophetic tradition, that these poets found prophecy's most vital conduit. Milton, they believed, took his place with the biblical prophets and stood, as Bishop Lowth once remarked, "next in sublimity"[4] to them; and Milton, they also believed, merited the designation of prophet because, like his predecessors, he played a significant role in the spiritual molding of his nation. More than any other precursor poet, Milton exemplified a tradition of art in which the poet and prophet were one ("Bards of Old / And Prophets were the same"[5])—in which the poet-prophet, both a legislator of reform and a transformer of the world, is charged with authoring poems that, apocalyptic in their intent, may be called more exactly by the name of prophecy.

However much Morton Bloomfield wished to claim *Piers Plowman* as an example of the apocalyptic or prophetic mode, he resisted doing so, explaining that "one must . . . accept as genres only literary forms defined as such before the time of the composition of the work being considered." "The chief objection to taking the form of *Piers* to be an apocalypse," Bloomfield concludes, "is that it is doubtful whether such a literary form existed."[6] Bloomfield's argument lends support to the popular supposition that the eighteenth century begins the research into prophecy that flowered during the nineteenth century; yet it ignores the fact that Renaissance commentators registered no doubts about the generic status of prophecy, tracing their understanding of the Revelation prophecy to medieval sources and then claiming it as the prototype for all true prophecy.

Of course, the process culminating in the recognition of a genre extends over a period of time and embraces several stages: poets make possible the birth of a genre, while critics ensure its acceptance. Understandably, then, an important distinction should be made between the accepted norms of literary criticism and the unwritten poetics of the same literary period. A new genre gradually becomes official, is slowly incorporated into the poetics of a period; and so, as Claudio Guillén argues, "a difference exists between the status of the model at an earlier and a later stage of the process."[7] Some evidence, certainly, suggests that the Book of Revelation came to be recognized as a genre during the Middle Ages; and the examples of both Dante and Langland suggest that, even if its poetics were uncodified, this Book had its effects upon the literature of that period. Unlike the Middle Ages, the Renaissance incorporates the Revelation model into its poetics, and it is noteworthy that the Renaissance accomplishes this codification by appealing repeatedly to medieval authorities.

5

Those authorities could easily have been literary, and for Spenser and Milton perhaps were so. They recognized, surely, that the problems consuming their attention had been faced before in poetry and that the devices appropriated for their art had been employed before. They must have recognized *Piers Plowman* as a poem full of speaking pictures; and they must have seen in its "odd and wondrous form" a difficult, complex, yet highly controlled design—a structure out of whose overlapping parts emerge new and developing patterns; a cumulative structure reflecting the "agonized unfolding of perception."[8] They must also have seen an analogous kind of structure in *The Canterbury Tales,* where each panel of story adds to what precedes it, introducing a new perspective and yielding a new perception. The prototype for such a structure is provided by the Bible, particularly by the Book of Revelation as it was interpreted by St. Augustine and St. Jerome.

From Augustine, the Renaissance commentators learned something about the design of John's Apocalypse; and, despite the reservations about this book expressed by Martin Luther, together with the fact that John Calvin demurred when it came to interpreting this book, commentators of the sixteenth and seventeenth centuries were fond of quoting Jerome to the effect that "the Revelation hath as many mysteries as words, and that in every word there is hidden manifold and secondary senses."[9] It may be that Luther held the Apocalypse "to be neither apostolic nor prophetic," arguing that "there is no prophet in the Old Testament, to say nothing of the New, who deals so out and out with visions and figures" as does John of Patmos. But then Luther leaves "everyone free to hold his own ideas"; and between 1522, when he registers these first impressions, and 1545, when he registers still others, his own idea of the Book alters. By 1545 Luther can acknowledge the Apocalypse to be a prophecy about "tribulations and disasters for the Church";[10] and he comes to regard the Apocalypse as a very special form of prophecy, composed exclusively of pictures or visions. Beginning with John Bale and continuing into the nineteenth century, exegesis on the

Apocalypse was frequent in its appearance, passionate in its beliefs, yet often divided both in its interests and conclusions. Even so, some beliefs about the work were widely shared; and the praise it elicited was often extravagant.

"Much more excellent then all the other prophecies"; "the conclusion & sum of the holy scriptures in and about those things that concerne prophecy"; "a Prophecy full of Majestie," wherein "all things are . . . delivered more distinctly and exquisitely, then ever before"; "the standard of all humane writings"; a work of "wonderfull artifice" and "singular workmanship" to which nothing in the Old Testament, not even the Psalms of David, is comparable—[11] encomia like these suggest that the Book of Revelation, attributable to Christ, had for the Christian poet more authenticity than did Aristotle's generic and aesthetic conceptions advanced in his *Poetics*. Those commentators who praise the Apocalypse for its variety and expansiveness typically argue that as a prophetic book it demands the highest veneration and attention because it "contains the most full and important series of prophecies ever bestowed on mankind" and because, "endued with a sublimer genius," it exhibits "all the splendour of poetry."[12]

Regarded during the Renaissance (as it would be in the age of Blake, Wordsworth, and Shelley) as a fully formed genre and as the source from which a Christian poetics could be derived, the Apocalypse—this "more than humane artifice"[13]—was distinguished both from other biblical prophecy and from the other literary kinds by the capaciousness of its form, by its thematic concerns and rhetorical strategies, by its distinctive structure and ideological fix. Together, these elements yielded the judgment that, excelling all other poetry in both style and subject, prophecy is necessarily the noblest of the kinds—a judgment shared by Milton himself.

In *Paradise Regained*, Jesus is emphatic: the classical forms, whether they be tragedy or oratory or epic, are far beneath prophecy, which better teaches "What makes a Nation happy, and keeps it so / What ruins Kingdoms, and lays Cities flat" (IV.363–64). Here, Milton's Jesus conveys sentiments expressed

7

by Milton himself in *The Reason of Church-Government.* There Milton writes that the prophets surpass the classical poets: "in the very critical art of composition," the prophets, he says, are "incomparable" (*Yale Milton,* 1:816). A similar view of prophecy, rooted in a reading of the Apocalypse, may have been held by Spenser—at least such a view was delivered to him by Gabriel Harvey. In a letter addressed to Spenser, Harvey writes, "I hearde once a Diuine, preferre *Saint Johns Reuelation* before al the veriest *Maetaphysicall Visions,* and jollyest conceited *Dreames* or *Extasies,* that euer were devised by one or other"; and having written this, Harvey concludes of this "superexcellent" work that it is "the verie notablest, and moste wonderful Propheticall, or Poeticall Vision"—that it is a model to which Spenser might aspire even if he does not fully realize its excellence (10:471). Milton's words, and those of Gabriel Harvey, invite a reconsideration of Michael Fixler's contention that "the imagery and themes of the Apocalpyse permeated the depths of his [Milton's] imagination, and though he may never have written vision poetry modeled on it, as Spenser had done in the *Theatre of Worldlings,* Milton owed his greatest literary debts to the imagery of the Apocalypse."[14] There is that debt, to be sure; but there is also a debt owed by both these poets to the Book of Revelation as a model: it provides the divine analogy to their art.

For poets like Spenser and Milton, the Apocalypse is the best rejoinder to Hobbes' claim that "Prophecy is not an Art."[15] To the contrary: as a model—"a faire copie . . . to write by"—the Bible, especially the Book of Revelation, exemplifies a style that is both cutting and searching, wherein "every word is . . . marshalled," every sentence given "its apt cadencie," and every syllable "so stuft . . . with substance" that matter and manner, sound and sense, always agree.[16] To take away a single word, says this commentator, is to take away the whole sense. Such an understanding extends forward in time, beyond the Renaissance into the eighteenth century. For as Frank Manuel explains (and he is following Sir Isaac Newton), there is "nothing left over, no random words . . . , no images that were superfluous."[17] Poets like Milton, about whom it can be said (as Coleridge did say) that to alter a word, or even the position of a word, is to destroy the artifact, or like Blake, who says on plate 3 of *Jerusalem* that "every word and every letter is studied and put into its fit place: the terrific numbers are reserved for the terrific parts—the mild & gentle, for the mild & gentle parts, and the prosaic, for inferior parts: all are necessary to each other"—such poets, quite understandably, turned to the Apocalypse as a model for their art. That model, they understood, "is no hastily thrown off pamphlet . . . , but a carefully studied product of tremendous . . . imagination."[18]

The Plenum of Vision

Recognizing the encyclopedic character of John's Apocalypse is an indispensable guide to understanding its genre; for that recognition unlocks the meaning of the fusion of epic and prophecy that, initiated by Spenser, is completed by Milton. Milton's idea of perfect form, like E. H. Gombrich's concept of total form, is attendant upon his discovery that individual forms, because they are pliable, submit to new combinations, new relationships, allowing for the creation of more complex orders. The very process Gombrich associates with the visual artist is by Milton associated with the prophet, who finds his archetype in Christ, his historical type in John of Patmos, and the model for his art in the Book of Revelation. That model is a composite order and in itself combines epic and prophecy which themselves are composite orders. As Bishop Lowth was to observe, epic is a mixed genre but so too, he says, is prophecy: "Some poems occur in the prophetic writings, which properly belong to the other classes of poetry," odes, for example, as well as elegies.[19] In union, as they are in Milton's poetry, epic and prophecy constitute the ultimate "transcendental form"; they represent "total form" by containing within themselves all other forms and by achieving a perfect harmony through a combination of styles.[20] The achieved form of Milton's epic-prophecies thus finds its analogue in the

9

perfect form of God's creation—a creation, as Milton describes it in *Paradise Lost,* that is teeming with "perfet formes" and mapped out in "various stile" (VII.455, V.146).

The affinities between epic and prophecy are most fully evident when epic theory of the Renaissance is juxtaposed with the aesthetic principles that biblical commentators of the same period inferred from the Book of Revelation. The modern understanding that epic, developing "from the older and commoner forms of poetry," is "the great matrix of all poetic genres," that, in keeping with the requirements for encyclopedic quality and variety, it "is one of the most complex and comprehensive kinds of literature, in which most of the other kinds may be included"[21]—this understanding is also the Renaissance understanding, and it points to an aspect of epic form evident from its very beginnings. Homer had combined epic and tragedy in *The Iliad* and epic and romance in *The Odyssey,* the two poems being so closely connected with one another that (as Lord Byron proclaimed in a note to *English Bards and Scotch Reviewers*) they may almost be classed as one grand historical poem. In both poems, Homer incorporates lyrical flights along with sustained moments of drama. Other amalgamations are attempted by Homer's successors, Virgil joining history and epic, and Dante merging comedy and epic. The Italian poets of the Renaissance combine epic with romance; and Spenser, as their principal successor in England, goes a step further, merging pastoral with the epic-romance he inherited—all this in accordance with Tasso's idea that epic, a composite form, develops by intermingling and tempering all elements and qualities.

Tasso is one poet-theorist (and I cite him because of the many congruences between his theory and the practice of Spenser and Milton) whose idea of epic attests to its inclusiveness. For Tasso, the poet's art allows great freedom—a point he demonstrates by reference to Homer, who taking "the greatest liberty, did not select a single idiom or a single style, but wanted to use them all, and did combine them all together."[22] The epic poet develops an assimilative style not by ignoring the dictum that the grand style is the appropriate one for this genre, the middle and the low

styles being the proper media for the lesser kinds, but by observing the full implications of such a dictum. If the epic poet is
to combine comedy and pastoral, history and tragedy, he is obliged
to appropriate with those forms their distinctive styles. These
various assimilations are exemplified by Virgil who, intermingling forms and styles, arranges them so that "they are, as it were,
the many steps of a theatre."[23]

Behind Tasso's view of the epic poem, which emphasizes its
dramatic character and predicates a movement toward new fulfillment and higher perfection, is his insistent belief that the poet,
like God, is a creator, and the corollary to this belief, that the
poet's universe is a replication of God's:

> I myself think it [variety] decidedly agreeable in the heroic poem
> and also possible to achieve. For just as in this marvellous domain
> of God called the world we behold the sky scattered over and
> adorned with such variety of stars, and as we descend from realm
> to realm, we marvel at the air and the sea full of birds and fish,
> and the earth host to so many animals wild and tame, with brooks,
> springs, lakes, meadows, fields, forests, and mountains, here fruits
> and flowers, there glaciers and snow, here dwellings and ploughed
> fields, there desert and wilderness; yet for all this, the world that
> contains in its womb so many diverse things is one, its form and
> essence one, and one the bond that links its many parts and ties
> them together in discordant concord, and nothing is missing, yet
> nothing is there that does not serve for necessity or ornament; just
> so, I judge, the great poet (who is called divine for no other reason
> than that as he resembles the supreme Artificer in his workings he
> comes to participate in his divinity) can form a poem in which, as
> in a little world, one may read here of armies assembling, here of
> battles on land or sea, here of conquests of cities, skirmishes and
> duels, here of jousts, here descriptions of hunger and thirst, here
> tempests, fires, prodigies, there of celestial and infernal councils,
> there seditions, there discord, wanderings, adventures, enchant-
> ments, deeds of cruelty, daring, courtesy, generosity, there the for-
> tunes of love, now happy, now sad, now joyous, now pitiful. Yet
> the poem that contains so great a variety of matters none the less
> should be one, one in form and soul; and all these things should

be so combined that each concerns the other, corresponds to the
other, and so depends on the other necessarily or verisimilarly that
removing any one part or changing its place would destroy the
whole. And if that is true, the art of composing a poem resembles
the plan of the universe, which is composed of contraries. . . .[24]

If God's universe subdues many forms and qualities to an order,
so too must the poet's. In consequence, poems in their conception
are like those pictures that portray the cosmos as a harmony of
discordant elements; and in their structure such poems resemble
those cosmological diagrams that, depicting the familiar hierarchy
of three worlds, emphasize the harmonies existing within and between these worlds (see fig. 1).[25]

This aesthetic, for those Renaissance commentators interested
in origins, was traceable to the Bible, which St. Jerome had already
celebrated as one grand epic poem,[26] and especially to the books
of the prophets, particularly of Moses and John of Patmos. During
the Renaissance, as now, the five books of Moses were regarded as
nobly varied, containing ballads and laws, concensus lists and
lyrics, all within books that are simultaneously a religious history
of Israel and its national epic. But today's question, "Could Moses
have been a master of so many literary forms?"[27] (a question now
answered in the negative), was then presented as a simple affirma-
tion: Moses excelled in many literary forms and is thus an
example for poets to follow. In the Pentateuch, Moses had successfully combined prophecy, history, and dogma; yet the very
elements here conjoined were seen in the Renaissance as the ones
that Homer and Virgil in their epics disjoined, their poems being
imperfect shadows, disfigurations, of the perfect form revealing
itself in Scripture. In *Paradise Regained* Milton has his Jesus make
precisely this point: "*Greece* from us these Arts deriv'd" (IV.
338), he says, and thereupon explains that, "ill-imitating" the
Bible, classical epics sing the vices, whereas Christian epics sing
the virtues, of their respective deities.

Milton's words here invite us to modify John Steadman's contention that Milton's own epics are "pseudomorphs." If, with

QVANT A CE QVE CHACVN DES TROIS

mondes eſt pourueu de ſa racine, quarré & Cube, tout ainſi que l'Vniuers, com-
me il apparoiſt par les nombres qui ſont hors les rondeaux, par là peux-tu enten-
dre l'Armonie & conuenance de tout, & comme peut eſtre vray le dire d'Ana-
xagore, qui mettoit omnia in omnibus & ſingula in ſingulis.

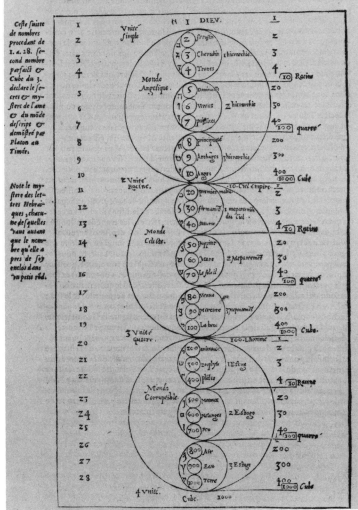

Fig. 1. A Drawing by Guy le Fèvre de la Boderie of the Numerical Structure of the World. Reproduced from Giorgio's *L'Harmonie du Monde*
(1579) by permission of the Trustees of the British Museum.

Steadman, we accept the notion that the epics of Homer and Virgil are Milton's models, then his conclusion follows. Yet Milton invites us to find his model in scripture; and if we follow Milton's lead, then we must regard the classical epic as the pseudomorph and, consequently, Milton's own epics as an attempt to return poetry to its unperverted model, which is the Bible. Steadman properly counsels that we should see the epic tradition as it appeared to men of the seventeenth century. To do this, though, is to arrive at a conclusion different from the one that he proposes; for both Spenser and Milton, it appears, selected a scriptural model for their epics and thus would revise Steadman's belief—that "epic appears to have been . . . a continuing pseudomorphosis"—to read instead that the epic effort they initiated was an attempt to break such a pattern of perversion and to return epic to the morph of scripture.[28]

For this reason, important distinctions were fashioned—between the classical epic of memory and the Christian epic of inspiration, between Old Testament prophecies and the New Testament prophecy of John. The Bible had a special place within epic tradition; and within the context of prophetic tradition, John's prophecy held unique status. Various books of the New Testament contained prophetic interludes and expatiated on the nature and efficacy of prophecy, but only the Apocalypse was wholly and expressly prophetic; or within the compass of the two Testaments. While other prophecies embodied the visions of their respective authors (of Isaiah, Ezekiel, and Daniel), John's prophecy recorded a vision, a revelation, of Jesus Christ.[29] The classical epic falls short of the perfect form of scripture; and Old Testament prophecy, no less, falls short of the perfect form achieved in and represented by the Book of Revelation. That Book, therefore, was thought to embody a vision, an aesthetic, and an ideology that earlier prophecy only approximated.

The Apocalypse, like epic, may lay claim to being "a posy of all flowers, a vision composed out of all visions" inasmuch as it participates in the general cunning of the New Testament which subsumes the classics, "the one . . . sunne to the other"; and inasmuch as "all the types in Moses's law, and all the stories and visions of the prophets, are borrowed to adorn it."[30] Like Hebrews, which "abridgeth all the Bible,"[31] John's epic-prophecy is a summation, an epitome, of all earlier visions and of all scriptural wisdom. "Nothing of importance can bee found in the Christian world, which may not be referred to some part of this booke"—a book, says William Symonds, that in its considerations is "more abundant than the sea" and in its "counsell profounder than the great deepe."[32] If everything coming before it could be said to relate the history of the world from Creation through the First Coming, this Book, in its brief compass, completed that history, extending from the advent of the church and recounting its history until the Second Coming. Epics may reveal the destiny of a nation; but the epic-prophecy of John's Apocalypse, in the words of Morton Scott Enslin, reveals a "vision of the destiny of the world."[33] This understanding, so often asserted by Renaissance commentators, persists into the late eighteenth century, which was reminded that the Book of Revelation "reaches from the day of St. John to the grand and final tribunal" when "time shall . . . be swallowed up in eternity."[34] Or if one wishes to accept Henry Bullinger's contention that the church is part of the first creation, then he is obliged to accept the corollary to that belief, that the Book of Revelation is designed to span all time—to encompass the history of the world.[35]

Regarded as an expansive vision, the Book of Revelation spread "infinitely farre and wide, like as in the heaven it selfe, that contayneth all things within the Circuit thereof";[36] it accorded, in every sense, with Tasso's insistence that epic embraces the world in all its variety:

> . . . this book is full of similitudes fetched from every thing: *from heaven,* sun, moone, and starres: *from* the rain-bow, windes, haile, thundering, and lightening; *from* the ayre, fire, water, sea, rivers, fountaines; *from* the earth, and earth-quakes, Ilands, and mountaines; *from* foules, fishes, beasts, and creeping things; *from* Angels, and men; *from* trees, grasse, greene hearbs; *from* wild wildernesses, and Cities inhabited; *from* warre hosts, and armies the sword, and battell, horses and Chariots, with triumph and victorie; *from* high callings, Princes, Kings, Priests, & Prophets, Merchants,

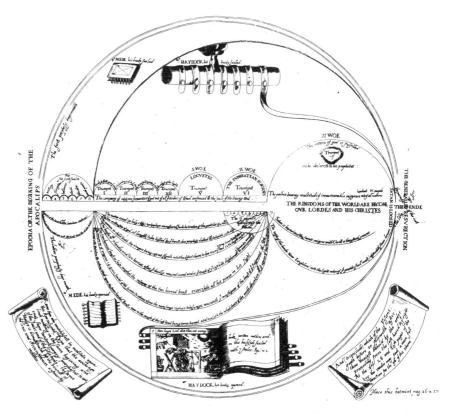

Fig. 2. A Diagram Illustrating Joseph Mede's Conception of Revelation's Structure. Reproduced from Mede's *The Key of the Revelation* (1643) by permission of the Huntington Library, San Marino, California.

and seamen; *from* thrones, crownes, and seates; *from* musicke, and musicians, pipers, trumpetters, harpes, viols, and sound of voices; *from* rayment, long robes, golden girdles, fine white linnen purple, silke, and scarlet . . .[37]

Yet this world of particulars, says Richard Bernard, is forever subordinate to a sense of world order: unity envelops multeity in an articulate order (see figs. 2 and 3).

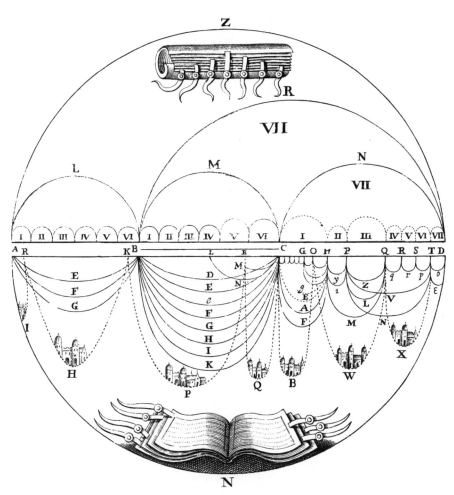

Fig. 3. A Diagram Illustrating Henry More's Conception of Revelation's Structure. Reproduced from More's *Apocalypsis Apocalypseos* (1680) by permission of the Folger Shakespeare Library, Washington, D. C.

In various ways, the Book of Revelation is, before the fact, a fulfillment of Tasso's idea of the epic poem. Not only does it join with history, representing all time under the aspect of eternity, but it spurns the rules of art, which, "knit[ting] up . . . dictates systematically," are a "human contrivance"[38] congenial enough to a poetry of imitation but incompatible with a poetry of inspiration. The inclusiveness that Tasso associates with epic derives from prophecy, which is "made by the fusion of all literary forms in one" and which, while giving "the realistic emphasis of dramatic presentation to its ideas," still remains "free at any point to abandon drama for discourse or lyric meditation."[39]

Like the epics of Homer and Virgil and the prophecies of the Old and New Testaments, the Book of Revelation encompasses the extremes of style, the one plain and simple in its opening chapters, the other difficult and enigmatic in its later ones.[40] It accomplishes by itself what the other books of the Bible achieve collectively: the fusion of literary and oral traditions, of borrowed literary forms and genuine prophetic forms of speech; the union, according to Hugh Broughton, of Aeschylean tragedy and Homeric epic, of lyrics and comedies, of history, philosophy, and oratory.[41] Like the *Sibylline Oracles,* it is a "mixture of hymns, ecstatic and mystical writing, historical narrative, and prophecy";[42] but unlike these oracles, its assimilation of various forms is not disorderly but part of an elaborate design founded upon a sophisticated conception of order. What has been perceived of *The Faerie Queene* may be extended backward to the Apocalypse and forward to the visionary poems of Milton and his Romantic successors: like Spenser's epic-prophecy, all these works reproduce the structure of the cosmos in its variety and extremes; like Spenser's poem, they are literary microcosms, gathering all forms into one central form,[43] thereby making, in Milton's words, "a kind of creation like to Gods" (*Yale Milton,* 1:721).

Poets, George Puttenham instructed the Renaissance, are "creating gods": like God, they contrive a universe out of their own brain.[44] God and the poet, then, are creators who relate to one another much as their respective creations relate each to the other.

Not a mere facsimile, or counterfeit creation, the poet is himself an image of God and his poem an inspired revelation of the Creation. The poet's objective takes him beyond simple, or even sophisticated, mimesis—beyond imitating existing forms into copying the perfect eternal forms. In this way, the poet can penetrate and express the secrets of creation; and by so fashioning literary analogues to God's creation, the poet identifies himself as a true visionary who both views "the sacred Forms" and *"perceives mentally* what the design of God is."[45] The literary microcosm thus becomes the prophet's chief credential: having penetrated the secret of creation—its design—he is uniquely qualified to speak of, to become a shaper of, history, which will bring God's design to fulfillment.

Yet, more than just an aggregate of forms, the Book of Revelation came to be understood as a multi-media performance, as a model for what Henry Howard termed "painted prophesies."[16] If medieval Christianity consecrated the book, it also, as Ernst Curtius has shown, resolved the perennial controversy between word and picture by urging the combination of the arts;[47] and such urgings found scriptural sanction in the idea that Revelation's prophecy, itself uniting the sister arts, was a scroll book. Thus Marjorie Reeves can speak of Joachim of Fiore's "pictorial prophesyings of new spiritual men" and of the vogue this mode of prophecy enjoyed in both the later Middle Ages and early Renaissance; and the same tradition, not without imitators, is remarked upon by Rupert Taylor in his study of political prophecy in England, especially during the English Revolution.[48] By the time of Martin Luther certainly, this alliance was a well-established fact. There are three kinds of prophecy, says Luther in his 1545 Preface to the Apocalypse: Moses' kind which consists only of words, Daniel's which combines words with symbols, and, lastly, John's which is purely visionary, consisting only of pictures, and which thus remains "a concealed and dumb prophecy" until the pictures, interpreted, are made to yield up hidden meaning.[49] Calvin expresses a similar idea when he distinguishes between revelation, which is often in words, and vision, which is presented directly to the eye.[50] The assumption, then, is that Christ's vision is presented initially as a picture; for John's sake (and ours) that vision is preserved as a book, this time with words accompanying the pictures; and this book, in turn, is translated by John into the Apocalypse, into its verbal icons.

The implication of all this for English art has recently been drawn out by Ronald Paulson: "Revelation in the New Testament is visual. . . . But in the Old Testament . . . it is aural. . . . 'Literary' England was a country that traditionally hewed to the religion and world view that preferred the word to the image," thereby forcing upon us the paradox of visionary sound.[51] There is an irony here that would not have escaped poets like Spenser and Milton and Blake: Christ came, the New Testament was written as a fulfillment of the Old; the New Testament then— prophecy as vision—should be the prophet's model. Assuming the New Testament as a model, moreover, meant turning to the Book of Revelation, where prophecy designed for human consumption is represented by the book given by Christ to John—by a book in which word and picture collaborate in the articulation of a prophecy.

This whole view of the Apocalypse is popularized by the various seventeenth-century editions of Joseph Mede's *The Key of the Revelation* (see fig. 4). One Mr. Haydock queried Mede on the nature of the sealed book, eliciting from him the admission that Mede himself had entertained the idea that "those visions concerning the Seals were not written by Characters in letters, but being painted in certain shapes, lay hid under some covers of the Seals; which being opened, each of them in its order, appeared not to be read, but to be beheld and viewed." The words of John, *Come and see,* agree with such an apprehension, says Mede; but still there is evidence for believing that some parts of this prophecy were verbalized, not perhaps in simple but in representational writing. For Mede therefore, as for Haydock, the sealed book, a picture-prophecy, is an exemplary emblem book conceived in such a way that the pictorial and verbal are joined together. Conceding this much to Haydock, Mede goes on to

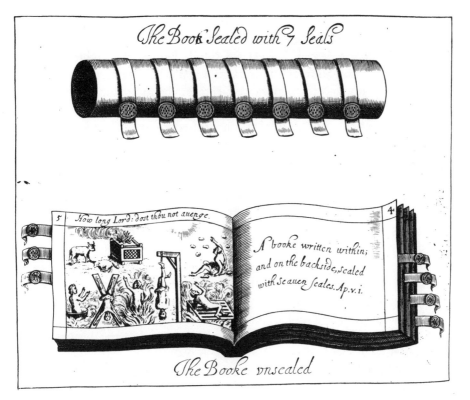

Fig. 4. Mr. Haydock's Idea of the Sealed Book. Reproduced from *The Works of Joseph Mede* (1664) by permission of the Huntington Library, San Marino, California.

argue, however, that John and Christ are so distanced from one another that John himself could not see into the book and so must have it translated verbally by Christ.[52] At issue here is not the nature of prophecy but rather the question of how prophecy should be transmitted; and at issue, too, is the nature of the book itself—what did it look like? how was it constructed, and thus what was it like once it was opened?

Adopted by Henry More and, subsequently, by most eighteenth-century commentators, Mr. Haydock's description of prophecy as a series of rolls, each to be opened in its order, provides an alternative to D. H. Lawrence's belief that the rolled up scroll "could not *actually* be opened till all seven seals were broken"; and Haydock's description clearly stands behind the eighteenth-century's explanation of the book as a roll where each seal, when broken, presents to the viewer certain hieroglyphic figures.[53] Samuel Langdon, for example, explains that "we may be sure that this roll consisted of a principal one, rolled inmost in the smallest size, which contained the most important matters, and was sealed separately; and of the six others rolled over it one after another, as so many covers to the principal one, each of which had also a separate seal: And so by breaking the seals of these covers, one after another, the contents of all were made known, before the inmost roll was opened."[54] Or as Thomas Newton proposes, "we should conceive this book, that it was such a one as the ancients used, a volume or roll of a book, or more properly a volume consisting of seven volumes, so that the opening of the one seal laid open the contents only of one volume."[55] Opening the seals, then, is like negotiating a labyrinth: when one reaches the center, when he comes to the innermost roll, he reaches the heavenly city, the source of all true vision (see fig. 3).

Mede is perhaps the most influential of the seventeenth-century commentators; but on the crucial detail regarding the nature of the book, Haydock rather than Mede seems to have prevailed, chiefly because the Book of Revelation came more and more to be seen under the lights provided by William Perkins' insistence that the kind of revelation experienced by John of Patmos is partly by vision, partly by voice.[56] Perkins' point is emphasized by various depictions of John composing (see fig. 5): he may be busy translating his vision into verbal equivalents, but the vision he experiences through the book given to him by Christ contains both pictures and words. The tradition of picture-prophecy, then, has the effect of prodding the prophet into getting back to origins, his objective being not the translation of vision into words but the experience of vision itself, which involves pictures together with words. Haydock and More were emphatic on this point, and so too was George Stanley Faber in the early nineteenth century.

Fig. 5. John of Patmos Composing. Reproduced from the extra-illustrated *Kitto Bible,* volume 60, by permission of the Huntington Library, San Marino, California.

23

Prophecy, says Faber, a mode of composing affecting "hieroglyphical grandiloquence," speaks by pictures quite as much as by sounds. And it is the Book of Revelation—"a continued hieroglyphic"— that Faber singles out as exhibiting "the most perfect and systematic specimens of Hebrew hieroglyphical composition."[57] This is precisely the proposition set forth by Blake in Night VIII of *The Four Zoas:* John *"saw* these things Reveald in Heaven / On Patmos Isle & *heard* the Souls cry out to be deliverd / He *saw* the Harlot . . . & *saw* her Cup" (my italics). Reaching back to origins, its purpose being to restore the Word, prophecy thus aspires to return poetry to it original condition—a condition under which all the arts partake of one another—thereby liberating the artist from the limitations, and his audience from the monotonies, of any single art form. All this proceeds from an aesthetic system, inferred from the Book of Revelation, which was said to involve a way of seeing, of "forc[ing] open our eyes";[58] and that system, in turn, imposes certain obligations on the visionary artist.

Poets who would designate themselves as prophets are expected to include visionary scenes figuratively (as Spenser and Milton do by letting verbal description be determined by iconographic traditions) or quite literally (as Blake does by creating poems that are firmly ensconced in this tradition of the pictureprophecy).[59] In this way, Spenser and Milton raise their poems to the status of word-pictures, while Blake, observing prophetic tradition to the letter, establishes a truly collaborative relationship between word and picture. His poems are, in the strictest sense, picture-prophecies.

The poetry of all these poets is "pictorially energized."[60] Not simply descriptive (indeed to be distinguished from simple description), this pictorialism involves the imitation of visual processes; it creates visual impressions, or images, in order to render visual experiences; and such experiences are a continual assault on the reader's mind, on his interpretive faculties. The effect of this pictorialism is to open the eye, guiding the mind through spaces it has not traveled before; the impetus behind such pictorialism is the poet's wish to encompass all experience and, attendant upon that wish, his search for a scheme to contain it. In either case, the poet is intent upon transcending the limitations of his medium by devising for literature a new optical system, an intention he accomplishes by spurning the boundaries of any single form, achieving an interpenetration of the arts, and in the process literalizing Sidney's metaphor, which portrays poetry as a speaking picture. All prophets, then, may at times feel as Byron's Dante does, that "I cannot all record / That crowds on my prophetic eye"—but they try. The prophet knows that sight which "is freed from all limitation embraceth at one and the same time each and every mode of seeing"; and consequently he regards prophecy as "the most adequate measure of all sights, and their truest pattern."[61] What Joan Webber describes as characteristic of epic poetry is the motive force behind prophecy: "To probe and extend the limits of human consciousness."[62]

For the prophet, partial consciousness is no consciousness—consciousness by his definition being infinite. If Roland Barthes is right, that poetry and painting represent completely different kinds of consciousness,[63] then we may conclude that either poetry or painting by itself is partial consciousness at best. That, in any event, seems to have been the conclusion of Spenser and Milton and, later, of the Romantic poets. Expanding consciousness, extending it into the infinite—these objectives require a transcendental form, one capable of subsuming all perspectives; they necessitate one central form capable of embracing all others. What is created, then, is a transcendental form whose objective is transcendental vision. Prophecy is, these poets would say with Blake, "Ideal Form, The Universal Mold." A perfect literary microcosm, prophecy is a new creation revealing the secret of all creation, whereby order is brought out of chaos and unity wrested from division.

Epic poets and prophets alike are theorists of vision, both concerned with expanding man's consciousness by emancipating his senses; but within that likeness there is this difference. If epic articulates a new stage of consciousness, prophecy is more ambitious still, attempting to bring man to the highest stage of consciousness that is possible, its objective being not to equip man to live in an advancing state of civilization but to enable him to enter the heavenly Jerusalem. Epic may record a culture's shift from one state of consciousness to another as the old culture is invaded by a new one, and as it discovers a need for values more permanent and enduring than those it is the heir to; but prophecy would alter the very eye by which the new culture has conceived of itself. This it accomplishes by altering the eyes of the populace on the assumption that the eye altering alters all—that by bringing individual men to the pinnacle of vision, the ultimate state of consciousness will be realized. Prophecy thus locks arms with epic—but only so that it may advance beyond it, so that it may become, in Wordsworth's phrase, "Of quality and fabric more divine."

The Strategies of Vision

Prophecy, for all its variables, contains a set of thematic constants: it postulates a providential pattern for a creation that in the course of history has become deformed. The prophet's objective is to re-form history—an objective dependent upon the renovation of individual men. Since apocalypse occurs only after mankind is readied for it, the prophet submits others to the processes of purgation and purification which, inwardly directed, result in mankind's transformation into a race of visionaries. Committed to brightening the mind, to exalting and purifying all its faculties, the prophet employs a series of strategies designed to force open the doors of perception, teaching men to see not *with* but *through* the eye. This master theme of prophecy is advanced through strategies and embodied in a structure that underpins the ideology of prophecy.

The themes and strategies of prophecy, the subject of much commentary on the genre, invite special attention—the kind of attention that caused Milton to observe of the Gospels, whose capstone is the Apocalypse, that they soar "to a Prophetick pitch in types, and Allegories" (*Yale Milton,* 1:714), and to say of the Book of Revelation that it is invested with a style that enables both ordinary men to assume the designation of angels and angels to adopt the name and person and very words of God—a style, moreover, that justifies the practice of holding the Father and the Son distinct and separate (as John of Patmos does in his Book of Revelation and as Milton, following John's example, does throughout *Paradise Lost*). Prophetic style is, for Milton, a vehicle for the "irksomnesse" of truth, which leads him to speak of "that mysterious book of Revelation which the great Evangelist was bid to eat" as an "eye-brightning electuary of knowledge, and foresight"—of knowledge at once painful and sublime—and which causes him to conclude that John's Apocalypse is "the majestick image of a high and stately Tragedy" (*Yale Milton*, 1:803, 815). Such proclamations accompany an impulse on Milton's part to identify with John of Patmos, Milton thereby asserting for himself a prophetic equality with John and so claiming for his art what already had been claimed for John's: that full of the deepest mysteries, it is made for elephants—"the very highest" ones, says Richard Bayly—to swim in but "not for Lambes to wade in."[64]

The fallen world, as Byron recognized in *A Prophecy of Dante*, consigns men to a condition in which they "are debased / By servitude and have the mind in a prison"; the intention of prophecy is to liberate men from such a condition—as Jesus explains in *Paradise Regained*, to liberate "inward slaves" so that they may be "outward free" (IV.145). Accordingly the prophet is a new Prometheus bestowing light from heaven—a bestower not of knowledge already disseminated through a culture but of knowledge about to be extended, as revelation, to it. The purpose of John's prophecy is to reverse the effects of the fall and, through the complications of its artistry, to bring individual men to their awakening—their first resurrection—so that mankind can be readied for the general resurrection. Poetry that is prophecy is thus fulfilled only when it can be said to precipitate man's entry into being. That is why prophetic poets, following the lead of John of Patmos, focus their attention so sharply upon man's first resurrection, an event accomplished only after man's senses have been purged and he has learned to see anew.

The Book of Revelation is what its title implies: a new vision set forth by Christ and set down by John, a vision that remains sealed until those visions it opens and expounds are comprehended. John's prophecy is about *seeing,* and thus the processes of understanding are involved in its various strategies. Indeed, those processes are focused by the book's title and then its prologue, both calling attention to the fact that the revelation proceeds from God to Christ, to the Angel who instructs John, to the Seven Churches which are instructed by him.[65] Furthermore, the Book's title asserts that John's Prophecy "is an Apocalypsis, and not an Apocrypsis"; not a sealing up of mystery but an unfolding of it, the Book of Revelation uses "concealment" as a device of "revealment."[66]

The prophet, as Bishop Lowth was to observe, is "naturally free, . . . too ardent a spirit to be confined by rule";[67] and so, just as prophecy does not endorse the orthodoxies of society, neither does it observe the rules of art that have been systematized into dictates. Henry More is emphatic on this point:

> . . . God has not made the Scriptures like an artificial Garden, wherein the Walks are plain and regular, the Plants sorted and set in order, the Fruits ripe, and the Flowers blown, and all things fully exposed to our view; but rather like an uncultivated field, where indeed we have the ground and hidden seeds of all precious things, but nothing can be brought to any great beauty, order, fulness or maturity, without our own industry. . . .[68]

The labor required in the course of reading a prophecy, also acknowledged by Ludowick Muggleton, testifies to the limitations of reason:

> . . . none of the seed of reason . . . can see the face of scriptures; that is the truth and spirit of them.
>
> But seeth them darkly, as in a glass; so that it may be clear that the seed of reason is always under a cloud, or seeth as in a glass.

. . . the letter of the scripture is as a vail before reason's face, because reason cannot see forth in the letter of the scripture by literal and temporal expression.[69]

Within this context, it should be remembered that often in prophetic literature the devaluation of reason is accompanied by the exaltation of the imagination. When prophecy becomes a philosophical problem, then, as Morton Bloomfield explains, imagination itself becomes a subject of concern: "All writers on prophecy had to give the imagination a place of some importance,"[70] as is attested to by the key role that Langland assigns to Imaginatif in the instruction of Will and that the Romantic poets give to this faculty in their poetry. According to *The Prelude,* a poem that declares itself to be a prophecy, imagination is the "auxiliar light" which bestows "on the setting sun / . . . new splendour"—which, "when the light of sense / Goes out," with a flash reveals the invisible world.

Though new vision is the prophet's final goal, his immediate strategy is to pull away the veils of deception that, clouding the spiritual eye, conceal the truth. Prophecy about deception (the enticement of the Whore), says Richard Bernard, employs deception as a surface glitter, thus scoring the idea that appearances are always being controverted by reality. The test of the hero in prophetic poetry, as well as the test of the reader, measures the ability of both to pierce appearances and to grasp reality. In *Paradise Lost* and *Paradise Regained,* no less than in *The Faerie Queene,* disguises engage protagonists and readers alike in an unmasking process: both experience, or should experience, an epiphany; and that epiphany is marked by an unveiling, a sudden recognition of error—an apocalypse. In such moments, protagonist and reader are able to say with the Jesus of *Paradise Regained,* "I discern thee other then thou seem'st . . . plain thou now appear'st" (I.348, IV.193). Una speaks comparably in *The Faerie Queene:* after Arthur's unveiling of the whore, the knights all stand "amazd" as Una says, "Such is the face of falshood, such the sight / Of fowle *Duessa,* when her borrowed light / Is laid away, and counterfesaunce knowne" (I.viii.49). In *Paradise Lost,* after his long and embarrassing deception by Satan (here even the angel Uriel is deceived), Milton's reader is brought to the same perception. Through such episodes, signally important to prophetic literature, Spenser and Milton would argue, as Richard Bernard does, that truth is to be sought after, and finally discovered, only through this mental exercise and only with the aid of great learning and knowledge, all this in keeping with the premise that "Spirituall things are spiritually discerned . . . and by the spirit must be taught, without which, though the words bee never so easie and plaine, the reader shall not see what is before him. If God open not our eyes, we shall remaine blinde, and not behold what is before us in the open Sun-shine."[71] The spiritual eye, not the natural eye, is what matters in the reading of prophecy —to open it is the prophet's obligation, which he meets by designing a set of strategies through which the reader, by labor, can achieve Jerusalem.

One of these strategies, generic mixture, has already drawn our attention; another is obscurity, a veil that can be penetrated only by the spiritual eye; and yet another is that "multifarious Allusivenesse"[72] which turns prophecy into a literature of contexts. Those allusions "make plaine the truth" by clearing away the obscurity of prophecy; and erecting the contexts that have been called "directing and multiplying glasses,"[73] they gradually enlarge and perfect man's understanding, having the effect, finally, of pushing the reader beyond the confines of any one prophecy— back into the earlier prophecy out of which the new one is made and forward into the world where it is eventually to be fulfilled. Both the obscurity of prophecy and its allusiveness are calculated to generate an antagonistic relationship between the prophet and his audience, a relationship founded upon that of a physician and patient, of a teacher and pupil. The Christ who appears to John, first in the Vision of the Candlesticks and then as the Mighty Angel with a book made for ingestion, comes as "the Sovereign Physician" and, in accordance with the formulation, "the Father creates, the Son *teaches,* the Holy Spirit exults," as man's teacher.[74]

The posture adopted by Christ in relation to his prophets is subsequently adopted by the prophet in the relationship he establishes with his audience.

Not only is prophecy *like* God's creation—a gathering of forms and styles; prophecy *is* creation—out of preexistent matter. Because the Book of Revelation was said to look back to all the visions of the Old Testament and to use them, the poet-prophets who took John for their model proceeded to study old prophecies by way of creating new ones; they gave to their precursors the same diligent study that Daniel gave to Jeremiah and that John gave to Daniel. Whichever pairing of prophecies is studied, the comprehension of the new prophecy is dependent upon first comprehending the old one. This understanding was commonplace during the Renaissance and persisted into the eighteenth and nineteenth centuries. For Thomas Newton, the prophecies of the Old and the New Testaments, when "considered and compared together, . . . mutually receive and reflect light from and upon each other" and so possess "a visible connexion and dependency," forming a harmony, with one prophecy augmenting another.[75] And Christopher Wordsworth observes that words and phrases are tenaciously repeated in the Book of Revelation so as to connect one portion of the prophecy with another; through these *"catchwords,"* he continues, not only is John's prophecy made to cohere in its various parts, but it is thus "interwoven with the prophecies of the Old Testament . . . , form[ing] a compact whole with them."[76]

In prophecy, what is important is not the truth contained by it but the truth to which it provides access. Prophecy is consumed—it is the ultimate "self-consuming artifact" in both senses that Stanley Fish attributes to his phrase—a phrase which finds biblical sanction in Revelation's metaphor of "eating the book" (10:9–10). "Eating the book," says Isaac Newton, "is becoming inspired with the prophecy contained in it"; it "implies being inspired with the prophecy of the whole book, and therefore signifies a living repetition of the whole prophecy by way of interpretation."[77] Prophecy, until it is comprehended, may turn back upon itself; but ultimately it points beyond itself—to the truths attainable through its underlying processes. Through them, as Fish well knows, "the reader's self (. . . his inferior self) is consumed," and because of them the artifact itself "is consumed in the workings of its own best effects"—"it becomes the vehicle of its own abandonment."[78] Such art battles against the mental obstacles that keep men entombed; it is engaged in a process of liberation that rolls stones away from the mind, thus allowing light to enter the mind and to stream forth from it. Behind the self-consuming artifact—behind all prophecy—is the notion that the reader's experience is primary; and his experience can be primary only if he can *hear* what is said and *see* what is shown to him.

For those who see with the spiritual eye, prophecy is decipherable; but deciphering it depends not just on the power of its allusions but on the discernment of the reader. Unless he penetrates the contexts of allusions, the book will remain sealed; it will stand as a self-enclosed, self-contained work of art (the static artifact prized by New Criticism) until by a successful reading its pages are opened and its visions consumed. Prophecy is a mode of reflection, operating in accordance with the precept that "Reflection about the prophets gives way to communion with the prophets."[79] Prophecy remains obscure, then, until the reader grasps a primary principle of its aesthetic: prophecy is a literature of contexts, depending upon the power of its allusions to return men to their source. Old prophecy thus sheds the light that will guide men on their "mental journey through the mazes and turnings and dark passages"[80] of new prophecy modeled on the Book of Revelation.

Contexts outside prophecy cast light upon its meaning but so, too, do the contexts developed within it. The various visions of any given prophecy act as interpreters for all that goes before them, so that the "third vision is as it were a Commentary or more cleere exposition of . . . the second vision" just as the second is a gloss on the first.[81] In prophecy, the movement is toward clarity, with the result that, while the first half of John's prophecy is enigmatic, the last half is "more plain and neerer matched and fitted to the events"; or, as Thomas Newton explains, the various visions that comprise the Book of Revelation receive light from one another, so that "together they are as it were a chain of prophecies, whereof one link depends on, and supports another."[82] Like the *Aeneid,* which was often said to exemplify the prophetic method, the articulation of John's prophecy "is conducted in such a manner as to open by degrees";[83] the breaking of each seal denotes a new discovery, an unfolding of visionary meaning, the breaking of yet another manacle as the mind moves progressively toward total consciousness. The prophetic method liberates the mind by combining individual prophecies with introductory visions that are shrewd directions for apprehending the structure and thus the meaning of a prophecy. Within each prophecy, vision combines with commentary, the obscurity of the one being mitigated by the clarity of the other. Yet any vision, once penetrated, moves the reader closer to the city; and progressing from vision to vision, the reader finds himself continually bursting confines, breaking seals. Each vision is, then, an exit into another higher vision. The process is continuous, each exit accomplished after a different set of obstacles has been negotiated, each entrance signifying a new stage in the purification of vision. Each portal is reached after more film has been removed from the eyes and opens into a vision that redefines what it succeeds, deepening its significance and purifying our understanding of its meaning. The design of these collateral visions, as Isaac Newton was to say very early on, makes one part of prophecy a key to another—"this is true opening scripture by scripture."[84]

The process, here ascribed to the Book of Revelation, is like the one that Stanley Fish traces to the Platonic-Augustinian tradition. Within the artifacts belonging to that tradition, Fish finds "a mimetic enactment of the reader's experience of the Platonic ladder in which each rung, as it is negotiated, is kicked away." In such artifacts, Fish says, words cease pointing to themselves or to other objects in the field of vision and instead become trained on the "vision developing *within* the reader-respondent."[85] Thus, by pointing away from itself, prophecy proclaims its own insufficiency as well as the insufficiency of the frame of reference from which it issues; and by pointing beyond itself, literally both in the direction of other prophecy and toward those who are its recipients, and metaphorically out into the world where it is to be accomplished, prophecy also reminds us that vision, unless it inspires action, is nothing, the mental activity involved in its interpretation being a correlative of the later activity that will effect its implementation.

Thus the prophet, like the epic poet, assumes a legislative function, which is embodied in Milton's belief that his poetry should be doctrinal to the nation, in Blake's idea that empire should be made to follow him, and in Shelley's insistence that the poet is the unacknowledged legislator of the world. After Tasso this legislative responsibility becomes increasingly more of an obsession to the poet, especially after epic joins with prophecy, whose history involves "the delicate problem of the interplay between word and action," and attests to the fact that the prophet, often thought to foretell the future, more exactly attempts to fashion it.[86] Like the epic poet, the prophet may recount history; but his purpose is less to record it than to bring it to an apotheosis. Historical patterns are drawn not for their own sake but to find a release from them. The "drama" of history is what preoccupies the prophet, who finds a source and an analogue for that drama in the structure of prophecy and in the relationship he strikes with his audience.

During the Renaissance, epic is gradually invested with the dramatic spirit of prophecy. Yet, while dramatic, prophecy was never thought to be dramatic in any ordinary sense; rather, its drama is like that of the Apocalypse—plotless. Not concerned with outward action, prophecy instead expresses and reveals the mind of a character, thereby interiorizing dramatic form. Prophecy, we shall see, is dramatically structured, its structure founded upon a dramatic tension first visible in the way the prophet responds to his source of vision and then evident in the posture he assumes toward his audience. So it is that Spenser's muse relates to him just as he relates to his reader. Within his poem, Spenser figures both relationships through the stories of Arthur's education by Merlin and even by Redcrosse. Both Spenser and Arthur receive from their teachers a vision; both, like John of Patmos, must either *write* what they have *seen* or translate it into act (see Revelation 1:19). But also, like Christ in the Book of Revelation, both deliver their visions in the form of a book, Spenser in *The Faerie Queene* deliberately invoking a comparison both between his gift to the reader and Redcrosse's gift to Arthur and the Mighty Angel's gift to St. John.[87] Similarly, through *Paradise Lost*, Milton gives to his readers a book correspondent to the visions extended to him by Christ, and to Adam (at different times) by Raphael and Michael.

The prophet, whether he be John of Patmos or Merlin, Spenser or Milton, does not search for God's vision; he is elected for it, and a condition of his election is that he must struggle first to apprehend the vision and then to give it form. This struggle is mirrored by the relationship that subsequently develops between the prophet and his audience, which now struggles to apprehend the vision that the prophet labored to articulate. Just as that vision once seemed obscure to the prophet, so it now seems obscure to his audience. Like him, the audience becomes engaged in mental exercise; through him, it becomes involved in a process currently called "reader harassment" but in the seventeenth century referred to as "the trial of the Reader."[88] That trial, first experienced by the prophet, is made to engage the reader as well. Just as the prophet requires an interpreting angel, who in the case of the Book of Revelation is Christ, so too does his audience. Consequently, John of Patmos assumes a strong presence in his prophecy just as Milton does in his epics, where the poet's highest office, misunderstood by A. J. A. Waldock but elucidated by Stanley Fish, is to serve as a commentator on the events he narrates.[89]

The prophet's method is to set narration and commentary on a collision course—the commentary serving, both in Milton's epics and in John's prophecy, as the *"Royal Key"* for unlocking visionary meaning. As Henry More explains, the reader must himself discover the connections between the narration or vision and the commentary; he himself must relate the components that do not seem to connect.[90] The prophet's method, moreover, pertains to his largest objective, which involves concretizing vision into word so that his audience may further concretize it into act. God needs the prophet to make manifest his Word, and the prophet requires an audience so that the Word may become flesh. This drama between the inspirer and the inspired—between God and the prophet, then between the prophet and his audience—dictates the form of prophecy, which, like all the other kinds, possesses, along with its rhetorical strategies, both a structure and an ideology. That structure, threefold or sevenfold, recalling either the three states or the seven ages of the world (and sometimes both) serves as an emblem for the subject of prophecy, which is history, and as a support for its theme, which is the renovation of history.

The Structure of Vision

The elaborate framework, the schematic architecture, the formal order of the Apocalypse does not elude Renaissance commentators; but neither does such an understanding burst forth in a moment, in a pulsation of an artery. Instead, developing from the premise that John's prophecy possesses "a certayne and distincte order," that all its parts are "knit together" so as to be "coherent and correspondent,"[91] that understanding evolves through the sixteenth and seventeenth centuries into the complicated expositions provided first by David Pareus and then by Joseph Mede and Henry More (see figs. 2 and 3 and Appendix A). Too often it is supposed that poets who reject narrative in favor of prophetic and apocalyptic structures necessarily bewilder their readers "because of their failure to conform to any expectations of a significant genre."[92] What Pareus, Mede and More show is that prophecy, by the seventeenth century, had established itself as a major genre and so possessed structural principles founded upon certain expectations.

By the middle of the sixteenth century, the threefold structure of the Apocalypse is sufficiently commonplace that it can be alluded to by William Fulke without elaborate explanation; and by this time the sevenfold organization of John's prophecy is widely enough accepted that Henry Bullinger cannot propose his own sixfold anatomy without conceding that more usually the Book of Revelation is regarded as a sevenfold vision, containing both a prologue and an epilogue.[93] This visionary structure is simply complemented by Bullinger with a coexistent rhetorical structure, his analysis ending with the concession, "Let the reader follow which [structure] he will"; for whichever structure he does follow he cannot but understand that in this prophecy everything is closely knit, "hangyng right well together."[94] The careful ordering which marks the Book of Revelation is thought, moreover, to mirror the dramatic experience that this prophecy affords. For Thomas Brightman, that experience is best described as "a most long & dolefull Tragedy," its last act introducing a "delightfull spectacle of perpetuall peace"; or, as Richard Bernard explains, the Apocalypse is a "tragicall Comedie," what is already accomplished being a tragedy and what is about to be accomplished being a comedy, all this set forth in "a delightsome coherence."[95] In our own century, Rosalie Colie has described pastoral "as *the* mixed dramatic genre" and thus regards it "as the official locus of tragicomedy."[96] Another locus, this one having scriptural sanction, is prophecy. Its conjoining of tragedy and comedy is an important subject in Revelation exegesis, commentators anticipating the modern understanding that these genres together constitute a culture's "dialogue . . . with itself and with the foundations of being."[97]

Assertions such as these are behind the generic labels and elaborate structural analyses of Joseph Mede and David Pareus, whose commentaries, first published in Latin, Pareus' before Mede's, were translated within a year of one another, Mede's in 1643 and Pareus' in 1644. Mede was a fellow of Christ's College when Milton attended Cambridge and may possibly be the "old Damœtas" (36) of *Lycidas;* and Pareus, referred to in the Preface to *Samson Agonistes,* is celebrated by Milton in *The Reason of Church-Government* for having provided an understanding of the Apocalypse that confirmed Milton's own (see *Yale Milton,* 1:815). Mede and Pareus, moreover, are both responsible for what Frank Manuel attributes to Mede alone, "something resembling a Copernican revolution"[98] in the world of academic commentary on the Book of Revelation. In defining their debt to these commentators, many attribute to them what has been claimed for Francisco de Ribera (1591), that they initiate a tradition of scientific study of the Apocalypse; and those who so regard both Mede and Pareus would doubtless appropriate for them the words by which Isaac Newton honored Mede alone: they "layed the foundation and I have built upon it."[99] In view of the vast body of Revelation commentary that antedates Mede and Pareus, such a claim may seem preposterous. It becomes less so, however, when it is remembered that earlier commentary was preoccupied with the theology of the Book, whereas Mede and Pareus, shifting attention to its aesthetics, open a wholly new tradition of commentary, the impact of which marks all subsequent commentary up to the present day.

Mede's commentary reiterates the idea that the Book of Revelation is a drama, calling it a "celestiall Theatre." Yet its immediate concern is with the structure of John's "holy *Labyrinth*" which it explores through synchronism, a device that enables "the things . . . designed . . . [to] run along in the same time." Conceding the importance of the number seven to the structure of John's vision (there are, for example, seven epistles, seven seals, and seven trumpets), Mede proceeds to study it within the arching order of the three prophecies. Insofar as this complex structure can be visualized, it may be seen as a series of overlapping arcs and concentric circles (see figs. 2 and 3) drawn to accord with the belief, first, that the Book of Revelation contains three entire prophecies and, second, that Chapter 11 provides a transition between the seals prophecy and the open-book prophecy:

The order of the Seales, and in them of the Trumpets, is certain . . . The rest therfore of the prophesies being compared first
between themselves, after ward with the Seals by way of Synchro-
nisme, the order of the whole Revelation will be clearly manifest. . . .

. . . the whole Revelation, from the fourth chapter . . . is dis-
tributed into two principall prophesies, either of which proceedeth
from the same time, and endeth in the same period. The first is of
the seales, and in them of the trumpets . . . The other prophecie
(or rather body of propheticall visions) is . . . of the little book
opened, which beginning at the same instant of the Apocalyptique
time, repeateth the time of the former prophesie. . . .

. . . I would the Reader should well observe: in this one vision of
the eleventh chapter (as being the first of the prophesie repeated
over again) the most wise Spirit runneth through, as the Weaver the
warpe with the woofe, the whole space of the prophecy of the seals:
and knitteth the same by the seventh trumpet, as it were with a
curious knot, to the order of the seals, for direction of the time.
But to what end, but that the other prophecies of the little book
being joyned by their characters to the first vision, so fixed and
compared with the seals, the whole body of the repeated prophesie
might bee aptly conjoyned with the seals.

John's prophecy is a series of "Apocaliptique visions . . . framed
by the characters of the Synchronismes" that open up its visionary
meaning; the whole book is a splendid artifice whose structure, for
Mede, is the key to its meaning. An analysis of this structure yields
not a linear but a labyrinthine design, wherein events instead of
succeeding one another are, through a system of synchronisms,
made to mirror one another. Apprehension of structure, says
Mede, provides the basis for interpreting visionary art; structure
is the device enabling the reader to become, along with its creator,
a fellow prophet (See Appendix A).[100]

The Book of Revelation has, for Mede, two distinguishing
marks: its special workmanship, which, when seen in relation to
all other prophecy, shows it to be the first universal prophecy;
and its dramatic character, which makes this "Apocalyptick

Theater" a "theater of the world."[101] The whole drama of cosmic conflict is played out on the stage of John's prophecy; and that stage, first in the prophet's mind, is shifted into the mind of the reader. Thus what Coleridge once said of *The Faerie Queene*, that its domain is neither history nor geography but mental space, is true of all prophecy. This point, fundamental to Mede's commentary, is presented even more assertively by Thomas Goodwin, a friend of Milton's in Parliament.

John's prophecy is not dramatic in the usual sense of showing characters in conflict with one another; rather, according to Goodwin, its drama is internalized, presenting a "true portrait of the Holy Ghost's mind."[102] Prophecy, as Mede and Goodwin understand, is not just mind centered: it is mind reflecting. Hence they anticipate what may seem a wholly modern perception, that in prophecy "mind makes a model of itself," mirroring its "very structure, as well as its principalities and powers."[103] Yet even here Mede and Goodwin are delineating the lines of an understanding of prophecy that derive largely from David Pareus and that, with the translation of Pareus's commentary in 1644, become widely disseminated.

Pareus' commentary epitomizes the tradition of Renaissance interpretation that tended more and more to regard the Book of Revelation as a dramatic poem. John's prophecy, accompanied by a prologue and epilogue, according to Pareus is divided into seven visions, each of them subdivided into four acts. The seven visions—implying an analogy with the seven ages of the world, each of them figured as a "play"—unfold the drama of world history, portraying the cycles of destruction and containing a promise of release from them:

Prologue	1:1–9
1 Vision	1:10–3
2 Vision	4–7
3 Vision	8–11
4 Vision	12–14
5 Vision	15–16

6 Vision	17–19
7 Vision	20–22: 6
Epilogue	22:7–end

What begins as an epistolary form becomes in Chapter 4 a "plainly . . . *Dramaticall* forme, hence the Revelation," says Pareus, "may truely be called a *Propheticall Drama,*" its closest literary analogue being with "humane Tragedies." The Book of Revelation resembles tragedy both in its substance and in its structure, representing "Tragicall motions and tumults of the adversaries against the Church of Christ, and at length the Tragicall end also of the wicked themselves," but also, according to Pareus, drawing from this genre its formal design: the diverse persons of tragedy are in the Apocalypse replaced "by diverse *shews* and *apparitions*"; the confrontations between characters, a feature of tragic structure, are replaced with confrontations of perspectives, one vision contending with another. Interspersed within and between visions are songs and hymns, which, functioning like a chorus in a tragedy, are intended "not so much to lessen the wearisomnesse of the Spectators, as to infuse holy meditations into the mindes of the Readers, and lift them up to Heavenly matters."[104]

The literal sense of the Apocalypse may operate "without constancy and coherency"; but, says Henry More, "in the *Propheticall* sense there is no such incongruity."[105] A similar point had already been made by Pareus. All the visions of Revelation cohere one with another; yet, says Pareus, Revelation is not one continued vision.[106] Throughout the prophecy linear movement is disrupted, forcing the reader into an attitude of contemplation and thus lifting him at each resting place to a new level of comprehension. This aspect of Revelation prophecy is emphasized through the exchange of letters between Mede and Haydock described earlier, which indicates, first, that the book given to John is a scroll and, second, that this book, combining verbal and visual images, is intended, some of it, to be read and some of it to be beheld and viewed (see fig. 4). There is, then, a double obstacle to linear movement in this prophecy: since the prophecy is not in any ordinary sense a book, all the seals need not be broken before an individual vision may be encountered; instead, each panel of the prophecy has its own seal and thus drops down to be read and viewed, to be scrutinized and interpreted, before another seal is broken. Moreover, within each vision the pictures arrest attention, delay movement, forcing the complex relationships between text and design to be unraveled before understanding can be achieved.

In various of their poems, Spenser, Milton, and Blake all draw out the implications of this device. Blake's epic-prophecies employ precisely these tactics; and those of Spenser and Milton, and of the Romantic poets who follow them, utilize analogous ones, which produce what Wordsworth will call the "clotting" of narrative. In *The Faerie Queene,* the alexandrine at the end of each stanza, the device of pictorialism, and that of intersecting one plot line with another—all disrupt the narrative flow; and in *Paradise Lost,* colliding image patterns, conflicting mythological identifications (at different times Satan, Christ, and Adam are all identified with Prometheus), clashing perspectives, contradictions between the story and Milton's commentary on it—all these are similar devices for achieving the same end. Each new vision— each new blast of a trumpet, as it were—expounds what precedes it. In each case, the poem is a sequence of visions: through the labor demanded by one vision we are prepared to encounter another, and through the labor required by it we are better able to grasp the meaning of the vision it succeeds.

In John's prophecy, then, linear movement is not only disrupted—it is minimized. It may exist within each vision, but the seven visions rather than relating to one another sequentially reiterate the same materials, each time from a different perspective and each time adding new materials that clarify, often amplify, what has gone before. This drama of perspectives, we have already said, develops out of the tension that once existed between the prophet and the source of his vision and finds its extension in the spirit of contention with which the prophet now approaches his audience. Employing techniques of harassment, using them to

initiate the educative process, the prophet, through the very structure of his vision, brings his audience to a new level of consciousness, investing it with a renewed capacity for vision. Structure,
then, is an agent in the process that culminates in our seeing all
things anew, this process finding its completion in the moment
when an audience, casting off the garments of orthodoxy, dons
the new ones woven by the prophet.

By 1650, owing largely to the commentaries by Mede and
Pareus, the Book of Revelation was commonly regarded as a
carefully defined structure, the appropriate model for all prophecy; and, through the efforts of Samuel Hartlib, the friend to
whom Milton dedicated *Of Education,* and those of Henry More,
what had become a commonplace remained one through the rest
of the century: the Book of Revelation was seen as an enfolding
of Vision, "All parts of it one with Another" so that there was no
"Loosing the Harmony . . . of the whole *Vision* . . . The design of one, is the design of all."[107] That is, the structure of one of
its visions is imitated by the others; and the structure of the entire
prophecy is there to be imitated by all those who would assume a
place in the visionary line—by those who, eschewing mechanical
forms, would create living ones.

Here one must differentiate sharply between the appropriation
of forms and the use of models. Appropriation usually involves
duplication, the simple transference of order from poem to poem.
Appropriation implies continuation and thus reinforces the established order. Models, on the other hand, serve the poet chiefly
as analogues: they are of interest to him less because they are
ready-made orders than because they provide the principles for
creating new orders that are subversive of established ones. Models are comparisons. There are models for the universe and also
models for poems—both closed models and open ones, both con-
stricting models and liberating ones. "A work is an *archetypus* before it is a reality," says Donald Howard; and its stated model
provides "an intrinsic key to perception."[108] Models like the Book
of Revelation are seized upon because they oppose and would
abolish reigning forms together with the orthodoxies those forms

43

symbolize. A model like the Book of Revelation suggests that form is a means to an end, which may "contradict . . . form and even deny it"; the final objective of form is not, then, to "prevail as . . . 'timeless designs' or eternal paradigms" but to effect liberation.[109] Appropriation of forms is tantamount to the appropriation of systems in order to uphold them. Prophets, in contrast, find their exemplar in Blake's Los, who builds a system, constructs an order, that would destroy all existing systems and abolish all existing orders. Milton, from Blake's point of view, is a historical manifestation of this archetype (see fig. 6).

On the surface, therefore, the Apocalypse appears to be a chaos, but then surfaces in this prophecy are deceptive—so much so that surface disorder stands in marked contrast to an ordered interior. What poets like Spenser, Milton, and the Romantics borrow from the Book of Revelation is not a structural mechanism that lends to their poetry a visible external design; instead, they borrow structural principles that by each poet are suited to his own special subject matter. In prophecy, structure is not openly revealed but, instead, is felt as a molding principle. Thus when Bishop Lowth writes of prophecy, he can contend that "in respect to order, disposition, and symmetry of a perfect poem of the prophetic kind" no easy definitions can be provided, even as he perceives "a certain accuracy of arrangement and symmetry of form," which reside in the internal structure of a prophetic poem.[110]

Through Lowth, the Renaissance understanding of prophecy is carried into the eighteenth century and then extended to the Romantic poets. Among the various genres of poetry prophecy is assigned to the first rank because it is said to excel all other poetry both in terms of its style and its subject. Like epic, which is itself a mixed kind, prophecy subsumes other classes of poetry—it contains complete poems of different kinds. A "perspicuous order" developing by repetition, amplification, and accumulation, prophecy, according to Lowth, is a "no plot, no action" genre: its concern is not with the imitation of an action but with the portrayal of a character's mind, with the projection and improvement of thought-processes.[111] In Lowth's century, the Apocalypse, still re-

Fig. 6. Plate 15 of Blake's *Milton,* Copy B. Reproduced by permission of the Huntington Library, San Marino, California.

garded as a work "wrapt and involved in figures and allegories," was called both "wild and visionary" and perceived as a work in which "Each op'ning leaf, and ev'ry stroke / Fulfills some deep design." The Apocalypse was still thought to be "a dark Aenigma," "an inextricable labyrinth." Its mazes are penetrable, though, because of perspectives that jostle against one another, enlarging the visions they individually succeed and because of those "visionary scenes" that help to interpret them. The Book of Revelation, according to this anonymous commentator, is a "grand system . . . formed of a number of parts, all of them tending to build up and perfect its greatness, and magnificence," and all culminating in a "grand revolution of things."[112]

"The sublime Prophecy," as it came to be called, interiorized a structure of "Circles or Spheres"—a structure characterized, first by an "elegant *Simultaneum,*" then by a pattern of gradually sharpening antitheses, and finally by the device of interlacing the separate visions. Very conspicuous throughout John's prophecy is a principle of "Gradation in which the *Evil* and the *Good* . . . advance and increase, till they come to the utmost conflict with one another," that conflict usually manifesting itself in a series of contrasting types that both adumbrate and find their culmination in the final battle between Christ and Satan. The various parts of John's prophecy, moreover, are beautifully interwoven, this part being replicated by that, but in such a way that "like the pipes and stops of an Organ," at times this part or that is silent, while at other times all the parts sound aloud together.[113] Even at the end of the eighteenth century, this understanding—usually presumed rather than fully delineated—is still commonplace. In the words of James Winthrop, the Book of Revelation is a connected work requiring "a connected view both of history and of prophecy"; or as James Bicheno would have it, this collection of visionary scenes contains one vision that is "a miniature picture of . . . history," the other scenes being "the same picture variegated . . . on a larger scale."[114]

However obscure the Apocalpyse may have seemed during the eighteenth century, there were those who continued to believe with Pareus, Mede, and More that John's design is palpable and certain, that it is the key to this prophecy's meaning. And still, John's Apocalypse is being described as a sacred drama, a dramatic prophecy. Yet this prophecy is also a special kind of play, one full of remarkable pauses that by arresting progression and instigating cogitation rouse men into action, such action bringing on those revolutions that culminate in "the dissolution of the reigning system of things," in the "ruin of the governing powers of a political system."[115] Fragmented on its surface and often discursive, prophecy nonetheless observes the law that "there must be a Consistency in the Whole"—a consistency that is made evident by the prophet's showing through his uneasy structure "a gradual working of Providence towards the Redemption of the World from the Curse of the Fall."[116] In this way, says George Stanley Faber, "the various coincident though dissevered parts of the Apocalypse are bound together."[117]

From the middle of the sixteenth century well into the nineteenth century the Book of Revelation was regarded as a finely formed genre. Though John's prophecy seemed structurally a chaos, it was understood to be, by design, an intricate Labyrinth, its various devices turning readers into pilgrims, its different paths all leading them to the same center, the city named Jerusalem. An image of the new but difficult order the prophet would wrest from the reigning disorder, this labyrinthine design was meant, first, to inspire the creation of a new order and, second, to serve as a foundation of support for it. The prophet, uniting his radical aesthetic with a revolutionary program, thus committed himself to "the building up of the walls of Jerusalem" in the mind of his audience that, he hoped, would construct those same walls in the world it inhabited.[118] This aesthetic of prophecy, both its rhetorical strategies and its structure, supported the revolutionary ideology that prophecy was meant to foster—an ideology focused in the Book of Revelation by the story of the angels, represented as stars, who, falling from heaven when they reject the Everlasting Gospel, embrace in its place "mens traditions," the orthodoxies of society.[119]

The Politics of Vision

The movement of the damaged angels of the Apocalypse toward orthodoxy is contrasted by St. John with the movement of the Mighty Angel, the true prophet, away from it. The Mighty Angel, Christ, is a perfect pattern of heroism; he is the great revolutionary who moves men from the sixth state into the seventh at which time "the whole system of prophecy shall be explained"; and as a revolutionary, it is said, he "confoundeth all traditions, and subverteth all constitutions" in accordance with the understanding that while history is reversed by Christ's First Coming it is brought to its culmination by his Second Coming.[120] Christ thus steps on the stage of the apocalyptic theater not as a spokesman for the reigning values of human culture but as the deliverer of a prophecy designed to subvert those values and to inaugurate new ones. Like his predecessors, he wields the prophetic lash, raising his voice in protest against all that is corrupt and meaningless in the existing order. Surfacing in times when religion dwindles into custom, when men's expectations are broken and the old order is crumbling, prophecy arises not to confirm men in their error but to release them from it. Distinguishing the sheep from the goats, those who worship in the outer court from those who worship in the temple, the prophet would transform the former into New Creatures treading down outward religion and thereby giving to "the formal Christian . . . an inward life."[121] True prophecy does not just instigate "commotions . . . that rise and sink, and are . . . forgotten";[122] it originates a new order of things. When "slavery clanketh her chains," we are told, it is "the indispensable duty of the oppressed people . . . to shake them off, and defend their freedom,"[123] to shatter the oppressive order and to erect a new one to replace it.

Prophecy encourages and justifies a particular course of political action. It appears in times when people are wandering in darkness and error, when their hopes are withered; and it attempts to show them the light, to buoy their spirits, to bring them back to the path, not one they have fully traveled before but one from which they have strayed before ever envisioning its destination. The world to which the prophet addresses himself is the world that King Lear and Cordelia, Prince Arthur, his knights and their ladies, and Milton's Lady and "uncouth swain" inhabit—a world of divisions (domestic, social, political, and spiritual). It is a world of confusion, destruction, warfare, and imprisonment, both physical and psychic: parents are hated by their children, husband and wife are at odds, sects and heresies abound, both church and state are marked by corruption.[124] " 'Tis all in pieces," as John Donne said, "all coherence gone." This upsidedown world the prophet undertakes to set right side up; and thus he comes as an Angel who will prepare the way and make plain the path by returning the hearts of fathers to their children, and the hearts of the children to their fathers.[125] Characteristically, the prophet corrects the errors of an impoverished kingdom, exposing the false prophets, destroying their errors, and subverting both institutionalized religion and monarchical government—both of which have grown corrupt, both of which must give way to a society founded upon the principles of a new community. An agent of revolution used for the fomenting of rebellions in the realm— God's vehicle for "subversion"[126]—prophecy rejects the established reality and, with it, the forms and structures, aesthetic and institutional, of a corrupt civilization. In its origins, at least, prophecy preserves this revolutionary cast; its history, however, involves those moments when orthodoxy intrudes upon it, making its cast conservative and so, some would say, perverting the entire genre. Such intrusions are equally a part of the history of literary prophecy, providing a basis for distinguishing between *The Faerie Queene* and Milton's last poems, between the later visions of Blake and Wordsworth, or even between the two versions of Wordsworth's *Prelude*.

The revolutionary intent of prophecy was openly declared by commentators who both supposed it would "undermine States and Churches" and "depress Parties of Men," thereby correcting what is amiss in the institutions of a society as well as in its members, and who proposed that reflection on the Book of Revelation will end in great revolutions, in church and state, within and without Europe.[127] Rather than being imposed upon John's prophecy, this radical ideology is inferred from it—both from its iconography and its narrative. The blaring trumpets were thought to signify the demise of the reigning system; and the smoke that issues from the bottomless pit was, by venerable tradition, associated with all manner of human traditions to which the fallen angels subscribe and which the Mighty Angel will scuttle. His garment dipped in blood was said to signify the overthrow of enemies, be they individuals or institutions; and the white garments worn by the heroes of the Apocalypse were said to emblematize the postrevolutionary state that the conquerors over custom and tyranny will inhabit. The angel flying in the sun, thought to symbolize those faithful ministers who in the last days will overthrow orthodoxy, was regarded as a new type of the Mighty Angel who appeared in John's apocalyptic drama to instigate a revolution, the tribulations of which are recorded in the story of the two witnesses, the event itself being symbolized by the earthquake—a "mighty commotion," "a great shaking of states," political and ecclesiastical.[128] Committed to delivering men from tyranny and servitude, the two witnesses spread the seeds of revolution by flooding their nation with light. In consequence, they are politically slaughtered, but so too are they politically resurrected, their death representing the cultural repression of visionaries and their resurrection representing a great turn of things— a hastening to the New Jerusalem. When their revolution is completed, we are assured, "the Saintes of the most High shall possess the Kingdom."[129]

Previously, we noted likeness between epic and prophecy, but there is also this distinction: the two forms, at least as they were perceived by a Milton or a Blake and by many of their commentators, are ideologically discrepant—epic written to preserve, prophecy to alter, the collective ideology of the culture producing it. This difference often gets blurred, of course, and usually in exact proportion to the degree that prophecy intrudes upon and then becomes incorporated into an epic poem. Expectedly, perhaps, the difference is most blurred in Virgil's *Aeneid* and Dante's *Commedia*. On the other hand, the difference is most apparent when we recognize that, while epic poets tend to strengthen the established order, prophets are bent upon over-turning it; epic poetry sounds like a chorus in which a whole cul-ture participates, but prophecy is only a monologue that the prophet hopes will one day be heard as a vast chorus; the prophet sings and, singing, would move a whole culture to a new vision of itself.

History is a fundamental concern of epic poet and prophet alike; yet both assume radically different stances in relation to history. Both embody historical patterns in their verse—epic poets so as to perpetuate them, prophets in order to reverse them. In epic, history is brought to the center of poetry; but in contrast, prophecy aspires to be at the center of history and to make all change emanate, reverberate, from that center. History, therefore, helps to make the epic poem, whereas prophecy, "a tradition at odds with the course of history,"[130] is bent upon remaking history and so, in accordance with its Revelation model, is intent upon showing good arising out of the evil that history unwittingly con-solidates.

Prophecy may take as its subject the past, but it finds its object in the future. That is, prophecy is "anticipatory History"—a per-spective which caused Thomas Newton to observe that, whereas history is "prophecy accomplished and dilated," prophecy is "his-tory anticipated and contracted."[131] Prophecy may not foretell the future (prediction is the function of prophecy only in its vulgar sense, says Shelley); but instead, by instructing the present, prophecy does help to shape the future. Thus epic records, often celebrates, the history that prophecy, in the act of reviewing it, seeks to transform. For the epic poet, a historical pattern is drawn so that it may be offered as a model for future history; for the prophet, the pattern is isolated and defined so that it may be al-tered. Epic is concerned with reformation; prophecy, with revolu-tion.

For Milton especially, it is not important that history repeats itself but that, as Mark Twain once said, it rhymes, and through its rhymes holds out the possibility of progress. Epic poets and prophets alike impose historical pattern upon historical pattern; but, whereas the epic poet translates pattern into model, the prophet searches beyond pattern for a new model, his search causing him to turn closed patterns into open ones, which become not emblems of perfection but gateways leading toward it. When the prophet looks at history he finds only a paradigm for tyranny, but when he turns inward he discovers, in his own psychic history, the possibility for becoming liberated from oppression.[132]

What stands to be achieved, as Milton saw as early as *Lycidas* and, subsequently, in *Paradise Lost* and *Paradise Regained,* is a paradise happier far than the one that had been lost, a paradise whose symbol is not Eden but Jerusalem. The radical implications of such a view are explained by Marjorie Reeves as she notes that although it may appear that the prophets seek to return to the primitive purity of the Apostles, this "motif of the backward aspiration" is grounded more fundamentally in a "myth of the future"; so much so that what is written as a prophecy of the past is in actuality a prophecy for the future:

> Their [the prophets'] reading of past history enabled them to complete the pattern of things to come in the Last Age and to find their own cosmic role within this pattern. Their models might be drawn from the past, but their belief was that the life of the future would far exceed that of the past. It was not so much a recapturing of the life of the first Apostles that they expected as the creating of the life of new apostles. It was this claim . . . which most shocked and offended the orthodox.[133]

It was also this claim that enabled politics to invade prophecy: the prophet regarded himself as the detector-general of the shortcomings of his age, as both the exposer of corrupt institutions and their executioner. Inheriting his revolutionary purpose from Christ as it was defined by Joachim of Fiore and his followers, the prophet was charged with joining that purpose to a revolutionary program, then with inspiring mankind to adopt it. The prophet, in this respect, is like St. John's eagle: he would have us burst through normal confines and travel with him into the light of the sun, where, after burning away the feathers of convention, we can return in the glory of the prophet. The eagle, of course, is an age-old symbol of the figure guiding man to the place of revelation and so became the prophet's emblem, signifying the lofty heights to which he aspires and to which he would have others aspire.

Temperamentally, the epic poet is a conservative, aiming at "eternalizing," and the prophetic poet, a revolutionary, aiming at "transforming," and their different temperaments find literary equivalents in epic and prophecy respectively.[134] For a long while (from the classical period into the Renaissance), these forms and their respective ideologies were disjoined until under the auspices of Spenser and Milton they are reunited. In these two poets, both of whom would lay claim to being prophets, we find examples of artists, temperamentally different, accommodating the medium of prophecy to their message. Their medium is founded upon the Book of Revelation, "a single and living unity from end to end"; but, turning from the Apocalypse to the use Spenser and Milton made of it, we must also challenge the conclusion of Austin Farrer, that, setting out to make "a new form of literature," St. John, because he was without influence, "had no success."[135] Spenser and Milton—and later the Romantic poets—show otherwise.

In any history of the alliance between literature and prophecy, Spenser and Milton merit special attention; for coming at the end of "a slow unfolding, in which the inherent potentialities of art are gradually actualized," together they create a "supreme moment"[136] marked by the emergence of a new form, the epic-prophecy, and subsequently by the emergence of a new literary tradition, a tradition of visionary poetics, that is later appropriated by the Romantics. Milton may seem to be—and in a certain sense is—the more important poet; for in literary tradition, he, rather than Spenser, occupies the position that in biblical tradition is held by Moses, that of "the common conduit through whom all pro-

phetical influence was conveighed to the rest of the prophets."[137]
Yet, as E. H. Gombrich urges, complex orders, such as Milton
achieved through prophecy, "can never be the work of one man,
even of one genius"; others join in the "working-out process."[138]
Because Spenser contributed so importantly to that process, Milton
assumed a relationship with him analogous to the one that the
Romantic poets were later to strike with Milton. These various
relationships are all best defined as Spenser, in *The Faerie Queene,*
defines his own relationship with Chaucer: "I follow here the
footing of thy feete" (IV.ii.34).

Spenser and Milton: Two Exemplars of Vision

That Spenser and Milton should both be drawn to the prophetic
mode may be explained by the way in which their culture viewed
both itself and the arts. England saw herself as the true center
of the Christian world, standing in the same relationship to Rome
that Christ stands in relation to Antichrist. Here, in England, as
one visionary put it, Christ will "begin to reigne . . . first";
"England . . . shall have first the revelation of truth."[139] That
revelation, both Spenser and Milton believed, was to be invested
in the poets who would transmit it through their poems, all with
a prophetic center.

Related to the question of how English Renaissance culture
viewed itself is another: how did Spenser and Milton view themselves and their art? Addressing himself to that question, Angus
Fletcher proposes that the chief precursor of Milton is not Spenser
but Shakespeare:

> That is, while much in Milton's poetry may be read as directly or
> indirectly influenced by Spenser . . . , a much stronger, deeper
> and more personally critical relation of influence exists between
> Milton and Shakespeare. The most powerful, and critical, extension
> of Shakespearean influence over Milton comes from the fact that
> Shakespeare writes plays, and Milton attempts to rival the dramatic
> economy of Shakespearean theatre.

Fletcher's proposition gives rise to two broad axioms: one is that "while Spenser wrote a very unusual kind of romance, in *The Faerie Queene*, . . . he must be accounted and understood as a prophetic poet"; the other is that "Milton throughout his career is centrally dramatic in his aims."[140] If it can be said that the poetry of both Spenser and Milton (and this Fletcher does say) issues from a prophetic moment, then it should be allowed, by way of focusing a distinction, that for Milton that moment was intensely dramatical—no less so than it was for Albrecht Dürer, judging from his electrifying portrayal of the prophetic moment in John's Apocalypse (see fig. 7).

The bifurcation of prophecy and drama is not one that prophetic tradition sanctions; nor, for that matter, is it one that Milton himself would countenance. The Book of Revelation, a prophecy, is for Milton a model of high and stately tragedy because of its dramatic character. In his Preface to *Samson Agonistes,* even as he apparently belittles Shakespeare as a dramatic model, Milton once again invokes the Apocalypse not only as an example of, but as an exemplary, drama. Indeed, the very phrases that Fletcher devises for the purpose of characterizing *Paradise Lost* are ones that in a broader sense characterize prophecy as we have here, through biblical commentary, described it. A "drama of information," but a peculiar form of drama since, in any usual sense, "practically nothing happens"; an example of "agonistic . . . dialectic narrative"; "a cosmic picture-show"; "the first epic which self-consumingly travels . . . to the boundaries of the informing quest," making "this trajectory of light in order, dramatically, to show the whole body of a concerted thought"[141]—less appropriate to Spenser's poem than to Milton's perhaps, these phrases nevertheless define the major features not just of *Paradise Lost* but of the Apocalypse as well.

As I am doing, Harold Bloom has also taken Spenser to be Milton's starting point, though such a recognition on Bloom's part is accompanied by the belief that Milton—not far from Spenser in his moral and theological beliefs—nevertheless "re-writes

Fig. 7. Albrecht Dürer's Illustration of the Mighty Angel of the Apocalypse Giving John of Patmos a Book. Reproduced from the extra-illustrated *Kitto Bible,* volume 60, by permission of the Huntington Library, San Marino, California.

Spenser so as to *increase the distance* between his poetic father and himself," thereby separating himself from the poet who inhibited him and distancing *Paradise Lost,* in the process, "from its most dangerous precursor, *The Faerie Queene.*" This proposition is credible only if we assume that the divisions between a conservative Anglican and a Christian belonging to "his own sect, a sect of one," are negligible and if, doing that, we are able to ignore the differences between a maker of images and a breaker of them, between a Queen's man and a hater of kings.[142] Those who believe the job of the critic is not to blur differences but to fashion minute discriminations will not find that an easy task.

Viewing Milton's achievement under the lights of Spenser necessarily returns us to the matter of prophecy's ideology—it is the dynamite laid in the structure of John's prophecy that none could ignore. Some like Spenser may wish to defuse it; but others like Milton waited, hoping for it to explode. Spenser, that is, could disregard the vast space between the first and second resurrections, the very space that by Milton had to be filled with a political vision. Thus, while Spenser and Milton both join prophecy to epic, Milton effects a merger different from and more complete than Spenser's: acknowledging the ideological discrepancies between epic and prophecy, Milton embraces what Spenser represses, restoring the hieratic relationship between epic and prophecy fostered by the Bible but subsequently ignored.

It has been said that every epic contains prophecy, but it should not be inferred, therefore, that every epic is a prophecy or even that Spenser's epic, and Milton's, are prophecies in the same degree. Other epics—the *Aeneid,* for example—have prophetic interludes or "prophetic Part[s]," as Robert Clayton calls them;[143] other poets—Homer and Dante, Ariosto and Tasso—employ prophecy as a device. In contrast, Spenser and Milton are the first poets after John of Patmos to harness epic to the prophetic mode. Both poets appropriate from prophecy its rhetorical strategies and structure; however, Spenser, bound to an ideology both "official and impersonal," endorses, as Yeats once remarked, "a system of life which [he thought] it was his duty to support."[144] Milton, unlike his precursor, embraces the revolutionary ideology of prophecy and so would agree with D. H. Lawrence:

> It is no use trying merely to modify present forms. The whole great form of our era will have to go. And nothing will really send it down but the new shoots of life springing up and slowly bursting the foundations. And one can do nothing, but fight tooth and nail to defend the new shoots of life from being crushed out, and let them grow. We can't make life. We can but fight for the life that grows in us.

De-radicalizing the genre of prophecy, Spenser uses a form ordinarily deployed against monarchs to celebrate them, and thus must be judged according to Tommaso Campanella's dictum that "the true prophet is one who . . . scolds princes for their wickedness and . . . peoples for their ignorance."[145] Still, in his apparent violation of prophetic tradition, Spenser is very much of his time. The ideological matrices of the Revelation prophecy, the book's revolutionary program, caused Protestants like Martin Luther to devalue John's prophecy (in his September Bible, Luther relegates the Apocalypse to an appendix). So strong was this impulse that by the end of the sixteenth century, the Book of Revelation had been emptied of its radicalism. No one really denied the subversive character of prophecy; it is just that subversion was thought to have already done its work: the Church, at least in England, had been purified, and a noble monarch was now ruling the State. The Reformation had been accomplished. Thus in 1593, acknowledging that prophets have "directed all their Admonitions generally to Kings, Princes, and Governours," John Napier suggests that, in dedicating his work to James VI, he is violating this convention in order to celebrate a good head of government who has had ennobling effects on his countrymen. Times have changed, Napier argues; and since the change is for the better, prophets and their commentators have a new obligation:

... it is ... the duty of Gods servants in this Age, Interpreters of Prophecies, ... to encourage and inanimate Princes, ... as also to exhort them generally to remove all such Impediments in their Countreys and Commonwealths, as may hinder that Work, and procure Gods plagues.[146]

A good ruler like James is thus a model for other rulers and a pattern for all mankind to emulate. Napier does not argue that the rulers of men are perfect, only that they become progressively better as they aspire to perfection. Through a process of purgation and purification, they reform themselves and thereupon their nations: the pattern of experience they undergo, beginning in the inward mind, makes them into princely prophets; and this pattern, when followed by the citizenry, transforms all men into prophets. Other men, such commentators imply, possess the perceptual faculties of the prophet; the prophets' charge is thus to cleanse those faculties, thereby enabling others to see with the same clarity with which they see.

The process described by Napier, involving the natural man's becoming the spiritual man, for Napier embodied by James VI, is transferred by George Gifford to Queen Elizabeth. The beast that once reigned with the monarchs of England has been pulled down by Elizabeth: because she has "made the whore desolate and naked," Gifford celebrates her as "the singular blessing of God," as "the greatest defender and protector of the holy worship, and true worshippers that is under heaven."[147] For Gifford, it is Satan, not God, who plots revolution, who seeks to subvert the monarchs of state and religion; and it is against these subverters of order that men must now take up arms. All men must become soldiers in the Lord's army; and this they do when as faithful shepherds they have cultivated the six virtues of labor, patience, zeal, wisdom, sincerity, and magnanimity.[148] Spenser defines the six virtues differently, but nonetheless a similar scheme informs *The Faerie Queene.*

Through its dedication and introductory prologue, *The Faerie*

Queene is firmly tied to the Book of Revelation. Spenser's dedication is insistent: Elizabeth, a paragon of virtue, is "Defender of the Faith" and, as a poet, he "Labours To Live With The Eternity Of Her Fame." Moreover, the epic itself instructs us to live with the Queen's virtues embodied in the knights and ladies who people Spenser's fairyland—virtues that, traceable to Arthur, are shown to have a long lineage indeed. The process involving heroes and heroines alike, in book after book of the poem, shows the natural man becoming a spiritual man; and nowhere is this process more sharply focused than in Book I where Redcrosse is transformed into a Christian knight. Here the "tall clownishe" Redcrosse, who "rested on the floore, unfitte through his rusticity for a better place" (*A Letter of the Authors*) and who, becoming entangled in error as his story begins, must be reminded to "Add faith unto [his] force" (I.i.19)—this knight who only "seemed a knight" (I.i.1) has by the end of his story become an exemplary Christian warrior. Not until his story is concluded, however, is there identity between the knightly apparel and the man.

The indebtedness of Renaissance poets to the Book of Revelation is still to be perceived. The John Harveys, of course, would discourage poets from, in any sense, prophesying: wishing to discredit prophecy, they would point to the Book of Revelation, arguing that it marks the cessation of prophecy and thus concluding that all modern claimers to vision—"Merlins, Pierce Plowmans, and Colin clowtes"—are "false prophet[s]."[149] But others, recognizing that prophecy is an ongoing process, encouraged poets to prophesy. Acquainted with Renaissance commentary on John's book, they quickly perceived evidence—implicitly in the case of Tasso, but explicitly in the case of Spenser—for aligning their epics, thematically and structurally, with John's prophecy.

For example, those committed to deciphering the historical allegory in the Book of Revelation pointed to Godfrey, the elected hero of Tasso's epic, as a type of the Christian warrior who by destroying one city would build up another. Leading an assault, he is the acknowledged type for Christ in his last battle with Satan, wherein one city is destroyed and another raised in its place; he is "a Christian Prince . . . made king at *Jerusalem*," where he "prospered mightily in . . . war."[150] Yet Godfrey is only a type (as are Redcrosse, Guyon, and Calidore), and thus his victory like theirs is temporary. After Godfrey, "Jerusalem was lost again with great slaughters of Christians."[151] This understanding of Godfrey was common enough in Spenser's time that, singling out Tasso in his letter to Raleigh, Spenser seems to have deliberately transferred this symbolic meaning to his own knights. All are in process of becoming Christian warriors and so, like Christ, must do battle with Satan. Of Spenser's knights, Sir Guyon possesses the most conspicuous resemblances with Christ, his story re-mythologizing Christ's encounter with Satan in the wilderness. But for Spenser's readers Redcrosse, who is finally identified with St. George, would be equally a Christ-type—and in exactly the same sense that Tasso's Godfrey is a type of Christ.[152]

It has been observed that the "identification of St. George with Christ, the dragonslayer of the Apocalypse, was probably not original with Spenser";[153] and it is true, this identification was not Spenser's invention. On some Renaissance crucifixes, for example, one face will show Christ on the cross and the other, sometimes St. Michael but often St. George slaying the dragon. In Book I of *The Faerie Queene,* opposing Una as the Church to "A goodly Lady clad in scarlet red," then opposing Redcrosse to Sansjoy (I.ii.13, 15), Spenser allows their battle to figure the last battle of the Apocalypse. So that this parallelism is not missed, Spenser reiterates it, first by insisting that in the battle between Sansjoy and Redcrosse "th' one for wrong, the other strives for right" (I.v.8, 9); then, having already made Redcrosse and St. George interconnecting figures, Spenser proceeds to associate Arthur, through the description of his helmet, with not only St. George but Michael and Christ, who themselves are regarded by Revelation commentators as interchangeable protagonists in Revelation's drama (see I.vii.31). Finally, having contrasted Una and Duessa, Redcrosse and Sansjoy, Spenser has Arthur, in imitation of Christ, unveil the whore after his conquest of Duessa's beast (I.viii.6, 7, 15–16, 25, 28, 46).

In his descent into the pit of Orgoglio's dungeon, Arthur is, moreover, like Revelation's Angel of the Bottomless Pit, who journeys into the dark regions of hell in order to annihilate evil, and like the Mighty Angel, St. Michael or Christ, who rescues man from the snares of the devil. Subsequent to his release, however, Redcrosse himself comes to be associated with the Mighty Angel, who like him is said to roar like a lion (see I.x.28; cf. Revelation 10:3); then, like the angel-heroes of the Apocalypse, having experienced a vision of the heavenly Jerusalem, Redcrosse, now resembling both the Angel of the Bottomless Pit and Arthur, must descend into an inferno in order to deliver Una's parents from the evil that has threatened them. Nevertheless, Spenser's heroes are only in a limited sense victorious: all wound but do not really slay the dragon of this world, and some like Redcrosse experience a vision of Jerusalem without ever establishing Jerusalem in this world (see I.viii.7 and I.xii.10). Thus Book VI ends just as Arthur's triumph, and Redcrosse's, end—with a dragon injured but not slain. This time, however, the beast, once subdued, escapes to resume his wanderings, Spenser, here in the conclusion of his poem, remembering a passage from John's prophecy: "And when the thousand years are expired, Satan shall be loosed out of his prison, and shall go out to deceive the people" (20:7–8). Yet the triumphant vision that closes John's prophecy is missing from the sixth book of Spenser's poem, where the wheel of history is not escaped but simply turns again.

First Josephine Waters Bennett and then John Erskine Hankins noted the correspondences between *The Faerie Queene* and the Book of Revelation, especially between John's prophecy and Book I of Spenser's poem, each critic attending not only to such deliberate borrowings as imagistic and allegorical patterns but also to structural parallels. Even so, perception of the relationship between John's prophecy and Spenser's poem is not of our century but of the seventeenth, when Henry More proposed that Spenser's Una is the church and that in Book I the poet is "lively set[ting] out the conditions of Christianity since the time that the Church of a Garden became a Wilderness."[154] Of course, what distinguishes More from these later critics is his refined understanding of Revelation's structure (see fig. 3 and Appendix A), and the evidence of *The Faerie Queene* suggests that Spenser himself possessed an understanding of Revelation's structure comparable to More's. To be sure, striking imagistic and allegorical patterns unite John's prophecy and the first book of Spenser's poem, and it may even be said that Spenser's plot derives from Revelation's drama. However, neither is Spenser's interest in the Apocalypse confined to "the latter half of the Revelation, from chapter 12 on," nor is it fully represented by discussions restricted to image and theme or allegory and plot.[155] For all manner of things—for image and theme, for allegory and plot, but also for drama and structure, for both rhetorical strategies and narrative ones—Spenser turns to his model. Its imprint is there, in one way or another, on every book of *The Faerie Queene* and on the design of the whole. In all ways, for example, the structure of John's prophecy is replicated by the structure of Spenser's; the devices of typology and synchronism, of dramatic and rhetorical structuring, of threefold and sevenfold organization—all find their equivalents in *The Faerie Queene.*

Structure, Joseph Mede and Henry More perceived well in advance of modern criticism, is a principal vehicle for meaning in prophecy; these words could easily be theirs:

> A quest for meaningful structures . . . may lead to sudden insight into major themes for the simple reason that these structures embody these themes. If a major poet has imitated the technique of creation so often attributed to the Deity—if he has devised a pattern in his mind before setting pen on paper—then inevitably a study of this pattern will take us right to the heart of his poetic vision. The pattern, so far from constituting a straight-jacket, will be a virtually inexhaustible fountain of inspiration.[156]

The outer structure of *The Faerie Queene,* its rhetorical design, is sixfold; but its visionary form is threefold and sevenfold. Books cluster together around their elected contexts: the classical group (I and II), the romance group (III and IV), and the Spenserian group (V and VI). Yet *The Faerie Queene,* as we have it, is a sevenfold vision, whose panels are the first six books, plus the seventh (the Mutabilitie cantos). As in the Book of Revelation, the first six visions, folding commentary into each vision, are followed by a seventh that, briefer than all the others, is a vision of "eterne in mutabilitie" (III.vi.47). The brevity of this last vision is in keeping with the idea that Revelation's concluding vision is briefer than all the others and, unlike the others, is unaccompanied by explanation or interpretation.

It was widely understood, of course, that prophecy contains both "vision" and "explanatory vision," to use Bicheno's terms;[157] and it was understood, too, that this latter aspect of visionary art was withheld from John's culminating vision, as it is from Spenser's, thus providing a test for the reader. All the other explanatory visions should have prepared the reader to interpret this final "apocalyptic vision."[158] There is nothing incomplete about this culminating vision, which, despite its distancing effects, shows the extent to which eternity is in love with the productions of time and which is, with both narrative and commentary pared away, a prophetic center to which narrative and commentary have already taught us to respond. Thus Spenser has given us a book (six of them to be exact) that enables us to read and interpret the vision we now behold—just as the Mighty Angel gave to John a book enabling him to interpret the final vision of the Apocalypse, and just as Redcrosse was in possession of a book, given away to Arthur, that assists him in penetrating the mysteries he beholds in the sealed book, the Book of Revelation, that Fidelia holds in the House of Holinesse. This last vision is intended to serve as a final check on the success of the process the reader has undergone. Milton administers the same kind of test through his purely visionary drama of *Samson Agonistes* that Spenser here administers through his cantos of Mutabilitie.[159] Moreover, each of Spenser's books, like his poem as a whole, is a labyrinth that culminates in vision (see fig. 3)—the vision of the Holy City that comes to Redcrosse finds one analogue in the culminating vision of John's prophecy and another in the final vision of Spenser's poem, which comes simultaneously to the poet and his reader.

The principle of synchronism is, moreover, built into Spenser's plan: the adventures of his protagonists begin on successive days, but there is overlap between one book and another, between one vision and its correlatives. The cumulative effect is not of a linear movement; instead, one episode flows into another, this character merges with that one. In the end, *The Faerie Queene* is one vision, variously repeated, each time from a different perspective, with each new angle of vision contributing to the poem's final clarity. For example, Orgoglio's dungeon in Book I is replicated in Book II by the Cave of Mammon; the triumph of both Redcrosse and Guyon is explained in terms of the saving power of grace (I.viii.1, II.viii.1), which in Book I is figured by Arthur and in Book II, by both the Palmer and the ministering angels.[160]

The same process that links book to book joins canto to canto. For within Book I, the various battles are all made to typify the last battle between Christ and Satan—Redcrosse's battles with Error and Sansfoy no less than Arthur's with Duessa's beast and Orgoglio, and these no less than Redcrosse's three-day battle with the dragon. Whether attention is fixed to one book or to them all, this process, relating episodes and characters within an elaborate system of typology, is admirably summarized by Kathleen Williams: one episode deepens, even while it explains, the meaning of another; and "the later books enrich the content of those which have gone before," says Williams, "so that from the first book to the fragmentary seventh the reader becomes increasingly aware of a clear and comprehensive vision, and of a steady purpose which impels him, through a mass of significant detail, toward a final unity."[161]

The model for the structure which channels and contains this process, in which "different views are given . . . of the very same periods,"[162] is John's prophecy as it was anatomized by Renaissance commentators both before and after Spenser. Like the Book of Daniel, after which it was fashioned, the Apocalypse was thought to be composed of multiple, overlapping visions: one vision impinges upon another, but to the extent that it does, the first is likely to be "more copiously enlarged upon" by the second, which, like a larger compass, introduces new materials for which subsequent visions may provide supplementation and expansion.[163] The movement of prophecy is, as Milton demonstrates and explains in *Paradise Lost,* "From Shadowy Types to Truth" (XII.303); and, though truth may seem to be hidden in darkness, prophecy promises, as Spenser does, that "time in her just terme the truth to light shall bring" (I.ix.5). Thus, what we confront in the end is not a poem composed of various books, but one book constituted of various layers—a book very like *The Faerie Queene* as Williams again describes it, "a comprehensive order . . . as orderly as a labyrinth," an "intelligible order" delineated by the poem's firmness of structure:

> Spenser marshalls all his organizing principles as one; the poem moves altogether, and moves unerringly towards unity . . . each aspect of the final unity is developed in itself.[164]

Spenser, everyone knows, projected a different plan for *The Faerie Queene:* "I labour to pourtraict in Arthure . . . the image of a braue knight . . . which is the purpose of these first twelve bookes"; he also pointed to other literary models: "first Homere, . . . then Virgil, . . . after him Ariosto . . . and lately Tasso" (*A Letter of the Authors*). In citing these models, of course, Spenser is concerned, as he explains in this same letter, with establishing precedents for presenting "doctrine by ensample" and for portraying heroism in a composite character. Precedents for both undertakings he could have found in the Book of Revelation: it, too, sets forth its doctrines "by ensample" and portrays both virtues and vices through a multiplicity of figures who, depending upon their proclivities, either for good or evil, delineate God and Satan respectively. Milton was probably encouraged by various Revelation commentators to portray both God and Satan through their various manifestations: God through Christ and the angels, Satan through Belial and Beelzebub, as well as Mam-

66

mon and Moloch. Spenser, like Milton, could have taken this much from the Book of Revelation; but he appears, again like Milton, to have taken much more—the very form in which his poem was finally to be cast. Yet, for all the similarities that exist in their respective handlings of prophetic tradition, there are important differences to be observed.

Two patterns consistently inform Milton's poetry—one of progression, the other of regression; and both are evident in the Nativity Ode, which Milton himself presents in the 1645 *Poems of Mr. John Milton,* and then again in the 1673 *Poems upon Several Occasions,* as a preludium to his poetic achievement. The Nativity brings a temporary end to the strife that again will be unleashed in the world after the Crucifixion. Civilization progresses into an era of peace only to regress from that peace into the agony and strife that have more typically marked it, back onto a "darkling plain," swept by confusion, "Where ignorant armies clash by night." *L'Allegro* and *Il Penseroso* succeed the Nativity poem and are, like the poems that Milton publishes last, companion pieces. These twinned lyrics project a pattern of progression that Milton's brief epic and tragedy reverse, *Samson Agonistes* ending not like *Il Penseroso,* with man at the pinnacle of vision, but like *L'Allegro,* in tragedy, with the chains of universal harmony untwisted,[165] this time by a cataclysm that promises more misery, more holocaust, more death. Not only do the visions of Milton's last poems collide with one another, then; but they collide, too, with the pattern of experience reflected in Milton's first set of companion poems, his point being not that one pattern now replaces the other but that, unless all men ascend to vision like the poet of *Il Penseroso* and the Jesus of *Paradise Regained,* a whole civilization may perish in a disaster like the one that befalls the Philistines (and Samson himself). It should not be thought that Milton in his last years sinks into despair or that his final vision is grimly pessimistic (*Samson Agonistes* is more exactly a warning). Rather, the aged poet, like the youthful one of *L'Allegro* and *Il Penseroso,* poses alternatives; and those alternatives necessitate choice. Go on in such a way, Milton seems

to be saying, and life will turn out in this way or that: a civilization which follows Jesus into the wilderness and, up, onto the
pinnacle of vision, will have a history different from that of a
civilization which follows Samson to the pillars and, down, into
the grave. Man's choices are nowhere more sharply drawn than
in the volume containing *Paradise Regained* "to which is added"
Samson Agonistes; but Milton's poetry is everywhere a "poetry
of choice,"[166] moving in *L'Allegro* and *Il Penseroso* from choices
that need not be made to choices, represented in *Paradise Regained*
and *Samson Agonistes,* that must be made, for on them depends
the survival of a nation—or its demise.

Not so in Spenser's poetry. At the end of *The Faerie Queene*,
there is just one pattern for history, one that is both emphatically
drawn and irreversible. Man does not in Spenser's poem shape
history, though he does shape the way he will live in history:
either succumbing to its deadly pattern or through his own life
opposing it and then suffering, however nobly, the consequences
of his opposition. Devoid of real alternatives, *The Faerie Queene*
is also devoid of clashing perspectives.[167] Different perspectives
provided by individual books tend to coincide rather than to
collide; and even if Spenser, like Milton, exercises the mind of his
reader, his objective is not to overthrow the reigning orthodoxies,
political or religious, but to effect a deeper understanding of them
and consequently to confirm them. In this sense, Spenser dimin-
ishes the dramatic possibilities inherent in his structure, contrasting with Milton who chooses to exploit them. Nevertheless, both
poets owe John of Patmos a debt both for their visionary structures and for their presiding themes of which their similar
strategies are a reflex.

Making the usual reference to Ephesians, quite explicitly in *A
Letter of the Authors* where Spenser identifies Redcrosse's armor
with "the armour of a Christian man specified by St. Paul," and
then, much more elusively, first in his description of Redcrosse
and later in the rebuke Redcrosse receives for becoming helplessly
entangled in error, *The Faerie Queene* begins where major Renaissance commentary on the Book of Revelation begins—with the

suggestion that "The lyfe of man . . . [is] a continual warfare on earth":

> . . . we are . . . in the middest of this difficulte and daungeouse fighte, compassed in on everye syde withe huge Armies of feyrce and cruell enemies, and also subjecte at every momet to the furiouse assaults and invasions of strange and subtill adversaries.
> . . . we wrastle not againste fleshe and bloud, but against principalities, against powers, and against the worldly governours, the Princes of the darkenesse of this world, against spirituall wickednesses which are in the high places.
> . . . the true souldiours of Christ [must] . . . put on all the armour of God; as to have there loynes gyrded about with veritie, having on the brest plate of righteousnesse, and to have there feete shood with the preparation to the Gospell of peace, to take the shield of faith, and the sword of the Spirite, the helmet of the Salvation. All which spirituall weapons, the Lord doth minister unto us by his holy woorde.[168]

This master-theme of Revelation prophecy, already focused by Tasso, is at the forefront of Spenser's epic as it will be, through exact quotation of Ephesians, at the beginning of Blake's *The Four Zoas*. The idea of warfare, figured in *The Faerie Queene* through the dragon battle, concludes its first book which, like the quotation prefacing *The Four Zoas,* is the context for the entire poem: "it is . . . ideological, the *significatio* or tenor embedded in the whole vast metaphor that is *The Faerie Queene*," says Isabel MacCaffrey; "it is the most comprehensive and resonant episode, allegorically, in the poem"—the one that roots it in history, "both far away and here and now, thereby opening a commerce between fiction and actuality."[169]

The same idea is at the structural center of Milton's epic, which, juxtaposing the celestial battle and the story of creation, explores the creative possibilities of Christian warfare. The same point may be made of the Revelation model. As a manual for God's army, its central chapters deal with the theme of warfare that has traditionally been the principal motif of epic poetry, but the

Apocalypse deals with this theme differently from Homer and Virgil. During the Renaissance and even into the Romantic period, the writers of classical epic were often thought to have celebrated carnal warfare whereas John was said to delineate, in accordance with St. Paul's epistle, a warfare that is spiritual and that has for its heroes men girded with truth, their breastplate being righteousness, their shield faith, and their weapon the Word of God (see fig. 8). These heroes will, like common soldiers, follow their captains even into death; but since their warfare is not carnal neither is their death,[170] for Christian warfare culminates in the annihilation of selfhood, in the transformation of its soldiers into new spiritual men (see fig. 6).

Spenser and Milton, under the aegis of John and with the prodding of Tasso, revolutionize the epic tradition of Homer and Virgil. In the classical epic, religion seemed an instigator and persuader to evil deeds, fostering the brutalities and cruelties by which Tasso was offended and which led Blake to speak of religion hid in war. Blake, of course, does not limit his criticism of religion to that of the pagans. Like Milton, he attacks institutionalized Christianity as well, whether it be Roman or Protestant: Christianity, no less than the religion of Homer and Virgil, has desolated Europe with wars. In this sense, Milton is closer to Blake than to Spenser, but in still another sense these three poets remain closely allied.

It has recently been argued that "in the epic tradition of the West, in the *Iliad* and the *Aeneid,* the 'true' God sends down real weapons in the service of his favored warrior. By contrast to Blake, who interiorized the struggle, Milton is a non-visionary . . . poet. There is in Milton no sentiment such as the Blakean 'mental fight,' which seems in fact to have derived as an imagined response to the failure of the historical Commonwealth."[171] *In fact,* the idea of spiritual warfare derives from St. John's Apocalypse and was made a central concern of *Piers Plowman*, where it is said that "any man who carries a sword, a lance, an axe, a dagger, or any kind of weapon, shall be put to death, unless he sends it to the smithy to be turned into a scythe, a sickle, or a

Fig. 8. The War in Heaven. Reproduced from the extra-illustrated *Kitto Bible,* volume 60, by permission of the Huntington Library, San Marino, California.

plow share."[172] Focused by biblical commentary of the Renaissance, this same theme is at the portal of Spenser's poem and at the center of Milton's (see fig. 8). In Book I of *The Faerie Queene,* Spenser repeatedly states that "bloud can nought but sin, and warr but sorrowes yield" (I.x.60); and in Book VI of *Paradise Lost,* Milton, like both John of Patmos and Spenser, sings of godly arms, of spiritual warfare, here associating physical combat with Satan, who in turn is defeated by the spiritual weaponry of Christ. The idea of spiritual warfare is also highlighted by Spenser, who has Guyon continually laying down his armour in Book II; and, lest we miss the implications of Book VI of *Paradise Lost,* Milton refocuses them in his brief epic, there taking for his subject "Christ combating with Sathan," that episode in Christ's life having already become an exemplum of spiritual combat.[173] Jesus, we are reminded, goes into the desert without a sword and, once there, speaks like the Milton of Sonnet XV: "what can War, but endless war still breed / Till Truth and Right from Violence be freed" (10–11). All "that cumbersome / Luggage of war" Jesus regards as evidence "Of human weakness rather than of strength" (III.400–02), and he has already told Satan as much:

> They err who count it glorious to subdue
> By Conquest far and wide, to overrun
> Large Countries, and in field great Battles win,
> Great Cities by assault . . .
>
> . . . . . .
>
> . . . if there be in glory aught of good,
> It may by means far different be attain'd,
> Without ambition, war, or violence;
> By deeds of peace, by wisdom earnt,
> By patience, temperance . . .
>
> (III.71–74, 88–92)

For Spenser and Milton (and later for Blake), mental fight is the only form of combat truly fitting to man.

It has been said that "the history of Western poetry has been that of its breaks and reconciliations with the revolutionary movement,"[174] and I would only add that it is against the backdrop of such a history that we come closest to understanding the inner dynamic of the Spenser-Milton relationship. All that has been said so far confirms Northrop Frye's distinction between Spenser and Milton (the one he calls a conservative, the other, a revolutionary artist)—but not in precisely the terms that Frye proposes:

> In English literature, Spenser seems to be a poet of . . . [the] conservative kind: he begins with experiment but moves toward . . . convention. . . .

> There is a radical or revolutionary temperament, however, also found among the greatest creators, and which contrasts with the conservative one. . . . It is clear that Milton belongs essentially to the radical group of artists . . .
>
> The revolutionary artist does not have to be a social and political revolutionary as well, but he often is if he lives in a revolutionary time. . . . For the revolutionary artist, it is precisely the continuity in tradition that he rejects in his art, and hence he tends to see his political situations also vertically, as a break with continuity.[175]

First of all, Frye's distinction is useful only after we postulate that all poets are traditionalists and thereupon proceed to distinguish between them in terms of the stance they strike in relation to tradition. Spenser and Milton belong to the same tradition; they hold a position in the visionary line, observing an aesthetic that both derives from the Book of Revelation and contributes to their poetry many of its distinctive themes. Moreover, like their model prophet, Spenser and Milton are poets, not theologians— poets whose concern is the meaning of history; yet Milton's understanding of history is closer to John's than to Spenser's. The unleashing of the beast at the end of *The Faerie Queene* is a telling detail, serving, on the one hand, to emphasize the misery of the human condition and, on the other, to distance Spenser's vision of eternity from it. For Spenser, eternity, though it may be glanced at from history, lies beyond it; for Milton, in contrast, history may be brought to an apotheosis—the apocalypse may be realized within it, not through violence but through poetry, which is to say not through civil war but through mental revolution. At least this is the attitude Milton ultimately adopts.

Both Spenser and Milton, we have said, assume the role of prophet; and prophecy, we have been told, has an "ultimate projection," which is sometimes beyond history and sometimes is a history radically transformed.[176] Spenser's poetry provides the first kind of projection; Milton's, the second. Milton's vision does not end in gloomy pessimism or in prophetic despair; the poet does not surrender his commitment to renovating history, but simply abandons one tactic for another, retreating from one form of revolution in *Samson Agonistes* and proselytizing another form of it in *Paradise Regained,* having learned through the failure of the Puritan Revolution that a paradise without succeeds, is dependent upon, a paradise within. The grandeur of Milton's vision derives, in part, from a profound sense of prophetic expectation that is unmatched by anything in *The Faerie Queene.* Indeed, it is as if Spenser wrote *The Faerie Queene* in order to conjure up such expectations so that they might be exorcised. "The Red Cross Knight's story," as Isabel MacCaffrey observes, "ends with a prophecy of apocalypse, and Arthur, if the poem had been completed, would have united with the Queen whom he had previously experienced in his vision. It is a definition of apocalypse that in it vision and reality become one."[177] Everything after Book I, however, subverts such a notion; and the fact of the matter is that, rather than not completing his plan, which was to have culminated in a marriage, Spenser revised it, thereby distancing vision from reality and in the process denying a connection between them—at least in the realm of human history. There, at the end of Book VI, hope seems scattered; and the poet is afflicted with doubt extending into the poem and reflected in its final musings on the state of the world. If there is a similar sense at the end of *Paradise Lost,* it is mitigated by the apocalyptic allusions in the last lines of that poem and utterly dispelled by *Paradise Regained,* where the ardor and enthusiasm of the youthful Milton, dampened for awhile by the failure of the Puritan Revolution, are now revived and strengthened as the poet, like his Jesus, comes forth exalted from his trial. Milton thus draws out from John's prophecy the Christian radicalism that Spenser would eliminate from it.

Even so, surrounding the Revelation model are opposing traditions of commentary that provide precedents for the differing postures Spenser and Milton adopt. Like each of the poets, the one tradition is conservative, the other revolutionary. Revolutionary doctrines deriving from the Book of Revelation, many of them popularized by Joachim of Fiore and his followers and familiar to Milton through the commentaries of David Pareus and Joseph Mede, were disregarded by Protestant conservatives even as they were appropriated by Protestant radicals.[178] Conservatives and revolutionaries alike attend to John's prophecy, then, but for different reasons and in different ways: the former because it denounces Babylon and rails at Antichrist, whom they regard as Rome and the Pope respectively; the latter because it proclaims a *renovatio mundi* and shows how, through subversion, to establish it. The conservatives invest their faith in the English monarchs who, as Anglican popes, represent the orthodoxies by which man may endure; the revolutionaries, possessing faith in neither, project their hopes into a *renovator mundi* who by overthrowing the reigning orthodoxies will establish new, enduring values, and thereby enable man to prevail. Monarchs and priests are thus the maintainers of the one civilization, while poets and prophets are the expected founders of the other. Insofar as the responding parties to John's Apocalypse are Spenser and Milton, the one aligns himself with this conservative tradition, the other with the revolutionary one; and, in the process, Spenser must force a distinction between John's radical aesthetic and revolutionary ideology—a distinction that Milton will extinguish.

Spenser and Milton alike manifest their culture's compulsion to make new combinations, to establish new relationships; yet new combinations, new relationships, mergers of any kind, involve adjustments, accommodations, and alterations of sorts. The process is adroitly explained by Rosalie Colie: "as subcultures continually melt into or are absorbed by a neighboring culture, so did the kinds . . . melt into one another—often to enrich the possibilities of literature taken as a system."[179] The ultimate objective of this inclusionist operation is to reform man by making him see with his spiritual eye. Thus Spenser and Milton, unlike their epic precursors, cease to be story-tellers and become visionary artists. Epic, as Northrop Frye allows, had always been "the most continuous form of poetry ever devised."[180] By joining epic to prophecy, Spenser and Milton disrupt its easy movement, employing visionary tactics to make their poetry and its recipients

75

more reflective. Essential to the reforming process, reflection culminates in a renewed capacity to see; but in Spenser and Milton that capacity is cultivated with different objectives in mind, the two poets leading their reformed man in opposite ways. Spenser would have him conform to the established orthodoxies; and Milton, believing those orthodoxies deformed, would have him spurn them and thereupon begin to remake the world.

Yeats once remarked that "all good criticism is hieratic, delighting in setting things above one another, Epic and Drama above Lyric and so on, and not merely side by side."[181] The Miltonic hierarchy of genres is different from Spenser's. Accordingly, if Spenser is, as Yeats suggests, the last epic poet of the old order, Milton is the first in the new order. Spenser writes a prophetic epic and Milton authors an epic prophecy. These different accents point to the essential differences between Spenser's and Milton's poems and ultimately to the differences between the two poets. Spenser embraces a vision that Milton transcends. Thomas Vogler points to this conclusion when he writes that "epic is in some sense encyclopedic" and thus "include[s] tragedy, or the tragic vision, as something that must be transcended."[182] Milton comprehends that prophecy is the ultimate transcendental form: that is, tragedy is to epic what epic is to prophecy—the thing contained within a larger compass, contained not so that its vision of life will be affirmed but so that it may be subdued within a larger, more expansive vision. Understanding what may seem a modern principle, that there are "countergenres—twinned yet opposite,"[183] Milton subdues one form within the other, epic within prophecy, at the same time that he subverts the established values, replacing them with new ones. Through this confrontation of genres, Milton himself asserts a principle for his time that Claudio Guillén has formulated for our own: one form, its norms, are "dialectically surpassed (and assimilated) by another, as a genre by a countergenre."[184] By Milton prophecy is made to subsume epic in a dialectic that also restores prophecy to its original preeminence; and with him it enters the annals of English literature, poetry and prophecy now being irrevocably allied. If it was still said subsequent to Milton that "we . . . possess only some ruins . . . of that magnificent fabric" called prophecy, it was said by those who for the moment forgot the generic revolution Milton had accomplished.[185]

Milton's writings, both his poetry and his prose, show that revolutionary art involves, finally, a unity of aesthetics and ideology. To embrace this proposition is to correct Frye's hypothesis without discarding his conclusion: Spenser the conservative contrasts with Milton the revolutionary. It is not necessary to pursue this distinction into the contention that when aesthetics and ideology are in conflict art is in a state of decay; but it is essential to observe the distinction and to extract two conclusions from it. "When a culture disintegrates, when we lose a world-view," then, as Christopher Caudwell observes, "aesthetics too disintegrates."[186] *The Faerie Queene* reflects the cultural malaise evident in Hamlet's "The times are out of joint"; yet the feeling, concentrated in Book VI, is not so open, so oppressive, so pervasive as it becomes in the seventeenth century, and when it appears in Spenser it is accompanied not only by the compulsion to hold tenaciously to the old order but also by the need to find a new support for it. Spenser's compulsion Milton was compelled to check, but the need for a new aesthetic system Milton felt too.

As Charles Jones notes, Milton did not think the matching of form and content inevitable in a fallen world;[187] yet probably Milton would himself speak of the need for matching aesthetics and ideology, which if not always achieved in poetry is a hallmark of genuine prophecy. Without such a correspondence, poetry remains one of time's deformities, lacking, according to the extent of its deformity, in integrity. Spenser, whom Milton regarded as a greater teacher than Aquinas, may have required correction by his student, but not nearly so much, from Milton's point of view, as did Homer and Virgil and some of his own contemporaries. They seemed to maintain the gulf between epic and prophecy that Spenser began to bridge. From one perspective, of course, Spenser provided a sense of an ending, but from another he marked a new beginning. From Milton's point of view, though,

77

Spenser was only a beginning, initiating the merger of forms that Milton accomplished. The new form of epic-prophecy is not complete—it has no claim to total form—until aesthetic and ideology harmonize as a chord. It is this union of epic and prophecy, achieved not by depressing the radicalism of prophecy but by exploiting it, that led to the Romantics' great celebration of Milton, enabling him to advance beyond Spenser to the head of the line of visionary poets. For his successors, Milton was not a poet who sat near the thrones of church and state but one who sang a higher song of freedom; Milton (the Awakener, Blake and Shelley call him) was the authenticator of poets and poetry —of their power to reform man and to transform his world. For his successors, moreover, that transforming power—an attribute of prophecy no less than poetry—was as evident in Milton's poetry as in his prose. These together form a two-handed engine wielded by the prophetic Milton in a world that once was, but could no longer afford to be, impervious to his word.

Chapter II

A Fabric More Divine:
Lycidas As A Prophetic Paradigm

A poet hath one step unto a prophet . . .

—Ariosto

If ever a poet wished to be a prophetic poet it was
Milton . . .

—Sir Herbert J. C. Grierson

The companion poems, *L'Allegro* and *Il Penseroso,* are an
early and obvious example of the interdependence of poetry and
prophecy in Milton's art; and they are the first occasion, of many,
when Milton acknowledges a hierarchy of genres, allowing the
kinds here to assume a place among the various symbols that,
like the tower, figure progression in these twinned lyrics. Proceeding by degrees through different orders of experience—in
L'Allegro out of pastoral into the fantastical world of "mask,
and antique Pageantry" and then onto "the well-trod stage" of
Shakespearean and Jonsonian comedy (128–34); in *Il Penseroso*
through "Gorgeous Tragedy" into the epic-romances of Chaucer
and Spenser, Ariosto and Tasso (97–120)—the poet says he will
continue to aspire until, through "old experience," he attains "To
something like Prophetic strain" (173–74). This culminating
reference to prophecy is prepared for by an earlier one to things
"too bright / To hit the Sense of human sight" (13–14) and by
allusions both to that art "Where more is meant then meets the
ear" (120) and to those ecstasies which "bring all Heav'n"

79

(166) before the poet's eyes. Here, as in *At a Vacation Exercise,* the poet hopes that his mind may be "transported . . . / Above the wheeling poles, and at Heavn's dore / Look in" (33–35); and here again, as in *Elegia Sexta,* the poet, "resplendent with holy vestments," is "sacred to the gods" and their priest (74, 86–87). Touched by the same "hallow'd fire" (28) that anointed him in the Nativity Ode and driven, as in *Elegia Quinta,* by "holy sounds . . . within," well trained, like Thomas Young in *Elegia Quarta,* in how "to feed the sheep" (17–18) and knowing, as he does in *Ad Patrem,* that the poet's task is "song divine" (19), the poet of Milton's earliest poems is also the poet of *Lycidas*—the poet as prophet.

A prophetic voice speaks through Milton's prose tracts, but that voice is not first to be found there; rather, it is achieved earlier, most notably in *Lycidas.* Here the voice of the prophet predominates as it had never quite done before. "There is a wide difference," says Walter Taylor Field, "between the poet of *Comus* and the prophet of *Paradise Lost,* yet in each [poem] are the two natures."[1] In *Lycidas* those two natures are mixed just as they will be in Milton's last poems. Milton makes this point himself—through the very title he assigns to his poem. The name "Lycidas," Louis Martz has shown, refers to a shepherd who having become a poet speaks with a prophetic voice.[2] Calling attention to his prophetic voice by the title he assigns to his poem and, as we shall see later, by the phrase *Yet once more* that opens his poem, Milton here composes his first poem that, besides assimilating prophetic elements, is itself a prophecy. One great pastoral alteration, the displacement of the shepherd by the poet-prophet, may be attributed to Spenser; but an even greater alteration, initiated by Virgil in his Fourth Eclogue, the transformation of pastoral into prophecy, must be attributed to Milton. Indeed, through the designation he gives his poem, Milton claims this transformation for it: *Lycidas,* not a "soft lay" or simple pastoral, is a *"Dorick* lay" (189)—a song, marked by "divine Inspiration," that is "grave, divine, . . . oraculous."[3] A "continuous reflection," *Lycidas* is written in the prophetic mode—the mode, according to Maimonides, that represents "the highest degree and greatest perfection man can attain."[4] In consequence, *Lycidas* is a poem that states immensely.

None of Milton's poetry before *Lycidas* is more fully engaged with the theme of artistic progress than is that "single utterance,"[5] *L'Allegro* and *Il Penseroso.* The progress contemplated in these lyrics is the progress realized in *Lycidas.* The latter poem is like the earlier ones in that it is "begotten of a struggle"—but unlike them in that they convey the impression of struggle only in their subsurface.[6] *Lycidas,* on the other hand, dramatizes a struggle—one not imagined, but experienced and resolved by the poet. In this poem, as William Riley Parker suggests, Milton holds "in anxious suspension all the happenings of the year 1637,"[7] confronting in King's death both his mother's death and his own possible death and bringing out of that confrontation a complete mastery of his situation.

If *L'Allegro* and *Il Penseroso* are about a progress anticipated, *Lycidas* is about a progress accomplished. In this, the greatest poem of his early years, Milton, having progressed from innocence through experience into a higher innocence, has learned that "common experience, intellectual experience, poetic experience are not enough."[8] Having progressed from " 'I' to 'eye' to 'eyes' " —his *eyes* open to a light that is "too bright to hit the sense of human sight"—Milton can now write out of crisis a poem that is, as Rosemond Tuve has so beautifully stated, "the most poignant and controlled statement in English poetry of the acceptance of that in the human condition which seems to man unacceptable"; a poem that, blending "pastoral" and "baroque apocalyptic," is, as David Shelley Berkeley labels it, a "dire prophecy."[9] The hermit-prophet of *Il Penseroso,* in *Lycidas* becomes the great emancipator—the chastizer and renovator of Christendom. Here, vision enters the world of action; his confidence in the power of song buoyed by the story of Orpheus' success in liberating Eurydice from Pluto, Milton now is ready to unleash his power, his poetry, upon the world.

As a prophecy, *Lycidas,* both in its themes and its concerns, resembles *L'Allegro* and *Il Penseroso*. Even more emphatically than these earlier poems, though, it develops the theme of expanding eyes: eyelids open, tears beclouding the eyes are wiped away, and clarity of vision represented by "pure eyes" (81) is achieved. Like the earlier poems, however, *Lycidas* also mirrors "the process of a whole day from morning, through noon, to evening and night"; and correspondingly, when vision is achieved, it comes to the poet not in the blaze of noon but when the sun is about to set, all this in accordance with John Smith's proposition that divine light rises on the horizon at the very moment that natural light goes out, in the moment that the prophet's own human light sets.[10] Vision is thus divorced from, and thereby contrasted with, the light of day and physical sight, although the moment marking the beginning of man's ascent, the time of his awakening, is made to correspond with the phenomenon of a rising sun.

In *L'Allegro,* after the exhortation, the cock crows, scattering the "darkness thin"; and a few lines later, the hounds and horn are said to "rouse the slumbring morn" (50, 55). The horn, the hounds, even the barnyard fowl, are objects in this landscape; but these objects are all, it seems, translated into symbols. As Pico della Mirandola acknowledges, the cock as a symbol represents the divine part of man's soul: when the cock crows, as light dawns, man comes to his senses; and the process of awakening to a new life begins. The genius of Milton's companion poems is that images at first seeming to be no more than literalistic detail suddenly burst forth as symbols, and through them the meaning of these poems is opened to us. The progress toward total consciousness, as *Il Penseroso* demonstrates, involves a retreat into contemplation—a withdrawal, Pico explains, "into the center of . . . [man's] own unity, his spirit," whereupon he becomes one with God. Not an end in itself, this ascent enables man to "descend, well taught and well prepared, to the functions of the active life."[11]

It was once thought that because *L'Allegro* and *Il Penseroso* represent "only moods, . . . only day dreams," Milton makes "no attempt . . . to link them, or to adjudicate between them in the context of a larger framework of thought."[12] Recent criticism, however, has shown otherwise: that these poems, like Blake's *Songs of Innocence and of Experience,* depict "the Two Contrary States of the Human Soul"; that those states, even if hierarchically valued, are interrelated and interdependent. These poems accord with Milton's thinking when, writing *Tetrachordon,* he observes that we must slacken "the cords of intense thought and labour," for "we cannot . . . always be contemplative . . . , but have need of som delightfull intermissions, wherin the enlarg'd soul may leav off a while her severe schooling" (*Yale Milton,* 4:596–97, 413). Furthermore, these poems reflect the careful discrimination between contraries advanced by Milton in *The Art of Logic.* By Milton's definition, *L'Allegro* and *Il Penseroso* are affirming contraries, which in this instance are to be seen as "adverses"—as states that are "diagonally" related to one another. Even in their opposition, however, such states are able to mingle; yet because they are contraries, they are never equal, their inequality being indicated in signs (*Columbia Milton,* 11:127, 149, 169). Life is process, Milton is saying, involving progression and regression, aspiration and retreat. Thus the poet of *Il Penseroso,* while valuing his superior state, does not repudiate the state represented by *L'Allegro,* for he must continually reenter that world. It is this temporal process with which Milton's twin lyrics and then *Lycidas* (in a somewhat different but even more emphatic way) are concerned.

In *Lycidas,* process is figured through the transformation of an uncouth swain into a princely prophet, a transformation that finds one precedent in Amos, the shepherd, who is told to go forth and prophesy on the assumption that "moral and spiritual rebirth is the only soil out of which a better world can grow."[13] Yet another precedent for the poet's transfiguration in *Lycidas* is provided by the parallel one undergone by Moses. To some, it has seemed that the line of development between *Lycidas* and *Paradise Lost* positions Milton within classical tradition, paralleling his literary career—its movement from pastoral to epic—with

Virgil's. However, the fact of the matter is that "the Christian poet advances his career by reversing the career of the classical poet";[14] and thus Milton probably had another analogy in mind, one that would set his poem within scriptural tradition and that would parallel both his intellectual development and literary career with Moses'. The prophet Hosea alludes to Moses when he says that "by a prophet the Lord brought Israel out of Egypt" (12:13); and Hosea's implication, rather than being that Moses merely asserts the birth of Israel, is that in and through Moses, who was once a shepherd but now is a prophet, Israel is born. Throughout Christian history, there has been a recurring interest in Moses, an interest accompanied by the sense that, because the mission of Moses went unfulfilled, there is a need for another Moses who will take up the task of the old Moses anew. *Paradise Lost* thus begins with Milton's proclaiming his muse to be the same one that "on the secret top / Of *Oreb,* or of *Sinai,* didst inspire / That Shepherd" (I.6–8), a claim that identifies Milton as a Second Moses and his audience as a Second Chosen People. Perhaps kings and priests were not to lead the battle against Antichrist or to be the realizers of messianic expectations; but England, says Christopher Hill, "was still the chosen nation"— was expected to "give a lead to Europe—*now.*"[15] In England, poets enlightened by revelation would have a crucial role to play: the spiritual sword, for a long time sheathed, would now be unsheathed; and the poets would bring forth the New Jerusalem. Adopting such an attitude—making apocalyptic exhortations to England and emphasizing "God's manner of dealing with the nations, and the spiritual role chosen for his Englishmen in the overthrow of antichrist"[16]—Milton shows himself to be like both Moses and Spenser, the prophetic poets he is now ready to rival.

The *locus classicus* for Milton's objective appears in *Areopagitica,* where England is portrayed first as "a strong man" rousing himself from sleep and then "as an Eagle muing her mighty youth" (*Yale Milton,* 2:558). "Nothing in Milton," says Frank Kermode, "is more Spenserian"[17] than this and other similar passages in Milton's early prose tracts. The passage here cited is best glossed—its implications most fully manifested—by a parallel passage in Dr. Twisse's Preface to Joseph Mede's commentary on the Book of Revelation. There, Twisse speaks of "God awaking . . . out of a sleep . . . like a gyant refreshed . . . : and the Lord Christ awaking, and stirring up his strength for the raising up of *Jacob,* and restoring the desolations of *Israel,* and blessing us with a resurrection of his Gospel." Twisse then proceeds to parallel the awakening of Israel with the awakening of England.[18] Equally pertinent is a passage from "The Prophecie of Thomas Rymour," who like Spenser delivers his visions from the shadows of fairyland and who like Milton understands that "A prophet . . . saythe, Awake englishmen," the prophet knowing that a great man "shall rise owte of his slepe a lyve man," that great men will "rise againe & live."[19]

In the passage from *Areopagitica* just alluded to, Milton conflates two symbols (the strong man and the eagle) and, with them, two myths (the one of individual regeneration, the other of national renewal). Following tradition in conjoining myth with symbol, Milton accentuates their interrelatedness, the promise of the one anticipating the other, its fulfillment ensuring the fulfillment promised by the other. Implicit in the tradition, as well as in Milton's works, is the idea that the functions of the prophet and legislator are united, but also the idea that only through Christ is there to be a fulfillment of prophetic expectations: Christ invades history, he incarnates, awakens, the prophet who, in turn, awakens his nation; Christ and the prophet together remake the world. Milton is like Moses and Spenser in that they all possess a vision; but he thinks of himself as being more like their antitype who is Christ, for like Christ Milton is prepared to deliver a vision that will free his nation from bondage. Writing his poetry as a plea for the illumination of the English people and their nation, Milton would translate vision into word, holding out the prospect that the word will initiate action.

Milton's prophetic poetry, then, exists within a larger prophecy for a nation; and thus what Octavio Paz would claim for Walt

Whitman may likewise be claimed for Milton: his poetry "is a great prophetic dream, but it is a dream within another dream, a prophecy within another prophecy that is even vaster and that nourishes it."[20] Not just an embodiment of the poet's highest aspirations, such poetry embodies the highest ideals existing within a nation; and, because Christ "worketh by the ministery of men,"[21] such poets become the implementors of those ideals, bringing individual men and thereupon their nations into Christ's glory. In these suppositions, *Paradise Lost* is not an advance upon *Lycidas;* it merely makes bold the claim underlying Milton's first prophecy, which is a preludium to this later, more expansive and more urgent one.

It may be said that pastoral poetry constitutes both "a symbolic and an actual entry into the poetic arena,"[22] but at the same time it should be acknowledged that *Lycidas* is not Milton's first pastoral poem and therefore does not represent his emergence as a poet. Rather, *Lycidas* is a poem in which an already accomplished poet assumes the role of a prophet—in which Milton makes prophecy not only an attribute of poetry but synonymous with poetry. This prophecy, which ought to be about Edward King, according to many of Milton's critics is really about Milton. Like all prophecy, though, however much it may look like history (even personal history), *Lycidas* is "written in the future tense"[23] and therefore is less about King than Milton, less about his past than his future, and finally less about Milton than the uncouth swain—all of us. *Lycidas* is about our capacity to rise out of sorrow into joy, to experience a second baptism, to be renewed through prophecy and to create in the here and now a new heaven and a new earth, just as Milton creates out of his prophetic consciousness the apocalyptic hopes of his prose tracts and the new paradise of his epics. It is, of course, a convention of prophecy to include—even sometimes to review—actual history; but this is done always with the same intention—that of making prophecy, already irrevocably involved in history, the maker of history.

Only after the fact of the Puritan Revolution, which seemed to so many a "lively performance of things hitherto abstruse and concealed"[24] in John's Apocalypse, and only after the fact of Milton's later accomplishments, does *Lycidas* look like history. In 1637, however, *Lycidas* is written to prophesy not just national but personal history, which for Milton are very much involved, each with the other. As a prophecy, *Lycidas* draws upon England's history and upon Milton's own personal history; it both assumes contexts and may be assumed as a context for Milton's prose works and last poems. Forging here the prophetic stance of the prose tracts, Milton also creates "a thematic paradigm, . . . a structural and stylistic model" for his last poems.[25] As a climax in Milton's maturing, *Lycidas* provides a particularly lofty perspective from which to view the poet's later work.

Lycidas *in Context*

Some critics, of course, attend only to the uniqueness of poetry: as Northrop Frye observes, they would reduce a poem "to a jangle of echoes of itself."[26] Others, however, mark only the conventional element in poetry; and they, like so many critics of *Lycidas,* would reduce a poem to a succession of echoes from other poets. *Lycidas,* for example, is often read (and too often dismissed) as a poem so "loaded with allusions" that it "can be fully enjoyed only by the classical scholar in the tradition of the Greek pastoralists."[27] *Lycidas,* indisputably, is loaded with allusions; it belongs to that class of literature which is "continuously, . . . explicitly, allusive."[28] Within its 193 lines is an astonishing range of reference; yet all of it is part of the poem's method and of the poet's methodology, which imposes upon his readers the obligation of examining any given text's relationship to sources and models.[29] Words, phrases, line clusters—even the poem's form—are allusive. Still, Milton's is no ordinary poetry of allusion. For here allusion operates not just to deepen the resonances and to complicate the meaning of a line but, more importantly, to indicate a relationship and thereby to unfold the meaning of the entire poem. Allusion is also the vehicle Milton employs to push *Lycidas* beyond local circumstance into the realm of the universal. In the process, one poet comes to stand for all creative men, a poem lamenting the death of one man becomes a universal lament and then celebration, a moment in history comes to speak for a pattern of experience that repeats itself through history.

If we need an analogue for the allusive character of *Lycidas,* it is to be found in the Book of Revelation, whose most striking compositional feature is its use of the Old Testament. Its 404 verses, we have been shown, contain 518 Old Testament citations and allusions, 88 to the Book of Daniel alone.[30] What the Old Testament is to the Apocalypse the pastoral tradition is to *Lycidas:* both works are rereadings of their contexts, and rewritings of them, in the light of a new prophetic moment. Thus what John's "poem," and Milton's, demonstrate is that in visionary literature, allusions in the form of repeated words, phrases, and ideas are both definers of contexts and authenticators of them, as Patrick Fairbairn remarks, "connecting the earlier with the later, certifying the existence of the earlier, and confirming [it] anew . . . [by] throwing new light on its import."[31] The new vision, then, brings light to the darkness of all the former visions; yet it also receives light from them.

If a prophecy is carefully conceived, its separate visionary panels, especially the first, will provide the key for interpreting what follows; and this same principle operates, through allusion, to connect one prophecy with another, the old prophecy containing the key that opens the new one, enabling the act of interpretation to begin. Possessing the gift of inspiration, the prophet also lays claim to the gift of interpretation, and so every new prophecy is an interpretation of what it succeeds and a vision requiring and receiving interpretation from the works it inspires. A poem such as *Lycidas,* for example, is both an interpretation of, let us say, *The Shepheardes Calender* and the recipient of interpretation from a poem like Shelley's *Adonais. Lycidas* is one of the poems that must have inspired Shelley's remark in *The Defence of Poetry*—a remark, it is seldom noticed, that refers specifically to the rich tradition of bucolic poetry. Such compositions, according to Shelley, may be perceived "simply as fragments and isolated portions," or they may be seen as "more finely organized, . . . as episodes to that great poem, which all poets, like the co-operating thoughts of one great mind, have built up since the beginning of the world."

That *Lycidas* is a link in this chain, like Spenser's *Calender* and Shelley's *Adonais;* that it is, as Shelley might say, an episode in the "cyclic poem written by Time upon the memories of men"; that Milton meant for us to consider his poem in such a light—all this is implied by the method of allusion in *Lycidas* which, says Lorna Sage, "leads the reader outside the formal limits of the poem into many other poems written before, and since. Thus it gathers meaning from the work of other poets who have explored the same mythological territory in search of some order to accommodate death."[32] Forcing upon the mind the question of where meaning is to be anchored, such allusions point not to *Lycidas*'s sources but to its context, which, in the broadest sense, is literature; yet literature, in turn, yields up less general but still generalized contexts for reading, and in the process for unraveling the meaning of, Milton's poem. These literary backdrops serve as an antidote to the obscurity of *Lycidas,* and they are established decisively by the different settings in which *Lycidas* appeared.

The poems in *Justa Edovardo King Naufrago,* themselves a backdrop for *Lycidas,* point also to *Lycidas*'s liturgical context; and *Arcades* and *Comus* (the poems surrounding *Lycidas* both in the 1645 *Poems of Mr. John Milton* and the 1673 *Poems upon Several Occasions*) similarly provide a setting for reading *Lycidas* even as these poems look toward *Lycidas*'s Spenserian context. Both the liturgical and Spenserian backdrops, moreover, gesture toward the Book of Revelation, where pastoral and prophecy are irrevocably allied. In *Lycidas,* therefore, context is doubly important, on the one hand serving as a key to the poem's meaning and on the other hand indicating the genre in which the poem's meaning is invested. Here, as in *Il Penseroso,* the prophet's vision is isolated from—is made to stand apart from and beyond—the pastoral world it is called upon to redeem.

It has been noticed that *Lycidas* begins, "almost as though it were specifically designed for the last position in the book in which it first appeared."[33] Just how much there is to that suggestion Michael Lloyd and J. B. Leishman have begun to show us.[34] Written in November, 1637, *Lycidas* was published in 1638, in the second part of a volume which, with its own title page, contains thirteen poems in English (see Appendix B). Those poems are entangled with one another—a poem here echoing a poem there, this poem rivaling that one. *Lycidas,* printed last in the volume, appears to participate in the collaboration, to be part of a comprehensive design; and thus Lloyd's perception cannot be overemphasized: Milton's "position, both as commentator and poet, permitted to reply to the other poems in the collection and to offer their poetic culmination, was a privileged one"; and so we shall miss a part of Milton's intention if we do not see that, besides developing his own themes, Milton is organizing those of the book as a whole—organizing them in such a way that the "Weep no more" of *Lycidas* is a turning point both in Milton's poem and in the larger poem to which *Lycidas* is the final contribution.[35] In this, Milton has the powerful precedent of Spenser—not only for mythologizing a dead poet's story, but for interlacing his own poem with all the others belonging to a memorial volume. In *Astrophel,* Spenser simply leads off a chorus of lamentation, whereas in *Lycidas* Milton brings such a chorus to its period, as Alastair Fowler explains, by writing a "coda . . . terminating the whole mourning rite."[36]

The introductory poem in the English section of the volume, by Henry King, sets the pattern for the others. Declining to "examine Gods decree," to "question providence," King nevertheless invites others to take up this theme, to "sing the world his Epicedium," "Pattern[ing] a grief," felt by "both Church and State / . . . and many thousands more," that may serve us all to mourn for future losses. Like the other poems in this volume

(*Lycidas* excepted), King's headpiece is an expression of grief, not an exploration of it—an assertion of providence, not like *Lycidas,* a questioning of it. Yet like *Lycidas,* King's poem focuses the paradox that it is the living who are dead, who are "shipwrack't," and the dead who through resurrection, "recover[ing] . . . from the first great fall," are truly alive. The tone of King's poem is determined throughout by its stern theology, portraying death as God's "executioner" and the sea (those "guilty waters") as his instrument; but it also establishes a perspective, adopted by some of the other poems, from which Edward King's drowning may be seen as a second baptism and from which King himself may be seen as someone other than himself—as perhaps "Some one of the celestiall Hierarchies." The second poem, signed by Joseph Beaumont, begins as King's poem ends, is thus "A faithfull Echo" of it; but then Beaumont proceeds to argue with King's conclusion, asserting that the sea is no destructive agent, no slave to him who wrought it. Raising hard questions, and itself a series of questions, this poem ends with an assuring voice that calls all those "questions into question"—one which tells the poet that, not imprisoned below, Edward King who soared so high in this world has now soared into heaven, becoming there a celestial flower, the amaranthus of *Lycidas.*

The resurrection motif, firmly established by these initial poems, is further developed by those succeeding them. The third poem, unsigned, commences with a reference to Phoebus Apollo and then continues by saying that in response to King's death, a "sad untimely fall," the stars go out and the sun lies down upon its western bed, only to conclude by associating Edward King with the sun that "by the deep / Didst climbe to th' highest heav'ns" where it is "crown'd / A King." In aftertimes, the poet concludes, it may be found that Edward King is "Edward the Confessour, or the Saint." This anonymous poem also develops the paradox that death, which seems a destructive agent, a slayer of poets, is actually a creative force, a maker of poets. The next two poems, written by John Cleveland and William More, similarly refer to King's resurrection from the deep; yet both these poets chide their precursors—Cleveland because, weeping in tune, employing rhymes, they have expressed their grief artificially; and More because, telling of King's life alone, they have not discerned the larger pattern—they have not comprehended, and therefore have not been able to celebrate, God's design. Edward King was bound for heaven, not Ireland, More concludes, and like Elijah, "Rapt in a fierie chariot," enters those fires above. William Hall, in the sixth poem of the volume, similarly chastizes the other poets for the formality of their grief ("Poetick measures have not learn'd to bound / Unruly sorrows"); yet, like Henry King, Hall uses the metaphor of the fatal bark, and like many of the other poets, he imagines King in his life to be like a setting sun that, once night has passed, will rise, showing its beams again:

> So did thy light, fair soul, it self withdraw
> To no dark tombe by natures common law,
> But set in waves, when yet we thought it noon,
> And thence shall rise more glorious then the sunne.

The seventh poem, by Samson Briggs, intersects through its imagery with some of the earlier poems: it begins with Phoebus, in a sable hood, mourning the death of Edward King who, by the end of the poem, has become a King; and, like Henry King's poem, it counsels that it is not for the poet to question Providence, thereby "Riddl[ing] us into atheisme." Yet such counseling comes after Briggs's own expression of disbelief at King's death. "How can my faith but startle now," he says, "that we / Are yet reserv'd another floud to see":

> . . . I scarce can find belief to think it done.
> For when because of sinne God opened all
> Heavens cataracts to let his vengeance fall
>
> .   .   .   .   .   .
>
> After his anger was appeas'd, he bound
> Himself, never again the world to drown:
>
> .   .   .   .   .   .
>
> . . . Could God forget

His covenant which in the clouds he set?
Where was the bow?

To avoid answering these questions, all of which Milton enter-
tains, Briggs must banish his muse, who has been asking them in a
poem where not just Phoebus, but all of nature and the entire
university join the poet in his mourning. These motifs, along with
others introduced to the volume through the next poem, by Isaac
Olivier, will be woven into *Lycidas,* especially Olivier's reference
to the dolphin and his mention of Arethusa, together with his
suggestion that King should have been "a lustie bridegroom" and,
like St. Peter, should have "trode the waves." Milton's strategy
here is identical with John's in the Book of Revelation: there,
John writes "a Christian Ezekiel or Zechariah *in the phrase of the
old*";[37] here, writing generally within the idiom of these precursor
poems, Milton similarly draws their various strands into his own
rope, in *Lycidas* creating a new poem out of old poems and simultaneously giving a new birth to poetic phrases, images, and
themes. *Lycidas,* like the Book of Revelation, is "stolen poetry"[38]
—but in this very special sense.

Yet Milton will not always reassert earlier themes, or appropriate images previously used. He will not, for instance, explain
providence as simply the grace that enables others to endure the
grief that comes with death, as John Hayward does in the ninth
poem of this volume; nor will he praise the church, thereby pay-
ing lip service to those who believe that vilifying it or its clergy
is the activity only of "Misguided people." He will not like Hayward, or like C. B. (Christopher Brembridge?) in the tenth poem
of the volume, turn from lamenting the deceased to celebrating
his living sister as none other than her "sex-transformed brother."
Milton will, however, seem to heed Hayward's advice that when
"verse and tears . . . sympathize" both will be without number;
and he will employ the reminder of the eleventh poem, by R.
Brown, that the nymphs were absent when King died, as well as
Brown's consolation, that purified by the waters of the sea King
revives. He will also allow his poem to rise out of the nadir—"a

planned depth of despair"[39]—that is reached in the twelfth poem, by T. Norton, where "Perpetual Night . . . / Puts on her mourning-weeds" and where Apollo, having gone to bed, leaves the whole world in darkness, all its members drowned in a general deluge. As the Book of Revelation was said to do, *Lycidas* "darts a beam of light through the solemn gloom" of the poem it succeeds, Milton knowing better than any of these poets that the elegiac poet plays "the Phisitian . . . making greef it selfe . . . cure of the disease"—*the despair*—with which death afflicts mankind.[40] Milton was probably not in the mind of Byron's Dante when he uttered the words, "his grief/Shall make an immortality of tears / . . . and his higher song / Of freedom wreathe him with as green a leaf"; yet those words aptly describe the poet's motive in composing *Lycidas,* as well as the poem's achievement.

Yet another tear shed for Edward King, *Lycidas* would hasten the time, also anticipated by Byron's Dante, "When Truth shall strike . . . [the] eyes through many a tear." In accordance with the idea that God gives man great comfort, even in the midst of tears,[41] *Lycidas* issues forth from the deluge, from total darkness, as a prophecy—as a clear light meant to release man from death into life; as a glorious light, a morning star, at once symbolizing God's providence and exemplifying his mercy. The sun is an image, Apollo a figure, in many of these poems; but only Milton recalls the identification of Apollo as "a leader of both Kings and people to a higher life," his role as "the dispenser of just retribution to all, from swineherds to Kings."[42] And only Milton develops the associations made in the *Hymn to Apollo,* where, identified as the source of all prophetic wisdom and as a god bestowing prophecy upon men, Apollo is also celebrated for guarding ships safely to shore. These associations, gathered into the typological system of *Lycidas,* enable Milton, in the very first movement of his poem, to begin meeting the challenge set for all these poets by Henry King: to take up the theme of God's providence and to pattern a grief that, serving men in their mourning of future losses, will awaken them from their own death-in-life.

Lycidas has sometimes been called an occasional poem, a designation that fits the other poems included in *Justa Edovardo King Naufrago* better than it fits Milton's; for it alone comprehends what Angus Fletcher calls the "pathos in the occasion . . . commemorating the moment of its loss" and thereby making the "poem . . . a tomb."[43] Paradoxically, by slighting the occasion and by turning King into Lycidas, Milton eternalizes the moment; by subsuming the patterns of the other poems within his own ritual, knowing that ritual promises continuance through repetition, Milton ensures that his own poem will live beyond the moment and simultaneously allows every other poem to live in the moment of his own. *Lycidas* is thus the only poem measuring up to what Henry King had hoped that all the poems would be— an invitation to participate in an elaborate ritual that would serve others in the mourning of all future losses. In these twelve poems, there is not a pattern of grief that *Lycidas* does not encompass, nor a thematic statement that Milton, even if he must alter or sometimes reverse it, does not expand. Indeed, *Lycidas* concludes by turning back to, by then turning on end, the very phrase that opens the English section of this volume, King's exclamation, "No death!" being rendered anew by the proclamation of *Lycidas:* that "Christ is the death of our death,"[44] that after the first resurrection, there is *no more death.* For all the similarities *Lycidas* shares with these other poems, still it finally relates to them as *L'Allegro* and *Il Penseroso* relate to each other: nearly every point of contact, upon scrutiny, becomes a point of contrast.

Seeming to rejoice in the spirit of rivalry that marks *Justa Edovardo King Naufrago,* Milton writes *Lycidas* (to borrow Henry King's phrase) in "a strain higher" than the other poems in this volume and as an open rejoinder to some of them. Resisting all the hyperbole in the poems preceding it,[45] *Lycidas* also does what many of them recoil from. Those that introduce the question of providence retreat from it, following King's declaration that "Discreet Religion binds us to admire / The wayes of providence, and not enquire." Those poems that are informed by theology adopt a rigidly Calvinistic position, supporting orthodoxies—even to the point of criticizing those who would impute corruption to the church or its clergy, who would see in either "the blatant beast." At most, the poems preceding *Lycidas* climax in a statement of belief, contrasting with Milton's poem which culminates in vision. All these poems, except *Lycidas,* are rhymed, usually in couplets, though some poets question the decorum of formalizing expressions of grief, artificializing them, in poetry; and John Cleveland very pointedly speaks of the impossibility of mourning in rhyme. No true mourner, he says, can confine his sentiments to "the Muses Rosarie"; grief knows no laws but runs its course like the waves. So formalized are most of these poems that, besides rhyming in couplets, they follow conspicuously the mechanical structure of the funeral elegy.

In every instance, *Lycidas* pursues the path from which the other poets waver: it confronts the overwhelming questions of existence that these poems, even when they raise them, resist— "was justice made so blind?" was Edward King only "partly blest"? is the sea to blame for his death, or, if it is guiltless, what of the nymphs? the muses? What of God?—did he "forget his covenant?" *Lycidas* is the one poem that questions providence so as to effect an understanding of it—that challenges orthodoxies, both theological and institutional, in the form of a wrathful, vengeful deity and of a corrupt church, Milton's intention being to subvert both. Acquiescing in Cleveland's belief that "The sea's too rough for verse," Milton spurns the laws of rhyming by way of warding off the charge of artificiality. Apparent wildness and irregularity run through *Lycidas;* but as John Thyer once remarked, these qualities give "the greatest grace to the whole," for instead of violating decorum they observe the principle, never understood by Dr. Johnson, that "Grief is eloquent, but not formal."[46] Thus representing through his artistry the heavy motions of his grief, Milton also uses the pattern of the funeral elegy as rough scaffolding for his poem; yet doing so, he underplays the narration, subsuming it within his double lamentation and thereby avoiding the excesses of the other poems.

No other poem in the volume *seems* so chaotic, so much a collection of "shattered fragments," so "filled with shocks of dis-

continuity" and metaphysical shudders;[47] but surfaces in Milton
are deceptive, for beside these other poems, *Lycidas* is more rigor-
ously controlled, more intricately patterned, more subtly and
strongly organized. In a word, *Lycidas* has massive unity. As a
poem, it is triumphantly affirmative; and therefore like *Paradise
Lost,* arises from chaos without ever being chaotic. Where these
other poets see only the shattering of the world by death, Milton
sees "the shape of the world in the dispersion of its fragments";
where these other poets can only sink further and further into
despair, Milton moves unremittingly toward "a startling penetra-
tion to a new perception of order."[48] It is the other poets in this
volume who descend, "rending . . . unity like Osiris into many
parts"; Milton is the poet who ascends, "with the force of
Phoebus collecting the parts like limbs of Osiris into a unity."[49]

If one can peel away perversity from genuine perception, then
with great reward he may study *Lycidas* (as Harold Bloom might
do) as "a psychic battleground" exemplifying the reliance of
texts upon texts, as well as the fact that because texts are so often,
and in such complicated ways, intervolved, "any poem is an inter-
poem."[50] Many of the poems in *Justa Edovardo King Naufrago,*
including *Lycidas,* assume a dialectical relationship with one
another; yet *Lycidas,* alone among these poems, is an active
complication of all the others. *Lycidas* is therefore the one poem
that is engaged in a mediating process; yet as a poem, it also
challenges the contention that "only weak poems, or the weaker
elements in strong poems, immediately echo precursor poems, or
directly allude to them,"[51] even as it confirms, in yet-to-be-
examined ways, the belief that the most vital and meaningful
links between poetic texts involve other than surface phenomena.

Some, but not all, of the poems in *Justa Edovardo King
Naufrago* are prophetic of *Lycidas;* and those which are reveal
that in *Lycidas* "the poem hidden in the earlier poem[s] comes
out from its concealment."[52] The extent to which this is so may
be suggested, first, by turning to *Lycidas* and noting how the
process that involves *Lycidas* with these other poems is written
into *Lycidas* itself: just as Milton's poem struggles to emerge from

beneath the covering of these other poems, so its consolation—the apocalyptic vision and promise—struggles to emerge from beneath the heavy grief and searing anger that dominate most of *Lycidas.* In Milton's poem, there *is* passion—concealed sometimes by a pastoral facade and "filtered through many runlets" so that, like Dr. Johnson, we are for awhile "blinded to the real fulness of the stream"; yet, from St. Peter's invective onward, Milton's poem surges with emotion that "runs in one current, and irresistibly."[53] The process by which *Lycidas* comes out from concealment is also suggested by the way that *Lycidas,* as a mourning ritual, issues forth as a restatement of those themes embedded in "The Order for the Burial of the Dead" as it appears in *The Book of Common Prayer.* Its opening declaration is reaffirmed in the penultimate verse paragraph of Milton's poem, "I am the resurrection and the life"; and like the church's mourning rite, Milton's poem uses another man's death to meditate upon the fact that in the midst of life we too are in death. Repeatedly turning its attention from the dead man to the living, *Lycidas,* like "The Order for the Burial of the Dead," proclaims that bodies terrestrial may become bodies celestial: man "is sown a natural body" and rises again, in this life, "a spiritual body"; in that moment, having been born in "the image of the earthy," man comes to bear "the image of the heavenly."

Lycidas is thus a poem buried in, but now issuing forth from, both the Bible and the Church's liturgy. The Church's mourning rite provides Milton's poem with its master-theme, while another set of liturgies, pointed to by the Edward King-King Edward-King of Heaven conceit, particularizes, as well as augments, the resurrection theme, even as this set of liturgies contributes to the design of Milton's poem. That conceit, explicit in some of the poems in *Justa Edovardo King Naufrago,* has resonances that, however muted, are still to be heard in *Lycidas.*[54] Nevertheless, not the conceit itself, but the context of meaning to which it led Milton should draw our interest, and here several facts are worth recalling.

Edward King, according to the record books, died on August

10, 1637; and it was said that he knelt in prayer while his ship was sinking. Milton wrote his poem, judging from his manuscript, in "Novmb: 1637." In November the feast of King Edward the Martyr is celebrated, his feast day designated as November 20 and his name, in most seventeenth-century liturgical tables, appearing simply as Edmund or Edward King (see fig. 9).[55] In *The History of Britain,* Milton remembers that Edward (like Lycidas) came to an untimely death (*Yale Milton,* 5:i, 317); and Milton must also have remembered that Edward was honored for having sacrificed himself for his people—an act that every prophet, by annihilating his selfhood, must repeat and that every prophet subsequently invites the unregenerate to undertake (see fig. 6). It should also be noted that Milton had previously drawn the inspiration for his poetry from the Bible, not by dipping into it here and there but by using it systematically—by using liturgical readings, allowing them to contribute thematically and structurally to the visions that became his poems. In the Nativity Ode he employed the Christmas liturgy, and in *Comus* he derived his vision from the readings assigned for Michaelmas Feast.[56] In *Lycidas,* it appears, Milton exploits the analogy between Edward King and King Edward both differently and more subtly than any other poet in *Justa Edovardo King Naufrago.* That is, the liturgical readings assigned for King Edward's feast day provide a setting for *Lycidas,* offering to Milton a reservoir of themes and solutions for his poem. Or more exactly: this liturgy combines with that for August 10th, the date of Edward King's death, these liturgies together offering alternately a pattern for lamentation and for consolation in *Lycidas.* In this, setting a course later to be taken by John Archer (1645), Milton "muster[s] together, the scattered ground of comfort in Scripture";[57] and doing so, he appears to subscribe to a view of the Bible very much like Goethe's, regarding it as a second world wherein we lose ourselves, enlighten and educate, find and create ourselves.

Especially noteworthy about the August 10th readings (Jeremiah 49, Acts 8, Jeremiah 50, and Hebrews 13) is the heavy accent placed on God's vengeance. Full of howling and lamenting ("gird you with sackcloth,"), Jeremiah 49, reporting Edom's fall into desolation, prophesies a last judgment: *"there is* sorrow on the sea; it cannot be quiet . . . I will bring evil upon them, *even* my fierce anger, saith the LORD and I will send the sword after them." Chapter 50 develops this prophecy. Here the situation is like that in *Lycidas,* and the prophet's sentiments correspond with those of Milton. "My people hath been lost sheep: their shepherds have caused them to go astray," says Jeremiah; but "their Redeemer *is* strong." Yoking together the themes of judgment and redemption, this prophecy promises that the weapon of the Lord— "his oppressive sword" (his engine), "his indignation"—will come forth to smite the infidels in a last, angry judgment, a prophecy that Milton allows to climax his invective against the clergy. Acts 8 similarly provides a precedent for that invective, since here, talking both of death and baptism, Peter lashes out at false teachers and false prophets, his invective aroused by the death of Stephen, as a part of the great lamentation for him; and one of the principal concerns of that lament is the making of the prophet.

The other reading prescribed for August 10th is similarly pertinent to Milton's poem. Hebrews 13 assures those who have faith in Jesus that in his resurrection they will find that timeless pattern which, delineated in *Lycidas,* is the ultimate justification of God's ways to men. Written in a prophetic style, Paul's epistle, especially its final chapter, teaches men to apply what is said about others to themselves: "Remember them that are in bonds, and bound with them; *and* them which suffer adversity, as being yourselves also in the body." Here Christ's resurrection, like Lycidas', is rendered as a type of our own; he is shown to begin "the Resurrection . . . [that] shalbee finished in us"; and our own resurrection, in turn, may be described as a "proeme unto the *second* or universal resurrection."[58] Ostensibly referring to the

Fig. 9. The Table of Saints for the Month of November. Reproduced from *The Book of Common Prayer* (1635) by permission of the Huntington Library, San Marino, California.

		Mor. Prayer.		Euen. Prayer.	
		1. Lef.	2. Lef.	1. Lef.	2. Lef.
1	f	Gyles.	Hof.13	Mat.2.	Hof.14	Rom.2
2	g		Ioel 1.	3	Ioel 2.	3
3	A		3	4	Am. 1.	4
4	b	Dogge	Am. 2.	5	3	5
5	c	dayes	4	6	5	6
6	d	end.	6	7	7	7
7	e	Enur.b.	8	8	9	8
8	f	Nat. of	Obad.i	9	Iona.1	9
9	g	Mary.	Ion.2,3	10	4	10
10	A		Mic.1.	11	Mic.2.	11
11	b		3	12	4.	12
12	c	Sol in	5	13	6	13
13	d	Lib.	7	14	Nah.1.	14
14	e	Holy cr.	Nah.2	15	3	15
15	f	Equin.	Hab.1.	16	Hab.2.	16
16	g	Autum	3	17	Zeph.1	1.cor.1
17	A	Lambert	Zeph.2	18	3	2
18	b		Hag.1.	19	Hag.2.	3
19	c		Zec. 1.	20	Zec.2,3	4
20	d	Faft.	4.5.	21	6	5
21	e	S. Mat-	Ecc.35	22	Ecc.38	6
22	f	thew.	Zec.7.	23	Zec.8.	7
23	g		9	24	10	8
24	A		11	25	12	9
25	b		13	26	14	10
26	c	Cyprian	Mal.1.	27	Mal.2.	11
27	d		3	28	4	12
28	e		Tob.1.	Mar.1.	Tob.2.	13
29	f	S. Mich.	Ecc.39	2	Ec.44.	14
30	g	Hierom	Tob.3.	3	Tob.4	15

		Mor. Prayer.		Euen. Prayer	
		1. Lef.	2. Lef.	1. Lef.	2. Lef.
1	A	Remige	(*⁎*)	Mar.4.	Tob.6.	1.co.16
2	b		Tob.7	5	8	2.cor.1
3	c		9	6	10	2
4	d		11	7	12	3
5	d		13	8	14	4
6	f	Faith.	Judit.1	9	Judit.2	5
7	g		3	10	4	6
8	A		5	11	6	7
9	b	Dennis.	7	12	8	8
10	c		9	13	10	9
11	d		11	14	11	10
12	e	S. in Sc.	13	15	14	11
13	f	Edward	15	16	16	12
14	g		Wif.1	Lu.di.1	Wif.2	13
15	A		3	di. 1.	4	Gal. 1.
16	b		5	2.	6	2
17	e	Ethel.	7	3	8	3
18	d	S. Luke	Ecc.51	4	Iob 1.	4
19	e	Euan.	Wif.9	5	vif.10	6
20	f		11	6	12	6
21	g		13	7	14	Eph.1.
22	A		15	8	16	2
23	b		17	9	18	3
24	c		19	10	Eccl.1.	4
25	d	Crifpin.	Eccl. 2	11	3	5
26	e		4	12	5	Phil.1.
27	f	Faft.	6	13	7	2
28	g	Sim. & Iu.	Io.24,25	14	Iob 42	3
29	A	Iude.	Eccl.8	15	Eccl.9	4
30	b		10	16	11	4
31	c	Faft.	12	17	13	Col.1.

		Mor. Prayer.		Euen. Prayer.	
		1. Lef.	2. Lef.	1. Lef.	2. Lef.
1	d	All	Wif.3	he.11.12	Wif.5	Reu.19
2	e	Saints.	Ecc.14	Lu.18.	Ecc.15	Col.2.
3	f		16	19	17	3
4	g		18	20	19	4
5	A	Pa.conf.	20	21	21	1.Th.1
6	b	Leonard	22	22	23	2
7	c		24	23	25 [¶]	3
8	d		27	24	28	4
9	e		29	Iohn 1.	30	5
10	f		31	2	32	2.Th.1
11	g	S. Mart.	33	3	34	2
12	A	S. in Sag	35	4	36	3
13	b	Brice.	37	5	38	1.tim.1
14	c		39	6	40	2. 3.
15	d	Machut.	41	7	42	4
16	e		43	8	44	5
17	f	Hugh b.	45	9	46 [†]	6
18	g		47	10	48	2.tim.1
19	A		49	11	50	2
20	b	Edmund	51	12	Baru.1	3
21	c	king.	Bar. 2.	13	3	Tit. 1
22	d	Cicely.	4	14	5	2
23	e	Clem.	6	15	Ifa. 1.	2. 3.
24	f		Ifa. 2.	16	3	Phile.
25	g	Kathe-	4	17	5	Heb.1.
26	A	rine.	6	18	7.	2
27	b		8	19	9	3
28	c		10	20	11	4
29	d	Faft.	12	21	13	5
30	e	And. ap.	Pro.20	Act. 1.	Pro.21	6

		Mor. Prayer.		Euen. Prayer.	
		1. Lef.	2. Lef.	1. Lef.	2. Lef.
1	f		Ifa.14	Act. 2.	Ifa.15.	Heb.7
2	g		16	3	17	8
3	A		18	4	19	9
4	u		20. 21.	5	22	10
5	c		23	6	24	11
6	d	Nicho-	25	dim.7.	26	12
7	e	las	27	dim.7.	28	13
8	f	Concep.	29	8	30	Iam.1.
9	g	Ma.	31	9	32	2
10	A		33	10	34	3
11	b	S. in Cæ.	35	11	36	4
12	c		37	12	38	5
13	d	Luci.	39	13	40	1.Pet.1
14	e		41	14	42	2
15	f		43	15	44	3
16	g	O fapi-	45	16	46	4
17	A	entia.	47	17	48	5
18	b		49	18	50	2.Pet.1
19	c		51	19.	52	2
20	d	Faft.	53	20	54	3
21	e	Thomas	Pro.23	21	Pro.24	1.Ioh.1
22	f	Ap.	Ifa.55.	22	Ifa.56.	2
23	g		57	23	58	3
24	A	Faft.	59	24	60	4
25	b	Chriftm.	Ifa.9.	Luke 2	Ifa. 7.	Tit. 3.
26	c	S Steuen	Pro.28	act.6.7	Eccl.4	Acts 7
27	d	S. Iohn.	Eccl.5	Reu.1.	Eccl.6	Reu.22
28	e	Innocen.	Ier.31.	Act.25	Ifa.62	2.Iohn
29	f		Ifa.61.	26	63	3.Iohn
30	g		63	27	64	Iude.
31	A	Silueft.	65	28	66	

Second Coming and the second resurrection, this epistle, like *Lycidas,* is really about the First Coming and man's resurrection in this life, a time when man recovers from "the death of sin, by Faith and Repentance, or, in a word, Regeneration."[59]

The epistle to the Hebrews counters the heavy emphasis given by the other liturgical readings to God's vengeance, arguing that the new covenant directs attention to forgiveness and, through that argument, asserting the preeminence of Christianity over Judaism, of Christ over Jehovah. It is the New Testament, not the Old, that perfects and renews us. Paul uses this occasion to proclaim the superiority of the Gospel over the Law, of the Mediator of the Gospel over the Mediator of the Law. Much more excellent than all his other types, "Christ is the ende of the Lawe"—the "ARCH-PASTOR, or Great Shepheard," who, bringing us to perfection, shows us that we too may be renewed into eternal life.[60] Repeatedly contrasting the God of Justice and the Christ of Grace, Paul teaches, in the words of David Dickson, that "without Christ we are kept under . . . : But, through Christ, we . . . climbe up":

> Without Christ, exposed to the wrath of the living God: Through Christ, admitted . . . in the Citie of the living God. Without Christ, affrayde, by the terrible sight of Wrath and Judgement. Through Christ, brought into Hierusalem, the Vision of Peace . . . Through Christ, Citizens of Heaven . . . Through Christ, admitted to the societie of innumerable Angels . . . Through Christ, our Names are enrolled in Heaven, amongst those who are written in the Booke of Lyfe elected unto . . . Grace, and Glorie.[61]

Moreover, in Hebrews 13, Paul explores the various implications of the "Yet once more" prophecy that immediately precedes this chapter and that by Milton is alluded to in the first line of his pastoral poem.

Concerned, like *Lycidas,* with Christ's pastoral function, with his ministers and their obligations, Hebrews 13 cautions against those who "have nothing but the bare title, and . . . do abuse this title of Pastor" and simultaneously urges that true ministers turn to Jesus for their pattern.[62] Neither vengeful nor capricious, Jesus is the same yesterday, and today, and forever, says Paul, who counsels further that suffering perfects man, readying him for salvation, that for this reason men should not harden their hearts on their day of testing in the wilderness, for that testing involves a chastening process that will turn grief into joy, affliction into happiness. The Word of God, Paul assures the Hebrews, is "sharper than any twoedged sword" (4:12); and it will be used for smiting the nations. This assurance he offers in an epistle of brotherly love that, describing Jesus as the great shepherd of the sheep, looks ahead repeatedly to the Book of Revelation, where its own vision of "the city of the living God, the heavenly Jerusalem, and . . . an innumerable company of angels" (12:22) is expanded and where its themes of love and mercy, of forgiveness and resurrection, are most fully expounded. This emerging interest in the Lord's mercy, also a principal concern of *Lycidas,* is the subject of the liturgical readings prescribed for the feast day of King Edward the Martyr.

Hope is the major theme of Ecclesiasticus 51, John 12, Baruch 1, and 2 Timothy 3. Ecclesiasticus 51 follows upon—is a response to—verses describing man alone and helpless, encompassed on every side by evil men and unrighteous tongues. Rejoicing in the Lord's mercy, this reading promises deliverance of the body from destruction to those who recognize in the Lord both their defender and preserver. Such men will be "lifted up . . . from the earth," will be delivered from destruction and "from the evill time"— will, by Jesus, be given their just reward. Developing the resurrection motif through the stories of Jesus' raising Lazarus and of his triumphant entry into Jerusalem, John 12 explains, through the voice of Jesus, that prophecy comes "not because of me, but for your sakes," its purpose being to open men's eyes, to lead them out of darkness into light, to effect in this world their first resurrection and thus ready them for their second, wherein they achieve life eternal. "Judgment of this world," "be[ing] lifted up from the earth," death in life and life in death—these themes are common to *Lycidas* and John 12, both of which testify to Jesus' words, "I come not to judge the world, but to save the world," and to Jesus's promise of life everlasting.

Like *Lycidas,* Baruch 1, a prophecy referring to the fury of the Lord and promising that the Lord will lighten our eyes, offers the assurance that God protects man against the corruption afflicting his world; and like Milton's poem, 2 Timothy 3 is an attack upon the clergy, an earnest pastoral emphasizing that "in the last days perilous times shall come," that in those days many men will be seen holding the form of religion but denying its power. In such times, the world will seem to have been turned upside down, says Paul: the just will suffer great affliction, and the wicked will flourish; this will be a time of great suffering, which, as good Christian soldiers, we must endure, for the general resurrection will be at hand. Having been brought to Jesus by Scripture, all men will now be delivered by Jesus from affliction. Thus John 12 and 2 Timothy 3 especially look ahead to last things, to the Apocalypse.

John's prophecy was said to reveal "the certaintie of God's providence," to be the Bible's fullest exploration, most complete anatomy of it; and, as both Frank Kermode and Michael Fixler have perceived, John's prophecy "is essentially a paradigmatic model of the imaginative encounter with death. It is a type of all 'fictions of the end'."[63] Within the Book of Revelation itself, there is progression—both thematic and generic progression: the movement is from lamentation to rejoicing, from a tragic perspective on life to a comedic one, from contemplation of a wrathful God to perception of a merciful one, from pastoral to prophecy. These same movements are apparent in *Lycidas* as well, and the last of them is underscored by Milton's turning from a liturgical context into a literary, Spenserian one, where pastoral and prophetic elements are combined, and then turning from it into the Book of Revelation where both pastoral and prophetic traditions are brought to their culmination. Not only does "the transposition of pastoral imagery into a transcendental key" derive from the Book of Revelation, Isabel MacCaffrey reminds us; but John's prophecy confers upon this mode of imagination, used by both Spenser and Milton, the sanction of the divine artist.[64]

Prophetic poets, though they may draw upon a whole tradition of literature, forge their most subtle effects, make their profoundest statement, through their interaction with a precursor. Consequently, they will align themselves not just with large traditions in which they write but with their last major precursor in those traditions—with those precursors who expand traditions in such a way as to open possibilities that the new prophet is ready to realize.[65] The major traditions Milton invokes are pastoral and prophecy; and Milton's last major precursor in each of these traditions is Spenser.

The Shepheardes Calender provides a general context for *Lycidas,* while *Colin Clouts Come Home Againe* and *Astrophel* provide very particularized contexts. Itself an experimental work, both in its form and prosody, Spenser's *Calender* anticipates the even more radical experimentation of *Lycidas,* as well as many of that poem's devices.

The May eclogue provides Milton with an immediate precedent for his invective against the clergy; but it also lays down the clue to what kind of poem *The Shepheardes Calender* actually is. Here, Spenser "is not writing history, but prophecy"; and A. C. Hamilton, in this pronouncement, claims no more than to echo Milton's belief that the May eclogue presages the reforming spirit of his own time, that Spenser's announcing "The time was once, and may againe retorne" (103) is prophetic. We can be fairly certain of Hamilton's claim that "Milton read the *Shepheardes Calender* in this way,"[66] as a prophecy, and fairly certain, too, that Milton understood why the prophetic elements in *The Shepheardes Calender* were so muted.

This point bears particular scrutiny that should begin with the recognition that *The Shepheardes Calender,* unlike *Lycidas,* was a poem, which for a decade at least, remained nearly anonymous. Its authorship, doubtless, was known to Spenser's closest friends, yet was concealed from others—so well concealed from them that, writing about this poem in *The Arte of English Poesie* (1589), George Puttenham can number its author among England's great pastoralists even while he is unable to specify who its author is.

Modern criticism has done with Spenser's poetry what, likewise, it has done with Blake's: reading late works by each poet, it has reached conclusions that it then transfers to early poems, which resist them—which cannot bear their weight. The Los of *Jerusalem* is a markedly different figure from the Los of Blake's early prophecies; and correspondingly, the Colin of *Colin Clouts Come Home Againe* and *The Faerie Queene* contrasts strikingly with the Colin of *The Shepheardes Calender*. Colin in the later works invites identification with Spenser, but the Colin of the *Calender* requires that we distinguish persona from poet: the one abandons his faith in time of trouble, while the other maintains it; the one, breaking his pipes or hanging them on a tree, surrenders his art, while the other, in the very act of writing his poem, demonstrates his dedication to art. Colin here is like his prototype in John Skelton's poem: he is a poet who exhibits no allegiance to prophetic tradition, contrasting with Spenser who would combine the roles of poet and prophet. There is thus a seldom noticed irony here that should not, for so long, have escaped Spenser's readers. He is writing a prophecy, then putting the political part of that prophecy into the mouth of a poet who is known to have abandoned his prophetic office. In a time when prophecy is outlawed, when therefore a poet must conceal his prophetic mission, it is wittily apt that Spenser should do this and that, further, he should protect himself by playing off Colin's ignobility against his own nobility.

Spenser's critics have long recognized that the poet derives his Colin from Skelton's poem, which bears Colin Clout's name as its title; they have not, however, acknowledged the extent to which Spenser's figure is a modification of the prototype provided by Skelton. Usually Skelton's Colin is treated as if he were a descendant of Langland's Piers—"honest, simple, a modern day Peter," says Stanley Fish, "in a world gone awry." But in fact, as Fish notices, Colin is a solitary, isolated figure aligned neither with the corrupt clergy nor with the reformers: he is "a poet-priest, but his priesthood has little to do with prophecy . . . and everything to do with responsibility (pastoral care) and endurance."[67] Indeed, Skelton's poem focuses upon the frustrations of a poet speaking to a world that never listens and that imposes demands upon its poets which seem to exceed their resources. In such a world, Colin endures and, preserving his faith—steeling himself with fortitude—finally prevails. In accordance with Psalm 93, Colin lives by the help of the Lord and so escapes dwelling in a grave; though lost in life, he nevertheless continues his journey through it; he is engaged in its processes and experiences through them a discovery that brings him like a ship into safe harbor.

Responsibility and faith, pastoral care and discovery—these same issues pervade Spenser's poem but are not a part of Colin's character or experience in that poem. No longer a flourishing poet, neither is Colin now (except ironically) a priest or prophet or reformer. No longer a pilgrim, Colin makes no progress; without faith and fortitude, he surrenders responsibility (pastoral care), now betraying Hobbinel just as he has been betrayed. In the *Calender,* Colin dwells in a grave and, at the end of this poem, looks at himself in that grave. Disengaged from life, from its processes, Colin is denied those discoveries and that growth which are a part of life. A false shepherd and a false poet, Colin contrasts with both Spenser and Cuddie, who is Spenser's example of the perfect poet—one who in the October eclogue submits to the counsel of Piers, a type of the prophet with whom poets, according to Spenser, must now join forces. The Cuddie of the February eclogue, so different from the Cuddie of the August and October eclogues, is generally thought to be a wholly different shepherd; but this is to miss Spenser's point: no less callow and no less foolish than Colin, Cuddie nevertheless remains engaged in life and is altered by its processes—is brought to those discoveries that enable him to make himself over and anew.

Later, in *Colin Clouts Come Home Againe,* Colin will be shown undergoing the same process. Reduced to nothing in the *Calender,* Colin ultimately makes something out of nothing, here rising up a new spiritual man, a rededicated poet. But this is a later development, having no real bearing on the Colin of the *Calender*. This Colin and the Colin of Skelton are different, then; and their differences point to essential differences between Skelton's and Spenser's poems. *Colin Clout* is a poem with a prophetic center—the so-called prophecy of Skelton that concludes the first part of the poem and that otherwise does not seem to have any real connection with the rest of this poem. *The Shepheardes Calender,* on the other hand, is a gathering of prophecies—Piers' of a time that will come, Morrell's of Algrind's restoration, Colin's of Elizabeth's, of England's, of his own annihilation. Those individual prophecies permeate this poem through and through, declaring it, as poem, to belong to the prophetic mode.

In *The Shepheardes Calender,* Spenser has pictured both the religious and political situation of England, particularly the prospect of the queen's marriage to the duke of Alençon and its consequences. Already the political prophets, troubled over the prospect of the queen's marriage, were announcing not only her death but the impending death of the English nation; and Elizabeth in turn became so agitated by this meddling in her affairs that she moved to abolish prophecy, even the religious prophecy that had been advocated by the Puritans and that later was to be encouraged and supported by Archbishop Grindal (Algrind in the July eclogue). John Stubbs, William Page, and the printer of *The Shepheardes Calender,* Hugh Singleton, all lost their right hands; and Grindal was discharged from his office and sequestered at Lambeth. Writing a prophecy, then, Spenser stood in double defiance of the queen, on the one hand for employing an outlawed mode of discourse and on the other for bringing up in that discourse the forbidden subject of her anticipated marriage to Alençon. It is no wonder that Spenser chose to veil his allegory and to conceal the prophetic intentions of his poem. Yet that allegory, once uncovered, makes clear that *The Shepheardes Calender* was conceived as a warning prophecy, Spenser knowing full well that the potential triumph for such a prophecy comes when it proves itself irrelevant—when impending disaster is averted because the prophecy is being listened to. As Spenser portrays the historical situation, the queen as Rosalind is about to break her covenant with the people, represented by Colin Clout. Her figurative death, therefore, is the subject of the lament in the November eclogue, where it is made to symbolize, as Paul McLane suggests, "the prophetic death that the Alençon marriage forebodes for England"; here in the death of Dido and in the approaching death of Colin Clout are figured the prophetic consequences of the queen's marriage: her spiritual death, together with the death of the English church, of England, of the people; and the death of poets and of poetry as well.[68]

The Shepheardes Calender, then, is a prophecy cast in the form of a modified pastoral elegy. Its center, which reaches out to encompass the entire poem, is the November eclogue. The lament for Dido, like the poem of which it is a part, resembles both in subject and purpose Bion's *Lament for Adonis.* Spenser replaces an actual physical death with an imagined spiritual death that, like a sea, rolls over, swallows up, an entire world. The traditional lament for a dying god is here turned into a lament for a dying ideal, and that lament turns finally into a poem like the *Lament for Bion,* a lament for the poet himself. In *The Shepheardes Calender,* there is, of course, the lament of the June eclogue for a dead poet, Tityrus (that is, Chaucer), whose virtues are extolled. Yet this very conventional elegy is, at the end of Spenser's poem, modified into a lament for a dying poet, Spenser in the December eclogue opening his poem to different interpretations. On the one hand, Spenser himself, if his prophecy is understood, may be silenced by the queen; but on the other hand, as the October eclogue implies, a country without worthies, a citizenry without the nerve for heroic deeds, leaves the poet speechless— may be said to have silenced him and thus to have killed his art. All this applies to Colin, but not, it should noted, to Spenser himself: *he* is not without a poetic subject, *he* is not like Colin silenced. He is rather like Blake's Los—a prophet who keeps his faith in times of trouble, who prophesies in order to avert disaster, who believes that by renovating the individual, even the queen, prophecy may inspire the rebirth of a nation. The aim of *The*

Shepheardes Calender, therefore, "is not merely that of turning some men to good but the betterment of the commonwealth."[69] That same aim informs *Lycidas,* which appropriately turns back into the November eclogue, Milton assuming Colin's lament for Dido as the prototype for the monody he designates his own poem to be.

In the November eclogue, there are two interlocuters, Thenot and Colin. Like Milton's uncouth swain, Colin sings the lament; and like Milton himself, Thenot concludes with a single stanza descriptive of the poet's departure. Colin's monody begins with an apology for its art: "my rymes bene rugged and vnkempt: / Yet as I conne, my conning I will strayne" (51–52); and like *Lycidas,* this earlier monody moves out of the lamentation that occupies three-quarters of the poem ("O heauie herse . . . O carefull verse"), into the rejoicing that concludes it ("O happy herse . . . O ioufull verse"). Again like *Lycidas,* Spenser's poem responds to a situation, created by death, which makes men feel that they "dwell in deadly night" (69). Moreover, in his manuscript Milton associates his poem with November, the same month to which Spenser assigns his monody—the month set aside for honoring England's monarch and the month, as E. K. explains, "when the sonne draweth low in the South toward his Tropick or returne" (7:110). Alongside these resemblances are the facts that, like Spenser, Milton mixes short and long lines, creating through his meter the rough, grating effects that are subdued by the binding together of stanzas through rhyme. The very devices of poetry are here transformed into symbols, Milton, again like Spenser, mirroring the disorder that rhyme overcomes. Each poem is what E. K. would call a "disorderly order"; and thus each poem testifies to his belief that, as in music, "a dischorde . . . maketh a comely concordaunce" (7:8).

There is, besides, an analogy to be noted between *Lycidas* and the October eclogue, which "set[s] out the perfecte patterne of a Poete" and which, developing the position probably taken in the lost prose treatise, *The English Poete,* explains that poetry is "no arte, but a diuine gift" deriving from celestial inspiration

(7:95). Poetry is—or should be—like *Lycidas,* indistinguishable from prophecy; and the poet, like the Milton of *Lycidas,* should be an aspiring prophet. That Cuddie here represents Spenser's thinking about poetry is suggested not just by E. K.'s notes to the October eclogue but by his letter prefatory to *The Shepheardes Calender.* In that letter, addressed to Gabriel Harvey, Spenser is represented as "our new Poete" in the classical line of Virgil and in the English line of Chaucer. He is said to be committed to an aesthetic that, in its rough rhymes and meters and rustic language, appropriates the "rudenesse of shepheards," restoring to the poet's vocabulary "naturall English words . . . almost cleane disinherited." In this E. K. again associates Spenser with "our olde Englishe Poetes" like Chaucer, who "were wont to comprehend all the skil of Poetrye, according to the Greeke woorde, ποιειν to make" (7:41–42); and he develops this association of the April eclogue in his notes to the October eclogue where poets are also said to be makers and poetry is said to be "a diuine instinct and vnnatural rage passing the reache of comen reason" (7: 100, 103). The real point of such a claim, of course, is that poetry is an emanation of the divine vision, a point that Spenser emphasizes by beginning his poem in January and that E. K. reemphasizes by calling attention to the fact that the end of each year and the beginning of the next are a memorial of Christ's birth and a monument to our salvation (7:13–14). January is the month of the epiphany; and *The Shepheardes Calender,* in turn, is "the poet's manifestation, his epiphany to the world."[70]

Epitomizing the pastoral tradition, *The Shepheardes Calender* brings that tradition to a new perfection; and thus according to E. K., in the appended argument for the November eclogue, "farre passing" Spenser's reach, this eclogue surpasses, too, "all other . . . Eglogues of this booke" (7:104), providing, as one modern reader has observed, "the source and end for all lesser visions."[71] This eclogue—indeed Spenser's "booke" as a whole—delineates a paradigm that in *Lycidas* Milton will observe; but Spenser's *Calender* also articulates a vision that *Lycidas* will reverse.

"The preference for radical allegory and 'iconographic ambiguity'; the search for a form that will contain variety and unity . . . ; the exploitation of a setting that can also serve as a complex controlling metaphor"; a unified design with a range so wide that the poet may travel into the "extreme borderlands" of epic and tragedy, satire and comedy; a design that is encyclopedic or cosmic and that contains both a "visionary geography" and a "circular groundplan"—all these features used by Isabel MacCaffrey to describe *The Shepheardes Calender* are attributes of *Lycidas*.[72] Both poems, similar in their design, have also the same design upon their readers: both would "teach the ruder shepheard how to feede his sheepe" (7:120). Yet, when these poems are considered together, not just similarities appear but also differences. Composed of the same elements, each poem mixes those elements differently; thus however alike these poems may seem, they are widely different in their effect.

Spenser's persona is an "antihero" who, though a pilgrim, never approaches the Heavenly City, his wanderings tracing instead "a movement which defines the failure of man to realize his *own* nature" and ending with the poet alone, awaiting death, in a winter landscape.[73] Spenser's is a despairing vision, showing that "the circle of time and the seasons . . . shut man up in a prison, from which he cannot break out," except intermittently through poetry and finally only by death.[74] Commencing his poem by seeing man and nature as congruent, Spenser concludes by acknowledging their fundamental incongruity. The September eclogue, an ironic commentary on naive efforts to regain paradise, and the November eclogue, concluding that only in death can man escape the cycles of nature, man then gaining access to a transcendental realm where reality, true destiny, lies—both contribute to the darkness of Spenser's vision. Spenser never bids adieu to pastoral, but here and later asserts its metaphoric, transcendental reality; Milton, on the other hand, in yoking pastoral and prophecy, asserts the relevance of pastoral as an image for the new world to be established through prophecy.

These differences point to still others which suggest that, instead of being a redaction of Spenser's vision, *Lycidas* is a reversal of it. Indeed Milton's intention is registered in a title that engages in ironic play with the whole pastoral tradition of which Spenser's *Calender* is the last great example. The name of Lycidas appears in the pastorals of Theocritus, Virgil, and Sannazaro—each of these poets allowing this shepherd to represent the ideal poet. By Theocritus Lycidas is portrayed as the best of the pipers: he is dear to the Muses, the perfect poet, and he sings of a happy voyage made possible by the harmonious relationship man enjoys with nature. However, in the pastoral world of Virgil, such harmonies are seen eroding. Still Lycidas sustains his optimism, continuing to trust in the power of song; and still a great poet, Lycidas is also portrayed as a special kind of poet—one who calls himself a bard and who is thus a self-proclaimed *vates*. Also inhabiting the pastoral world of Sannazaro, Lycidas, now associated with the sea, laments from the shore the burial of his loved one. Rather than sinking into despair though, Lycidas asserts through his lament that this death in no way weakens his song or wrecks its harmonies.

Milton's poem appears to turn this whole tradition on end. The ideal poet, the bard, now is dead. The harmony of man and nature, the harmony of song which is its emblem, both are destroyed. The sea from which Lycidas had earlier reaffirmed the power of song has now overwhelmed the poet. But the most startling ironies surface when *Lycidas* is read within the context of *The Shepheardes Calender*. Colin Clout is spiritually dead, having betrayed his song and the world over which song wields its power; Lycidas is physically dead, having been betrayed by a world that wielded its power to accomplish the destruction of the poet and the silencing of his song. The whole pastoral tradition is thus made to look to an uncouth swain for its reaffirmation and, finally, for its authentication. Colin Clout surrendered his art by breaking his pipes, contrasting with Milton's swain, who, still not fully accomplished as an artist, perseveres in his commitment to art. In the course of Milton's poem the swain will therefore be restored by art and, reciprocally, will restore it to dominion—

to the eminence from which with Lycidas' death it seemed to have fallen. Milton's uncouth swain has the same trappings of the antihero possessed by Spenser's persona; yet by the poem's end he achieves heroic status, not by being caught in a maze that ends in darkness but by journeying through a labyrinth that ends in light. Milton's poet may have not yet achieved Jerusalem, but he has moved toward it by experiencing a first resurrection that promises his second; instead of inhabiting a winter landscape and awaiting his own death (this is where *Lycidas* begins, of course), the poet looks "to fresh Woods, and Pastures new" (193), thus typifying not man's failure but his success in realizing his own nature and also holding out the prospect that this world may be made over and anew.

Milton never inhabits a purely pastoral world. Spenser, how-ever, in one of his last poems, *Colin Clouts Come Home Againe,* retreats into a pastoral world, producing "a classic example of the pastoral paradigm."[75] This poem (more than *The Shepheardes Calender*) sets in relief the extent to which Milton moves beyond Spenser—and beyond pastoral. Yet again, as it did with the *Calender, Lycidas* reverses the patterns of experience and, doing so, rejects the dichotomies that this precursor poem delineates. Milton thereby suggests, as Isabel MacCaffrey almost alone has understood, that " 'mere' pastoral . . . is . . . too vulnerable and limited to account for the brutalities of life; but [is] shown, finally, to contain the possibility of deeper, or higher, strains more fruitful to 'reality.' "[76]

In *Colin Clouts Come Home Againe*—a poem described by Spenser as a "simple pastoral" (1:47) and one that is both a sequel to *The Shepheardes Calender* and a poem prefatory to the elegies commemorating the death of Sidney—the shepherd, hav-ing journeyed across the Irish Sea to London and back again, re-counts his experiences to his friends, telling them a fearful story of his sea voyage. This poem about a poet who does not die is published first in a volume with poems commemorating a poet who does die. The irony is deliberate, and it must have sounded for Milton as he began to write *Lycidas.* In Spenser's poem, a poet journeys eastward, across the Irish Sea to London—he undergoes a perilous journey from which he returns, reborn as a poet. In *Lycidas,* Milton must sing of a poet's journey westward, from England to Ireland, a destination he never reaches, for once again the rough seas are an obstacle, this time to a poet whom they overwhelm and defeat. The simple optimism of *Colin Clouts Come Home Againe* is thus translated by Milton into the initially tragic vision of *Lycidas;* and the despairing vision of *Astrophel* is, in *Lycidas,* elevated by degrees to the divine comedy with which Milton's poem ends. In the volume containing Spenser's poems— a volume, like *Justa Edovardo King Naufrago,* containing poems by various hands and one possessing a careful plan that a master- poet executes—Spenser fiercely dichotomizes pastoral and elegy, along with the simplistic visions of life those forms presume. Milton's task is like Spenser's in that he, too, must weave his poem into the plan of the volume of which his poem is only a part.[77] Unlike Spenser, however, Milton, rather than distilling one perspective from all the other poems, incorporates all per- spectives within *Lycidas,* thereby implying not that man is frozen into one perspective or another but that by encompassing them he also transcends them all through prophecy. In prophecy, man is not batted to and fro—between joy and grief, between the worlds of innocence and experience, between comedy and tragedy; but he passes through those states into the higher innocence figured in this world by the transfigured swain and in the next by the apotheosized King.

Progression operates in Spenser's poems, but not as it does in Milton's. The movement from January to December in *The Shepheardes Calender* involves a progress from innocence to ex- perience, a progress represented again, even more dramatically, in the juxtaposition of *Colin Clouts Come Home Againe* and *Astrophel,* both poems about poet-shepherds, the first about one who triumphs over nature and the second about one who is de- feated by that same nature. *Lycidas* is a profound commentary on the claims made both by pure pastoral and plaintive elegy; and thus it begins, appropriately enough, where *Astrophel* ends, with the pastoral world brutally shattered by the death of a poet. Spenser's elegy, as well as all the others accompanying it, is written as "mournfull verse," "not to please the liuing but the dead" (7:177); like all the others, Spenser's elegy, full of wailing and weeping, ends in tears. Those tears cannot be wiped away, grief is unassuageable in a world, like that portrayed in the *Dolefull Lay of Clorinda,* where heavenly powers are the authors of man's "vnremedied wo"—where, "subject to the heauens ordinance," man is "Bound to abide what euer they decree" (5, 7–8, 14–15). In such a world, the poet can merely mark the discrepancy between those who use physical death as a ladder to the skies and those like himself who, racked by inward woe, must mourn in another their own misery. The elegiac world of Spenser, whether represented by the *Astrophel* poems or Spenser's earlier *Daphnaida,* is a world where joy fast becomes grief—where daily, it seems, happiness is swallowed up in tragedy; it is a world that repeatedly beckons, "Weepe Shepheard weepe . . . Weepe Shepheard weepe" and from which man can go forth only "With staggring pace and dismall lookes dismay," having just seen death "in the face" (*Daphnaida,* 294, 343, 563–65).

Lycidas confutes this whole vision of life. Like Spenser, Milton uses his elegy to confront the nothingness that is death; but Milton, loathing necessity, brings out of that confrontation a perception unfocused in Spenser's elegies but one shared with Milton by the modern poet, Octavio Paz:

> Nothing is more affirmative than this facing [of death], this continuous coming out of ourselves . . . Death is the void, the open space, that permits the passage forward . . . If being born implies dying, dying also implies being born . . . It is said that we are surrounded by death; can it not also be said that we are surrounded by life?[78]

Paz's question Milton would answer affirmatively, and so in *Lycidas* mournful verse becomes joyful verse, weeping ceases, tears are wiped away, lamentation gives way to rejoicing, *because* figured in the resurrection of the dead man into eternity is Milton's own (our own) resurrection in this life. The natural man, the uncouth swain, in the course of Milton's poem is transfigured; his "song . . . sung," his vision realized—with his "hard-won insights"[79]—he rises up a new spiritual man. *Lycidas* thus unfolds the revelation that confrontation of death, of man's nothingness, "leads . . . to the creation of being. Thrown into the nothing, man [Milton, all of us] creates himself in the face of it";[80] and creating the self anew is an act both coexistent with the creation of poetry and prefatory to remaking the world—a world that, once remade, finds its most powerful symbol, as Dr. Johnson never realized, in the pastoral image.

The Genres of Lycidas

In his life of Milton, Johnson presents a series of indictments against *Lycidas:* "the diction is harsh, the rhymes uncertain, . . . the numbers unpleasing"; the poem "is not to be considered as the effusion of real passion," for "where there is leisure for fiction there is little grief," and where the exhausted imagery of pastoral is used, there is nothing new; indeed, the allegorical character of the genre renders "true meaning . . . uncertain and remote" and is responsible for that "grosser fault"—the mingling of pagan fictions with the most sacred truths of Christianity. These various indictments reduce to Johnson's fundamental objection to Milton's poem: *Lycidas,* written in the "form . . . of the pastoral," is "easy, vulgar, and therefore disgusting."[81]

Such an objection may have receded over the centuries, but even today it has not disappeared. Indeed it now reappears as an objection leveled not against *Lycidas* but against those critics of *Lycidas* who, invoking pastoral to explain Milton's poem, have produced a "scandal of literary scholarship": according to Louis Kampf, since Milton's use of the pastoral tradition "is a foolish irrelevance," that tradition "will hardly lead . . . to reflections on the meaning of death."[82] Sounding no less cranky than Dr. Johnson, Kampf, instead of dismissing *Lycidas* because it is a pastoral, dismisses pastoral because, for him, it is a tradition irrelevant to the meaning of Milton's poem. To his credit, Kampf would push us beyond pastoral believing that *Lycidas* is first a response, a reaction, to death and not simply another rendering of the pastoral tradition. He would do so, however, without acknowledging: that in its inception, pastoral was devised "to insinuate and glaunce at greater matters"; that as a tradition, pastoral had become, during the 1630s, irrevocably bound to the idea of death through the "Et in Arcadia Ego" theme; that since Theocritus, pastoral was continually pushing beyond itself, aspiring to be something other than itself; that (and here Kampf is less culpable than Dr. Johnson) for purposes of initiation and discovery, pastoral—"the place of vision"—is also *the* place where "the Individual Talent is brought into confrontation with . . . Tradition."[83] However different their estimates of *Lycidas* may be then, both Johnson and Kampf reject pastoral and so reject the reason for which *Lycidas,* years before Johnson blasted it, had been praised.

Such praise came to *Lycidas,* in Milton's own century, through an anonymous commentary which describes the poem as "an Elegy . . . incomparable"[84] and, in the early eighteenth century, through Thomas Purney's treatise on pastoral, one purpose of which is to rescue pastoral from those who, defining pastoral according to the rules, would isolate it both from epic and tragedy. If pastoral has become a problematical genre, says Purney, that is because too many poets have "gone in exactly the same Track, without once endeavouring to raise . . . [the genre] to any greater Perfection," without even recognizing that pastoral, like epic and tragedy, can develop only if it engages poets in generic competition with their predecessors.

Typically, the pastoral poet has relied on classical precedents. Purney proposes that he turn from them to Scripture; that, recognizing the genre's potential for embracing a full range of human emotions, he remember his largest obligation which is to "spread a Calm over the Mind." Milton, Purney concludes, is the great example of such a pastoral poet—of one who, ignoring classical precedents and established rules, grounds his poetry in Scripture.[85]

And Purney might have continued, as Edward Tayler does, by asserting that in *Lycidas* Milton has recapitulated the entire history of pastoral—a history that, encompassing pastoral from its classical beginnings, through its Old Testament modifications, and its final development in the New Testament—is made to correspond with the three structural units that comprise Milton's poem. The form of the poem, Tayler remarks, imitates its theme; and its structure reflects its meaning,[86] showing Milton sinking into, then rising out of—Milton progressing beyond, then returning to—the pastoral tradition. The point of all this, of course, is that Milton is in the process of effecting one of the great revisions of the pastoral pattern: he explores its limits, as well as territory beyond, incorporating the pastoral pattern within the all-subsuming paradigm of prophecy. *Lycidas* is thus a classic example of a poem that, assuming a tradition, vaults beyond its limits.

The significance of Milton's turning from classical examples of pastoral to scriptural ones is suggested by Edwin Honig: the only way of keeping pastoral alive after its infection by "a literary plague"—once it becomes "broken and mute"—is to bring to pastoral "a strong sense of commitment to circumstances of living actuality" and, simultaneously, to create for pastoral a new aesthetic.[87] Milton accomplishes the former by letting the bitter reality of Edward King's death shatter the pastoral world at the beginning of *Lycidas;* and the latter he does by becoming, as Blake was later to do, a biblical poet and by consequently cultivating a critical interest in the Bible—an interest that turned Milton to the prophets and that showed him how prophecy itself could be called upon to restore the atrophying form and fading dream of pastoral.

Lycidas is a triumph of the imagination; and its triumph, involving the transcendence and transformation of pastoral, occurs within the context of a tradition—"a continuing tradition"[88]—whose unrealized potentiality Milton brings to fruition. Pastoral is the tradition Milton receives; prophecy is the sometimes unseen presence in that tradition which, writing *Lycidas,* Milton makes manifest. Like so many of Milton's other poems, *Lycidas* is the decisive turning point in the history of a genre; and the turn it makes has its own history, which can be neither written nor understood apart from the long history it presumes. For our purposes, that history is especially worth recalling since, as Scott Elledge reminds us, "Milton knew well nearly all the poems of the genre, both classical and renaissance" and since, as Claudio Guillén observes, "the trajectory of a genre," which "constitutes some sort of historical series," conditions and molds both literature and its history.[89] But Guillén also cautions that a poet, even one who invokes the whole history of a genre, may be more intent upon "the interaction between a contemporary model . . . and his own poetic efforts and gifts."[90]

Pastoral is historically the oldest of the genres. The usual view is that Theocritus establishes it; nevertheless, Thomas Rosenmeyer has shown that Theocritus's real achievement is to have isolated pastoral elements in earlier literature, thereby creating a pure form. Theocritus is an "implementer," not the creator or fore-runner of pastoral, a genre that before the Renaissance—from Aristotle onward—was regarded as sometimes a component, but more often as a type, of epic. Even when Renaissance critics de-termined that pastoral was a genre in its own right, they were formulating a conclusion that some like Milton would have to revise, and adopting an "exclusiveness," as Rosenmeyer remarks, that was not destined to last.[91] Not an exclusive but an inclusive form, pastoral was by Theocritus extrapolated from epic, to which Virgil returned it. The Virgilian combination had, however, been preceded by another: no sooner had Theocritus distilled a pure form than Bion and the poet who wrote Bion's lament began anew the process of assimilation, joining together pastoral and elegy. Subsequent to Virgil, pastoral was allegorized and Christianized, and thereupon still other assimilations occurred, pastoral com-bining here with satire and invective, there with drama and ro-mance.

In the last great pastoral before *Lycidas,* Spenser's *The Shep-heardes Calender,* many of these same elements are evident. Within Spenser's microcosmic world, there are tragic movements and comedic ones, there is the satire of the May eclogue and the elegy of the November eclogue. And *The Faerie Queene,* as Milton must have noticed, begins and ends in a pastoral world, Spenser in his greatest literary microcosm allowing pastoral to sit comfortably within a poem imbued with elements of romance, epic, and prophecy. In *The Shepheardes Calender,* Spenser may not radically alter the pastoral tradition he inherits; but here, and later in *The Faerie Queene,* he makes "pastoral a thing of significance for English writers"[92] and so suggests the potentiality of the tradition of which *Lycidas* is an historic transformation. Kathleen Williams puts it succinctly when she says that Spenser senses the limitations of the forms that Milton subjects to more radical criticism; and saying this, Williams explains that *Lycidas* is richer than the *Calender* because all that Milton's poem responds to is there in the earlier work: "Without it, *Lycidas* could not be what it is."[93] Milton's indebtedness to Spenser is, of course, no discovery of modern criticism; for in the eighteenth century, Philip Neve proposed that *Lycidas* was formed by Spenser, singling out *Astrophel* as the poem that probably gave rise to Milton's.[94]

Assimilation, then, describes the process by which pastoral, subsequent to Theocritus, aspired to a higher condition. That process is noted by Harold Toliver when he speaks of pastoral's "capacity to devour elegies, lyrics, plays, fairy tales, masques, odes, and even to gnaw ambitiously at romances, epics, and novels"; and the same process, Angus Fletcher has shown, is already operating in Milton's poetry—in *Comus*—where Milton finds in the masque form "an unrivalled chance to mix all the modes already brought together" in other dramatic or quasi-dramatic genres.[95] An even greater opportunity for mixing the genres, and thus for not only rivaling but transcending his achievement in *Comus,* Milton found in prophecy—a form that more than any other is predicated upon assimilation.

Lycidas is ample evidence that Milton must have believed with Thomas Hobbes that all the incidental genres "are but . . . parts of an entire Poem";[96] for in this poem Milton allows pastoral to climb the ladder of the genres, assimilating to itself various lyric forms like elegy, canzone, and madrigal, and various dramatic perspectives like tragedy, comedy, and satire, achieving dimensions that are epical and strains that are prophetic. Forms within forms, visions within visions, each mediating the others, *Lycidas* achieves what has recently been credited to Coleridge: the extension of pastoral to its outermost bound.[97] In the process, Milton demonstrates "the lowest of forms . . . to be capable of articulating the loftiest insights";[98] and part of that process involves Milton in the strategy of creating various and shifting perspectives, which, though they represent different angles of vision and also different attitudes toward the human condition, reflect a clash between different cultures, classical and Christian, and imply the triumph of the one over the other.

In pastoral, as Milton inherited it, there is a perfect blending of the two cultures; but in pastoral, as Milton here uses it (in juxtaposition with prophecy), those two cultures are seen at odds. The crossing or mixing of the genres, Ernst Curtius has remarked, is part of the crossing of pagan and Christian canons;[99] what Curtius does not say is that out of such crossings often arise confrontations. A form here, and its perspective, may complement or augment—or even conflict with—a form there, and its very different perspective. A series of perspectives and an aggregate of forms, *Lycidas* is also an assimilation of styles appropriate to them; yet between perspectives, forms, and styles there is also a contention which, enabling *Lycidas* to burst the boundaries of pastoral, "dilate's and widen's the Mind, and put's it upon the Stretch."[100] In its various multiplicities, then, *Lycidas* "comprehends . . . almost too big for it's Reach," exemplifying that kind of poetry, described by Thomas Purney, wherein "the Mind is most stretch'd."[101]

Another element contributing to the design and thereby enlarging the dimensions of *Lycidas* is pictorialism. Not only the various literary forms and their individual styles, but all the arts are evident in the Bible, even if those arts have subsequently become isolated and deformed. Still, as one eighteenth-century commentator explains, by returning to scriptural models the artist may use poetry and song, in conjunction with pictorialism, "to check and divert every species of corruption" that now infects both church and state.[102] In harness with poetry, pictorialism may be used to awaken the mind: it imitates the process of visualization, which is to say that it imitates the mental expansion that poetry would induce. In *Lycidas,* following the precedent of the Bible and the lead of Spenser, Milton "makes images that are like pictures in significant ways": he translates images into iconographic symbols but also shatters images in such a way that the whole poem resembles a mosaic whose pieces, though broken, are also interlocking.[103]

Pictorialism is inextricably a part of prophecy; and prophecy, we should here remember, at least as it is exemplified by John's Book of Revelation (see fig. 4), was understood to be written in scrolls, to be a form of picture-writing. It should, therefore, be regarded as one of those "programmatic attempts," spoken of by John Hollander, "to reunite [the arts] in their original unfallen relation."[104] In this context, it is interesting that the prophetic center of *Lycidas,* before introducing Peter to voice his own prophecy, presents Camus who, wearing a mantle, appears with a bonnet "Inwrought with figures dim, and on the edge / . . . inscrib'd with woe" (105–06). The "hairy" mantle invokes the image of the grieving prophet, and that image is reinforced by a hidden reference to the Revelation angel who flies in the heavens crying "Woe, woe, woe" (8:13; and see fig. 10). At the beginning of the fourth book of *Paradise Lost* (1–12), Milton will again remember that warning voice of prophecy, which, in *Lycidas,* is about to be heard through the utterance of St. Peter—a voice that in both poems is associated with revenge for the wrecking of innocence. But in *Lycidas,* in the description of Camus's bonnet, Milton makes specific reference to those written scrolls that combine pictures and words, that use pictures to serve up prophetic meaning.[105] Like Camus' bonnet, *Lycidas* itself is "Inwrought with figures dim"; it is a prophecy combining hearing and seeing in words.

Pictorialism enters *Lycidas* through its sea imagery and fractured structure. In its association with Neptune, for example, the

Fig. 10. The Revelation Angel Crying "Woe, woe, woe." Reproduced from the extra-illustrated *Kitto Bible,* volume 60, by permission of the Huntington Library, San Marino, California.

sea symbolizes, as Kathleen Williams documents, "the divine power existing through the waters"; an emblem of danger, flux, chance, and death, the sea is also (and more importantly) an emblem for the justice of providence and thus becomes, in iconographic tradition, coextensive with justice, with the nature of the universe, and with the divine mind controlling it. The sea, says Williams, "figures . . . the ultimate justice which prevails through the apparent meaninglessness."[106] Not only is the sea a verbal image in *Lycidas;* but in its rough surfaces and turbulent rhyme patterns the poem itself issues forth as an image of the sea. Simultaneously, Milton's poem articulates, acts out, figures forth, this emblem.

The same sense of turbulence, of roughness, manifests itself in the fragmented structure of Milton's poem—a structure that mirrors on its surface a shattered world. This technique of what John Bender calls "fragmented visualization" involves "the shattering of perceptual experience into a sequence of relatively small and concentrated units"; intended to fix "concentration upon the distinct parts of . . . [a] visionary world," it is employed by artists who, wishing to encompass everything within a difficult order, use this scheme to contain it. The fragmented units of Milton's poem, often linked by common images, accord with Bender's notion of "imitat[ing] the eye's discovery of more and more about what confronts it" so that the sea at the beginning and end of Milton's poem signifies differently.[107] This surface incoherence, a feature of pastoral poetry as Thomas Purney describes it, is only that, for there is connection underneath it all.[108] Thus, at the end of *Lycidas,* with fragments regrouping, having fallen suddenly together, a deliberately structured chaos appears as a new-found order. The poem's process is admirably described by Stewart Baker: "The success of the poem's structure . . . consists in organizing its different pastoral modes under the flexible but controlling perspective of the speaker, which assimilates and transvalues their variety into a pattern, and finally a vision, of unity."[109]

Hoping for the renewal of all things, attempting through art to repair the ruins of our first parents, Milton must figure both the fragmentation of the fallen world and the unity he would restore to the world through his art. One manifestation of the fall, Milton fully understood, is division, which reflects itself everywhere in the universe, even in the division of the arts. By joining pictorialism and song in his poem, by reintegrating the arts, Milton aspires to a unity, like that represented in the Bible, through which he can assert an *"intimate correlation between poetry and the universe,"* the one creation mirroring the other.[110] *Lycidas* is a pastoral perhaps—but one that by assimilating more than had ever been assimilated before also aspires to more than any pastoral had achieved before. In this "pastoral," not only are all the major forms gathered together within the central form of prophecy, but the arts—poetry, painting, and song—are reunited in Milton's verbal idiom.

Lycidas has always been thought a difficult poem, and much of its difficulty derives from the complexity emanating from this mixing of genres and art forms and from the multiple perspectives generated by such mixtures. This generic complexity may be both assessed and understood through distinctions devised by Kenneth Burke. He argues for a discrimination between forms of acceptance and rejection and then, comprehending the relative simplicity or complexity of the world-view contained within any one genre, arranges them hierarchically.[111] The simplest forms of acceptance and rejection, according to Burke, are pastoral and elegy respectively. *Lycidas,* however, escapes the simplicity of either world-view by subsuming both visions of life within the complicating perspectives of satire, tragedy and comedy and the containing form of epic heightened to prophecy.

Milton, at least the early Milton, is often said to be the pastoral Milton; and, accordingly, *Lycidas* has been described as "the most pastoral in form of all Milton's English poems, more so considerably than the *Arcades* and *Comus.*"[112] Yet this generalization, like so many others that have been used to explain the poet, oversimplifies and, oversimplifying, distorts the poems belonging to the period between 1629 and 1637. Already we have observed that in *L'Allegro* and *Il Penseroso,* which have their pastoral moments, the poet moves beyond pastoral, reaching, in his own words, for the "Prophetic strain." This same movement, this same reaching, the same impulse toward transcendence, is evident in *Lycidas*. That poem did not always appear in the same setting; but whatever its setting, *Lycidas* always marks a generic progress. So important is this progress that Milton has *Lycidas* call attention to itself by the boldness of the typeface given this poem in "The Table of the English Poems" included in *Poems upon Several Occasions* (see fig. 11).

All the poems in the Edward King memorial volume are elegies; but *Lycidas* alone is a pastoral—and at that, a pastoral which, maturing into vision, moves on "the plane of vision and prophecy."[113] No less than *Justa Edovardo King Naufrago,* the 1645 *Poems of Mr. John Milton* has "an impressive and peculiar sense of wholeness," which, as Louis Martz has shown, derives from a purposeful "arrangement" that exhibits "the growing awareness of a guiding, central purpose."[114] Both *Justa Edovardo King Naufrago* and the 1645 *Poems,* then, possess integrity as volumes; and Milton's description of the latter volume, in an ode to John Rouse, serves equally well as a description of the earlier one: each is a book in twin parts, "rejoicing in a single robe, yet with double leaves" (1-5); that is, each volume is divided into two sections— one of English, the other of Greek and Latin poems; and each of those sections has its own title page and pagination. In each volume, there is a sense of generic progress heightened by a parallel thematic movement. It is as if *Justa Edovardo King Naufrago* inspired both the physical layout and organizational plan of the 1645 *Poems.* In any event, the progression implicit in the earlier volume is made explicit, then is magnified, in the later one. Both volumes, carefully designed, are directed toward a common end— the representation of Milton as a rising poet and predestined bard,[115] as a poet who, though indebted to his English predecessors, is ready to move beyond them. This competitive spirit is noted by Humphrey Moseley when, in a word to the reader, he praises Milton as Spenser's successor, one who not only "imitated" but "sweetly excelled" his precursor. Milton, it should be noted, never thought of Spenser as a threatening poet, but instead turned to him as a creator whose genius was to expand, instead of restrict, the individuality of those who followed after him.[116] Yet finally even Spenser must yield precedence to the prophetic parts of Scripture, particularly to John's Apocalypse, various parts of which, as James Holly Hanford long ago noticed, became "the center of . . . [Milton's] imaginative activity."[117]

Profoundly Spenserian, the poems surrounding *Lycidas* are also poems that, like *Lycidas*, portray generic progress: *Arcades* commemorates one historic transformation of pastoral—the modification of classical into Christian pastoral, while *Lycidas* commemorates yet another—the transformation of pastoral into prophecy. The transformation is like the one achieved three years before, when in writing *Comus* Milton gave to his pastoral masque visionary dimensions. In *Comus,* as in *Lycidas,* pastoral is harnessed to prophecy, and that harnessing is accomplished by Milton's allowing both poems to spring from John's Book of Revelation, which itself yokes pastoral to prophecy and simultaneously, even as it interconnects the two forms, implies a progression from the one to the other.[118]

Edward Tayler, we have said, acknowledges a progression that moves *Lycidas* beyond classical and Old Testament pastoral into the pastoralism of the New Testament; and, similarly, Louis Martz notices a generic progression in *Lycidas,* speaking of "the poem's movement beyond the limitations of pastoral elegy into the border reaches of the pastoral eclogue, with its awareness of the world of history."[119] This progression is most precisely marked by Stewart Baker, who describes the poem's process as a "mediation to prophecy," as a pressing beyond pastoral into the "apocalyptic prophecy" of St. Peter and then up "the mount of prophecy," whose pinnacle is reached in the tenth verse paragraph of Milton's poem.[120] Here, as both Thomas Warton and Henry John

Fig. 11. The Table of Contents for Milton's *Poems upon Several Occasions* (1673). Reproduced by permission of the Huntington Library, San Marino, California.

THE TABLE.

Todd perceived, is the place of *"great Vision"* where the Apparition of St. Michael is said to have appeared and from which the vision of Lycidas emanates.[121] This same progression is dramatized within Milton's poem by the constant pressing forward toward vision which, once achieved, seems to throw the poet back into the pastoral world, albeit with a different understanding of it. Three times the poet reaches "that fearsome crest of prophetic vision"; and each time, Martz observes, the poem draws back into the mode of pastoral.[122] Milton's point is not to reject one mode, or one world, for another, but rather to assert the interconnection between them, to assert that through prophecy a new world, emblematized by the pastoral image, is to be born.

Pertinent here is William. Empson's remark that pastoral is "a puzzling form which looks proletarian but isn't":[123] pastoral is about the people, Empson concludes; but it is not, like proletarian literature, by and for the people. Milton knew, however, that "prophecy belongs not to the prophet but to the people";[124] and so, by joining pastoral to prophecy, he allows a form about the people to modulate into a form by and for the people. Just as the poet in *Lycidas* is at one with the prophet, the uncouth swain and the miscellaneous rabble are "one," and in their metamorphosis they become another "higher one." All the Lord's people, like the poet, are becoming prophets; and in the process, pastoral modulates into prophecy. The meaning of that modulation is grasped in the realization that "the art of pastoral is the art of the backward glance," the pastoral poet "revers[ing] the process (and the 'progress') of history."[125] The art of prophecy, in contrast, is the art of the forward gaze, and in consequence the process and progress of history are set in motion again: prophecy would thus move history to a last judgment, would bring history to its apotheosis.

For this reason, the pastoral world is a dominant but not an omnipresent image in Milton's poem: it is invoked in the opening lines of *Lycidas* only to be shattered by the knowledge that *"Lycidas* is dead, dead ere his prime" (8). Death shatters, disrupts everything in Milton's poem, as the world of experience invades the world of innocence; still, in the course of Milton's poem, the pastoral image obtrudes here and there only to be banished again and again until, in its epilogue, the pastoral world is reestablished. In the process, *Lycidas* shows how, through prophecy, the pastoral world can be reestablished in human history—how, through the agency of prophecy, the world is to be created anew. For a poet like Spenser, the pastoral world is finally relevant to men only as an image of life after death, as an emblem of immortality; for Milton, the pastoral world retains that symbolic significance but, equally, is a symbol for the world once all the Lord's people, having become prophets, establish the Lord's kingdom in history. If the pagan dies out of glory, the Christian dies into glory—not just at the end of time when the second resurrection occurs, but also within time, within history, where the first resurrection is accomplished.

Stating the occasion for *Lycidas* as King's drowning in 1637, Milton firmly establishes the Revelation context through the epigraph he adds in the 1645 *Poems,* explaining he has used that occasion to "foretell," to *prophesy,* "the ruine of our corrupted Clergie then in their height." It continues to be argued, of course, that Peter's invective is a digression, "a poem within a poem" that both "detracts from the harmony of the whole" and is "at variance with the niceties and the discretion of its genre":

> There is no doubt that Milton's introduction within the major poem, which is a literal pastoral, of a minor poem, which is an allegorical one, must be viewed as a grievous error, yet such an error should not be seen as a religious and moral fault . . . but simply as a poetic and literary mistake.[126]

Peter's invective is, more exactly, a prophecy within a larger prophecy, a focusing and an expression of what the poem is. The tradition of Christian pastoral, certainly, sanctions Milton's decision to inveigh against the clergy, but so too does the visionary tradition represented by Langland's *Piers Plowman,* Dante's *Paradiso,* and Spenser's *The Shepheardes Calender*—a tradition that finds its source in John's Apocalypse.

In all these works, richly imbued with pastoral elements, there is prophetic vehemence, that prophetic zeal through which an upside-down world can be turned right side up. Langland, Dante, and Spenser, like Milton, return to the Book of Revelation not because their concern is with dead history but because it is with the ongoing drama of history. Milton is therefore not the first poet to give utterance to a prophecy such as Peter delivers: Langland's Piers and Anima, Dante's Peter, and Spenser's Piers (who, when the May eclogue is translated into Latin, becomes Lycidas) utter comparable prophecies, which are traceable to the Old Testament prophets and which belong to the radical prophetic tradition charted by Norman Cohn. "The Lord God will come with strong *hand*," says Isaiah (41:10); and in Zechariah the Lord himself says, "Mine anger was kindled against the shepherds . . . Awake, O sword, against my shepherd . . . : smite the shepherd" (10:3, 13:7). And in Mark: "I will smite the shepherd" (14:27). Recalling the prophecy of Hans Hut, the Anabaptist, Cohn reminds us of those, claiming to be prophets, who said that "Christ would return to earth and place the two-edged sword of justice in the hands of the rebaptised Saints. The Saints would hold judgment on the priests and pastors for their false teachings."[127] Poets who are also self-proclaimed prophets can thus denounce the failings of their own time through biblical prophecy and, in the process, can mythologize that history—they can translate it into *figurae*. The figures of Piers, Peter, and Christ are intervolved, Piers being a representative of Peter just as Peter is a representative of Christ. As representatives, Piers and Peter are laborers sent by Christ to prepare for the harvest: they are the new providers for society who plough the way to the truth and who would thereby effect the reformation of the natural man. With one modification, that in the modern world the poet is the new provider, this I take to be the crucial point in the following lines of *Lycidas*:

> He shook his Miter'd locks, and stern bespake,
> How well could I have spar'd for thee, young swain,

Anow of such as for their bellies sake,
Creep and intrude, and climb into the fold?
Of other care they little reck'ning make,
Then how to scramble at the shearers feast,
And shove away the worthy bidden guest;
Blind mouthes! that scarce themselves know how to hold
A Sheep-hook, or have learn'd ought els the least
That to the faithfull Herdmans art belongs!
What recks it them? What need they? They are sped;
And when they list, their lean and flashy songs
Grate on their scrannel Pipes of wretched straw,
The hungry Sheep look up, and are not fed,
But swoln with wind, and the rank mist they draw,
Rot inwardly, and foul contagion spread:
Besides what the grim Woolf with privy paw
Daily devours apace, and nothing sed,
But that two-handed engine at the door,
Stands ready to smite once, and smite no more.

(112–31)

In his Commonplace Book, Milton remembers Dante's open censure of the clergy in the *Inferno* (*Yale Milton,* 1:366); and he doubtless recalled the fiery diatribe in the *Paradiso,* where Peter denounces Boniface and prophesies vengeance:

Rapacious wolves in shepherds' garb behold
In every pasture! Lord, why dost Thou blink
Such slaughter of the lambs within Thy fold.

(XXVII. 55–57)

But providence, Peter concludes, "will swift lend aid": Christ will come again, through his prophets restoring order to Church and State. Even more immediate analogues are provided by Spenser in his May and June eclogues. Spenser and Milton alike use pastoral to focus an attack on clerical abuses, equating "pastor" and "minister" by way of distinguishing true prophets from false ones. In the May eclogue, Piers, like Milton's Peter, complains

133

that the Lord's task has been abandoned, the flocks are unfed (indeed are being devoured) by those who "under colour of shepeheards . . . / . . . crept in Wolves, ful of fraude and guile" (44, 53, 126–28). Or as E. K. explains, the ministers of the Church, namely "the Pope, and his Antichristian prelates, . . . in steede of feeding their sheepe . . . feede of theyr sheepe" (7:57). A dichotomy is drawn by Spenser to differentiate Catholic from Protestant ministers and by Milton to distinguish true pastors, who are also poets, from the various ministers in England's Protestant churches. Also pertinent here is Spenser's July eclogue which, praising good shepherds and chastizing proud and ambitious ones (7:66), alludes to "S. Michels mount" (41–42) and the feeding by that "great God *Pan*" of "the blessed flocke of *Dan*" (49, 51), that is, according to E. K.'s notes, the feeding of the entire English nation by Christ (7:55–56, 73). Spenser's point is identical with Milton's, and both their statements are traceable to the Book of Revelation, where Christ is shown to be a pattern and where it is argued that so too should his ministers "be paternes to the flocke."[128]

Spenser's theme here is also Milton's theme in *Lycidas,* where the poet takes on Christ's pastoral mission, proclaiming with Ezekiel, "Woe *be* to the shepherds . . . that do feed themselves" (34:2, 8). The theme finds repeated articulation in the writings of the prophets—"My people hath been lost sheep: their shepherds have caused them to go astray" (Jeremiah 50:6), but "the Lord God . . . shall feed his flock like a shepherd" (Isaiah 41:11); and the theme is also woven through Milton's prose works, both early and late ones, and, deriving from the Book of Revelation, accords with the then current idea that bishops are not only limbs of Antichrist but are themselves Antichrist.[129] Indeed, Milton's prose tracts are a manifestation of Revelation's struggle between Christ and Antichrist, which in *Lycidas* expresses itself as a struggle between true and false prophets. In *Of Reformation,* Milton chastizes *"Priests* [for] not perceiving the heavenly brightness, and inward splendor of their more glorious *Evangelick Ministery,"* calling them *"Wolves,* that wait and thinke long till they devoure thy tender *Flock*" (*Yale Milton*, 1:593, 614). In *Animadversions*, such ministers are said to "have fed themselves, and not their flocks . . . They have fed his sheep (contrary to that which Saint *Peter* writes) [see I Peter 2–3]," says Milton, "not of a ready mind, but for filthy lucre, not as examples to the flock, but as being Lords over Gods heritage" (1:726–727). Such ministers, Milton insists in *An Apology for Smectymnuus*, are false prophets, who "chase away all the faithfull Shepheards of the flocke" (1:952); and they should be called, says the Milton of *Defensio Secunda*, "Sheep, rather than shepherds," for "they are fed more than they feed" (4, i:650). In *The History of Britain*, Milton reiterates his indictment, again in language and imagery reminiscent of *Lycidas:*

> Unlerned, Unapprehensive, yet impudent; suttle Prowlers, Pastors in Name, but indeed Wolves; intent upon all occasions, not to feed the Flock, but to pamper and well line themselves: not call'd, but seising on the Ministry as a Trade, not as a Spiritual Charge: teaching the people, not by sound Doctrine, but by evil Example: usurping the Chair of *Peter,* but through the blindness of thir own worldly lusts, they stumble upon the Seat of *Judas.* . . . (5, i:175)

The epigraph added to the 1645 printing of *Lycidas* does not allow us to forget the poem's occasion, or even its original setting; however, through its references to drowning at sea and to the corrupt clergy, that epigraph points to the Book of Revelation, establishing it as *Lycidas's* primary context, the religious matrix out of which Milton's poem, like some poems by Spenser, issues. Time and again, John's Apocalypse was said to be about the Church's drowning at sea and subsequent revival; and John clearly used his seven epistles, with which he begins his prophecy and which themselves were understood to be a miniature prophecy, for the purpose of analyzing the follies of the church and its ministers, for when the spirit of God leaves the church, not only is it dead but so are its members. However, apocalyptic notes are sounded not just in Milton's epigraph but throughout

St. Peter's prophetic invective. They may not always be heard today, but they were heard by John Ruskin, who says of the keys borne by Peter that "Milton makes one, of gold, the key of heaven; the other, of iron, the key of the prison, in which the wicked teachers are to be bound," Ruskin then explaining that "he who is to be bound in heaven must first be bound on earth. That command to the strong angels of which the rock-apostle is an image, 'Take him, and bind his hand and foot, and cast him out,' "[130] issues forth from the prophetic center of *Lycidas,* which, in form, is a perfect judgment oracle, beginning with an indictment and concluding with a sentence.

Lycidas should remind us of Milton's delight in hearing that poets themselves are "made . . . by divine Providence" (*Yale Milton,* 1:381) and so may be said to exemplify the providence to which they testify. Such delight was probably generated for Milton, as it later was for John Rogers, by the understanding that poets are now the recipients of God's revelations, which are, in turn, "a wonderful Scheme of Providence derived down, with great Consistency, from the Beginning of the World, and gradually open'd thro' a long Succession of Ages."[131] As a prophet, Milton knows his charge, which is to bear witness to the highest truths of Christianity; and meeting that charge, he invites the praise that in the nineteenth century was bestowed upon him: He stood, at the head of his generation in literature and theology, and so might be called upon (as Ruskin called upon Shakespeare and Dante), to "put . . . [his] creed into articles and send *that* up into the Ecclesiastical Courts!"[132]

First and last lines in poetry are usually important, and they are especially so in *Lycidas,* for here they open into—they assert and reassert—the context from which the meaning of Milton's poem unfolds. An ironic commentary on the vision of the other poems in *Justa Edovardo King Naufrago* and on Spenser's pastoral and elegiac visions—an inversional transformation of all these poems—*Lycidas* finds its most important context in the Book of Revelation, which is both *a* context and *the* model, a generic analogue, for *Lycidas.* Here it is worth remembering, with John

Crowe Ransom, that "Milton *intended* his effects," especially "this one of indebtedness to models."[133] But Milton knew, too, that models and the norms they imply demand "both a reaffirmation of their validity and a renewed perception of their nature"; for as Claudio Guillén observes, " a form can never be 'taken over' " but "must be 'achieved' all over again, from the start, with each single work."[134]

Lycidas *and the Book of Revelation*

Lycidas shares with Milton's later poems a common purpose, the justification of God's ways, the assertion of eternal providence, which for Milton, as later for Blake, is opposed to and distinct from divine vengeance. Like its model, that "admirable Looking-Glass of Providence" called the Apocalypse,[135] Milton's poem is inspired by men's questionings, and it would allay such questionings in the manner of John of Patmos—by testifying to providence and ensuring that there will be ministers of it. If such testimony is "the First great Fruit and Use of the Apocalypse,"[136] that is also its yield in Milton's poetry, where providence is asserted not by invoking a god of justice and wrath but by countering such depictions with a god of love and mercy. Like another of his prophetic contemporaries, Milton would insist that God moderates his justice with his mercy, believing with Henry More that the vengeful God of Christian orthodoxy was an "imagination" of the false prophets, which they would erect within "the Temple of every mans Minde" and which it is the duty of every true prophet to destroy.[137] This Milton undertakes to do, not by advancing the notion that God is the arch-destroyer, but by promulgating the idea that he is the master-creator whose presence gives order, however intricate and involved, to the world and to its finest facsimile, the poem.

With calculation, Milton brings *Lycidas* into accord with the scriptural book that, enmassing "so many cleare arguments of . . . providence," puts aside all the questioning of it in earlier prophecy—the book that was alleged to supersede all earlier prophecy by explaining God's justice, which earlier prophecy allowed but admitted it could not comprehend.[138] Like the Book of Revelation, *Lycidas* testifies to God's providence by invoking the theme of man's redemption, a theme that Milton's poem, following the instruction of the Geneva Bible, yokes to information concerning "what things the Spirit of God alloweth in the ministers [of the church] and what things he reproveth." Moreover, by casting himself into the role of witnessing to providence, Milton arrogates to himself the power attributed to God's witnesses in scripture—power over water. If Christ's pastoral function involves his rescuing the church when she is drowning, Milton's prophetic role engages him in rescuing men from a similar fate. He wishes for nothing more than to be numbered with those who like Moses brought his people "out of the sea with the shepherd of his flock" (Isaiah 63:11). Christ presides over the second resurrection, receiving Lycidas into the heavenly kingdom; and correspondingly, the prophet, in this case Milton, presides over the first resurrection, raising up his audience of readers into a new spiritual life. Since the " 'Apocalyptic' lyric retains the epic intention,"[139] in scope, *Lycidas* may look like an epic; but in purpose Milton's poem, as both its first and last lines suggest, strains beyond epic—aspires to prophecy. Itself a revelation, the poem takes the Book of Revelation as its primary context.

The "cell" of a poem, "its simplest nucleus," says Octavio Paz, "is the poetic phrase."[140] "*Yet once more,* O ye Laurels, and *once more*" (my italics) recalls other occasions in Milton's poetry when the italicized phrases reappear. One setting for the first phrase is Sonnet XXIII ("as *yet once more* I trust to have / Full sight of her in Heaven without restraint")—a setting that underscores its visionary associations; and such associations are preserved in the one variation on the phrase that occurs in *Paradise Regained,* where Milton speaks of Elijah, that "great *Thisbite* who on fiery wheels / Rode up to Heaven, *yet once again* to come" (II.16–17). When the phrase, *yet once more,* reappears in *Paradise Lost,* sometimes in clipped form, it is almost always given apocalyptic overtones. Thus of "the mighty Combatants," Sin and Death, the narrator remarks, "For never but *once more* was either like / To meet so great a foe" (II.719, 721–22; cf. I.268), an obvious reference to the roles of Satan and Death in the Apocalypse and a reference rendered even more explicitly in the last books of *Paradise Lost* where an angel sounds a "Trumpet, heard in *Oreb* since perhaps / When God descended, and perhaps *once more* / To sound at general Doom" (XI.74–76; cf. XII. 211). In *Paradise Lost,* however, the most revealing setting for the phrase is God's second speech in Book III, where he proclaims, "*once more* I will renew / His lapsed powers . . . / . . . *yet once more* he shall stand / . . . By me upheld . . . / . . . and to me ow / All his deliv'rance" (175–76, 178–82). In this setting, the phrase is associated, as it is in *Lycidas,* with man's deliverance and, specifically, with his first resurrection which promises a second; and in both *Paradise Lost* and *Lycidas, Yet once more* recalls St. Paul's admonition to the Hebrews, not only his advice that if they are to achieve the heavenly city they must not turn away from the prophets who speak on earth or from heaven, but also his words:

> . . . *Yet once more* I shake not the earth only, but also heaven.
> And this word, *Yet once more,* signifieth the removing of those things that are shaken, or of things that are made, that those things which cannot be shaken may remain. (12:26–27)

In Milton's line, there may be the suggestion that, having written many elegies, the poet is about to write another. More likely, however, Milton here refers not to his own poetry but to the ritual of lamentation to which his own poem is a contribution and which it terminates: yet once more (*for the thirteenth time*) Edward King is being lamented—"but ONCE MORE, and no oftener."[141] There is "something decisive"[142] about the phrase, both as it is used in the Bible and as it appears in Milton's poem; and in both cases there is the suggestion that what is written is, as the Geneva Bible explains, for "no one man, citie or countrey" but for all men, all nations, and all times. The phrase, seeming to imply repetition, really signifies cessation; built into the phrase is the sense of an ending, the promise that a beginning ensures an end: there will be but one more lamentation of tears; it will be uttered by Milton "once for all, once and but once, once and no more"—"no other tears shall follow after it."[143] The lament this time, then, will be different; for King, translated into a symbol and so called Lycidas, yields through his own fate a pattern that, associated with Orpheus and St. Peter, with St. Michael and Christ, is generalized, universalized, mythologized into a pattern of experience relevant to all men. King's death and resurrection repeat the death of all men in Adam and, simultaneously, the resurrection of all men in Christ. "His victory is our victory"—a victory over both physical and spiritual death.[144] What is lost in Adam, Milton is saying, is regained in Christ; the paradise lost by the one is restored by the other. That assurance comes in the vision of "the blest kingdoms meek of joy and love," where Lycidas is entertained by all the Saints above who wipe the tears for ever from his eyes:

> Weep no more, woful Shepherds weep no more,
> For *Lycidas* your sorrow is not dead,
> Sunk though he be beneath the watry floar,
> So sinks the day-star in the Ocean bed,
> And yet anon repairs his drooping head,
> And tricks his beams, and with new spangled Ore,
> Flames in the forehead of the morning sky:
> So *Lycidas* sunk low, but mounted high,
> Through the dear might of him that walk'd the waves
> Where other groves, and other streams along,
> With *Nectar* pure his oozy Lock's he laves,
> And hears the unexpressive nuptial Song,
> In the blest Kingdoms meek of joy and love.
> There entertain him all the Saints above,
> In solemn troops, and sweet Societies
> That sing, and singing in their glory move,
> And wipe the tears for ever from his eyes.

(165–81)

In Milton's first line, there is the clear echo of Hebrews—of a passage from it that was said to signify "the removing of the Law or Old Covenant, given by Moses, and the immutabilitie and unchangeableness of the Gospel, or New Covenant"[145] and that by biblical commentators was repeatedly joined to the great promise in the Book of Revelation, that a time will come when man can wipe the tears forever from his eyes, that at that time a new Jerusalem will rise in the place of the old one. This coupling of Hebrews and the Apocalypse was common enough, especially among those like Isaac Newton who believed that Hebrews, succeeding the Apocalypse in time, was written as a commentary on it—as an assurance that there would be an "end of weeping and of all troubles," an end signaled by the ruin of wicked men and by the abolition of corrupt institutions.[146] As Henry More explains, this is the time for wiping away the tears, and it is signified by the fact that no one is any more oppressed with grief, nor does anyone any more express his grief by tears.[147] Now the witnesses of Christ, liberated from injustice and cruelty, from the abuses of institutionalized religion, rise up, like Milton's uncouth swain, doffing their sackcloth and revealing the garments, the mantle, of the resurrection; now the witnesses can testify to God's providence. Having thus "array[ed] himself . . . as a shepherd putteth on his garment," the swain, Milton and his readers, can "go forth . . . in peace" (Jeremiah 43:12). The epistle to the Hebrews thus anticipates, through "Prophetic Language" and in "Metaphors of the highest Excellencies," man's triumph over the beast,[148] a triumph won through the mental warfare that the true prophets like Milton wage against the false prophets, in Milton's poem represented by the corrupt clergy. It is no accident that Milton prophesies in an elegy; for true prophets, wearers of sackcloth, appear as mourners; nor is it an inconsequential detail that the poet, in the epilogue, assumes the prophet's mantle, for the man (who and what he is) is known by his apparel. Milton's point is simple enough: prophets are "set out by their *condition,* which is in sackcloth and mourning"; and they are called upon to prophesy, to feed the church, in those periods when she is in the wilderness.[149]

As if to underscore the implications of his modest beginning,

Milton starts his poem anew with the words, "Begin then, Sisters of the sacred well / That from beneath the seat of *Jove* doth spring, / Begin, and somewhat loudly sweep the string" (15–17). Echoing directly, emphatically, Virgil's Fourth Eclogue, Milton appears to be claiming for his poem what the Middle Ages and Renaissance had already attributed to Virgil's: it is a supplement to Holy Writ, a new version of the prophetic books. This was the poem, as Renato Poggioli explains, in which pastoral poetry "tried and succeeded in becoming, at least once, prophetic and oracular." Seeming to replicate the visions of the Hebrew prophets, the Fourth Eclogue reversed the pastoral pattern, says Poggioli: "in content, from the private sphere to the public one; and in form, from the mode of elegy . . . to the mode of . . . hymn." At the same time, Virgil's eclogue, as Poggioli describes it, projects the Golden Age into the future, thereby "introduc[ing] into the bucolic a metaphysical vision, and a messianic dimension."[150] *Lycidas,* like this poem, proclaims that a new order of things is imminent but, unlike it, follows not Old but New Testament prophecy, thereby excelling Virgil as John of Patmos had excelled Daniel. Within the context of pastoral poetry, Virgil shows to Milton the prophetic and oracular possibilities of a genre that Milton is ready to implement and to realize. Both first lines of Milton's poem, then, proclaim it to be a prophecy, and prophecy invariably explores the process whereby man is created anew.

That *Lycidas* is about the making of the prophet, the natural man becoming the spiritual man, is insinuated in the first lines and confirmed by the poem's final lines. In its coda, Milton asks us to observe, and share in, the expansion of the swain's understanding; in these last lines, the uncouth swain, drawing his mantle about him, stands transfigured by the experience he has undergone just as we, Milton's readers, are to be transfigured by it. The primary allusion here is to the relationship of prophets: just as Elijah passes on his mantle to Elisha, Lycidas bestows his mantle on the uncouth swain and Milton passes on his to us; and Elijah, we should remember, is the prototype in the Old Testament of the new spiritual man.[151] Alastair Fowler makes a similar point when, alluding to the swain's mantle, he writes that "It is the robe of a rededicated student body, the bands of a *Musarum sacerdos,* even a prophetic mantle fallen from the ascended King to Elisha-Milton below."[152]

If the first lines of *Lycidas,* apparently an easy reference to pastoral convention, have hidden in them a reference to prophecy, a key for unlocking the poem's meaning, so these last lines, seemingly wrapped in pastoral cliché, have encapsulized in them a reference to the very process that *Lycidas* involves—the natural man's becoming the spiritual man, which is a matter of opening his doors of perception. The theme of *Lycidas,* having been asserted figuratively by the vision of King's second resurrection, is here in Milton's epilogue reasserted by the swain who focuses the belief that those who "rise in the first resurrection are priestes to God, to his Christ, and they shall raigne with him."[153] Thus "within the sad and shaken opening of Milton's poem"—within the phrase, *Yet once more*—lies "a secret promise of redemption," of the resurrection, so movingly portrayed in the conclusion of Milton's poem.[154] Coming as they do within the prologue and epilogue to *Lycidas,* these opening and closing lines have special force; for in the pastoral poem, Thomas Rosenmeyer tells us, "the introduction and epilogue are emphatically separated from the . . . poem proper," allowing the poet to speak in his own voice and thereby to make his own feelings, his own intentions, manifest.[155] The prologue to Milton's poem, very much a part of the swain's song, may violate this convention; but Milton's epilogue, wrenched from the poem proper, scrupulously observes it.

This fact causes William Empson to remark that "the trouble about Milton conceived as a writer of pastoral is that he keeps so great a distance between himself and the swain."[156] Yet, in the concluding stanza, it is as if Milton, having read Joyce's *A Portrait of an Artist,* decided to use these last eight lines to illustrate one of Stephen's propositions:

The simplest epical form is seen emerging out of lyrical literature when the artist prolongs and broods upon himself as the centre of an epical event and this form progresses till the centre of emotional gravity is equidistant from the artist himself and from others. The narrative is no longer purely personal. The personality of the artist passes into the narration itself, flowing round and round the persons and the action like a vital sea.

In the concluding stanza of *Lycidas,* whose distancing effects find a precise analogue in Spenser's November eclogue, Milton is not so much distancing himself from the swain as he is mediating between himself and the reader, who now is figured in the poem by the swain, though until the startling verse, "Thus sang the uncouth swain" (186), the reader has assumed that he was to perceive only Milton in the swain. Now, as that identification is discouraged, another is encouraged. In this way, *Lycidas* exemplifies the belief that because poetry is "participation," the "poet and the reader are two moments of a single reality."[157] Both are participants in the process of regeneration that the poem celebrates and by which the reader, like the poet, will be remade.

The experience recorded in *Lycidas* had raised Milton's consciousness before his poem was written; the circles of expanding consciousness are represented within the poem by the swain, and they are fostered by the poem in the reader. Milton's point is simple enough: a limited consciousness is no consciousness, as Ludwig Feuerbach was later to say; for consciousness is something infinite by nature. To make this point, Milton juxtaposes his own all-inclusive, prophetic consciousness with the swain's—with our —evolving consciousness. Thus the very jolt that momentarily separates Milton from his swain simultaneously identifies Milton's swain with his reader, invites the reader to develop in himself the same consciousness that enabled Milton to write this "crisis-lyric,"[158] which dissolves that crisis into poetry—which turns questions into answers as it works joy out of grief and wrests order from chaos. The point is made succinctly by Donald Bouchard: Milton and the swain, or Milton *in* the swain, sets the pattern of regeneration for the reader.[159]

First lines sometimes have hidden in them a poem's resolution

—they prophesy its conclusion. But *Lycidas,* we have been told, "almost alone among Milton's important poems, does not suggest at the beginning how it will end": "Of the poem's conclusion we are given no hint," says Isabel MacCaffrey, largely because "no literary context" is developed by these initial lines.[160] Such an argument misses Milton's strategy in *Lycidas* and, moreover, ignores the evocative images introduced very early in the poem, which, as Samuel Palmer once observed, hold a vast store of suggestion—the mind is meant to be enchained by them.

There is, first, "the sacred well, / That from beneath the seat of *Jove* doth spring" (15–16). The reference here is to poetry as sacred song, as prophecy, which, as Thomas Lodge had explained, "commeth from above, from a heavenly seate of a glorious God"; and the passage itself is a thinly veiled allusion to the sea of glass before the throne of God, which is a renowned emblem for "the *Spiritual Kingdom* of Christ, . . . of Regeneration,"[161] so movingly envisioned both in the penultimate chapter of John's Apocalypse and in the penultimate verse paragraph of Milton's apocalyptic poem. Even more pointedly, there is the implied metaphor of the first five lines—Milton's poem is a garland —a metaphor that, in the language of prophecy, identifies Milton as a Christian poet and that builds, or should build, the expectations for the consolation which comes at the close of his elegy. But most important of all is the very first line of *Lycidas*—an allusion to an allusion that, once penetrated, points to the poem's ultimate resolution, "And wipe the tears for ever from his eyes" (181).

Commentators like David Pareus and George Gifford interpret this verse, which Milton lifts from the Book of Revelation just as John of Patmos had earlier lifted it from Isaiah (7:27, 21:4; cf. Isaiah 25:8), to mean that, though this life is *"a vale of teares,"* God "will make it, that we shall weepe no more, by taking away all cause of teares, turning our teares into joy according to the promise: *They which sow in teares, shall reape in joy."*[162] Milton's consolation implies, even further, that "it is much better to weepe here in afflictions for a little time, and to rejoyce for evermore in the world to come . . . , then to have delight . . . for a season, and afterward to mourne for ever."[163] If joy is liberating to the soul, sorrows are weights that depress and fetters that manacle it.

Nevertheless, affliction and sorrow have their purpose and deliver up their own rewards. God tries us by affliction and sorrow —tries our faith in both his love and justice "whilst he so afflicts the good, and letts the wicked prosper."[164] By repeatedly focusing this irony, and then magnifying it in the invective against the clergy, Milton makes his poem a trial of its reader, turning it into what his own age would have recognized as "a tryall of Faith" and into what Milton himself, in *De Doctrina Christiana,* describes as "Good temptations." By exercise God proves our righteousness and effects our restoration; he enables us to become "regenerated and born again and created anew," says Milton (*Yale Milton,* 6:338, 394), whose formulation here is in perfect accord with the idea, expounded by Thomas Taylor, that every Christian is engaged in "a twofold battell. 1. Of Christian redemption. 2. Of Christian exercise."[165] By means of the exercise, administered by *Lycidas,* man can reach toward the state of redemption promised by *Lycidas.* In this poem, Milton shows that affliction and sorrow can be seeds yielding a harvest of joy: the trial of the reader, as it is conducted in *Lycidas,* moves us toward the realization that the Covenant of Grace and the promise of redemption by Christ remove all grounds for sorrow; and bringing us to that realization, the trial itself may be said to have brought us closer to the crown of life. Out of sorrow comes the perception that such a crown is "wrought unto us by the afflictions of this life"—and, with that perception, the realization that this crown is the only one that matters, for connoting eternal life and happiness it never fades away.[166] As Tertullian assures us, "Blessed . . . are those who weep and mourn . . . To such . . . is consolation and joy promised."[167] To such men both come as a reward.

Wiping away the tears—an activity customarily associated with Christ's pastoral function—drives home the message of Milton's poem, which is the message of the Apocalypse as George Gifford related it:

> . . . he [Christ] is the shepherd over the whole flocke, which shall be even to the worlds end. And seeing we be now in exceeding great dangers in these evill dayes (as the last times are perilous) assure your selves he hath a special care over us.[168]

In *Lycidas,* the priest who has turned the garments of Christ's word filthy is made to surrender his duties, as shepherd and ploughman, as minister and prophet, to the poet who, becoming a prophet, acquires great power over water. Ariosto's poet who is one step from the prophet becomes in *Lycidas* identical with the prophet: poet and prophet are now indistinguishable; they are one. Poets who were "the first Prophetes or seers" and "the first . . . ministers" now have their religious function restored to them.[169]

Christ's pastoral role, then, is appropriated by Milton who, in the act of writing his poem, raises up the reader just as Christ raises up Edward King. Thus, the nominal subject of *Lycidas* is King's second resurrection—a raising up into life and eternal glory; but the poem's real subject is the reader, his first resurrection, which occurs in this life, through the agency of the poem, and involves moving out of the desolate prison habitated by the natural man into the mental spaces traveled by the prophet.[170] As in all prophecy, the real subject of *Lycidas* is its reader, the real locus of the poem, the reader's mind, represented within the poem by the uncouth swain. *Lycidas,* whose "true landscape . . . is the speaker's consciousness,"[171] that same mental landscape of the Apocalypse, is about his (our) metamorphosis into glory, which ensures the still greater one realized by King.

Christ, both in *Lycidas* and in the Book of Revelation, is man's saviour. As commentators so often noted, he made man when he was nothing and saved man when he was lost; he restored him to life when he was dead and raised him up to heaven.[172] Literally, this is true for Lycidas, and metaphorically it is true for his mourners; for in *Lycidas* the poet is made to take on Christ's function, must now minister to man's religious and secular needs as well. *Lycidas* (and this point needs to be made because it is so often ignored) is a poem written for the living, not for the dead, though it is of course lodged in the paradox that it is we, the living, who are dead and King, the dead man, who is truly alive. Just as Christ rescues King from the ocean's floor, so through his prophets he rescues the rest of us from our death sleep, restoring us to new life and raising up a paradise in the mental wilderness we have until that moment been inhabiting. *Lycidas,* therefore, like the Book of Revelation, is about two resurrections, the first in which the living rise from error and the second in which the dead rise up into eternal glory. Ostensibly a celebration of the latter, *Lycidas* is actually an invitation to and exploration of the former—a poem that figures forth through the second resurrection (the moment when men take possession of eternal life) the first resurrection (the moment when they take possession of divine truth and, thus entering into what Blake calls the Divine Vision, begin to remake the world).

Some of Revelation's commentators, of course, believed that the first resurrection was "not of particular persons, but of whole Churches and nations"; they are "spiritually quickened; . . . raised from the death of sin, to the life of grace."[173] Judging from his comments in *De Doctrina Christiana,* Milton, however, had more sympathy with commentators like John Alsted who, proposing that "the State of the Church after the fall is, either *Internall,* and perpetuall; or *Externall,* and temporal," says that the former consists in man's inner "Union and Communion with *Christ,*" who through his prophets provides man with the enlightenment and guidance that effect his regeneration.[174] A poet like Milton, for whom each man was his own church and who consequently belonged to a sect of one, could thus be expected to make the resurrection of nations contingent upon the regeneration of its members. In this way, having already aligned poetry and revolution so that all his poems are dramatic acts of resistance,

Milton achieves an "equivalence between 'internal' and 'external' revolution."[175]

The promise of Milton's poem relates first to the achievement of a paradise within and then to the building of one without, an idea which is focused by the epigraph for *Lycidas* and subsequently developed within the invective against the clergy; an idea which is carried out only when the deceits of the false prophets are wiped away and the church or its individual members are again purified. This is what is meant, says Richard Bernard, when John speaks of a time when there will be no more crying. Like the Book of Revelation, *Lycidas* is written to assert God's providence in a world where the wicked seem to prosper and the innocent are afflicted with all sorts of punishments, even untimely death. To show, as John does, that "lies, falshod, violence, tyranie false and franticke opinions, idolatrie and superstition, raign every where," says Bartholomew Traheron, while "trueth, righteousenesse, vertue, & all honestie, is trodden under foote, and lieth wounded, maimed, and mangled in the mire of the streates"[176]—to show this is to invite the revolution that will set an upside-down world right side up; and that revolution will occur not by employing the tactics of Antichrist but by manifesting the virtues of Christ.

In *Lycidas,* lamentation begins with the "forc'd fingers rude" (3) that pluck berries not yet ripe, a gesture rich in prophetic suggestion and pertinent to the largest objectives of Milton's poem, which are "to root out, and to pull down . . . to build, and to plant" (Jeremiah 1:10). The pastoral image, shattered and seemingly lost at the beginning of the poem, is restored by the end of the poem as an emblem of what is to be built. An image of what is desirable and possible, the pastoral world, as William Empson perceives, "is highly useful in that it facilitates the arousing of a revolutionary attitude towards reality, an attitude of practically changing the world."[177] The end of *Lycidas,* therefore, in its sudden shift from the first to the third person, does not catch Milton nodding; it does, though, show his concern for relationships—"of seer to his vision and seer to his community and community to the vision"—which as E. S. Shaffer suggests in another context, "is represented by the mobility . . . of the personal pronoun."[178]

In this strategy, Milton finds a way of reminding us that the sheep follow their shepherd: when he falls asleep so do they, yet when he awakens he can also awaken them.[179] This reminder is in keeping with the proposition that prophets awaken themselves first, and thereupon awaken others. The process completed by the prophet is now to be undergone by others, and in that process the outward man will decay as the inward man is renewed—"the winter of the one, is the Spring of the other."[180] This inner apocalypse, moreover, will effect an apocalypse in history. At one time it was thought that *Lycidas* was a great poem because, preceding Milton's prose tracts, it excluded "the repulsiveness [i. e., the revolutionary, subversive character] of his ecclesiastical and political theories." *Lycidas,* says Paul Elmer More, was written before Milton "flamed with a . . . zeal to make his own life a true poem and so to train himself for creating such a work of art as would lift his people from the ugly slough of faction and greed."[181] Intent upon telling us through such a statement "how to read *Lycidas,*" More actually exemplifies how *not* to read a poem that is notable for its quietly revolutionary and subversive doctrine.

Milton's revolutionary objectives, fully evident in the coda to *Lycidas,* are also manifested in the very first line of his poem. *Yet once more,* especially in later echoes charges *Lycidas* with emotion and also, taken by itself, charges *Lycidas* with meaning.[182] That meaning accretes to the phrase as the themes of *Lycidas* progressively manifest themselves; thus by the time we complete our reading of the poem, the phrase *Yet once more* has lost its neutral, prosaic quality. The original phrase has been restored—has been reinvested with its spiritual meaning.

Typically the phrase, *Yet once more,* was used to connect the prophecy of Hebrews with the prophecy of a last judgment in the Apocalypse—was thought to promise, according to John Diodati, a "universall and finall change and annihilation of the state and form of all the creatures, at Christs last appearing in judgement."[183] These judgment scenes, moreover, find their counterpart in Revelation's great scene of heavenly Sabbath: in the Apocalypse, as in *Lycidas,* visions of judgment find their "unmistakable companionpiece" in the vision of the heavenly city;[184] and in both works, these complementary scenes point downward —into this world. And inward—toward the spiritual history of everyman in this life. Already commentators were reading the Apocalypse as a book whose reference points were in the human psyche; they were reading it, much as Blake was later to do, as a spiritual drama involving everyman and climaxing in Christ's reign here on earth. In consequence, they were inclined, like Henry Archer, to argue that the establishment of Jerusalem "may fitly be called a day of judgement" because on that day *"God saves the Saints from the wicked."*[185] Here in the wilderness Christ will set up his throne of judgment; and here through his prophets he will build a new heaven and a new earth, first in man and then in history. Since the world to come cannot be described, says John Smith, no prophecy relates to it; rather, prophecy "must concern some state *in this world,*" and so "we must understand all those places that treat of a new heaven and new earth. . . . And so," Smith concludes, "we must understand the new Jerusalem mentioned in . . . that propheticall book of the Apocalypse."[186]

John Calvin had already found in the phrase, *Yet once more,* the promise of man's "deliverance." Bestowing upon man "the gift of regeneration," Christ, says Calvin, will also change "the whole state of the world."[187] In 1642, moreover, Henry Archer made the phrase fundamental to his argument that, once the kingdom of God is established within, through revolution a new monarchy, Christ's Monarchy, will be established in this world. Christ's kingdom, Jerusalem, Archer explains, "is not heaven, for *it comes downe from God out of heaven"* and so must refer to "a change . . . in this world, on earth."[188] Attributed to Christ himself, the phrase was said to sound the trumpet of a prophecy and to prove that, still speaking from heaven, Christ continued through his prophets to speak from earth as well. Alluding to the state of the church especially, the phrase also promised a change of earthly monarchies and governments; it was meant to ensure man of the overthrowing of some kingdoms so that, through his prophets, Christ might set up another.[189]

Such an understanding persisted in England from Milton's time well into the eighteenth century. Writing in 1785, for example, Robert Ingram says that *Yet once more* should remind us that, like the Book of Revelation, this phrase constitutes a "prophecy concerning the great revolution in all the kingdoms of the earth"—"revolutions which God was going to cause" and which would affect especially the church. To this conclusion, an explanatory note is appended: *Yet once more* "certainly implies some things of the same Nature yet are or have been done before. And thus it gives St. Paul an Opportunity of Shewing more fully the meaning of this Prophecy . . . , viz. that besides those changes which had been made in the Religions of the Jews & Gentiles" others will follow, and they will so perfect religion that "no other changes will succeed them."[190]

A paradise within thus precedes—stands in a causal relationship with—a paradise without; or as William Erbery puts it, God will dwell within his people, a nation of prophets, and dwelling within them, will guide his nation of visionaries into the new Jerusalem.[191] The same argument is advanced by Jacob Boehme:

> Zion shall not be from without; but in the new man: it is already born . . . let him enter into himselfe, and so he shall finde Babel, and her workings in him: those he must destroy, and enter into Gods Covenant, and then *Zion* will be manifest in him. . . .[192]

And thereupon, Milton would add, Zion stands a chance of being manifest in the world. *Lycidas* is thus a poem written not to consecrate history but in the hope that it one day will be history.

Lycidas possesses all the earmarks of Revelation prophecy and, besides, many of the more general signatures of prophetic writing.

In this poem, there are the salient features of Revelation's prophecy, cataloged by Austin Farrer: "the many-sidedness of the continuous symbolical theme," "the internal building up of pattern out of the elements of previous pattern," "the systematic use of echo," and an astonishing skill in "piling up climax."[193] In addition, there is the lonely hillside occupied by the uncouth swain in the sorrowful absence of Lycidas, a setting in which the poet experiences and from which he transmits his theophany. At the end of the poem, there are "the guarded mount" and "the Genius of the shoar" (163, 183), Milton here recalling the biblical tradition of the guardian deity. That tradition, as Martin Buber observes, is fundamental to prophetic literature, wherein the guardian deity, entrusted with a vision, "goes with those He guards, not only on moonlit nights, but also on the nights without moonlight, and on winter days too. He is a God that *tells* a man He is leading him," and who would lead, as well, a community of men, a whole nation.[194] There are also the seasonal markers of prophecy: August, the month of mortality and of Edward King's death, a time of devastation and devouring, of affliction and woe, is set against November, the month in which *Lycidas* is composed and during which the feast of two King Edwards is celebrated, a month signifying the dawning of peace and presaging the coming of Christ. There is the cryptic art of prophecy evident in both the poem's rhyme scheme and its numerical symbolism; and more conspicuously, there is the tripartite structure and within it a repeated pattern of "mental music,"[195] this pattern mirroring thought processes as they shift in the movement from panel to panel of Milton's poem.

The Art of Lycidas

If *Lycidas* is art, says William Hazlitt, "it is perfect art";[196] and such art, for Milton, finds its best analogy in music. That is fitting for a poet who imagines himself to be a prophet and who would have us designate his poem as a prophecy. Prophesying, after all, refers to "the art of playing poetry to a tune upon any instrument of music": "We read of prophesying with pipes . . . , with cymbals, and with every other instrument of music then in fashion," says Thomas Paine; "prophets were a company of musicians and poets, and . . . the concert . . . was called prophesying."[197] But the analogy Milton implies between *Lycidas* and music has still other ramifications. As Sigmund Spaeth explains, while noting Milton's love of "lofty fugues," this poet was pleased by "a bewildering series of passages . . . because of the mathematical order which lay at the bottom of their confusion, and because of the demands made by it upon the analytical powers of the listener."[198] Not only was *Lycidas* set to music in the eighteenth century, but throughout his poem Milton purposefully maintains the fiction that *Lycidas* is a song with musical accompaniment. No longer a singer of "soft lays" (44), the poet presents an "Oat" (88), he warbles a *"Dorick* lay" (189), that in the poem's epigraph is called a "Monody." A monody, John Alsted explains, is a simple melody carried forward by a series of different voices: it is "a simple Disposition of musical Voices," wherein words (the text) do "give . . . a soul to an Harmonical Song, or to the Image thereof." In a monody, Alsted continues, the musical accompaniment expresses the text, creating an "Image" that points to "the Archetype."[199] In *Lycidas,* as we shall see, the image is the circle, and the archetype toward which it points is Christ. Since all the images of the Bible are made to fuse in Christ's very existence, so too are the images of *Lycidas* gathered into their archetype who is Christ: he is the perfect pattern figuring the resurrection of all men; he is the inward and the new man that *Lycidas* would create;[200] and he is also the breath and finer spirit of true prophecy, which, as an emblem of mercy and forgiveness, is the ultimate vindicator of God's ways to men and thus the ultimate testimony to God's providence. *Lycidas* therefore is a special kind of song, its string accompaniment inducing the harmony, ensuring that the passions will be allayed and that a calm of mind, an inner paradise, will be established.

Perhaps the finest example in English poetry of that historical process described by John Hollander, "whereby *song* became a figurative term" by "internaliz[ing] music in the sounds and textures of its verse,"[201] *Lycidas* is also a form of sacred poetry, recalling a passage from Ephesians that refers to "Speaking . . . in psalms and hymns and spiritual songs"—a passage that connects with another in Corinthians, which proclaims sacred poetry to be divine song, one of God's gifts to man: "I will sing with the spirit, and I will sing with the understanding also" (14:15; cf. Revelation 5:8, 14:2; Colossians 3:16; Ephesians 4:32). But most importantly, by designating his poem a song, Milton reminds us of the fact that pastoral poetry was consecrated at the time of the Incarnation by the song the angels sang to the shepherds, and of the fact, too, that those who come to the Lord "with song . . . shall obtain joy and gladness and sorrow and sighing shall flee away" (Isaiah 35:10). Like a musical composition, moreover, *Lycidas* is deliberately designed to strain the mental powers of its audience; emanating from the mind's deepest recesses, it also penetrates "the Interiors of the mind,"[202] and it does so by employing what Milton, in *The Art of Logic,* calls "a crypsis of method."

Crypsis, Milton says, is "concealment"; and it is signaled both by "digressions" and by seemingly needless "lingerings," as well as by the rejection of certain commonplaces: "And especially the order of things will be inverted" (*Columbia Milton,* 12:297, 485). The "digression" wherein Milton rails at the corrupt clergy, his "lingering" in the flower passage, his introduction of pastoral *topoi* only to subvert them, his inversion of the standard form of the funeral elegy, his burying of narration in lamentation, and his concealment of rhymes—all these devices should alert Milton's reader to the "crypsis of method" that underlies the art of *Lycidas* and that finds one notable precedent in what Henry More calls "the Artifice of Concealment in the Apocalypse."[203] In *De Doctrina Christiana,* Milton is quick to clarify why he uses such a device: "I do not seek to conceal any part of my meaning"; rather, through such a device, he hopes to identify his audience as "mature, strong-minded men who thoroughly understand the teaching of the gospel" (*Yale Milton,* 6:122). The device of obscurity, of course, implies a measure of artificiality, and that has bothered artists who prize spontaneity. When is the artificial acceptable in art, they asked; and one answer to their question came from George Puttenham: "only in the subtlities of . . . arte . . . when . . . [the poet] is most artificiall, so to disguise and cloake it as it may not appeare, nor seem to proceede from him by any study or trade of rules."[204]

One such device, not unique to *Lycidas* but deriving from its biblical source, is that of cross-referencing images not just from Hebrews and Revelation but from Genesis and Revelation—a device that, as Isabel MacCaffrey explains, "was regularly regarded as proof that the beginning and the end are one."[205] Through its epigraph and through allusions within its verse, *Lycidas* thus invokes the first and last books of the Bible, both the works of prophets, and both prophecies rich with pastoral elements. In Genesis, the pastoral world is shattered only to be restored in the Apocalypse through prophecy. One dimension of meaning created by these allusions is suggested by Edward Tayler, who says that "the ideal landscape of pastoral is meant to recall the harmony of Eden, the moment in scriptural history when Nature operated without impediment and had no need of Art to attain perfection."[206] To this assertion, we may add a corollary: the perfection figured by the pastoral world is still to be sought after, is still attainable in this world; and its attainment is dependent upon art, upon prophecy, which regenerating man also restores to him the paradise he once lost.

By thus referring to the first and last books of the Bible, Milton stretches the past tense of his poem back to Creation and its future tense forward to Apocalypse. This movement toward extremities, however, is also a movement toward convergence; for last things and first things meet so that "the backward journey is also a journey ahead to the paradise regained that awaits us."[207] In this, Milton's strategy is like that of John of Patmos: through the pastoral image, he recalls the Edenic world about to be infested with Sin and Death at the beginning of the Bible; and through the genre of prophecy in which that allusion is made, he explores, like John, how man may be released from his fallen condition. The structure of the one experience (represented by the Book of Genesis) is negated by the structure of the other experience (represented by the Book of Revelation). This John makes clear by inverting in his own prophecy the structure of Moses'; and Milton in his prophecy follows suit by pitting against the structure of pastoral that of prophecy. In the process, Milton ensures that, through prophecy, the pastoral world will come to be regarded as "a foreshadowing, not an echo,"[208] that instead of looking backward it will gaze into the future. Pastoral, it may be said, projects Eden backwards, while prophecy, in contrast, projects Eden forward in time. Apocalyptic prophecy adumbrates, as Michael Fixler suggests, what is yet to be completed: "the regeneration of mankind, the redemption of Nature, the restoration of the Saints to the bosom of God, and the fulfillment of the whole drama of human existence in such a way as to make triumphantly manifest the justice of God's ways to Man."[209] These are the adumbrations of *Lycidas*.

Pastoral, like any other genre, has a set of conventions that provides a poet with a formulaic structure. In *Lycidas,* each verse paragraph turns upon a pastoral convention; and the three panels comprising the poem's overriding thematic structure, each practically equal in length and parallel in pattern, give accents to three of these conventions—the lament of nature, the procession of mourners, and the apotheosis of the lamented. This threefold structure, discovered and anatomized by Arthur E. Barker, is accompanied by a prologue and an epilogue;[210] and this structure, combining with others, becomes the key that fits *Lycidas* into its Revelation model. Like that model, no single part of *Lycidas* can contain the whole—at least none but the last part, which "gathers up the substance of all the preceding parts"; and like that model, "articulating itself stage by stage,"[211] *Lycidas* is a poem not of one but of many structures, a poem whose large structures are no less intricate and intervolved than the design provided for its verse paragraphs by their rhyme. The design of

Milton's poem is thus a facsimile of the design of John's.

As a pastoral and an elegy, *Lycidas* draws organizational principles from both genres. Not only are its three main panels controlled by a pastoral convention, but so too are its eleven verse paragraphs:

    1. statement of occasion
    2. ritual of mourning
    3. personal reminiscence
    4. lament of nature
    5. questioning of the nymphs
    6. answering of questions
    7. procession of mourners
    8. invective against the clergy
    9. flower passage
  10. the apotheosis
  11. singer's departure.[212]

Lycidas, of course, was not always so divided. When first published in *Justa Edovardo King Naufrago,* it was divided not into eleven verse paragraphs but into six: lines 1–14, 15–36, 37–131, 132–64, 165–86, 186–93. One does not lose the pastoral scaffolding in this early version, but here one is made much more aware of the elegiac patterning that so conspicuously organizes all the poems in *Justa Edovardo King Naufrago*—the pattern of narration, lamentation, and consolation.[213] When the threefold pattern of *Lycidas* is perceived according to Barker's analysis this elegiac pattern, though not lost, is greatly complicated. Milton's poem moves through two tentative consolations into a final one; and each of Barker's thematic divisions is itself tripartite in its pattern, being composed of elements that correspond to narration, lamentation, and consolation. The emotional progress of *Lycidas* is therefore marked by Milton's allowing one of these elements to predominate in each panel of his poem—narration in the first, lamentation in the second, and consolation in the third. Patterns are thus repeated, each time in a different key and each time with a new set of accents. Moreover, the pattern of threes—of the three sections and of the tripartite organization in each of those sections—together with the effect of structure within structure, of vision within vision, causes *Lycidas* to resemble those cosmological diagrams that represent the universe as ten circles—orb within orb (see fig. 1).

Extending into the prosody of Milton's poem, this patterning turns *Lycidas* into a work exactly correspondent with Octavio Paz's contention that a "poem is a shell that echoes the music of the world, and meters and rhymes are merely correspondences, echoes, of the universal harmony."[214] The customary marking of rhymes by arcs, or half-circles (see fig. 12), which in complicated structures overlap and intersect, reinforces this point. George Puttenham explained to his age that there were then two ways of marking rhyme: either by a "plaine and cleere compasse not intangled" or by "enterweaving one with another by knots." Indicating rhyme through "a compast stroke or semicircle," Puttenham concluded that the greater the distance between rhymes, the more compasses and interweavings.[215] If the rhymes of *Lycidas* were to be so marked by us, we would produce for Milton's poem a visual pattern analogous to those produced by Joseph Mede and Henry More to represent the complex patterning of the Book of Revelation, which is both a microcosm of the Bible and of the world (see figs. 2 and 3). All this accords with the contention that "theologians . . . habitually attributed meaningfulness to structures described in the Bible . . . or to literary structures formed by the text itself . . . [which] were related to the structure of the universe," and this should cause us to remember with Donald Howard that "the circles-in-circles design displays the complexity of the universal order."[216]

The design of *Lycidas* finds a general analogy in the tripartite structure of the Book of Revelation, and especially in Revelation's juxtaposition of its condemnation of the church with its vision of "the unconceiveable happinesse of all Gods chosen in the Heavens for evermore."[217] The second and third movements of *Lycidas*— its eighth and tenth verse paragraphs particularly—replicate this away and fo often returne agayne, as their tunes are neuer loft, nor out of the eare, one couple fupplying another fo nye and fo fud-denly, and this is the moft vulgar proportion of diftance or fitua-tion, fuch as vfed *Chaucer* in his Canterbury tales, and *Govver* in all his workes.

Second diftance is, when ye paffe ouer one verfe, and ioyne the firft and the third, and fo continue on till an other like diftance fall in, and this is alfo vfuall and common, as

Third diftaunce is, when your rime falleth vpon the firft and fourth verfe ouerleaping two, this maner is not fo com-mon but pleafant and allowable inough.

In which cafe the two verfes ye leaue out are ready to receiue their concordes by the fame diftaunce or any other ye like better. The fourth diftaunce is by ouerskipping three verfes and ligh-ting vpon the fift, this maner is rare and more artificiall then po-pular, vnleffe it be in fome fpeciall cafe, as when the meetres be fo little and fhort as they make no fhew of any great delay before they returne, ye fhall haue example of both.

And thefe ten litle meeters make but one *Exameter* at length.

-- , -- , -- , -- , -- , -- , -- , -- , -- , -- ,

There be larger diftances alfo, as when the firft concord falleth vpõ the fixt verfe, & is very pleafant if they be ioyned with other diftances not fo large, as

There be alfo, of the feuenth, eight, tenth, and twefth diftance, but then they may not go thicke, but two or three fuch diftãces ferue to proportiõ a whole fong, and all betweene muft be of other leffe diftances, and thefe wide diftaunces ferue for coupling of ftaues, or for to declare high and paffionate or graue matter, and alfo for art: *Pe-trarch* hath giuen vs examples hereof in his *Canzoni*, and we by lines of fundry lengths & and diftances as followeth,

And all that can be obiected againft this wide diftance is to fay that the eare by loofing his concord is not fatisfied. So is in deede the rude and popular eare but not the learned, and therefore the

M ij

Poet muſt know to whoſe eare he maketh his rime , and accommodate himſelfe thereto,and not giue ſuch muſicke to the rude and
barbarous, as he would to the learned and delicate eare.

There is another ſort of proportion vſed by *Petrarche* called the
Seizino,not riming as other ſongs do, but by chuſing ſixe wordes
out of which all the whole dittie is made, euery of
thoſe ſixe commencing and ending his verſe by
courſe , which reſtraint to make the dittie ſenſible
will try the makers cunning, as thus.

Beſides all this there is in *Situation* of the concords two other
points,one that it go by plaine and cleere compaſſe not intangled:
another by enterweauing one with another by knots,or as it were
by band,which is more or leſſe buſie and curious, all as the maker
will double or redouble his rime or concords,and ſet his diſtances
farre or nigh,of all which I will giue you ocular examples,as thus.

Concord in

Plaine compaſſe Entertangle.

And firſt in a *Quadreine* there are but two proportions,
for foure verſes in this laſt ſort coupled,
are but two *Diſticks*, and not a ſtaffe quadreine or of foure.

The ſtaffe of fiue hath ſeuen proportions as,

whereof ſome of them be harſher and vnpleaſaunter to the eare
then other ſome be.

The *Sixaine* or ſtaffe of ſixe hath ten proportions,wherof ſome
be vſuall, ſome not vſuall,and not ſo ſweet one as another.

The ſtaffe of ſeuen verſes hath ſeuen proportions,whereof one
onely is the vſuall of our vulgar, and kept by our old Poets *Chau-*
cer and other in their hiſtoricall reports and other ditties: as in the
laſt part of them that follow next.

The

George Puttenham's *The Arte of English Poesie* (1589) by permission of design. But Milton also finds a very precise analogy for *Lycidas'* structure in David Pareus' contention that God's is metaphorically a threefold book—one of his providence, another of his universal judgment, and a last which is the book of life. In its first section, *Lycidas* introduces the question of providence, "Where were ye Nymphs when the remorseless deep / Clos'd o're the head of your lov'd *Lycidas?*" (50–51), concluding as Pareus did, "That one & the same crowne is promised to all that are faythful," this crown "promised not of desert, but of grace, as a reward freely bestowed on them that are constant in faith." Those are Pareus' words, which should be compared with Milton's:

> *Fame* is no plant that grows on mortal soil,
> Nor in the glistering foil
> Set off to th' world, nor in broad rumour lies,
> But lives and spreds aloft by those pure eyes
> And perfet witnes of all-judging *Jove;*
> As he pronounces lastly on each deed,
> Of so much fame in Heav'n expect thy meed.
>
> (78–84)

Here Milton is no less insistent than Pareus had been: no man is rewarded for good works, which "merit not life" since "all are due to God."[218]

In the second section of *Lycidas,* Milton banishes the philosophy that, ascribing all unfortunate occurrences to destiny, is but a fond dream making "fatall periods the cause of all changes and crosse-accidents."[219] The stoicism of paganism allows the answer, "It was that fatal and perfidious Bark / Built in th' eclipse, and rigg'd with curses dark, / That sunk so low that sacred head of thine" (100–02); but Christianity demands another resolution, which comes through the theme of justice figured by the "two-handed engine," the "Two massy Keys," the two-edged sword—instruments not of mortal warfare but of those, like Peter, who are invested with the power of the divine word. Here again Pareus provides a relevant gloss as he explains that *"Gods wayes* are his counsells and judgements about the Church and the enemies thereof":

. . . though he suffers the godly to be afflicted and . . . troubled, and the enemies to bear sway and flourish . . . [he is] *righteous*: . . . for in the end he performs his promise to the Saints, in preserving and delivering the Church, and in punishing and destroying their adversaries.[220]

Through his judgments, God weakens Antichrist and brings both the church and its members into the liberty of Christ. This assurance is provided in the third section of Milton's poem, which is modeled on God's third book, the book of life, and which contains a vision of life everlasting, achieved for all the faithful by "the dear might of him that walk'd the waves" and emblematized by the "sweet Societies / That sing, and singing in their glory move" (173, 179–80).

Within Milton's threefold structure, there is prophetical progression, his poem proceeding from obscurity to clarity, from shadowy types to truth—from Orpheus, to Peter, to Michael, to Christ; from type, to type, to manifestation, to the reality—each new vision interpreting the one it supersedes, just as in Revelation each new blast of a trumpet expounds what has preceded it. This procession of types, together with the manifestation of Michael (who by most biblical commentators was understood to be Christ), brings Christ to the center of this prophecy, just as he is at the center of John's. And, as in John's prophecy, each visionary panel contains a type of the Last Judgment until it is overwhelmed by the vision of the new Jerusalem. The Book of Revelation, subsuming the whole structure of the Bible, is, says E. S. Shaffer, "the climax and summation of the typological method."[221] Yet typology is not synonymous with prophecy, but rather, as John M. Evans observes, an aspect of prophecy: types, like prophecy itself, look forward to future fulfillment; both typology and prophecy "can exist only in a universe in which the progress of events follows a discernible and meaningful pattern, in which prophecies come true and types are fulfilled."[222] The fulfillment of the one ensures the realization of the other, the antitype representing the figure or the state that the type promises.

Typology, however, is but one of several aspects of prophecy that reveals itself in the structure of *Lycidas*. Besides the structures we have already observed, there are the poem's time structure and its numerical structure, both of which find a precedent in, and are to be explained by, the complicated patterning of prophecy.[223] Prophecy is historical—but in a special sense: it contains all time (past, present, and future) within its moment, and thus the prophet past, present, and future sees simultaneously, though the prophet also takes that moment and, like Eno in Blake's *The Four Zoas,* stretches it out in time. The Book of Revelation, for example, is said to look backward to Christ's passion and resurrection and to see in them the present tribulations and imminent renewal of the church and its members; the operation of providence in current history, moreover, is said to ensure a final judgment—a decisive victory over Antichrist.[224] These same time perspectives are evident in *Lycidas,* where Christ's resurrection anticipates King's, and the reader's, and where the resurrection of both promises a last judgment, as well as a resurrection into eternal glory.

In *Lycidas* two time perspectives are early and firmly established—time past when Lycidas was still alive, and time present when Lycidas, having died, is being lamented. But no sooner established, these perspectives are complicated and modified: there is the remote past when Lycidas was still alive, and the immediate past marked by Lycidas's death; there is the immediate present, the time of the poem's composition, the time of lamentation, and the new present, a time of rejoicing and of consolation. Finally, there is the future, pointed to by the poem's concluding line, "To morrow to fresh Woods, and Pastures new" (193), a future that is itself imminent and remote, this line pointing simultaneously to a new world, a reformed world, that is to be realized in history, and to eternity, a life of resurrection and joy beyond history, to be realized at the end of time. In *Lycidas,* then, our ideas of past and present are continually being modified and, once modified, begin to modify our sense of the future: they reveal its possibilities.

The past is a burden only to those who, believing that it must die, are repeatedly confronted by the fact that it never properly dies; the prophet would thus lift from man's shoulders the burden of the past by demonstrating through his art that the past "is perpetually resumed and carried forward in the future."[225] For this reason, especially, "the manner of the Prophets, in speaking of future events, is," as Thomas Taylor observes, "to propound them in the time past," thereby interconnecting past and future, making the one the harbinger of the other.[226] Yet the prophet always places the accent on the future. As a prophecy, the movement of *Lycidas,* therefore, is out of the past, beyond the present, into the future. Milton's poem is shot through with the future. Though the poem repeatedly looks into the past, it begins in the present: *now* "I come to pluck your Berries harsh and crude" (3); but it ends with a forward gaze, first by the swain (". . . thou . . . *shalt* be good . . ." [184]) and then by Milton (*"To morrow* to fresh Woods, and Pastures new" [193]). The prophet looks ahead to *tomorrow,* realizing that his role has not been to predict the future but to present a "renewed vision . . . of the past for the future."[227]

Typical of prophecy, this whole process is eloquently described by Ernst Cassirer when he writes that "in human beings the awareness of the future undergoes the same characteristic change of meaning which we have noted with regard to the idea of the past":

The future is not only an image; it becomes an "ideal." The meaning of this transformation manifests itself in all the phases of man's cultural life. So long as he remains entirely absorbed in his practical activities the difference is not clearly observable. It appears to be merely a difference of degree, not a specific difference. To be sure the future envisaged by man extends over a much wider area, and his planning is much more conscious and careful. But all this still belongs to the realm of prudence, not to that of wisdom. The term "prudence" (*prudentia*) is etymologically connected with "providence" (*providentia*). It means the ability to foresee future events and to prepare for future needs. But the *theoretical* idea of the future—that idea which is a prerequisite of all man's higher cultural activities—is of a quite different sort. It is more than mere expectation; it becomes an imperative of human life. And this imperative reaches far beyond man's immediate practical needs—in its highest form it reaches beyond the limits of his empirical life. This is man's *symbolic future,* which corresponds to and is in strict analogy with his symbolic past. We may call it "prophetic" future because it is nowhere better expressed than in the lives of the great religious prophets. These religious teachers were never content simply to foretell future events or to warn against future evils. Nor did they speak like augurs and accept the evidence of omens or presages. Theirs was another aim—in fact the very opposite of that of the soothsayers. The future of which they spoke was not an empirical fact but an ethical and religious task. Hence prediction was transformed into prophecy. Prophecy does not mean simply foretelling; it means a promise. This is the new feature which first becomes clear in the prophets of Israel—in Isaiah, Jeremiah, and Ezekiel. Their ideal future signifies the negation of the empirical world, the "end of all days"; but it contains at the same time the hope and the assurance of "a new heaven and a new earth." Here too man's symbolic power ventures beyond all the limits of his finite existence. But this negation implies a new and great act of integration; it marks a decisive phase in man's ethical and religious life.[228]

Another of the multiple patterns evident in *Lycidas* is that of numerology. Neither as consistent nor as rigorous in his employment of this device as he was in the Nativity Ode or as he will be in *Paradise Lost,* Milton nevertheless uses it not only to pattern *Lycidas* but also to invest that pattern with meaning. Eventually divided into eleven verse paragraphs, *Lycidas* observes a convention whose basis "lay in the ancient association of 11 with mourning and specifically with its termination" and in the Christian association of eleven with resurrection.[229] The Bible itself, Henry More had explained, conveys truth by "a method of concealment which is *Numeral*,"[230] a method particularly evident in the Book of Revelation where the numbers three and seven are made to figure the Book's subject and theme. Following Revelation's method, Milton employs such symbolism, though apparently as an afterthought, to emblematize the subject of his poem, which is both King's resurrection and our own, and the purpose of his poem, which is to terminate mourning through the discovery that if death is to be found in life, then life is to be found in death. Like its model, Milton's poem is sown in sorrow but culminates in gladness—in a vision of the marriage feast; in this moment, when all things once again center in God and the Lamb, man wipes away the tears, achieving at last what Richard Bernard calls a "quiet peace."[231] The presence of these various structures—the prominence here of Revelation's design—makes clear that *Lycidas* is a prophecy, and Milton's intention that we designate it as such is made further evident not just by such features as numerology but by the art of crypsis informing the rhyme scheme of his poem. The poem's rhyme scheme is perfected in the various revisions of *Lycidas;* but paradoxically those revisions, instead of focusing the rhyme, are part of a process of "subduings."[232] Yet even here, in the poem's rhyme scheme, we find a secret coherence.

No element in *Lycidas* has generated more bewilderment (and in the case of Dr. Johnson, displeasure) than the uncertainty of its rhyme. Still, there is much in Milton's poem that Johnson could not see and even more, as Edward Weismiller observes, "that Dr. Johnson simply could not hear."[233] *Lycidas* possesses a formal, circular pattern carefully articulated by its rhyme scheme and supportive to its presiding themes. The chief control for the poem's pattern is the English madrigal, the practices associated with it providing the rigorous technical tradition that makes a subtle art possible. The poet who used this form could assume an audience, few though fit, familiar with madrigal conventions and trained to appreciate them; and such a poet, if asked to comment on rhyme in his poetry, would probably remark as Yeats once did: "to him who ponders well / my rhymes more than their rhyming tell."

For the Elizabethan and seventeenth-century poet, the pleasure of rhyme did not preclude the intricacy of structure. The primary function of rhyme was to convey the emotional effects of verse;

and with this end in mind, the poet's first concern was with the audience he was addressing. The distance of his rhymes, the intricacy of his rhyme patterns, depended entirely upon the sophistication of his audience. What escaped the untutored ear, the poet reasoned, could be taken in by the trained ear. The poet who distances his rhymes "doth intende to shew himselfe more artificiall then popular," says Puttenham; and the only real objection to be raised against wide distance is that the poet may have to sacrifice the pleasure of sound for the greater pleasure that comes from intellectual apprehension of harmony.[234] The poet may have to sacrifice the vulgar in his audience for the esoteric few. Such a sacrifice Milton was prepared to make in *Lycidas,* a poem initially addressed to an academic audience.

Among the subtler verse forms available to poets—and thus to Milton—was the madrigal. It was one manifestation of resistance to conventional stanzaic forms that were so often convenient devices for concealing loosely structured and unrhythmical verses. The form, moreover, offered the poet an opportunity for internalizing his structure and thus for imparting "some sense of integral relationship between matter and manner."[235] Just as importantly, it provided the poet with maximum technical freedom within what was nevertheless a convention with certain settled principles. The poet was free to set the number of lines for each stanza, or to vary them if he wished; he could create as intricate a rhyme scheme as he chose. His efforts, however, were ultimately engaged in transforming the seeming irregularities of his rhyme into regularity through persistently repeated patterns. The rhymes, because distant, were not obtrusive; but neither were they hesitant. They occurred, or were supposed to occur, "with the quiet confidence of perfect art."[236]

Like other forms of the English lyric, the madrigal was originally accompanied by a musical score. And, as was the case with other lyrics, the score dropped silently away as the form became increasingly more complicated; yet the poet maintained the fiction that his poem was a song with musical accompaniment. So it is that Milton in the final lines of *Lycidas* tells us, "Thus sang the uncouth Swain" (186); so it is that his muse "loudly sweep[s] the string" (17) as the first movement of the poem commences; and so it is that all the designations Milton provides for his poem—it is a "Monody" and a "Dorick lay"—find their reference in music. Still, the most distinctive feature of the madrigal tradition—and the one of special relevance to *Lycidas* —is that, despite the clearly marked divisions between stanzas or verse paragraphs, the poet, interested in the binding effects of rhyme, works out a single, continuous rhyme scheme. Thus instead of beginning a new rhyme scheme with each new stanza, the poet treats those stanzas, or verse paragraphs, as if they did not exist at all. The divisions did exist, of course, and existed, in part, as an afterthought to conceal the carefully articulated pattern inscribed by the rhyme. In this way, the madrigal provided the poet with the pleasure of making his own regularity rather than the task of accommodating his verse to an established pattern. Moreover, the madrigal extended to the poet a form that, compelled by rhyme, moved, however haltingly, toward conclusion.

This complexity contributes to the madrigal's place as a forerunner of the most sophisticated types of hieroglyphic poetry. Within the tradition, the poet discovered a means of employing the artifice of poetry to image forth the archetypal pattern of the universe. It was, of course, one thing to arrange the lines of a poem to suggest the subject of a poem, but an infinitely more difficult assignment to marshal meter and invent rhyme patterns that might successfully duplicate the divine order. The madrigal, however, was well suited to the task. Its tenaciously repeated rhymes, simultaneously looking forward and backward, could easily be made to suggest the circle, the traditional symbol for perfection and order brought out of chaos. The circle, says Donald Bouchard, symbolizes "the order of disorder" and "stands for the mirrored structure of the universe."[237]

The rhyme scheme of *Lycidas,* when worked out according to the principles of the madrigal tradition, forms a carefully articulated and highly ritualistic pattern of order that extends over the entire poem as if the verse paragraphs and *ottava rima* stanza did not exist at all:

Visionary Poetics

Roman Numerals = Verse paragraph.
√ = Unrhymed lines according to analyses of rhyme scheme worked out paragraph by paragraph.
* = Unrhymed lines according to my analysis.
( ) = Line references.
————— = Original verse paragraph divisions (see *Justa Edovardo King Naufrago*).

	(Prologue)		
I	more	A√	
	sere	B	
	crude	C	
	rude	C	
	year	B	
	dear	B	
	due	D	
	prime	E	
	peer	B	
	knew	D	(10)
	rhyme	E	
	bier	B	
	wind	F√	
	tear	B	

	(First Movement)		
II	well	G√	
	spring	H	
	string	H	
	excuse	I	
	Muse	I	
	Urn	J	(20)
	turn	J	
	shroud	C√	
	hill	K	
	rill	K	
III	appear'd	L	
	morn	M	
	heard	L	
	horn	M	
	night	N	
	bright	N	(30)
	wheel	G	

	mute	O	
	flute	O	
	heel	G	
	long	P	
	song	P	

IV	gone	Q	
	return	J	
	Caves	R√	
	o'ergrown	Q	(40)
	mourn	M	
	green	S	
	seen	S	
	lays	T	
	Rose	U	
	graze	T	
	wear	B	
	blows	U	
	ear	B	
V	deep	V	(50)
	*Lycidas	W√	
	steep	V	
	lie	X	
	high	X	
	stream	Y	
	dream	Y	
	done	Z	
	bore	A	
	son	Z	
	lament	A'	(60)
	roar	A	
	sent	A'	
	shore	A	

VI	care	B′	
	trade	C′	
	Muse	I	
	use	I	
	shade	C′	
	hair	B′	
	raise	T	(70)
	mind	F	
	days	T	
	find	F	
	blaze	T	
	shears	D′	
	praise	T	
	ears	D′	
	soil	E′	
	foil	E′	
	lies	F′	
	eyes	F′	
	Jove	G′√	
	deed	H′	
	meed	H′	

(Second Movement)

VII	flood	I′	
	reeds	J′	
	mood	I′	
	proceeds	J′	
	Sea	K′	
	plea	K′	(90)
*winds	L′√	
	swain	M′√	
	wings	N′	
	Promontory	O′	
	story	O′	
	brings	N′	
	stray'd	C′	
	brine	P′	
	play'd	C′	
	Bark	Q′	(100)
	dark	Q′	
	thine	P′	

VIII	slow	R′	
	sedge	S′	
	edge	S′	
	woe	R′	
	pledge	S′	
	go	R′	
	lake	T′	
	twain	M′	(110)
	amain	M′	
	bespake	T′	
	swain	M′	
	sake	T′	
	fold	U′	
	make	T′	
	feast	V′	
	guest	V′	
	hold	U′	
	least	V′	(120)
	belongs	W′	
	sped	X′	
	songs	W′	
	straw	Y′	
	fed	X′	
	draw	Y′	
	spread	X′	
	paw	Y′	
	said	X′	
	door	A	(130)
	more	A	

(Third Movement)

IX	past	Z′	
	Muse	I	
	cast	Z′	
	hues	I	
	use	I	
	brooks	A″	
	looks	A″	
	eyes	F′	
	showers	B″	(140)
	flowers	B″	

dies	F′			head	X′	
Jessamine	P′			Ore	A	(170)
jet	C″			sky	X	
violet	C″			high	X	
Woodbine	P′			waves	R	
head	X′			along	P	
wears	D′			laves	R	
shed	X′			song	P	
tears	D′	(150)		love	G′	
lies	F′			above	G′	
ease	D″			Societies	D″	
surmise	F′			move	G′	(180)
Seas	D″			eyes	F′	
hurl'd	E″			more	A	
Hebrides	D″			shore	A	
tide	F″			good	I′	
world	E″			flood	I′	
denied	F″					
old	U′	(160)				
*Mount	G″√					
hold	U′			(Epilogue)		
ruth	H″		XI	rills	I″	
youth	H″			gray	J″	
				Quills	I″	
X more	A			lay	J″	
dead	X′			hills	I″	(190)
floor	A			bay	J″	
bed	X′			blue	D	
				new	D	

The traces of regularity evident in such an analysis should cause us to ask whether there is really point in talking about the uncertainty of *Lycidas*'s rhyme scheme. Thomas Warton raised this question for the eighteenth century, and answered it by asserting that the poem's "irregularities . . . must not be tried by modern criticism"; and Richard Hurd, despite Dr. Johnson's censuring of the art of *Lycidas,* proclaimed that he saw "no extraordinary *wildness* and *irregularity* . . . in the conduct of this little poem." What irregularity there is, Hurd concludes, "is owing, not to any disorder in the plan," for "Milton's ear was a good second to his imagination."[238] Still, one may wonder as he ponders the art of *Lycidas,* "How many readers *hear* these harmonies and near-harmonies? . . . are such textures chance . . . [or] esthetic intention?"[239] These questions are, to a certain extent, answered by Milton himself—in his revisions to *Lycidas* in the Trinity manuscript. Whereas Ransom argues that Milton's revisions of the poem betray his impatience with rhyme, and with any formal design, those revisions instead confirm the contention of Merritt Y. Hughes: that actually Milton's "revisions did not add even one to the original ten unrhymed lines."[240] In fact, through revision, Milton eliminates some rhymeless lines from his poem.

The rhyme scheme of *Lycidas,* according to my analysis, is uncertain in the opening verse paragraph, but drives relentlessly toward certainty and regularity achieved in the tenth paragraph and made conspicuous in the *ottava rima* stanza that comprises the poem's epilogue.[241] By ignoring the stanzaic divisions and thus the general practice of devising a separate rhyme scheme for each unit, Milton has moved toward a realization of his belief that sense should be variously drawn out from verse to verse. At the same time, he clearly compensates for the uncertainty of rhyme in the early verse paragraphs by using internal rhyme, extensive repetition, and elaborate alliterative patterns. Most importantly, however, in concealing his rhyme pattern, Milton takes the reader unaware. Blurring his design with the eleven separate units of unequal length, Milton achieves the effect of irregularity and spontaneity. Here, too, we should again remember that *Lycidas* was not always divided into eleven units; in *Justa Edovardo King Naufrago,* it appeared as a poem divided into six units. In either case, however, it is clear that the rhyme is obviously and strongly organized and that it relates meaningfully to the architectonics of the poem, and to its theme. *Lycidas* exemplifies John Hollander's belief that "a poem's shape . . . may be a frame for its picture of the world."[242]

Something of Milton's method here had already been understood in the eighteenth century by Francis Peck, who believed that Milton's rhymes are dispersed in *Lycidas* because Milton so designed it:

> This Poem . . . tho' wrote in Rhime, is very remarkable for a great many of those Rhimes not being either successive, alternate, or triple, but often thrown off from each other, by the intervention of other lines & Rhimes, to a great distance . . .

By this very manner of writing, Peck concludes, Milton "attempts to give us, tho' secretly, a poetical image or draught of the ma hematical Canon of Music. The fancy is very singular; but, I think, may be thus made out."[243] Peck makes no claims for interstanzaic connections but nonetheless suggests something of the method of rhyming Milton employs in *Lycidas*—and something of its purpose. For through rhyme Milton insinuates his belief that a poem is an unformed Chaos wrought into order by rhyme, meter, and stanzaic patterning—that the poet "raiseth beauty even out of deformity, order and regularity out of Chaos and confusion."[244] It is true, as S. K. Heninger has observed, that an artist who wishes "to confirm prevalent disorder . . . must fashion an art work which embodies the principle of random occurrence"; but once that principle is surrendered, as it is toward the end of *Lycidas,* so too is the idea of the universe it would convey even as another conception is put in its place:

> Our universe is a poem written in careful meter by the creative godhead. . . . Under such an assumption, God as poet and nature as poem are not arbitrary similes, but rather descriptive facts. To accord with these facts, the metrics, stanza form, and total structure of a man-made poem should therefore image the divinely-decreed orderliness of the cosmos.[245]

F. T. Prince has demonstrated that Milton builds many of his individual units upon the scaffolding of the *canzone.*[246] Milton's decision to use the *canzone* as an informing principle in *Lycidas* is no less daring than Spenser's employment of it in his *Epithala-*

mion. "The length and complexity of the stanza," Thomas Greene explains, tend "to strengthen the autonomy of each unit and to render the concluding line more of a conclusion."[247] Given Spenser's drive toward unity in this poem, which parallels Milton's rage for order in *Lycidas,* we should also observe that the use both these poets make of the *canzone* is "a deformation of its spirit":[248] that is, to write in this form is to encourage and evince both fragmentation and division; yet these are the very principles that Spenser and Milton, in their respective poems, would transcend. Thus Milton uses the *canzone* in much the same way that he uses the Italian sonnet. He approaches the form, scalpel in hand, cutting it to pieces and then reassembling it in a way that expresses his own genius rather than that of his models. He enjambs lines, and breaks up the rigid *fronte-coda* division, just as he runs lines together, and ignores the rigid octave-sestet division of the sonnet. In short, the sense spills over from one part of each unit into the other; and going a step further in accordance with madrigal practices, the sense is carried from verse paragraph to verse paragraph, from one thematic division into another. Milton abandons the *canzone* before the end of his poem, turning from its principles to those of the madrigal tradition, which more nearly support the impulse toward unity that drives through, and finally drives together, the fragmented units of *Lycidas.* It is this movement that finds its precedent in and that is supported by the single, continuous rhyme scheme characteristic of the madrigal and brilliantly described by Thomas DeQuincey's phrase, "solemn planetary wheelings."[249]

According to my analysis, there are fewer unrhymed lines in *Lycidas* than ordinarily thought. Rhymes fall together leaving a total of only *three* unrhymed lines (51, 91, 161), one in each of the *three* thematic units and always in the verse paragraph immediately preceding the consolation for that movement.[250] "The difficulty of finding rhymes," observes Edward Bysshe, has often caused "the best of our Poets to take up with rhymes that have scarce any consonance, or Agreement."[251] This was not the case with Milton, however. Though spurning rhyme as a mere ornament, he remained surprisingly exact in his use of it. Milton has substantial historical precedent for the rhymes he chooses. Some of those rhymes may be less precise, and less common, than others; but none are unique to Milton. Furthermore, those that are remote, like *-ude:-oud,* seem to be intentionally so. The dissonances they create—deliberately sounded in the early lines of the poem—are in keeping with Milton's uncouth persona and with E. K.'s belief that the "rusticall rudenesse of shepheardes" is to be conveyed by "rough sounde" and "rymes more ragged" (7:8). Thereafter, the rhymes become increasingly more exact and thus contribute significantly to the poem's final harmony.

The unrhymed lines, it appears, mark the three major disjunctions in the poem; but these divisions are paradoxically held together by rhyme and by the figures of Phoebus Apollo, St. Peter, and St. Michael, all of whom are typologically related to Christ, who, dominating the third movement, spans the enormous gap between humanity and perfection. Each figure, introduced in consecutive even-numbered paragraphs (6, 8, 10), provides the poet, and hence his audience, with the increasingly more satisfactory consolation that comes with an ever-deepening understanding of King's death. And according to my analysis, the first line of Milton's poem—contrary to Ransom's belief— does not constitute a gesture of rebellion, but turns out to be the most significant and most commonly used rhyme in the poem.[252] The *-ore* rhyme is not completed until the introduction of the Orpheus image (58), a key image in the poem and the one that begins the deification of Lycidas. This rhyme is picked up again at the end of the second movement, at which point Milton finds intellectual justification for King's death, and appropriately frames the apotheosis passage where, in that apocalyptic vision, Milton finds ultimate emotional calm. Rhetorically, then, the *-ore* rhyme brings emphasis to prominent images, and structurally it marks off the great consolation passages.

Appropriately, Milton completes one alphabet just before the end of the first movement and completes the second alphabet six lines into the third movement. The rhyme scheme, then, serves as a guide to the poem's tripartite structure; but rather than marking the three main divisions precisely, it serves instead to bind them together. With the second alphabet, beginning in the first movement and ending in the third, Milton unites the great massy units that comprise his poem, while at the same time roughly identifying them.

The rhetorical and structural use of rhyme is most obvious in the last three divisions of Milton's poem:

Roman Numeral = Verse Paragraph
NR = New Rhyme
OR = Old Rhyme
( ) = Structural unit to which rhyme returns
* Rhyme suspended until this point

	IX				X		
-ast	NR			-ore	OR	(I)	
-use	OR	(I)		-ead	OR	(III)	
-ooks	NR			-igh	OR	(I)	
-eyes	OR	(II)		-aves	OR	(I)	*
-owers	NR			-ong	OR	(I)	
-ine	OR	(II)		-ove	OR	(II)	*
-et	NR			-ies	OR	(III)	
-ead	OR	(II)		-ood	OR	(I)	
-ears	OR	(II)					
-ease	NR						
-url'd	NR				XI		
-ide	NR						
-old	OR	(II)		-ills	NR		
-ount	NR			-ay	NR		
-uth	NR			-ue	OR	(I)	

This analysis brings attention to several devices used conspicuously here but operative throughout the poem. As the third movement commences, Milton begins to draw his poem toward conclusion. His technique is to introduce a new rhyme, look back to an old rhyme, move forward again, then backward again. Significantly, he breaks the pattern in the central lines of paragraph nine, thus drawing our attention to the amaranthus, which, as a symbol of God's love and mercy, introduces to the poem the concept of a benevolent Deity. Just as God transplants the most beautiful flower of Eden at the moment of the Fall, he takes Edward King from a corrupt world and, doing so, preserves his innocence. Then, through a quick succession of new rhymes interrupted only once and then to recall the earlier pattern, Milton forces us to move unhesitatingly into the apotheosis passage. Once there, we discover that new rhymes drop silently away and that two rhymes, until now suspended, are completed, one from each of the previous movements.

It is in the epilogue, however, that Milton makes his most concerted effort to return us to the first movement, and then to the first lines of the poem. The *-ills* rhyme, thrice repeated, echoes the *-ill* rhyme (23, 24), while the *-ay* rhyme reverberates the *-ays* rhyme (44, 46). The final *-ue* rhyme that closes the epilogue reiterates the *-ue* rhyme of the prologue (7, 10) to which the rhyme scheme and image patterns invite us to return. In *Lycidas,* then, Milton achieves his most poignant effects through a gesture that gains its force from his initial pronouncement that we should not expect such a gesture from an immature poet (3–5). That is, Milton accomplishes with consummate skill precisely what his opening lines ask us not to expect—a subtle and sophisticated art. Ritualistically, the rhyme scheme of *Lycidas* inscribes a series of interlocking and concentric circles; and this pattern, in turn, makes its own symbolic point.

With its separate verse paragraphs and larger thematic units inextricably bound together by a single, enveloping rhyme scheme, *Lycidas* appears not so much as a series of panels, but rather as one unified structure. A principle of cohesion, the rhyme creates a meaningful pattern of order, inscribing the figure of a circle and conveying Milton's theme that in our beginning is our end, in our end a new beginning. Just as the rhymes in Milton's epilogue and apotheosis passage echo or reiterate rhymes from the prologue and first movement, so the imagery, too, returns us to the poem's beginning. The flames bursting "in the forehead of the morning sky" (171) look back to "the opening eye-lids of the morn" (26); the sun's dropping into the western bay (191) recalls "the Star that rose, at Ev'ning bright" and "Towards Heav'ns descent had slop'd his westering wheel" (30–31). And so the twitching fingers (192) renew the image of the fingers that "loudly sweep the string" (17) and of the "forc'd fingers rude" (4) that brutally shatter the leaves of plants not yet ripe. Corresponding images such as these are, as Denise Levertov suggests, "a kind of non-aural rhyme";[253] and they reinforce and are reinforced by the pattern created by rhyme.

The imagery of *Lycidas* has been classified in various ways—with varying success. The point to make, however, is that the imagery is essentially biblical and that it invites us to consider the Book of Genesis and the Book of Revelation, the beginning and the end; the alpha and the omega. The two books stand in splendid contrast, polarizing the worlds of tragic defeat and spiritual triumph, the worlds of innocence and of experience yielding a higher innocence. These are also the worlds that pull oppositely in *Lycidas*. The myths of the Golden Age and of Eden before the Fall combine within the pastoral to recall Genesis, while a whole complex of apocalyptic imagery encourages us to meditate upon the Book of Revelation. There is, moreover, an important correspondence yet to be noticed between John's Apocalypse and Milton's poem: both are revelations that climax in mystical union. The Book of Revelation has in its background the Book of Genesis, as well as the sinister power of the Roman Empire that was threatening the entire Christian Church. Correspondingly, *Lycidas* has in its "background" the pastoral world of Genesis, as well as the corrupt clergy that was threatening Christianity in England.

Furthermore, there is a striking parallel between the great visions of John the prophet and Milton the poet. The same verse paragraphs (6, 8, 10) that are typologically related through the figures of Phoebus Apollo, the Pilot of the Galilean lake, and the Guardian of the Mount, contain the great visions from the Book of Revelation. The judgments of God are prophesied by Phoebus (82–83) and then again by St. Peter (130–131). The tenth verse paragraph embodies "the vision of God and the Lamb," "the vision of the lamb and his redeemed host," and "the triumph songs in heaven" (see Revelation 4, 14, 19, 21). Similarly, the poem's epilogue anticipates the New Jerusalem that descends from the seat of God as He wipes away all tears from the eyes of the faithful. Toward this moment, everything in the poem tends. These examples—and there are many more—suggest how thoroughly saturated *Lycidas* is with apocalyptic imagery, which, when set against the more familiar pastoral imagery, combines with the rhyme pattern to convey Milton's theme that after the first death, there is no other.

Coleridge comments, with his usual incisiveness, that the natural forms, like the pastoral, possess their own unity, which is addressed to the outward senses, to reason rather than understanding. The poet who deviates from these forms so as to re-create them appeals to imagination rather than the senses in order to contemplate man's "inward nature, and the workings of the passions in their most retired recesses." The poet who accepts literary forms and dwells within them, as it were, holds firmly to the here and now. Conversely, the poet who attempts to transcend such forms reveals an abiding interest in "eternal truths," which like "the endless properties of the circle" have little "connection . . . with this or that age, with this or that country."[254] Appropriately, Milton holds his poem together with the circle image, which he insists that we apprehend imaginatively rather than sensorily.

Like Philo and St. Paul, like many medieval theologians and Renaissance poets, like his immediate predecessors Donne and Herbert, Milton believed the world was created according to a pattern conceived by the Father and executed by the Son—a pattern symbolized by the circle of perfection. The creation of the world, and by analogy the creation of a poem, are preceded by the creation of a pattern. Thus in Book VII of *Paradise Lost,* the Son is seen, golden compasses in hand, his brooding wings outstretched across the great abyss (225–42); and so in Book I,

Milton, identifying himself with the Creator, is seen brooding over his materials as the act of poetic creation begins. In either instance, there is first the mental impression that derives from God, then the execution by His agent. So it was with the First Creation; so it is with every subsequent creation. Always the pattern is hidden only to be discovered by the mind's eye. The poet's task is to reveal what is not readily apparent to the undiscerning eye, to create out of the chaos of language and of experience a form that reflects his apprehension of order, proportion, and harmony in the universe. The original pattern, that of the circle of perfection, symbolizing totality, infinity, God himself, is, in short, impressed upon the mind of the poet-prophet whose poem becomes a shadow of that original circle.

By finally dividing *Lycidas* into ten verse paragraphs, plus an epilogue, and then grouping the paragraphs into thematic units, Milton deliberately conceals the pattern engraved upon his mind and so carefully etched by the poem's rhyme scheme. By doing so, he insures that the pattern, if apprehended, will be apprehended intellectually rather than sensorily. The circular pattern of the perfectly executed madrigal is thus made to adumbrate "the Charm of the Circle of Perfection."[255] In the process, *Lycidas* becomes a sophisticated hieroglyphic poem that, through its rhyme pattern, images forth eternity. The poem insists that order lies beneath apparent chaos and is perceived in all its glory by the eye that pierces the surface into the heart of things.

It is not without purpose that final consolation comes in the *tenth* verse paragraph. The number ten, through numerological tradition associated with totality and perfection, emphasizes "the poem's completeness, its circularity, its perfection, and its unity."[256] Besides being the numerological symbol for the geometric figure of the circle that the rhyme scheme inscribes and that the imagery supports and helps to define, the number ten possesses a special religious significance that derives from the Book of Revelation and that figures prominently in this verse paragraph. In the Apocalypse, *ten* stands for divine control and completeness; it represents the day when, after having withstood the tribulations of an earthly life and having remained faithful unto death, the Christian receives the crown of life (2:10). *Ten,* says William Fulke, is "the number of fulnesse or perfection" and signifies that life in this world culminates in "eternall blessednes in heaven."[257] The *tenth* day, then, is the day of transcendence when, with the destruction of earthly kingdoms and temporal systems, everything centers in God and the Lamb. Milton asks us to contemplate the moment of mystical union and, as we do that, to apprehend the full significance of images and activities that until now were only vaguely suggestive. The amaranthus—a symbol of God's love and mercy and the immortal flower once in Paradise—inwreathes with beams the resurrected soul of King. The new garland, bestowed "in the blest Kingdoms meek" (177), recalls the temporal garland angrily fashioned with "forc'd fingers rude" (4) as the poem commences.

It is not accidental that Milton should rely so heavily upon repetition, imagery, and sound; for repetition imitates the immortal world. The movement of the heavenly bodies, the cyclical pattern of the seasons, the day-night-day sequence, the spherical imagery (especially the wheel and the tear), and the movements associated with the circle (rising, falling, mounting, climbing) reinforce the circular pattern of the madrigal form. Anne Ferry has properly observed that the circle is the geometric figure most aptly suited to Milton's needs, because it is itself "a repeating pattern, turning endlessly upon itself, and because it is the traditional symbol of divine perfection, unity, eternity, infinity."[258] The circle, which has neither beginning nor end, is the pattern that joins microcosm, geocosm, and macrocosm and that moves the understanding from the terrestrial to the celestial. It is a figure that suggests the archetypal movements of the universe: contraction and expansion, expiration and inspiration, death and rebirth. The point had already been made by Proclus: *"In any divine procession the end is assimilated to the beginning, maintaining by its reversion thither a circle without beginning and without end . . .* This reversion of the end upon the beginning makes the whole order . . . convergent upon itself and by its convergence revealing unity in multiplicity."[259] Or as M. H. Abrams suggests, while identifying the spiraling circle as a distinctive feature of Romantic thought and imagination, "the self-moving circle . . . fuses the idea of the circular return with the idea of linear progress . . . 'Every development moves in a spiral line, leaves nothing behind, reverts to the same point on a higher turning.' "[260]

Once used as a mock-prophetic form,[261] the madrigal is made by Milton to serve once again the serious objectives of prophecy. The circular patterns of the madrigal gesture toward the subject of Milton's poem, which is divine providence, and toward the very image that is the emblem of prophecy. The wheel, the circle, in its association with Ezekiel's chariot, symbolizes both the subject and the process of prophecy. Prophecy as represented by the Book of Revelation was called "an exact map . . . *of Providence";* and the wheel or circle was said to reflect that subject since, "like the *index* of the clock," it possesses "necessary connection with internal movements."[262] Those internal movements are, moreover, like those of an ever-widening circle, figuring the mind-expansion that prophecy induces; and simultaneously, the circle image reinforces the analogy between God's creation and the prophet's, the one being patterned like the other. The meaning of that pattern is expressed by George Puttenham as he explains that the circle is "the most excellent of all figures Geometrical," first because, "even and smooth, without any angle, or interruption," it signifies continuous motion which is the author of life; and second because, containing "the commodious description of every other figure," it resembles not just the world or universe but in its "indefinitenesse[,] having no speciall place of beginning nor end, beareth a similitude with God and eternitie."[263] The similitude between Milton's poem and the Godhead is underscored by its tripartite structure and by the trinitarian symbolism inherent in such a structure. Correspondingly, the similitude between Milton's creation and God's is captured within the very process that *Lycidas* delineates.

Writing of providence in *De Doctrina Christiana,* Milton says that God produces something good out of the evil and corruption in the world. In his own creation, a facsimile of God's, Milton not only creates order out of chaos but, like God, "creates as it were, light out of darkness" (6:333). Bringing good out of evil, light out of darkness, order out of chaos—in the Book of Revelation and in Milton's poem, these are the marks of God's providence. Like God, the poet exhibits his wisdom and power by turning evils to good—by showing himself to be "not the authoure and proper worker, but the orderer, and disposer of evill."[264] In this way, Milton and his poem exemplify the providence to which poet and poem are a testimony.

Variations on the Paradigm in Milton's Last Poems

Lycidas is a prelude poem—in the Wordsworthian sense: one that records the history of a poet's mind to the point where his faculties are sufficiently matured that he may enter upon more arduous labors. As such, *Lycidas* may also be said to confirm Blake's belief that the productions of youth and of mature age are equal in all identical points. Like *Lycidas,* Milton's last poems take shape, substance, and strategies from their Revelation model; yet these poems, in their "vast Design" (the phrase is Andrew Marvell's), also produce structural variations not evident in · *Lycidas* but nonetheless sanctioned by the complicated ordering of the multiple visions that comprise the Apocalypse.

Isabel MacCaffrey has remarked that "in Books XI and XII [of *Paradise Lost*], Milton develops on a grand scale the movement from disaster to redemption adumbrated in *Lycidas.* The vision that completes the cycle of history in the epic" is the same one, says MacCaffrey, that had completed the cycle of meditation in the elegy.[265] Without fear of distortion, we may generalize upon this formulation: *Lycidas* anticipates what is to come—not just in *Paradise Lost* but in Milton's last poems as well. Its concern with divine providence—with good resulting from evil and with a new world emerging from the one corrupted by the fall—manifests itself again and again in the epics and in *Samson Agonistes* where in each instance, following the example set by

Lycidas, Milton makes "doctrine coalesce with aesthetic pattern,"[266] letting that pattern generate and project his meaning.

Still, the most notable repetition of the thematic content of *Lycidas* occurs in the culminating vision of *Paradise Lost.* The extent to which this is so is made evident by Raymond Waddington in his masterly interpretation of Books XI and XII. "The typological scheme which overshadows the concluding books is that of the two Adams," says Waddington; "the figural scheme of world destroyed and restored, therefore, overlaps the temporal patterning with Book XI dominated by the sins of the Old Adam and XII with the prophecies of the second Adam."[267] The scheme Milton employs here is the same one set forth in 1649 by Richard Coppin. Here Satan is said to inhabit the natural man and Christ to inhabit the spiritual man; and correspondingly, Adam in his fallen state is said to be a type of Satan and in his perfect, and then resurrected, states a type of Christ:

> The first *Adam* in his purity was but a type or figure of the second *Adam* in his humane nature, . . . and the second *Adam* in his humane nature was but a type or figure of Christ in the divine nature, which type was swallowed up by the coming of Godhead upon it: And now Christ in the divine nature . . . is the end and the substance of both the other types, nay, of all types from the beginning to the end.[268]

In Christ, Adam comes to discover what he has lost—he comes to resemble his former self; for as Jacob Boehme once observed, the "angelicall Image, which did disappeare in *Adam,* was again manifest in the humanity of Christ."[269] Books XI and XII may allude to Adam's drowning, to his physical death and resurrection at the end of time; but what these books stress is Adam's spiritual death and resurrection in this life. *Lycidas,* it should be remembered, was written out of a nadir wherein the whole world had been drowned in a general deluge; its objective, and that of the final books of *Paradise Lost,* is to turn grief into joy. Adam, "all in tears" (XI.674), is eventually drowned in them: "thee another Floud, / Of tears and sorrow a Floud thee also drown'd, / And sunk thee as thy Sons" (XI.756–58). But Adam also learns to rejoice as he comes to understand the promise of "A gentle wafting to immortal Life" (XII.435), a promise that, in the moment of his exile, enables Adam to wipe tears from his eyes.

These various patterns are set forth in the miniature prophecy with which Book XI begins, and the whole process of awakening to a new life here on earth is explored in the visions that follow. It is these concluding books, more than any others, that give to *Paradise Lost* its cosmic dimensions. Moving from Book X into Books XI and XII, we find ourselves moving out of a myth into a total mythology: until now our attention has been riveted to the story of creation and fall; now, in a moment of expanded vision, the myths of redemption and, more dimly, of apocalypse are brought before our eyes. And here, just as it is in the Apocalypse, the number seven is particularly significant: there are six cycles of history, six ages of the world, that once broken and transcended introduce a seventh age. The unveiling that occurs in these books anticipates the unveiling at the end of time—this apocalypse promises another just as the first resurrection ensures a second.

Paradise Lost itself is a sevenfold vision. Perhaps those visions are not so cryptically involved with the seven visions of the Apocalypse as Michael Fixler would have us think,[270] but the poem divides quite readily into seven visionary panels: the vision of Hell (I and II) followed by the vision of Heaven (III); the vision of Eden before the Fall (IV–IX), which embraces the visions of both the celestial warfare (VI) and the creation (VII); and the vision of the Fall (IX–X) succeeded, finally, by Adam's vision of future history (XI–XII). Book XI, moreover, contains not six but seven visions: the six of biblical history that are always counted, plus a seventh, which comes first in the sequence, wherein Adam sees, but does not discern the meaning of, the prophet Michael's coming in majesty. The analogy, of course, is with the Mighty Angel's coming in majesty and appearing with the book of prophecies that he gives to St. John. Full of the various signatures of visionary literature, *Paradise Lost* proceeds from the most common of visionary scenes, those of Hell and Heaven, adding to them a sequence of other visions. Put simply, Milton's epic, like its final two books, begins and ends in vision. As part of a summary vision, recapitulating the entire epic, Book XI begins with Adam's viewing "One of the heav'nly Host, and . . . / . . . some great Potentate" (XI.230–31); then as *Paradise Lost* draws to conclusion, Adam sees the flaming sword; and finally, looking back after having left the garden, Adam beholds the whole eastern side of Paradise (XII.590–93, 641–42). The progress from hearing to seeing, so beautifully charted in *Lycidas,* repeats itself here in *Paradise Lost.*

Once regarded as "an untransmuted lump of futurity,"[271] the concluding books of *Paradise Lost* are a vital part of Milton's design. As a summary vision within the poem, they act as commentary on all the others, even as they duplicate the pattern of the entire epic. *Lycidas* took its structural model from those who had anatomized the Book of Revelation as a tripartite structure; *Paradise Lost* takes its from those who saw the Apocalypse as a sevenfold structure. This culminating vision repeats the pattern of the entire epic (it is not only the seventh vision but also a sevenfold vision[272]); the prophetical progression operating throughout the epic, encapsulized in Milton's phrase, "From shadowy Types to Truth" (XII.303), is the subject of this vision, which though it may be a brief epic within a diffuse epic is also, and more importantly, a small prophecy within a larger one. The visions of the future all prophesy—they culminate in—the coming of Christ. Each of the visions is invested in typological significance; and those types are "a silent Prophecie of him; each Prophecie a speaking Type."[273] As they are unfolded, these visions prophesy Christ's First Coming which, for Milton and his readers, is itself a prophecy of his Second Coming. Yet Books XI and XII also take their start by reminding us that the Fall has overthrown a noble mind; and this reminder, in turn, points to much of their substance, the books themselves showing the extent to which that mind has been impaired and the ways in which it may become restored. In keeping with this purpose, as Waddington remarks,

Michael's narrative technique is itself an internal mimesis of Milton's own poetic strategies throughout his poem.[274] Those strategies, moreover, have two components, the first focusing on the interiority of prophecy and the second, on the fact that vision is accompanied by—indeed requires—commentary.

Objecting to these last books of *Paradise Lost* as monotonous and inartistic, C. S. Lewis denies them the very quality that gives them their meaning: a profound dramatic significance.[275] The drama in these books has two sources. On the one hand, it derives from an inversion of the relationship between Adam and the reader that has operated throughout most of the epic. Adam in his perfection stands superior to the fallen reader, though the gap between them is appreciably narrowed by the signs of susceptibility to falling that Adam displays in Books IV–VIII, and the gap is then closed when Adam does fall in Book IX. At the end of this book and throughout Book X, Adam and the reader, in their fallenness, occupy the same ground; but suddenly in the eleventh book, the reader finds himself in the position of superiority. He already can do what Adam is about to learn: he is able to read typologically, something that Adam cannot do until the end of Book XI; he also knows the history that here is unfolded to Adam and understands the implications of that history.

The tension between Adam and the reader is one source of drama; yet the real center of drama in these books is the mind of their protagonist. The pattern is always the same: Adam is shown a vision, he misinterprets it, and each time Michael corrects Adam's misunderstanding. Not until the end of the sixth vision is Adam able *to see.* In Book XII, the process repeats itself; yet this time, responding to narration, Adam is taught *to hear.* Only after the organs of perception have been cleansed and after Adam comes to resemble Milton's ideal reader, only then is Adam exiled to the wilderness. Dramatic in intent, these books are likewise marked by a pattern of ironies that alert us to Adam's failure both *to see* and *to hear.* Further, as a commentary on all that they succeed, these books are a part of Milton's doctrine of accommodation that is both "unusually daring and thorough-going"[276]—a doctrine, we should note, that acknowledging the primacy of vision also allows the possibility of its failure, and so searches its limitations for man in the fallen world. Prophecy began in the Garden and continues to the end of time; it may be extended to the prophet in the form of a vision, but to be comprehensible it must then be translated into pictures and words; it must make its entry through the eye and the ear before the mind can be set in motion—before understanding can commence. The point is handsomely reinforced as we turn from Book XI into Book XII and thus move, it is said, from vision to narration. Mortal sight may begin to fail Adam, his senses having become wearied; but Michael (now called "Prophet" and "Seer blest" [XII.375, 553]), appears throughout as one beholding a vision that he must then translate into words for Adam: "I *see* him, but thou canst not, . . . I *see* his Tents" (XII.128, 135; my italics). On occasion, Michael even forces Adam to rely again on his eyes, to take in the vision for himself: "each place *behold* / In prospect, as I point them . . . *See* where it flows" (XII.142–43, 158; my italics). It is in this book, moreover, that Adam proclaims: "now first I finde / Mine eyes true op'ning, . . . *now I see*" (XII. 273–74, 76; my italics). "All his senses bound" (XI.265) before the visionary experience of these concluding books, in the course of that experience Adam's senses become unbound—he learns to see anew.

Critics have expressed dismay at Milton's shifting here from vision to narration without noting how incomplete that shift actually is, nor how commonplace such shifts really are in prophecy. The device Milton here employs is identical to the one employed by Christ as he delivers his prophecy to St. John; and it exemplifies God's way which, as biblical commentators so often noted, is to let explication follow the vision itself:

> . . . he utters . . . his narration as a chorus, or as an interlocutor in a comedy useth to do his speech, and not by vision only; wherein he opens and explains what could not by vision well have been understood, and therefore gives it by word of mouth.[277]

That Milton attributes the same strategy to Michael is to be expected: Michael was, after all, identified by most biblical commentators with Christ. The pattern that, in this instance, arches over the last two books is the same pattern that dominates the individual visions that comprise Book XI: first there is the vision followed by Adam's imperfect interpretation of it; then, accompanying Michael's correction of Adam's imperfect response, there is a fuller, subtler explanation of what the vision means. Book XII breaks the pattern, offering still further amplifications of what these visions contain, Michael now drawing from them their doctrinal implications. Moreover, in accordance with the Revelation model, the biblical visions of Book XI share a common pattern: each portrays, typologically, a conflict between Christ and Satan, dramatizing the struggle that plays itself out in human history and thereby moving the reader, along with Adam and Eve, to the awareness that this battle is not unending; that Christ, at various moments victorious, will be ultimately victorious. This drama of types, informing Book XI, also frames the narration of Book XII, extending from Nimrod, the great Antichrist of history, to Christ, in history, triumphing on the Cross over Satan. There is, finally, a seventh vision, this one extended to the reader, revealing Adam and Eve, repentant, being expelled from the Garden: wiping away their tears, "They hand in hand with wandring steps and slow, / Through *Eden* took thir solitarie way" (XII.648–49). This vision is both prologue and epilogue to the others. In time it precedes them, but also in time it looks beyond them—beyond Christ's first coming to his second coming, to the time when all things will center in God and the Lamb, when man can wipe away the tears forever from his eyes.

Paradise Lost ends with the same promise that brought consolation to the poet in *Lycidas*. In both poems, consolation comes from the promise of a "Heav'n and Earth renewd" (XI.66; cf. XI.900–01). Prologue and epilogue to Book XI, that same promise climaxes Book XII: the world will go on, Adam is told, until "New Heav'ns, new Earth . . . / . . . bring forth . . . Joy and eternal Bliss" (XII.549–51). Adam leaves Paradise wiping away the tears. Like *Lycidas,* this poem draws upon the Book of Revelation for many of its images and most of its themes: it asserts eternal providence by demonstrating that God is just, because he is loving, forgiving, and merciful, these qualities finding their embodiment and manifestation in Christ. It is unsurprising, therefore, that Milton's last epic should be an anatomy of Christian virtues, celebrating in Christ their perfect pattern and through him the moment in which, after trial, they become fully manifested. Indeed, these two epics relate to one another in much the same way that the Old Testament was said to relate to the New: the first is the dress rehearsal for the second; it contains the whole gospel—but as a number of intellectual propositions that, once accessible only to the enlightened, are now being made accessible to all. Prophesied by what precedes it, *Paradise Regained,* like the New Testament, is itself a prophecy of what is to come. It is commentary on *Paradise Lost* but, itself a prophecy, it also requires the commentary provided for it by *Samson Agonistes,* which, albeit in a negative way, illuminates Milton's brief epic even as it is illuminated by that epic. Thus *Lycidas* and *Paradise Lost* reverberate the prophetic tradition that informs both *Paradise Regained* and *Samson Agonistes.*

Poets are sometimes their own best critics—and sometimes not. Milton was not, or so it would seem, if we set his judgment of his epics against history's evaluation of them: Milton preferred the epic that history has since devalued. In such circumstances, it is better that we ponder what *Paradise Regained* is rather than proclaim what it is not: it is, most importantly, a poem with its own integrity, yet one that is linked through its prologue to *Paradise Lost* and through its publication to *Samson Agonistes.* We need not here concern ourselves with when these poems were written; for even *if* they were not composed sequentially, they were published that way. Any conjecture about the significance of their joint publication, however, must be in large part a response to Arthur Barker's probing questions: "Should not Samson's fallen . . . experience rather precede Christ's making possible the regaining of Paradise . . . ? Or is there some deep significance in this apparently inept reversal? Can we interpret our poems in a way which will demonstrate that . . . they are properly sequential?" And if we assume a close connection between *Paradise Regained* and *Samson Agonistes,* then what of the fact that we find Milton's brief epic "beginning by attaching itself, as in some sense a sequel, to *Paradise Lost*"? Barker's answer to these questions provides a starting point for further conjecture: "In some sense we are involved with the last two items in a trilogy, rather than merely with a pair of companion or contrasting poems."[278] Milton, of course, may have published these two poems together because he had nothing better to do with them; but as Balachandra Rajan so perceptively remarks, "the sterile hypothesis should not drive out the creative one. We must at least explore the proposition that Milton put the two poems together because he meant to say something through the juxtaposition."[279] While exploring that proposition here, we may not be able to offer a full-scale interpretation of these poems, though, keeping in mind that Revelation commentary is concerned with how prophecy was written in order to instruct us in how it should be read, we can conjecture about how these poems, once written, were meant to be read.

Paradise Regained, often called a pendant to *Paradise Lost,* has usually been read as if it were a footnote to it; that is, the first epic is treated as a final, definitive vision and the second one as if its every line and episode were to be glossed by the earlier poem. This is, of course, an inference we can make from the fact that Milton uses the prologue of the second poem as a device for linking it to the first. But there is another inference that is possible, especially if we are exploring these poems in the light of prophetic tradition: every new vision is just that, but it is also a commentary on what it succeeds. Thus *Paradise Regained* may be understood as a poem that interprets, rather than as one interpreted by, *Paradise Lost;* and it, in turn, is interpreted by *Samson Agonistes.* These three poems, as integrated as the three prophecies that comprise the Book of Revelation, are, like those prophecies, parts of a multifaceted vision.

Milton's final vision, composed of *Paradise Lost, Paradise Regained,* and *Samson Agonistes,* is, like the Book of Revelation, tripartite in its structure; and Milton's two epics, like John's first two prophecies, are each sevenfold. This pattern, deciphered in *Paradise Lost,* is even more clearly evident in *Paradise Regained,* where a prologue and an epilogue frame (1) the stone temptation, (2) the banquet temptation, (3–5) the *three* kingdom temptations, (6) the storm temptation, and (7) the pinnacle temptation. *Samson Agonistes,* expectedly, breaks the sevenfold pattern: parodying the Book of Revelation (its open structure), Milton's tragedy reverts to the closed form of its Greek models, its vision being not of man's release from the cycles of history but of man's being ground down by them. Such structural continuities unite Milton's last poems in an encompassing vision at the same time that they imply an analogue between it and the vision emerging from the three great classical epics.

It has been said that Homer's epics, as well as Virgil's *Aeneid,* begin at the nadir of the total cyclical action of history.[280] The *Aeneid* also ends in a nadir, in tragedy. Milton, of course, would shatter the cyclical pattern of classical literature: opening the epic form by elevating it to the status of prophecy and thereby showing how man can break through the cycles of history, Milton also complements his epics with a tragic vision, with a prophetic warning, that shows how easily man can be caught up again in the onrush of history and be imprisoned in its patterns. In Milton's trilogy of poems, the vision of paradise restored is framed on either side by a fall, first Adam's and then Samson-England's. The first fall is a pattern for all others, and its pattern swallows up individuals and nations alike. Any one of Milton's last poems, as Frederick von Schlegel perceived of *Paradise Lost,* is marked by "incompleteness."[281] Yet together these poems form a totality, spanning history from the beginning of the world to Restoration England and extrapolating from that history a predominantly tragic pattern that Milton would translate into the finally comedic pattern of the Book of Revelation. Here in his last poem, Milton steadfastly refuses to intermix tragedy and comedy because what he anticipates is the annihilation of the one form accomplished through the eventual triumph of the other.[282]

Samson Agonistes remains Milton's most problematical poem, and criticism of it has advanced by repeatedly invoking new contexts for reading the play—contexts, as it happens, that have become less and less historically remote from the play. In the process, we have been turned from the background of Greek tragedy to the Christian exegetical tradition and, most recently, to the treatment of Samson in the Puritan literature of the 1640s and 50s.[283] At the same time, however, other possible contexts, while noted, have been rejected. A. S. P. Woodhouse, for example, allows that commentators "debated . . . the righteousness of Samson's revenge," but then declares that this question troubles Milton not at all. Milton, we are told, would approve of Samson's motives because they directed him to kill not just his own enemies, but also God's: "To Milton this seems self-evident: at least he assumes it in silence."[284]

For the most part, critics of *Samson Agonistes* have likewise assumed a silence, with the consequence that we have yet to be turned to the play's context in prophetic literature, probably because it would revise the very interpretation that these other contexts have been used to uphold. A new interpretation of Milton's tragedy might begin, first, by acknowledging with Irene Samuel that *Samson* is just that, *a tragedy;* second, by remembering with Northrop Frye that criticism should neither leave *Samson* sitting in the seventeenth century, nor "annex it to our own age, ignoring its original assumptions"; then by realizing with Christopher Hill that in *Samson,* no less than in his epics, Milton is "wrestling with the problem of the failure of the Revolution, trying to apportion blame and to look forward from defeat";[285] and finally, in the light of this proposal, by suggesting as an epigraph for criticism of the play the following scriptural passage: "thou shalt grope at Noon days as the Blind gropeth in darkness, and thou shalt not prosper, but be oppressed and spoiled, and no man shall save thee" (Deutoronomy 28).

The Book of Judges, especially the verses "the child grew . . . And the spirit of the Lord began to move him at times" (13:24–25), was sometimes cited as evidence that the motions from God working through the prophet "are gradual and progressive; not violent and instantaneous,"[286] thereby providing a basis for distinguishing discerning spirits from erring ones and, in the process, instructing men that they should not cry out for revelation. In this context, the speeches Milton assigns to Samson are as significant as Samson's catastrophe at the end of the play. Both may cause us to question whether Milton was among those who regarded Samson as a revolutionary hero emblematizing the idea that God's soldiers, the people, must follow Samson in his violence, even unto death, and pull down the Whore of Babylon.

There were those, of course, who read the Book of Revelation as a call to arms and who, accordingly, found in Samson a heroic example. Samson figures with special prominence, therefore, in those commentaries that regard war as an expression of God's justice and a nation's soldiers as ministers of his wrath.[287] The question, however, is whether Milton read the Book of Revelation in such a way and whether he would therefore invoke Samson as such a model—whether, like J. B. Broadbent, Milton would say that "it is a failing of Christian mythology, that its vital parts do not include violence, physical power," and whether he would thus proceed to "humanize" Christianity by roughening it up.[288] Joseph Boden was one of those who counseled that men must use "the sword, and the speare, as well as the pen, and the pulpit to destroy Antichrist";[289] and, it is true, Milton sounds very much like Boden when in *Defensio Secunda* he writes:

> And so I concluded that if God wished those men to achieve such noble deeds, He also wished that there be other men by whom these deeds, once done, might be worthily praised and extolled, and that truth defended by arms be also defended by reason—the only defence truly appropriate to man. Hence it is that while I admire the heroes victorious in battle, I nevertheless do not complain about my own role. (*Yale Milton*, 4:i, 553)

Even if Milton exalts mental over carnal warfare, at this point in his life he also invokes the Samson story to argue, in *Pro Populo Anglicano Defensio,* that "whether prompted by God or by his own valor" (Milton pointedly does not say which prompted Samson) he "slew at one stroke not one but a host of his country's tyrants, having first made prayer to God for his aid." According to Milton, Samson, at least, "thought it . . . pious to kill those masters who were tyrants over his country, even though most of her citizens did not balk at slavery" (4:i, 402). Earlier, in *The Reason of Church-Government,* Milton had also invoked the Samson story, this time representing the figure's "puissant hair" as "the golden beames of Law and Right" and allowing that even if Samson brings his evil counselors to ruin, he does so "not without great affliction to himselfe" (1:859). In the early 1650s, then, Milton is willing to see in Samson a revolutionary hero and probably would be willing to argue, like Boden, "What losse is it [if you die at war] to be translated from earthly persons, to heavenly enlargements?"[290] Yet what Milton might have said during the late 1640s and early 50s, he clearly would not have said in the 1660s when *Paradise Lost* was published and *Paradise Regained* written. The poems of Milton's late years validate the claim made for the poet a century later: he moves into "realms unknown to pagan lays: / He sings no mortal war."[291]

It would be helpful to know when *Samson Agonistes* was written; as it is, all we know conclusively is when it was published. But I at least have been persuaded that this is an early work, though what is important for our purposes is that it was published late—"added" to a volume containing *Paradise Regained.* Thus whatever statement the play was intended to make, that statement is greatly qualified by the contexts provided for it in Milton's later poems, especially in Book VI of *Paradise Lost* and *Paradise Regained.* Indeed, it would be hard to object to an argument which proposed that, having written *Samson* early, Milton came to see the Samson story, and hence his play, in a wholly different light and that he deliberately chose to place that play in a context that would reveal his own earlier intellectual and moral failings. After all, to defend the army's part in the Revolution, Milton had to modify a position held by him when he wrote *The Reason of Church-Government,* where he says that "the approved way" is spiritual warfare, fought with *"spiritual weapons"*—warfare not carnal *"but mighty through God to the pulling downe of strong holds"* (1:848). Milton's position here is emphatic, and it accords perfectly with the one assumed in Book VI of *Paradise Lost* and with the one articulated by Jesus in *Paradise Regained.* If Milton's epics teach us anything, it is that the poet came to understand that "the condemnation of violence . . . is a major theme in the prophets' speeches," that "the prophets were the first men in history to regard a nation's reliance upon force as evil."[292] And neither Milton, England, nor for that matter Samson had to rely upon the New Testament for a message that is there in the Old, the prophet Hosea proclaiming in the name of the Lord, "I will not deliver them by bow, nor by sword, nor by war"; rather, "I will break the bow and the sword and the battle out of the earth . . . I will have mercy upon her that had not obtained mercy; and I will say to *them which were* not my people, Thou *art* my people; and they shall say, *Thou art* my God" (1:10, 2:18, 23). Milton also had the letter from Moses Wall, with its counseling:

> . . . let us pity humane Frailty when those who made deep Protestations of their Zeal for our Liberty . . . when . . . being instated in power, shall betray the good Thing committed to them, and lead us back to Egypt, and by that Force which we gave them, to win us Liberty, hold us fast in Chains. (*Columbia Milton,* 12:334)

Not only did Milton's attitude toward Samson probably change after the failure of the Puritan Revolution, but the treatment of Samson in biblical commentary also changes. Samson is no longer the saviour whom the people are to follow—they have followed him too well already. Thus the moment that the revolutionary dream fades, many commentators begin to speak as Roger Williams earlier had done, of "God's own people, fast asleep in antichristian Delilah's lap."[293] Moreover, as it became increasingly evident that Antichrist could and perhaps, during the Revolutionary years, did disguise himself as a zealous church member so as to appear in the world as a saint,[294] Samson himself came to look like Antichrist. This realization served as a check upon the tendency to see Samson as one of the saints against whom Antichrist wages battle, for it was now more evident than ever that the Lord's battle would not be fought out in history but was to be waged within every Christian. The true exemplar of Christian warfare, therefore, was not Samson but Christ; and the scene of the battle was not at the pillars but in the wilderness.

Rather than appearing simply as type and antitype, Samson and Christ now appear as representatives of two different ways of life, two radically different patterns of behavior.[295] If the Christian was obliged to choose between Christ and Mammon, he could make that choice by distinguishing Jesus as a true prophet from Samson, the false prophet. Such a hypothesis may discourage a typological reading of *Samson Agonistes,* but no more so than does the play itself. As *Paradise Lost* and *Paradise Regained* both show, Milton knew how to exploit the tradition of typology when he wanted to. The fact that the brief epic does not mention Samson and that *Samson Agonistes* does not mention Christ suggests, alternatively, that Milton knew how to repress such a tradition in order to cancel it out (he does precisely this with the Crucifixion story in *Paradise Regained*). And these facts should be coupled with another: however positive the references to Samson in the prose tracts may be, in *Paradise Lost* there is only one reference, and that negative, comparing the fallen Adam with the *"Herculean Samson"* who "wak'd / Shorn of his strength" (IX.1060–62). Accompanying *Paradise Lost,* in Andrew Marvell's poem, is another reference (this one also negative) distinguishing Milton as a "strong" poet from Samson who "groap'd the Temples Posts in spight." Marvell, it appears, anticipated the unfortunate construction that in our century Christopher Caudwell has put upon Milton's motives: *Paradise Lost* is full of noble defiance which returns to Milton in *Samson*

Agonistes where, recovering his courage, the poet "hopes for the day when he can pull the temple down."[296] Marvell anticipates the construction—and he rejects it; and he would reject, consequently, any suggestion that would attribute to Milton's Samson "a boundless energy" capable of creating all things anew.[297]

At issue in the Samson story (and Milton makes this an issue, too, in his epics) is the nature of Christian warfare: as William Perkins had earlier asked, what is "the right way of fighting in the spirituall battell"? Such a question necessarily provoked discussion, like Perkins', about the warriors who are locked in combat—"the tempter, and the Christian souldier"—and about the temptation itself which figures that combat and which, when withstood, defines resistance as "an action."[298] Not only does the Christian warrior resist temptation by abstaining from evil, but simultaneously he *actively* pursues the good. He must be more than "Stupidly good" like the Satan of *Paradise Lost* (IX.465). It is not enough to stand, like Satan, "abstracted . . . / From . . . evil" (IX.463–64); for as Milton explains in *The Reason of Church-Government,* "vertue that wavers is not vertue, but vice revolted from itselfe, and after a while returning. The actions of just and pious men do not darken in their middle course, but . . . they are as the shining light, that shineth more and more unto the perfet day" (*Yale Milton,* 1:795). Christ is thus repeatedly invoked to exemplify spiritual combat—he carries no sword with him on to the desert, we are reminded, but nonetheless resists all of Satan's temptations. Samson, on the other hand, is invoked to exemplify a man engaged in physical warfare and capable of "smit[ing] downe a thousand Philistines." Yet Thomas Taylor, who here portrays Samson in a favorable light, must explain that Christ is the *true* Samson "who with the jaw bone of his owne mouth smites them [the Philistines] downe, heaps upon heaps," even as he warns: there are those who "under the name and colours of Christ fight against Christ."[299]

More often, however, Samson is portrayed in terms used much earlier in the century, as a representative of those who "flye to their owne wisdome, and their owne strength, and their owne policy, and their owne knowledge."[300] Within this context, it is ironic that *The Souldiers Pocket Bible,* explaining that "the battell is the Lords," should, using virtually the same words (*A Souldier must denie his owne wisdome, his owne strength, & all provision for war*), cite Samson as an exemplary soldier—one who prays before doing battle. Frequently, of course, the illustrative episode for displaying the negative side of Samson's character is his surrendering to the harlot; yet what is true of Samson's behavior here could easily be extended to, could even be inferred from, subsequent episodes in his life, especially from his hurling down of the pillars. In that moment, Milton's hero appears as one of those men, described by John Bale, who "runne hedlong to . . . [their] owne destruction."[301]

In his prose works and throughout *Paradise Lost,* Milton is engaged in—and thus engages us in—distinguishing the false from the true prophets. Such a distinction, especially as it was developed in prophetic literature, involves separating the former who adhere to the doctrine of God's wrath and justice from the latter who subscribe to the doctrine of his love and mercy. Since false prophets, like Satan, assume the appearance of angels of light, the real test is implied by the question, "do they resemble God, or Satan, in word and deed"; and that test is administered according to the understanding that the Beast's way is violence and the Lamb's way, love.[302]

The question raised here is central to the concerns of both *Paradise Regained* and *Samson Agonistes*—poems through which Milton focuses, just as sharply as he had done in Books I and II of *Paradise Lost,* the whole problem of distinguishing between true and false prophets. In his last poems, Milton shows that it is Jesus, not Samson, who is the heavenly Champion.[303] The common soldier may be one who follows Samson unto violence and unto death; but the Christian soldiers "scorne to revenge themselves" and will do much more: they will follow Christ into mental warfare.[304] Implied by Milton's last poems is the very distinction drawn by William Perkins as he contrasts Samson with Christ: "he slue more by his death, then by his life: so Christ . . . saved more by death then by his life."[305] Christ, that is, submitted to the Crucifixion in order to save—Samson hurled down the pillars in order to slay—his enemies. Thus Samson in his climactic act confuses, as Henry More might say, the slaying of bodies with the converting of souls.[306]

The terms of the contrast between Christ and Satan, between Jesus and Samson, between the redeemer and the destroyer, are laid out most fully by Richard Bernard. The former, a proponent of mental fight, subdues his enemies by the sword which comes out of his mouth; the latter, by force and violence, using the carnal sword (see fig. 8). But Bernard also amplifies this antithesis by way of further differentiating the true from the false prophet: the one has his wife, the other only his whore; the one rises into new life, the other goes down to destruction; the one lives by the waters of the Gospel, while the other is drunk with the blood of murder and sacrifice. Such antitheses, when set against the stories of Jesus and Samson, also set those figures in dramatic contrast, discouraging the sorts of typological associations that were often used to link them. And Bernard advances still other antitheses, contrasting those who go forth with the everlasting gospel and those who ignore it; those who are killed for preaching God's word and those who put others to death, thereby exalting the sacrifice of blood over the gospel of love. The former, Bernard concludes, are virgins, while the latter are spiritual and corporeal fornicators; the former are Christian in deed, while the latter are Christian in name only. Given this context, it is noteworthy that Bernard should later invoke the Samson story, representing Samson as a type of the great Dragon, Antichrist, and Delilah as a type of the Great Whore.[307]

During the 1640s, it may have been convenient to follow Thomas Taylor in his modification of this equation, turning Delilah into the dragon, that power both within us and outside us that, like Samson, every Christian must overcome—by whatever means. But after the failure of the Revolution, commentators suddenly found too much that militated against such a reading of the Samson story. Thomas Taylor's conception of Christian warfare is still held to:

> The nature of the Christian war is divers from other warre. In other fields the enemie is without, here the strongest enemie is within: there the enemie is another person from the souldier, here the enemie is the same person with the Christian souldier . . . . : the Christian souldier hath more adoo to conquer himselfe . . . and is then the greatest conqueror.[308]

However, Christ in the wilderness, struggling with and overcoming his own humanity, was ultimately a better illustration of Christian warfare than was Samson who succumbed once and then again, first to the Satan without, then to the Satan within.

Such a realization had caused John Trapp, before the Revolution, to say: "follow the way of Christ, assume his burden, take up the cross" rather than "runn[ing] away with it as did Sampson with the gates of *Gaza.*" Christ enables men to escape the destruction to which Samson had doomed himself, and to avoid the afflictions of spiritual blindness, imprisonment, and violent death that are visited upon Samson. According to Trapp, Samson's life is marked by "continuance in an evill course"; and thus he is punished, "one Sinne with another."[309] Similarly, though from one point of view Thomas Goodwin can see in Samson a figure who begins the deliverance that Christ accomplishes, he also feels compelled to emphasize that as a strong man Samson is but a shadow of the true strong man who is Christ and who really has the power to overcome all our enemies. Unlike Christ, Samson is a backslider, slipping again and again into sin. Were it not for the fact "that we find his name in the list of those worthies, Heb. xi," says Goodwin, we probably never would have thought Samson "a godly man"; for only those who do what Samson did not do—repent, and turn from their folly—can take comfort from his negative example.[310] Such a view of Samson, gaining prominence during the 1650s and 60s, persisted into the nineteenth century, when it was conceded that Samson is often treated as a regenerate hero, but then allowed that after his death "we find the people again in idolatry, accompanied by social crimes of horrible character":

> . . . Sampson . . . did not, for all his strength, deliver his countrymen from the Philistines. Strength is the only extraordinary quality which he is recorded as possessing. He was not very moral or very wise.[311]

This is the Samson who, in Edith Sitwell's words, stood at the pillars of the world, "emptily calling"; and he may be judged according to Martin Buber's proposition, that any action or "reform that did not reform the life of the people is nothing in God's eyes."[312]

Such a reading of the Samson story brings us very close indeed to the most recent reading of Milton's play. *Samson Agonistes,* we are told, is a theater—and the theater as a symbol of order is what Samson manages to destroy at the end of the play. But we need not turn to modern criticism to learn that "Order of any kind is threatened by the violence . . . exemplified by Samson," or that "violence toward others, such as Samson has shown, is ultimately self-violence."[313] Those sentiments are very much in England's consciousness at the time that *Samson Agonistes* is published, and they would be very much a part of the consciousness of any reader who approached Milton's tragedy after having just listened to Jesus' sentiments expressed in *Paradise Regained* (III.388–440).

Contexts are not a substitute for interpretation, but they can lead toward an interpretation. The particular context, here outlined, is one that the prophetic Milton surely knew; and it is one that, admittedly, will alter received readings of Milton's play, for it underscores Donald Bouchard's recent complaint that Milton's critics have been "all too eager to discount the *hero's* shortcomings and his all too human character," which, when measured against that of the Jesus of *Paradise Regained,* appears to be fashioned on the Satanic model.[314] It should cause us to consider with Arthur Barker that "Perhaps we need . . . to be a little more objective about the ongoing choral comments throughout, and even its wondering comments in the end, in terms of what these now-liberated Hebrews are going on to."[315] If Samson were simply a villainous character, then of course the laws of tragedy, which Milton promises to observe, would have been sorely violated. Milton understood with Aristotle that there is nothing tragic in seeing the downfall of a wicked man; rather, the tragic hero is an intermediary man, and this particular hero was subject to radically different assessments. Once a hero, however, Samson was falling into disrepute. *Why* is the question that Milton turns into the subject of his tragedy, which, insofar as he himself had identified with Samson, is a personal tragedy and which, insofar as a whole nation had done so, is a social tragedy. What is important, above all, is to remember that Milton's play, as Bouchard reminds us, is not a "theology" but a "theatre."[316] And like *Samson, Paradise Regained* may also be described as a theater whose message, again like *Samson*'s, has not always been heard because it, too, has been isolated from the traditions that might best illuminate it.

Paradise Regained has generally been read in terms of the gospel accounts of Jesus' journey into the wilderness and, usually, in terms of the exegetical tradition that considers the wilderness story under the lights of the triple equation. It is likely, however, that Milton perceived the life of Jesus and especially this event as a visionary drama and it is probable that, like Blake, his interest was less in redacting Scripture than in providing clarification of the prophetic visions of the Messiah, which he then uses to fill in the white space left in John's Gospel where the wilderness episode is an untold story. Certainly Milton could have found a precedent for treating this story as a drama of illumination in Joachim of Fiore who, rather than imposing the usual exegesis on the wilderness story, advances another which seems remarkably like Milton's own; Christ's journey is, therefore, read as a summoning of all men to spiritual adventure, which, beginning in self-transformation, ends in cultural renewal:

Clear the eyes of the mind from all dusts of earth; leave the tumults of crowds and the clamour of words; follow the angel in
spirit into the desert; ascend with the same angel into the great and
high mountain; there *you will behold high truths hidden from the
beginning of time and from all generations.* . . . For we, called in
these latest times to follow the spirit rather than the letter, ought
to obey, going from illumination to illumination, from the first
heaven to the second, and from the second to the third, from the
place of darkness into the light of the moon, that at last we may
come out of the moonlight into the glory of the full Sun."[317]

That Milton had something of this idea in mind as he introduced
the most revolutionary of his poems is suggested by its proem,
by its claim "to tell of deeds / Above Heroic . . . / And *un-
recorded left through many an Age, / Worthy t' have not remain'd so long unsung*" (I.14–17; my italics). We might even
conjecture further: that *Paradise Regained* adumbrates the understanding of this episode that will be popularized during the
eighteenth century and that accords with Milton's belief, expressed in *An Apology for Smectymnuus,* that "Christ had . . .
open'd the kingdome of heaven before he had *overcome the
sharpnesse of death*" (*Yale Milton,* 1:940).

Within a century after the publication of *Paradise Regained,*
the story at the center of Milton's poem was to be interpreted as
a series of visionary scenes wherein Satan is used as the symbol
of temptation and which themselves are understood as an expansive prophecy of Jesus' future trials, once his ministry begins.
As Hugh Farmer observed in 1765, "the several scenes were distinct prophecies and symbols of the different temptations which
were to occur in the course of his ministry"; that is, the various
visions are "mental illuminations" whose "prophetical design"
was grasped by Jesus. The wilderness story becomes another great
testimony of God's providence, showing "wise conduct in the
Deity . . . because his intention was to forewarn Christ of his
danger and to arm him against it"; and as "a *spiritual* and mental
transaction" this story emphasizes elements and symbols in a
vision that do not necessarily refer to real objects or have exact

external archetypes.[318] Rather than proving that Satan is a historical personage, this story shows that he is a principle manifesting himself from within, a character in a symbolic drama that plays itself out in the theater of the mind. Satan, then, is just another symbolic component in a drama wherein all the symbolic components are like the figures in the apocalyptic vision of St. John.[319] This understanding of Jesus' temptations, if not popularized until the eighteenth century, is nevertheless to be found prominently articulated in English literature before the supposed time of *Paradise Regained*'s composition. In his *Leviathan,* Thomas Hobbes asks: what can be the meaning of this temptation, "other than that [Jesus] went of himself into the Wildernesse; and that this . . . was a vision?" The biblical recounting of this episode, moreover, "suiteth with the nature of a Vision."[320]

Like John's drama, *Paradise Regained* plays out its drama in the arena of the world; and focusing on the temptation story, Milton's poem has reference points everywhere in history, its story recapitulating the total experience of the human race. This understanding of Milton's poem and of the story from which it derives explains, for example, why Christ is finally subjected to temptations that may seem inappropriate to him; and this understanding, we should note, may be found in literature contemporary with Milton. In 1642, Henry Archer explained that by the Gospel story of Christ's temptations "is not meant onely his Personall Temptations, but . . . his misticall, that is all the Temptations which in his Name & Members do fall him," as well as the rest of the human race.[321] Christ's temptations thus agree with—they figure forth—everyman's temptations and, at the same time, ensure that all those who live in the first resurrection will rule the world, will rise yet once more in a second resurrection.

Moving from the epics to *Samson Agonistes,* from Genesis and the Gospels into the Book of Revelation, is moving from narrative into drama, from epical into tragic literature—is moving, as Milton would have understood, from a mode which provides commentary into one which requires commentary. Ignoring this fact, Donald Bouchard has proposed that *"Samson Agonistes* is

a literary product and *Paradise Regained* its interpretation"—
Milton's brief epic, in other words, is the "plain word" written
after *Samson Agonistes.*[322] Perhaps. But presumably Milton controlled the arrangement of the 1671 volume and, through his
arrangement, defined the relationship between these two poems,
making *Paradise Regained* the context for *Samson* and *Samson,*
in turn, the interpreting poem for *Paradise Regained.* As here, so
with *Lycidas* and the pastoral tradition: pastoral is a context for
Lycidas, and also the norm from which Milton's poem deviates;
Paradise Regained is positioned as a context for *Samson* and supplies the norm which Samson violates. Yet *Samson Agonistes,* if
it offers commentary on *Paradise Regained,* offers a sad commentary, both on men and civilizations that have repeatedly
reverted to the ways represented by Samson from which Jesus,
as an example, provided them with a release.

Thus the very meaning of *Paradise Regaind* finds its demonic
parody in *Samson Agonistes,* Milton's tragedy showing not a man
freeing other men from the cycles of history but a "hero" binding
men down to them. Milton's "tragedy" is just that, showing a
false apocalypse, resulting from a commitment to "mortal fight"
(1175), and contrasting with the true apocalypse whose harbinger
is Christ and which comes only when mankind, undergoing the
experience of self-annihilation, toppling the Antichrist who has
enthroned himself within the temple of the mind, begins to
build, through mental fight, a Jerusalem in England's green and
pleasant land (see fig. 6). Samson is a type of those apocalyptic
angels who fall from the divine vision; Christ, and Milton with
him, a type of the Mighty Angel who, restoring to mankind the
Everlasting Gospel, makes manifest our destiny.

The restoration of the Word, the restoration of the forms that
would contain it—this is the undertaking of all prophets and
the purpose of all their prophecies. Accordingly, prophets are
not the authors of single poems but the shapers of large visions
that would contain them all, their own and those of others.
Insofar as any prophet (or any poet who aspires to be one) is the
maker of a definitive vision, that vision is the canon and not a

single poem within its boundaries; and insofar as that vision bursts into clarity, it does so progressively, prophetically. To speak of "the Miltonic labyrinth," as Donald Bouchard does, is to call attention to this fact by comprehending *Paradise Lost* as a poem in which "the darkness of the prose is illuminated" and as a poem whose own preoccupation with interpretation is equally evident in *Paradise Regained* and *Samson Agonistes.*[323] Milton's poetry, like Blake's, "removes the barriers between poetry and criticism"; and it thus testifies to the belief that "Truth lies in the progressive expansion of meaning."[324] There is, therefore, reciprocity, interdependency, among poems—those within the canon and those invoked as a context for it: one poem, or a whole collection of them, opens the way into what succeeds it, but then the later poem also rolls away the obscurities from the precursor poems, sharply focusing their meaning, on occasion doing this by posing against them an alternative or contending perspective, or sometimes by creating for them a subsuming perspective. This principle for Milton criticism is firmly asserted by Balachandra Rajan: "the rich meaningfulness of the poems is made evident by the manner in which they reach out to what surrounds them."[325]

Lycidas contributes meaning to *Paradise Lost,* as do many other poems and polemics that precede the epic. However, whereas *Lycidas* vies with the other poems in the Edward King memorial volume, *Paradise Lost,* taking its inspiration from the Book of Genesis, advances biblical themes and details the theology that in *Paradise Regained* Milton will seek to revise. In short, rather than setting *Paradise Lost* on a collision course with the Bible and thereby making his poem vie with *it,* Milton's strategy is to let *Paradise Lost* epitomize the orthodoxies that *Paradise Regained* will subvert. In this way, Milton makes his later poem enter into contention with his earlier one. Itself a subsuming structure, *Paradise Lost,* in turn, serves as a gateway into the brief epic and the tragedy; yet these poems are much more than recapitulations of the diffuse epic, and certainly they are not redactions of one another's visions. In no case does the perspective of one poem duplicate that of the other: the diffuse epic is a focusing of the orthodoxies that *Paradise Regained* proceeds to demolish; the brief epic is a formulation of a new system of religion, more perfect and enduring than the one it supersedes, but one that is tested against the contrary vision of Milton's tragedy. *Paradise Regained*, having shown how the paradise within may be achieved, is complemented by a tragedy that shows how it may be lost, and the effects of its being lost; but this fact should not be construed to mean that Milton's faith in, or hopes for, an outward apocalypse are abandoned. Rather, because his faith had been so deeply challenged and because his earlier hopes had been so completely dashed, Milton distances apocalypse in the future, making it contingent upon the spiritual man's rising up against the natural man and thereupon establishing for himself and his society a new system of values.

Thus far, we have stressed Milton's indebtedness to the Book of Revelation and, more generally, to prophetic tradition for the design that is replicated in his major poetry. However, Milton's last poems and their vast design are emanations of biblical patterns; here the whole Bible comes into play, Milton recreating in these poems the major myths—creation and fall, exodus and wandering, resurrection and return—that comprise the total Christian mythology. The relationship of these poems to the Bible is not as simple as it may seem, however; for Milton is a myth-maker in precisely the sense that Roland Barthes would attach to that phrase:[326] he uses myth to expose, and especially in the case of *Samson Agonistes,* to explode the myths by which a society falsely sustains itself. In *Paradise Lost* Milton scrutinizes the view of God that emerges from the Genesis story, superimposing, in accordance with Revelation commentary, the image of God reflected in the Jesus of the New Testament; moreover, here Milton explodes, along with mythologies, also cosmologies, turning the center of his epic into a gigantic pun, for the Son-centered theology put forward in the epic and asserted through the Son's position in Book VI implies the heliocentric cosmology advanced in Books VII and VIII. Here, at the center of *Paradise Lost,* cosmology supports and is supported by theology. The diminished position of man (for which Copernicus is held responsible) and man's diminished heroism (for which Milton so often is made responsible) are made perfectly congruent. Aesthetic design, new cosmology, revisionist theology—all converge in the middle books of Milton's epic. In *Paradise Regained,* another Christocentric poem, Milton amplifies a story only sketched in three of the gospel accounts by way of filling in the gap left in John's Gospel, which does not even mention the temptation episode.[327] In *Samson Agonistes,* finally, the poet assumes the Book of Revelation as his context by way of showing that precipitous action only forestalls the true apocalypse. This poem, instead of being an amplification of its source, is an inversional transformation of it, *Samson* portraying a false apocalypse and Milton, through such a portrayal, distancing apocalypse into the future. Milton's last three poems, but *Samson Agonistes* especially, reveal his concern with helping an entire culture cope with its broken expectations, with expectations that Milton himself, through his prose works, had helped to build. Thus when Frank Kermode speaks of the "readjustment of expectations in regard to an end which is so notable a feature in naïve apocalyptic," he leads us to the very heart of the significance with which Milton's suite of poems is invested; and when Kermode refers to apocalypse merging with tragedy, he speaks a truth that Milton in his last poem comprehended.[328]

In this trilogy of poems, Milton replicates the whole structure of literature as it is represented in the Bible, presenting greatly expanded visions of Genesis and the Gospels. Portraying only a counter-apocalypse, however, Milton leaves to other poets the task of presenting "the expanded vision of apocalypse and Last Judgment"—a task, as Northrop Frye has shown, that Blake was the first to assume as the Romantic movement got underway.[329] Like Blake's later poems, Milton's also attach themselves to the tradition of the Everlasting Gospel—a tradition that would move us beyond the Old and New Testaments, beyond the first and second ages of the world, into a third. Yet this tradition promises not a new book but rather a new revelation of the spiritual sense of the Bible. In this age, of which Milton's poems are written as a harbinger, "God will be with man," rendering "all existing forms of worship, ceremonies, churches, legal and moral codes . . . superfluous." No longer appearing as a source from without, says A. L. Morton, "God will now be within, and the unity of God and man will be freely accomplished."[330] Once expecting this end to be realized through revolution, Milton, subsequent to the Revolution's failure, came to see that end as something that could be legislated through his poetry which, as a commentary on the Bible, would be a new revelation of its meaning.

Marked like the biblical books by an "intense interrelatedness,"[331] Milton's last poems, as Roland Barthes might be expected to say, oppose ideology to culture: they erect a new system of religion by way of delivering men from all other such systems; they make new myths, enabling us to see through the myth about which they are written; and in the process, they turn the old myths into "corpses." Milton, better than any poetic precursor, understood that the best way to combat a myth is to reconstitute it; for as Barthes explains, "the power of the second myth is that it gives the first its basis as a naivety."[332] The new myths also force choices, and this is doubly true when they are made to sit side-by-side as they do in Milton's 1671 volume. By this time, Milton knew what his own errors had been and what those of recent history had been; he knew—and therefore attempts to make us see—that "to fail to choose is to be bound to the past," to be imprisoned in its mistakes; in Donald Bouchard's words, "to be a captive of history."[333] In an important way, as we have seen, epic had become just such a captive; and so in *Paradise Regained* and *Samson Agonistes* Milton bursts its boundaries, now writing purely prophetic poems, presenting here the "visionary forms dramatic" that he had distilled from the Bible and that, in the course of a lifetime, he had seen playing themselves out in English history—and in his own psychic history.

Paradise Regained and *Samson Agonistes* are Milton's most radical statements in poetry, and they may remind us of the proposition: "there is not a finer sight than to see an old man thus strip himself of the darlings of half a century in order to educate and refine his country." The prophet, says Abraham Heschel, is "an individual who said No to his society, condemning its habits and assumptions, its complacency, waywardness, and syncretism."[334] The prophet may even like Milton be called upon to say "No" to himself, condemning his own past mistakes. The prophetic Milton knows that others can know, finally, only if they examine "the relationship between truth and its types but also between truth and its parodies"; only then can man apprehend that "Right action—and the emphasis falls upon action—is discovered through rejection of the wrong roles."[335] Readers of these last poems too often forget what Henry John Todd felt compelled to tell his own century—that Milton, aware of the public's distaste for *Paradise Regained,* attributed that distaste to a people with a strong sense of the loss of paradise but not an equal gusto for regaining it.

Waiting for apocalypse—that was Milton's posture both when he completed *Lycidas* and *Paradise Lost* and when he published his brief epic "to which is added" *Samson Agonistes.* That is also the posture from which Milton's Romantic successors have written their greatest poems. For the Romantics, *Paradise Lost* is still the great epic projection. Yet *Paradise Regained* and *Samson Agonistes* are equally important models for their poetry: Milton's brief epic provides a pattern for the mental journey that is at the heart of the Romantic epic; and *Samson Agonistes* exemplifies the sardonic apocalypse figured in poems like Blake's *Europe,* Byron's *The Vision of Judgment* and *Don Juan,* and Shelley's *The Cenci.* For this reason, it may be said that Milton's poetry, restoring the tradition of prophecy to perfection and then delivering that tradition to future generations of writers, looks beyond itself with forward gaze.

A. S. P. Woodhouse once remarked that "it is the duty of the critic to try . . . every reasonable hypothesis that will cover the phenomena and save the poem."[336] *Lycidas,* along with Milton's epics and tragedy, requires saving—not from oblivion, but from systems of criticism that ignore genre and context and thus Milton's artistry; that, consequently, obscure more than they clarify Milton's vision and that themselves possess no real vision of Milton's place in, or contribution to, the history of English poetry. Prophecy is the rubric that best explains the phenomena of Milton's poetry and that will best save his poetry for future generations of readers. To understand prophecy is to begin to understand the nature and meaning of Milton's poetry; but it is, likewise, to begin to comprehend the legacy that Milton, through his poetry, left to future generations of writers. Prophecy is Milton's gift to the Romantic poets; and their gift to him is one of understanding his achievement through which they are able to realize their own.

The tradition of prophecy, some would say, had its swan song in the eighteenth century; and they would argue further that despite the uninterrupted existence of a tradition that goes back to the early centuries of Christianity, this type of literature became increasingly "the refuge of cranks and an occasional poetic or artistic genius."[337] On the contrary, many poets in England, from the Renaissance onward, lived in the tradition of prophecy and in their writings that tradition continues to live. From the standpoint of literary history, prophecy may be described as a bridge thrown up over time, uniting Milton's poetry with that of his Romantic successors. It might even be proposed that Milton is a living presence in Romantic poetry because the tradition of prophecy had lived so prominently in his own. Two traditions, then, coalesce in Romantic poetry—the Milton tradition and the tradition of prophecy. That coalescence is finally so complete that it is difficult to separate these traditions; and for that matter, it is unlikely that the Romantic poets would have wished for their separation. After all, they married the traditions and thus could be expected to resist any effort that would tear them asunder.

There is no more evident link between the tradition of prophecy, the Milton tradition, and the Romantic poets than the eagerness of these poets to elevate historical figures, Milton and themselves, into the eschatological position of apocalyptic angels. This constellation of poets, whose greatest star is Milton, regarded themselves as the spiritual men who would usher in a new order and a new age: like their precursor, they saw it as their calling to embody in themselves the spiritual life of the new age and, at the same time, to lead the pilgrimage toward it. The correlative to the centuries-old tradition of historicizing Antichrist, of seeing him in Pope or High Priest, in Monarch or Ruler, is the historicizing of Christ, which involves the belief that he will reign over the new age in spirit, through the apocalyptic angels (the poets and prophets) who, as "Authours," are "guides and Captains"—Christ's emissaries effecting the reformation of mankind.[338] For Blake and for the other Romantics, Milton is a type of the *renovator mundi,* a liberator rather than an oppressor, who, like other such figures, appears under a number of guises— as *Corrector, Reparator, Reformator.* Milton, for these poets, is the great prophet who stands between the ancient and the modern world.

Notes

Chapter I

[1] See Marjorie Reeves, *The Influence of Prophecy in the Later Middle Ages: A Study of Joachimism* (Oxford: Clarendon Press, 1969), p. 508; and Austin Farrer, *A Rebirth of Images: The Making of St. John's Apocalypse* (1949; rpt. Boston: Beacon Press, 1963), p. 306. Frank Manuel, allowing the Book of Revelation a somewhat larger range of influence than does either Reeves or Farrer, speaks of "the continued fascination of great European intellects of the seventeenth and early eighteenth centuries with the interpretation of Daniel and the Apocalypse" (*The Religion of Isaac Newton* [Oxford: Clarendon Press, 1974], p. 88); and Lafcadio Hearn, noting the "tremendous character" of Revelation's imagery, as well as the Book's more general influence, observes that it possesses a unique ability to shape literary taste (*On Art, Literature, and Philosophy,* ed. Ryuji Tanabé *et al.* [Tokyo: Hokuseido Press, 1932], p. 10).

I concentrate upon the Book of Revelation in this chapter because, despite the modern tendency to differentiate prophecy (Old Testament) and apocalyptics (New Testament), *historically* the Apocalypse has been dealt with as the "classic example of Christian prophecy" (see M. H. Shepherd, Jr.'s comments in *The Interpreter's Dictionary of the Bible,* ed. George Arthur Buttrick *et al.* [4 vols.; New York and Nashville: Abingdon Press, 1962], 3:919). Moreover, as Michael Fixler explains, "the Apocalypse was a literary model of extraordinary authority for one who was both a Puritan and a poet" ("The Apocalypse within *Paradise Lost,*" in *New Essays on Paradise Lost,* ed. Thomas Kranidas [Berkeley and Los Angeles: Univ. of California Press, 1969], p. 139). For the modern distinction between prophecy and apocalyptics, see both Frank Kermode, *The Sense of an Ending: Studies in the Theory of Fiction* (1967; rpt. London and New York: Oxford Univ. Press, 1968), p. 30, and Tony Stoneburner, "Notes on Prophecy and Apocalypse in a Time of Anarchy and Revolution," in *Literature in Revolution,* ed. George Abbott White and Charles Newman (New York, Chicago, and San Francisco: Holt, Rinehart, and Winston, 1972), pp. 246–82. Throughout my own study, I will follow the historical assumption that the Book of Revelation is the culmination of Christian prophecy and the best example available to those who would write in the prophetic mode. Here, though, I should also acknowledge that the most recent commentator on the Book of Revelation believes it "does not fit into the Christian apocalyptic genre"; rather "more akin to Jewish apocalyptic literature," this commentator proposes, the Book of Revelation "might be a Jewish apocalypse redacted by Christians who altered the text" (J. Massyngberde Ford, *The Anchor Bible: Revelation* [Garden City, N. Y.: Doubleday, 1975], pp. 4, 22, 27). Implicit here is yet another distinction, one between ancient and modern apocalyptic, which has been studied by Amos N. Wilder, "The Rhetoric of Ancient and Modern Apocalyptic," *Interpretation,* 25 (1971), 436–53.

² *Apocalypse* (Florence: G. Orioli, 1931), pp. 9, 15, 20, 35.

³ Speaking of John's Apocalypse, A. B. Van Os remarks that it surpasses ". . . anything that has come down to us of visionary literature" and that its influence is strongly felt in the Middle Ages (*Religious Visions: The Development of the Eschatological Elements in Mediaeval English Religious Literature* [Amsterdam: H. J. Paris, 1932], p. 8). Nevertheless, it is with strong doubts that Morton W. Bloomfield points to the Book of Revelation as a context for *Piers Plowman* (see *Piers Plowman as a Fourteenth-century Apocalypse* [New Brunswick: Rutgers Univ. Press, 1961]); whatever Bloomfield's doubts, they are effectively dispelled by Barbara Nolan, *The Gothic Visionary Perspective* (Princeton: Princeton Univ. Press, 1977). In *The Prophetic Moment: An Essay on Spenser* (Chicago: Univ. of Chicago Press, 1971), Angus Fletcher observes that during the Renaissance "poetry and prophecy combine forces" in *The Faerie Queene* (p. 6); see also Michael Murrin, *The Veil of Allegory: Some Notes Toward a Theory of Allegorical Rhetoric in the English Renaissance* (Chicago: Univ. of Chicago Press, 1969). More recently, Kathleen Williams has placed *The Faerie Queene* within the tradition of "the prophetic epic [which] runs parallel . . . to Holy Writ, and to the Book of Revelation itself" ("Milton, Greatest Spenserian," in *Milton and the Line of Vision,* ed. Joseph Anthony Wittreich, Jr. [Madison: Univ. of Wisconsin Press, 1975], p. 32), and Raymond B. Waddington discusses Chapman in the light of prophetic tradition (*The Mind's Empire: Myth and Form in George Chapman's Narrative Poems* [Baltimore: Johns Hopkins Univ. Press, 1974]). My own essay, " 'A Poet Amongst Poets': Milton and the Tradition of Prophecy," in *Milton and the Line of Vision* (pp. 97–142), assesses Milton's debt to the Book of Revelation, a debt that is also suggested by David Shelley Berkeley, *Inwrought with Figures Dim: A Reading of Milton's Lycidas* (Hague and Paris: Mouton, 1974) and studied by Austin C. Dobbins, *Milton and the Book of Revelation: The Heavenly Cycle* (University: Univ. of Alabama Press, 1975). Also relevant here is William Kerrigan's *The Prophetic Milton* (Charlottesville: Univ. Press of Virginia, 1974). The fullest accounts of Blake's place in prophetic tradition are provided by my essay, "Opening the Seals: Blake's Epics and the Milton Tradition," in *Blake's Sublime Allegory: Essays on The Four Zoas, Milton, and Jerusalem,* ed. Stuart Curran and Joseph Anthony Wittreich, Jr. (Madison: Univ. of Wisconsin Press, 1973), pp. 23–58, and by my book,

Angel of Apocalypse: Blake's Idea of Milton (Madison: Univ. of Wisconsin Press, 1975). Long ago Wordsworth was positioned in this same tradition by Sir Herbert J. C. Grierson, *Milton and Wordsworth, Poets and Prophets: A Study of Their Reactions to Political Events* (New York: Macmillan, and Cambridge: University Press, 1937); and, though Shelley's *Defence of Poetry* remains the best statement on his place in prophetic tradition, some useful suggestions are provided by Stuart Curran, *Shelley's Annus Mirabilis: The Maturing of an Epic Vision* (San Marino: Huntington Library, 1975), and earlier by Harold Bloom, *Shelley's Mythmaking* (1959; rpt. Ithaca, N. Y.: Cornell Univ. Press, 1969), and Earl R. Wasserman, *Shelley: A Critical Reading* (Baltimore: Johns Hopkins Press, 1971). In *The Inclusive Flame: Studies in Modern American Poetry* (Bloomington: Indiana Univ. Press, 1965), Glauco Cambon proposes that prophecy is a "main fuel of the 'inclusive' flame that is American poetry" (p. 52); and my former colleague Raymond Olderman is at work on a book, *Waiting for Apocalypse,* that explores this same tradition in relation to the contemporary American novel. Less the theoretician and more the practitioner, John Martin has been described as the nineteenth century's "most typical apocalyptic painter" and then aligned with that century's apocalyptic poets: the Book of Revelation, says James G. Nelson, "was not only a source for Martin and the Apocalyptics but it was also a model of great religious poetry." For Nelson, however, that "great" poetry is exemplified not by the major Romantics or eminent Victorians but, oddly, by the spasmodic school of poetry and its immediate forbears (see *The Sublime Puritan: Milton and the Victorians* [Madison: Univ. of Wisconsin Press, 1963], pp. 45, 53).

[4] Robert Lowth, *Lectures on the Sacred Poetry of the Hebrews,* trans. G. Gregory (Boston: Printed by Joseph T. Buckingham, 1815), p. 352. Lowth's lectures, under the title of *De Sacra Poesi Hebraeorum,* were delivered at Oxford, beginning in 1741. The first Latin edition and a translation of the first lecture appeared in 1753, and other editions followed in 1763, 1766, 1770, 1775. The first full translation of the lectures, often reprinted, appeared in 1787.

[5] These lines from Virgil's ninth eclogue appear as an epigraph to the anonymous work, *The Prophets: An Heroic Poem* (London: Printed by A. Baldwin [1780]), pp. i, ii; here we are reminded that "the Word *Vates* was the Appellation of both Prophet, and Poet, it being universally believed of old, that good Poetry was Inspiration" (pp. i–ii). The characters of poet and prophet, of course, are not always associated; see, e.g., George Hickes, *The Spirit of Enthusiasm Exorcised,* 4th ed. (London: Printed for Richard Sare, 1709), p. 3; but during the Romantic period, as M. H. Abrams argues, Milton was the chief model of the poet-prophet in England (*Natural Supernaturalism: Tradition and Revolution in Romantic Literature* [New York: W. W. Norton, 1971], p. 12). And Milton understood, certainly, what Thomas Paine had to tell a later age: that "the word *prophet* . . . was the Bible word for poet, and the word *prophesying* meant the art of making poetry. It also meant the art of playing poetry to a tune upon any instrument

of music" (*The Age of Reason* [1795; rpt. London: J. Watson, 1845], p. 13, but see also pp. 42–43, 50).

It may be that, during the Renaissance, "Sidney could only gesture vaguely towards the *vates*" (see Murray Roston, *Prophet and Poet: The Bible and the Growth of Romanticism* [Evanston: Northwestern Univ. Press, 1965], p. 157); yet it is clear that for both Spenser and Milton the poet and prophet are one. See, especially, Spenser's October eclogue in *The Shepheardes Calender;* and note, too, that Milton's famous description of the function of poetry, "to allay the perturbations of the mind, and set the affections in right tune" (*Yale Milton,* 1:816–17) is exactly correspondent to the function John Smith ascribes to prophecy, to compose the mind and to allay turbulent passions—indeed all kinds of perturbations of the mind ("Of Prophecy," in *A Collection of Theological Tracts,* ed. Richard Watson [6 vols.; London: J. Nichols, 1785], 4:359; Smith's treatise, well known in the eighteenth and nineteenth centuries, both in England and America, was first published in 1631).

The one lamentable feature in Kerrigan's *The Prophetic Milton* is his curious insistence that *he* has discovered the prophetic Milton; he does not admit to being preempted in the early nineteenth century by William Blake or William Ellery Channing (the prophetic Milton is, of course, the subject of Blake's *Milton*), nor to having been anticipated in his own century not just by Grierson's *Milton and Wordsworth, Poets and Prophets,* Charles Roden Buxton's *Prophets of Heaven and Hell: Virgil, Dante, Milton, Goethe* (Cambridge: University Press, 1945), and Merritt Y. Hughes's "Milton as a Revolutionary," in *Ten Perspectives on Milton* (New Haven and London: Yale Univ. Press, 1965), esp. pp. 243–44, 247, but most signally by Angus Fletcher's *The Transcendental Masque: An Essay on Milton's Comus* (Ithaca: Cornell Univ. Press, 1971). The prophetic stance, it should be emphasized, is not unique to Milton's poetry but is equally important and prominent in his prose tracts as both my essay and Michael Lieb's demonstrate; see, respectively, " 'The Crown of Eloquence': The Figure of the Orator in Milton's Prose Works" and "Milton's *Of Reformation* and the Dynamics of Controversy," both in *Achievements of the Left Hand: Essays on the Prose of John Milton,* ed. Michael Lieb and John T. Shawcross (Amherst: Univ. of Massachusetts Press, 1974), pp. 3–54, 55–82. Such a perception does not, however, belong to modern criticism alone: William Ellery Channing noted long ago that Milton assumes the posture of John of Patmos as he writes *De Doctrina Christiana,* addressing himself to "All the Churches of Christ" (see *Remarks on the Character and Writings of John Milton,* 2nd ed. [London: Printed for Edward Rainford, 1828], p. [5], and also *Yale Milton,* 6:117).

⁶ *Piers Plowman as a Fourteenth-century Apocalypse,* pp. 8, 10. In the same book, Bloomfield speaks of "the somewhat dubious literary form of the apocalypse," saying that "If we do not use the term too strictly, we may say that *Piers Plowman* is a fourteenth-century English apocalypse"; despite these reservations, for Bloomfield Langland is indisputably a prophetic poet (pp. 34, 154, 173). Contrary to Bloomfield, Eugène Vinaver, also working prin-

cipally with medieval materials, concludes that "prophecy assumes a significantly concrete form" (*The Rise of Romance* [New York and Oxford: Oxford Univ. Press, 1971], p. 111, see also p. 116), as does Nolan, *The Gothic
Visionary Perspective,* esp. pp. 3–34, 205–58. Importantly, Martin Rist allows that apocalyptic visions are "conscious literary productions" and that the
Book of Revelation specifically is a "careful . . . literary structure" (*The
Interpreter's Bible,* ed. George Arthur Buttrick *et al.* [12 vols.; New York
and Nashville: Abingdon Press, 1952–57], 12:350, 360). Though his description of prophecy is insufficiently pointed and generally unsophisticated,
Rupert Taylor perceives that it is a carefully, clearly defined literary genre,
explaining that as prophecy evolves it develops elaborateness and complexity
of form (*The Political Prophecy in England* [New York: Columbia Univ.
Press, 1911], pp. 90, 92). Taylor's conclusions are extrapolated from non-
biblical prophecy, however; and the form he describes has but one characteristic—obscurity.

Taylor's claim, along with the argument advanced by Iain H. Murray—
that, while the eighteenth century represents a great awakening to prophecy,
"the seventeenth century was the formative period of the differing schools of
thought on prophecy"—counters the view expressed by Roston, that it was
only in the eighteenth century that the theory of biblical aesthetics was re-
discovered (Roston explicitly denies any relationship between this aesthetic
and Milton's poetry), as well as the view expressed by Claus Westermann,
that prophecy as a rhetorical form is a modern conception. See Murray's *The
Puritan Hope: A Study in Revival and the Interpretation of Prophecy* (London: Banner of Truth Trust, 1971), p. 55; Roston's *Prophet and Poet,* pp.
18, 54, 131; and Westermann's *Basic Forms of Prophetic Speech,* trans. Hugh
Clayton White (Philadelphia: Westminster Press, 1967), p. 21. Murray also
speaks of what no student of the Book of Revelation from the Renaissance
into the Romantic period can fail to notice: "the remarkable unanimity of
prophetic views to be found among the multiplied ranks of evangelicals after
the 1740's," which, he says, "is . . . indicative of the formative influence of
the Puritan school" (*The Puritan Hope,* p. 150).

[7] *Literature as System: Essays Toward the Theory of Literary History*
(Princeton: Princeton Univ. Press, 1971), p. 125.

[8] William M. Ryan, *William Langland* (New York: Twayne, 1968), p.
13; and Elizabeth D. Kirk, *The Dream Thought of Piers Plowman* (New
Haven: Yale Univ. Press, 1972), pp. 2, 205.

[9] See, e.g., George Gifford, *Sermons upon the Whole Booke of the Revelation* (London: Printed by Richard Field and Felix Kingston, 1599), p. 2.
Renaissance commentators also purport to draw their view of Revelation's
structure from Augustine. See, e.g., John Mayer, *Ecclesiastica Interpretatio:
or the Expositions upon the Difficult and Doubtful Passages of the Seven
Epistles Called Catholike, and the Revelation* (London: Printed by John
Haveland, 1627), pp. 248, 255. Augustine himself said:

   . . . the Apocalypse contains many obscure texts that exercise the reader's intelligence, and only a few so clear that one may rely on these in laboriously

studying out the remainder. This is due chiefly to the fact that there is multiform repetition of the same themes—so various that, whereas John seems to be saying constantly new things, you find out that he is repeating the same themes now this way, now that. However, the passage, 'And God will wipe away every tear . . . ,' so luminously concerns the world to come, immortality and eternity of the saints . . . that no one who finds this text obscure should look for clarity anywhere in Holy Scripture or hope to find it.

For Augustine's statement, see *The City of God,* trans. Gerald G. Walsh and Daniel J. Honon (3 vols.; New York: Fathers of the Church, 1954), 3:294.

[10] See "Preface to the Revelation of St. John," in *Works of Martin Luther* (6 vols.; Philadelphia: A. J. Holman, 1932), 6:481, 488.

[11] I quote from John Bale, *The Image of Both Churches* (1548; rpt. London: Thomas East [1570]), sig. Aiii^v; James Brocard, *The Reveled Revelation of Saint John After Divers Learned Authors* (London: Thomas Barth, 1582), sig. B2^v; Thomas Brightman, *The Revelation of S. John* (Leyden: Printed by John Class, 1616), p. 7; John Trapp, *Gods Love-Tokens, and the Afflicted Mans Lessons* (London: Richard Badger, 1637), sig. a; Joseph Mede, *The Key of the Revelation,* trans. Richard More, 2nd ed. (London: Printed for Phil. Stephens, 1650), pt. I, p. 92; pt. II, p. 108 (Mede's commentary was first published in 1627 under the title, *Clavis Apocalyptica ex Innatis et Insitis Visionum Characteribus Eruta et Demonstrata;* a second edition appeared in 1632, another in 1649, the first edition of More's translation, in 1643; and finally in 1650 Joseph Mede's *Remaines on Some Passages in the Revelation* [London: Printed for John Clarke, 1650] was published); see also Arthur Dent, *The Ruine of Rome, or an Exposition upon the Whole Revelation* (London: Printed for Simon Waterson, 1633), p. 24. For a quick summary of sixteenth-century Protestant attitudes toward the Book of Revelation, see Josephine Waters Bennett, *The Evolution of The Faerie Queene* (Chicago: Univ. of Chicago Press, 1942), pp. 110–12. And see also Isabel G. MacCaffrey who observes that "the loftiest role in which they [poets] have cast themselves has been that of the seer or visionary; for Christian authors, the model is the author of the Apocalypse" (*Spenser's Allegory: The Anatomy of Imagination* [Princeton: Princeton Univ. Press, 1976], p. 23).

[12] I quote from Samuel Langdon, *Observations on the Revelation of Jesus Christ to St. John* (Worcester, Mass.: Printed by Isaiah Thomas, 1791), pp. 23, 24; the anonymous commentator, *Prophetic Conjectures on the French Revolution, and Other Recent and Shortly Expected Events* (London: Printed by W. Taylor, 1793), p. 2; and Lowth, *Lectures on the Sacred Poetry of the Hebrews,* p. 293.

[13] See the anonymous commentary, *An Illustration of Those Two Abstruse Books in Holy Scripture . . . Framed Out of the Expositions of Dr. Henry More* (London: Printed for Walter Kettilby, 1685), sig. Y2.

[14] *Milton and the Kingdoms of God* (London: Faber and Faber, 1964), pp. 71–72. See also Fixler's essay, "Apocalypse," in *A Milton Encyclopedia,* ed. William B. Hunter *et al.* (8 vols.; Lewisburg: Bucknell Univ. Press, 1978–79), 1:57–60.

[15] *Leviathan,* ed. C. B. MacPherson (Middlesex, Eng.: Pelican, 1968), p. 458 (III.36).

[16] Trapp, *Gods Love-Tokens,* sig. A8–A8ᵛ.

[17] *The Religion of Isaac Newton,* p. 98.

[18] Morton Scott Enslin, *The Literature of the Christian Movement: Part III of Christian Beginnings* (1938; rpt. New York: Harper and Row, 1956), p. 364.

[19] *Lectures on the Sacred Poetry of the Hebrews,* p. 274.

[20] Angus Fletcher introduces his conception of transcendental form in *The Prophetic Moment,* p. 301, and develops it in *The Transcendental Masque,* pp. 116–46; and E. H. Gombrich explains his idea of total form in *Norm and Form: Studies in the Art of the Renaissance,* 2nd ed. (London and New York: Phaidon, 1971), esp. pp. 63, 73, 79. Both ideas derive ultimately from scriptural exegesis and are canonized as part of a critical idiom during the Romantic period. In his 1815 *Preface,* listing the various genres, Wordsworth acknowledges that some poets create a "composite order" from them; and Hazlitt, in *The Plain Speaker,* allows that the productions of Milton, more "multiform" even than Shakespeare's, "were of the *composite order*" and "sometimes even amount to centos" (see *The Romantics on Milton: Formal Essays and Critical Asides,* ed. Joseph Anthony Wittreich, Jr. [Cleveland: Press of Case Western Reserve Univ., 1970], pp. 128, 397). Henry Fuseli reminded the Romantics that "as the mind and fancy of men . . . consist of mixed qualities, we seldom meet with a human performance exclusively made up of epic, dramatic, or pure historic elements" ("Lecture III," in *The Life and Writings of Henry Fuseli,* ed. John Knowles [3 vols.; London: Henry Colburn and Richard Bentley, 1831], 2:179). Fuseli's observation is borne out by much criticism.

Chaucerians have long recognized the impulse toward total form in *The Canterbury Tales,* and Morton Bloomfield finds the same impulse in Langland's *Piers Plowman* (see *Piers Plowman as a Fourteenth-century Apocalypse,* esp. pp. 3–43). Turning attention to the Renaissance, O. B. Hardison laments that so many literary historians subscribe to "the idea that each literary type is autonomous and self-perpetuating, and that it can therefore be studied in isolation from other types" (*The Enduring Monument: A Study of the Idea of Praise in Renaissance Literary Theory and Practice* [Chapel Hill: Univ. of North Carolina Press, 1962], p. 68). Rosalie Colie, with eyes fixed fast to Renaissance literature (especially to *The Faerie Queene, King Lear,* and *Paradise Lost*) discusses the phenomenon of *genera mista* as an attribute of Renaissance poetry in *The Resources of Kind: Genre-Theory in the Renaissance,* ed. Barbara K. Lewalski (Berkeley and Los Angeles: Univ. of California Press, 1973); and the weighty theory of both Bernard Weinberg and Angus Fletcher supports her conclusions (see *A History of Literary Criticism in the Italian Renaissance* [2 vols.; Chicago: Univ. of Chicago Press, 1961], 2:1103–05, and *The Transcendental Masque,* esp. pp. 97, 116–17, 124). Colie develops her idea of *genera mista* in relation to Shakespeare in *Shakespeare's Living Art* (Princeton: Princeton Univ. Press, 1974). For discussion of this phenomenon in seventeenth-century poetry, see Norman K. Farmer, Jr., "A Theory of Genre," *Genre*, 3 (1970), 293–317, and also Barbara K. Lewalski, *Donne's Anniversaries and the Poetry of Praise: The Creation of a Symbolic Mode* (Princeton: Princeton Univ. Press, 1973), who recognizes Donne's *Anniversaries* as complex, mixed-genre works, Donne here "creating a new coherence out of the elements of several generic traditions" (pp. 7, 11). For discussion of *genera mista* in Romantic and modern poetry, see Herbert Lindenberger, *On Wordsworth's Prelude* (Princeton: Princeton Univ. Press, 1963); E. S. Shaffer, *Kubla Khan and the Fall of Jerusalem: The Mythological School in Biblical Criticism and Secular Literature 1770–1880* (Cambridge: University Press, 1975); Curran, *Shelley's Annus Mirabilis;* and Edward Engelberg, *The Vast Design: Patterns in W. B. Yeats's Aesthetic* (Toronto: Univ. of Toronto Press, 1964). Blake's poetry has not yet been explored formally in the light of this tradition, though Kay Parkhurst Easson commented provocatively on Blake's involvement in it at the 1973 Modern Language Association meeting (Seminar: Blake and the Moderns). Also pertinent here is Barthes' observation that, like culture, poetry is a system of forms, marked not so much by its harmonizing of form and content as by its "absorption of one form into another" (*Mythologies,* p. 133n); so too is J. V. Cunningham's argument that a literary work "is a convergence of forms, and forms of disparate orders. It is coincidence of forms that locks in the poem" ("The Problem of Form," in *The Journal of John Cardan* [Denver: Allan Swallow, 1964], p. 15).

[21] See W. P. Ker, *Epic and Romance: Essays on Medieval Literature* (1897; rpt. New York: Dover, 1957), p. 13, and Susanne Langer, *Feeling and Form: A Theory of Art* (New York: Charles Scribner, 1953), p. 304.

[22] *Discourses on the Heroic Poem,* trans. Mariella Cavalchina and Irene Samuel (Oxford: Clarendon Press, 1973), p. 295. For an illuminating discussion, see Annabel M. Patterson, *Hermogenes and the Renaissance: Seven Ideas of Style* (Princeton: Princeton Univ. Press, 1970), esp. pp. 176–213.

[23] *Discourses on the Heroic Poem,* p. 192.

[24] *Ibid.,* pp. 77–78. See S. K. Heninger, Jr., *Touches of Sweet Harmony: Pythagorean Cosmology and Renaissance Poetics* (San Marino: Huntington Library, 1974), and Annabel M. Patterson, "Tasso and Neoplatonism: The Growth of His Epic Theory," *Studies in the Renaissance,* 18 (1971), 105–33. Heninger observes quite rightly that few poets attempted to reproduce the metaphor of God's creation *in toto* (p. 341). That goal, I am arguing, is the province of epic poets and, more so, of prophetic ones. See also Ernst Robert Curtius, *European Literature and the Latin Middle Ages,* trans. Willard R. Trask (New York: Pantheon, 1953), pp. 544–46; Maren-Sofie Røstvig, "Structure as Prophecy: The Influence of Biblical Exegesis upon Theories of Literary Structure," in *Silent Poetry: Essays in Numerological Analysis,* ed. Alastair Fowler (New York: Barnes and Noble, 1970), esp. pp. 32–35; and Don Cameron Allen, *Mysteriously Meant: The Rediscovery of Pagan Symbolism and Allegorical Interpretation in the Renaissance* (Baltimore: Johns Hopkins Press, 1970), esp. pp. 145, 265.

[25] See S. K. Heninger, Jr., *The Cosmographical Glass: Renaissance Diagrams of the Universe* (San Marino: Huntington Library, 1977), esp. figs. 13 and 79; and see also *Yale Milton,* 2:272.

[26] Curtius observes that the Christian Biblical epic is older than the Christian hymn (*European Literature and the Latin Middle Ages,* p. 241). Milton is associated with this tradition of epic by Anselm Bayly, who writes that the Bible "may be considered as forming one grand epic poem, under the conduct of a mighty hero, and finishing with an event or action, in which the whole world is interested." Bayly also calls epic poems "Poetic Prophecies" and urges epic poets to go to the Book of Revelation for instruction (see *The Alliance of Musick, Poetry, and Oratory* [London: Printed for J. Stockdale, 1784], pp. 132, 135, 267; and also Charles M. Jones, "Milton's Brief Epic," *Studies in Philology,* 44 [1947], 209–27, Barbara K. Lewalski, *Milton's Brief Epic: The Genre, Meaning, and Art of Paradise Regained* [Providence: Brown Univ. Press, and London: Metheun, 1966], esp. pp. 3–129; and D. F. Raubner, "Observations on Biblical Epic," *Genre,* 3 [1970], 318–39). Martin Buber notices the links between epic and prophecy in *The Prophetic Faith* (1949; rpt. New York, Harper and Row, 1960), p. 88.

[27] See Alice Parmelee, *A Guidebook to the Bible* (New York: Harper and Row, 1948), p. 6.

[28] See "The Epic as Pseudomorph: Methodology in Milton Studies," *Milton Studies,* 7 (1975), 18.

[29] Johann A. Bengel, *Bengelius's Introduction to His Exposition of the Apocalypse,* trans. John Robertson (London: J. Ryall and R. Withy, 1757), p. iv. In *The Revelation of S. John,* Brightman observes that "there is a difference between the auncient inscription of Prophecyes, & that of this. There, *the vision of Isaias, and the vision of Obadiah, The Booke of the vision of Nahum; The Prophecy which Habakuk saw;* but never till now, *the vision, or Revelation of Jesus Christ"* (p. 7). The same point is made by Richard Bernard, *A Key of Knowledge for the Opening of the Secret Mysteries of St. Johns Mysticall Revelation* (London: Felix Kyngston, 1617), p. 1, and earlier by William Symonds who says that the Book of Revelation is the one place in Scripture where the prophetic spirit "doth fully shew it selfe" (*Pisgah Evangelica* [London: Felix Kyngston, 1606], dedicatory epistle).

[30] I quote from Goodwin's *The Exposition of the Revelation* (1639), in *The Works of Thomas Goodwin,* 12 vols. (London: James Nisbet, 1861–66), 3:33; see also Hugh Broughton, *A Revelation of the Holy Apocalyps* ([London]: n. p., 1610), pp. 70–75. The headnote to the Book of Revelation in the Geneva Bible describes John's prophecy as "a summe of those prophecies, which were written before, but shulde be fulfilled after the coming of Christ." (Goodwin was a friend of Milton's in Parliament, but his commentary was not published until 1683). Just as Goodwin believes that the perfect prophecy is made by collating the best features of earlier prophecy, Tasso believes that the perfect epic will evolve from a similar process of collation; again Patterson comments importantly in "Tasso and Neoplatonism," pp. 112–16, as does Gombrich in *Norm and Form,* p. 3.

[31] See Brightman, *The Revelation of S. John,* p. 225, and also Henry Bullinger, *A Hundred Sermons upon the Apocalipse of Jesu Christ* (1557; rpt. London: John Daye, 1573), p. [1]. Bullinger describes the Apocalypse as "an abridgement of hystories . . . unto the worldes end" (p. 6). Observations like these readily explain why the Apocalypse, "the most sublime book of the Bible," lent itself "to the eighteenth-century conception of the epic as sacred song" (Shaffer, *Kubla Khan and the Fall of Jerusalem,* pp. 70–71, also pp. 20, 65).

[32] *Pisgah Evangelica,* unpaginated dedicatory epistle and the author's Preface to the Lord Bishop of London, p. 5.

[33] *The Literature of the Christian Movement,* p. 355.

[34] I quote from an anonymous commentary, *A Paraphrase, Notes, and Observations, upon the Revelations of St. John* (London: Printed by T. Spilsbury, 1790), p. 33; but the same idea may be found in John Diodati's *Pious Annotations upon the Holy Bible* (London: Printed for Nicolas Fussell, 1643), p. 98. For other expressions of this idea, see Robert Clayton, *A Dissertation on Prophecy, Wherein the Coherence and Connexion of the Prophecies in Both the Old and New Testament Are Fully Considered* (London: Printed by J. Watts, 1749), p. ii, and Thomas Newton, *Dissertations on the Prophecies, Which Have Remarkably Been Fulfilled, and at This Time Are Fulfilling in the World,* 2nd ed. (3 vols.; London: J. and R. Tonson, 1759), 3:200. Here, Newton observes that when the books of Daniel and Revelation are taken together they may be said to present "a summary of the history of the world" (3:439).

[35] See *A Hundred Sermons,* sig. Aii.

[36] Brightman, *The Revelation of S. John,* p. 212 .

[37] Bernard, *A Key of Knowledge,* pp. 10–11.

[38] John Smith, "Of Prophecy," in *A Collection of Theological Tracts,* ed. Watson, 4:359.

[39] Richard G. Moulton, *The Literary Study of the Bible,* rev. ed. (Boston: D. C. Heath, 1905), p. 435.

[40] See Brocard, *The Reveled Revelation,* sig. Cl^v.

[41] See both Claus Westermann, *Basic Forms of Prophetic Speech,* p. 56, and Broughton, *A Revelation of the Holy Apocalyps,* p. 70. As Shaffer remarks, "the Bible was the original of all forms," containing all classical genres; always a source for poetic genres, it had the capacity to assume all forms (*Kubla Khan and the Fall of Jerusalem,* pp. 66–67). See also East Apthorp, *Of Sacred Poetry and Music* (Boston: Printed by Green and Russell, 1764), pp. 12–16, and Alice Parmelee, *A Guidebook to the Bible,* p. 5. James Muilenburg notes the "heterogeneity" of form in prophecy (*The Way of Israel: Biblical Faith and Ethics* [1961; rpt. New York: Harper and Row, 1965], p. 46); and according to Charles Roden Buxton, in the Book of Revelation, as in Job and Isaiah, "a mingling occurs of direct oratory, of dramatic interchange of dialogue, of choric strophe and antistrophe, of prose and poetry, of repetition and alternation" (*Prophets of Heaven and Hell,* p. 27).

[42] Taylor, *The Political Prophecy in England,* p. 31. See also Westermann, who observes that prophecy is composed of "foreign genres," appropriating as it evolves various forms of profane and religious lyrics and intermixing with the different genres various styles (*Basic Forms of Prophetic Speech,* pp. 26, 28, 43).

[43] See Heninger, *Touches of Sweet Harmony,* p. 372. Kathleen Williams' discussion of *The Faerie Queene,* especially of Books III and IV as an analogical universe built into a harmony through a system of contraries, is relevant here (*Spenser's Faerie Queene: The World of Glass* [London: Routledge and Kegan Paul, 1966], pp. 87–89). Williams' remarks are predicated on the belief that the poet as a maker is the creator of his own universe, which resembles the shape of the world we know (pp. xi–xii).

[44] *The Arte of English Poesie,* ed. Edward Arber (1589; rpt. London: English Reprints, 1869), p. 20.

[45] I quote from Lowth, *The Geneology of Christ* (London: Printed for J. Jackson, 1729), pp. 7–8, and Adam Clarke, *Holy Bible . . . with a Commentary and Critical Notes* (3 vols.; New York: Daniel Hitt and Abraham Paul, 1820), 3:1.

[46] *A Defensative Against the Poyson of Supposed Prophecies* (London: Printed by John Charlewood, 1620), p. 116. Shaffer comments pertinently: "The visionary tradition had a picturesque perspective built into it" (*Kubla Khan and the Fall of Jerusalem,* p. 97).

[47] *European Literature and the Latin Middle Ages,* p. 315; and see all of ch. 16.

[48] See both Reeves's *The Influence of Prophecy in the Later Middle Ages,* esp. p. 73, and Taylor's *The Political Prophecy in England,* p. 119.

[49] "Preface to the Revelation of St. John," in *Works of Martin Luther,* 6:480.

[50] *Commentary on the Epistles of Paul the Apostle to the Corinthians* (2 vols.; Edinburgh: Calvin Translation Society, 1849), 2:366.

[51] *Emblem and Expression: Meaning in English Art of the Eighteenth Century* (Cambridge, Mass.: Harvard Univ. Press, 1975), p. 12. On the paradox, see John Hollander, *Vision and Resonance: Two Senses of Poetic Form* (New York: Oxford Univ. Press, 1975), p. 24.

[52] See the unpaginated translator's Preface in *The Key of the Revelation.*

[53] See both Lawrence's *Apocalypse,* p. 141, and Langdon's *Observations on the Revelation,* p. 62.

[54] *Observations on the Revelation,* p. 62.

[55] *Dissertations on the Prophecies,* p. 49.

[56] *Lectures upon the Three First Chapters of the Revelation* (London: Printed by Cuthbert Burbie, 1604), sig. B2.

[57] *The Sacred Calendar of Prophecy: or a Dissertation on the Prophecies,* 3 vols. (London: C. and J. Rivington, 1828), 1:12, 15, 226. Comparable views of the Apocalypse are expressed by the anonymous commentary, *A Key to the Mystery of the Revelation* (London: W. Goldsmith, 1785), p. 96, and James Bicheno, *The Signs of the Times; or the Dark Prophecies of*

Scripture Illustrated by the Application of Present Important Events (West Springfield, Mass.: Printed by Richard Davison, 1796), p. 14. (Though printed in America, Bicheno's tract was written in England between 1793 and 1795.) See also James Winthrop, *An Attempt to Translate the Prophetic Part of the Apocalypse of Saint John into Familiar Language* (Boston: Printed by Belknap and Hall, 1794), pp. 3–4; Clayton, *A Dissertation on Prophecy,* p. 88; an anonymous commentator, *Prophetic Conjectures on the French Revolution,* p. 4; Robert Fleming, *A Discourse on the Rise and Fall of the Papacy* (London: Printed for Robert Fleming, 1793), p. 233; and Edward King, *A Supplement to the Remarks on the Signs of the Times* (London: Printed for George Nicol, 1799), p. 27. Also pertinent are Bernard, *A Key to Knowledge,* p. 130; William Cowper, *Pathmos: or, a Commentary on the Revelation of Saint John* (London: Printed by George Purslow, 1619), p. 16; the anonymous tract, *Catastrophe Mundi: or, Merlin Reviv'd* (London: n.p., 1683), pp. 60–61; and Thomas Beverley, *The Prophetic History of the Reformation; or the Reformation to be Reform'd* (n.p.: n.p., 1689), p. 53.

[58] Trapp, *Gods Love-Tokens,* sig. A12.

[59] Spenser's pictorialism is the subject of John B. Bender's *Spenser and Literary Pictorialism* (Princeton: Princeton Univ. Press, 1972); and Milton's pictorialism, already commented upon by Hollander (*Vision and Resonance,* p. 272), is the subject of Roland Mushat Frye's *Milton's Imagery and the Visual Arts: Iconographic Tradition in the Epic Poems* (Princeton: Princeton Univ. Press, 1978). It should be remembered here that, in a letter to Gabriel Harvey reprinted in the Spenser Variorum edition, Spenser describes his early poetry as poetical visions illustrated by pictures and thus prompts Harvey's letter, also reprinted in the Variorum, advising him that the Book of Revelation was "a super-excellent" model for a poet with Spenser's ambitions (3:18, 471). *The Faerie Queene,* of course, is not pictorial in the same way that much of Spenser's early poetry is; yet it does contain "allegorical centers" that are planned as "enigmatic pictures" (see Frank Kermode, "The Cave of Mammon," in *The Prince of Poets: Essays on Edmund Spenser,* ed. John R. Elliott, Jr. [New York: New York Univ. Press, and London: Univ. of London Press, 1968], p. 260). Northrop Frye makes an important comment on Blake's pictorialism in "The Road of Excess," in *The Stubborn Structure: Essays on Criticism and Society* (Ithaca: Cornell Univ. Press, 1970), p. 166.

[60] I borrow the phrase from Bender, *Spenser and Literary Pictorialism,* p. 154.

[61] Gerald Snare (quoting Cusanus), "The Poetics of Vision: Patterns of Grace and Courtesy in *The Faerie Queene,* VI," *Renaissance Papers 1974,* ed. Dennis G. Donovan and A. Leigh Deneef (Spain: Printed for the Southern Renaissance Conference, 1975), p. 5. See also Octavio Paz, *The Bow and the Lyre,* trans. Ruth L. C. Simms (1973; rpt. New York: McGraw-Hill, 1975), p. 253. The prophetic poet, to use Paz's words, aspires to write "a poem that will be the Book of books"—thus the plural perspective through which he ensures that his vision will be a "total view of the totality . . . not

only a vision of the world, but . . . made in its image: . . . a representation of the shape of the universe, its copy or its symbol" (pp. 241, 253). Carol V. Kaske provides the fullest discussion of plural perspectivism in *The Faerie Queene;* see "Spenser's Pluralistic Universe: The View from the Mount of Contemplation," in *Contemporary Thought on Edmund Spenser,* ed. Richard C. Frushell and Bernard J. Vondersmith (Carbondale: Southern Illinois Univ. Press, and London: Feffer and Simons, 1975), pp. 121–49.

[62] *Milton and the Western Tradition of Literary Epic* (forthcoming from Univ. of Washington Press). The primary goal of such art, to use Marcuse's phrases, is "the emancipation of *consciousness*" accomplished through "the emancipation of the senses" (*Counter-Revolution and Revolt* [Boston: Beacon Press, 1972], pp. 74, 132).

[63] *Mythologies,* trans. Annette Lavers (New York: Hill and Wang, 1972), p. 110.

[64] *The Shepheard's Starre* (London: Printed for John Rothwell, 1640), p. 2. On Spenser's attitude toward the Book of Revelation and on his familiarity with its commentators, see Bennett, *The Evolution of The Faerie Queene,* pp. 111, 114–15, and also Frank Kermode, *Shakespeare, Spenser, Donne: Renaissance Essays* (London: Routledge and Kegan Paul, 1971), esp. pp. 39–44. Neither Spenser nor Milton would share in Thomas Paine's contempt for prophecy, but both poets would probably concur in his observation that the Apocalypse is a "book of riddles that requires a revelation to explain it" (*The Age of Reason,* p. 10, also p. 17).

[65] See John Napier, *A Plaine Discovery of the Whole Revelation of Saint John* (Edinburgh: Printed by Robert Walde-grave, 1593), p. 69.

[66] See Bernard, *A Key of Knowledge,* sig. D6ᵛ; see also pp. 85–99.

[67] *Lectures on the Sacred Poetry of the Hebrews,* p. 211.

[68] More, *An Explanation of the Grand Mystery of Godliness* (London: Printed by W. Morden, 1660), p. 4.

[69] Ludowick Muggleton, *A True Interpretation of the Eleventh Chapter of the Revelation of St. John* (1662; rpt. London: E. Brown, 1833), p. 29.

[70] *Piers Plowman as a Fourteenth-century Apocalypse,* p. 174. Also relevant here is MacCaffrey's reading of *The Faerie Queene* as an anatomy of imagination; see *Spenser's Allegory.*

[71] Bernard, *A Key of Knowledge,* p. 80.

[72] I borrow the phrase from Henry More, *An Exposition of the Seven Epistles to the Seven Churches* (London: Printed for James Flesher, 1669), p. 143.

[73] See Bernard, *A Key of Knowledge,* p. 137, and Samuel Hartlib et al., *The Revelation Reveled by Two Apocalyptical Treatises* (London: Printed by William Du-Gard, 1651), p. 20.

[74] See William Guild, *The Sealed Book Opened* (London: Printed for Anthony Williamson, 1656), unpaginated dedicatory epistle, and Reeves, *The Influence of Prophecy in the Later Middle Ages,* p. 136 (my italics).

[75] *Dissertations on the Prophecies,* 3:370, 437. The idea had found notable expression in Dr. Twisse's Preface to Mede's *The Key of the Revelation*

where Revelation's "congruitie with *Daniels* text" is acknowledged (sig. A3).

[76] *The Apocalypse* (London: Francis and John Rivington, 1849), p. xiii. See also Patrick Fairbairn, *Prophecy, Viewed in Respect to Its Distinctive Nature, Its Special Function, and Proper Interpretation* (Edinburgh: T. and T. Clark, 1856), esp. ch. 6, "The Inter-Connected and Progressive Character of Prophecy."

[77] *Observations upon the Prophecies of Holy Writ, Particularly the Prophecies of Daniel, and the Apocalypse of St. John,* in *Opera* (5 vols.; London: John Nichols, 1785), 5:460–61.

[78] *Self-Consuming Artifacts: The Experience of Seventeenth-Century Literature* (Berkeley and Los Angeles: Univ. of California Press, 1972), p. 3. Fish's concept of an "anti-aesthetic" is particularly troublesome; for, if accepted and pursued, it spells the end not just of the artifact but of art. Marcuse provides the proper alternative perspective, observing that the abolition of aesthetics is, as a notion, "false and oppressive"; what the revolutionary artist—*what the prophet*—strives for is rather "Permanent aesthetic subversion" (see *Counter-Revolution and Revolt,* p. 107).

[79] Abraham Heschel, *The Prophets: An Introduction* (1962; rpt. New York: Harper and Row, 1969), p. xiii.

[80] See the anonymous commentary, *Prophetic Conjectures on the French Revolution,* pp. 39–40; and cf. Richard Brothers, *Wonderful Prophecies, Being a Dissertation on the Existence, Nature, and Extent of the Prophetic Powers in the Human Mind,* 6th ed. (London: n. p., 1795), p. 4. Bengel comments somewhat differently: "the Revelation . . . is yet so contrived that the other Prophets are *not* necessary for the understanding of it; but it is rather necessary for the understanding of them. This very regularly dispersed System brings it's key along with it" (*Bengelius's Introduction,* p. 65; my italics).

[81] Dent, *The Ruine of Rome,* p. 201; see also Gifford, *Sermons upon the Whole Booke,* pp. 157, 166, 217.

[82] See Diodati, *Pious Annotations,* p. 98, and Newton, *Dissertations on the Prophecies,* 3:200–01.

[83] Clayton, *A Dissertation on Prophecy,* p. 35. For further discussion of Virgil's prophetic method, see Lowth, *Lectures on the Sacred Poetry of the Hebrews,* p. 125, and Fletcher, *The Prophetic Moment,* p. 76.

[84] "Fragments from a Treatise on Revelation," in Manuel's *The Religion of Isaac Newton,* p. 120.

[85] *Self-Consuming Artifacts,* pp. 13, 14.

[86] I am quoting from Reeves, *The Influence of Prophecy in the Later Middle Ages,* p. 135, but see also Tasso's comments on poets and legislators in his *Discourses on the Heroic Poem,* p. 37. Octavio Paz comments pertinently when he describes poetry as a "movement that engenders movement," as an "action that transmutes the material world. Animated by the same energy that moves history, it is prophecy and the actual consumation, in real life, of that prophecy" (*The Bow and the Lyre,* p. 236).

[87] The fact that Arthur, taking the keys, descends into hell is significant

(I.viii.34–40): this detail relates him to the Angel of the Bottomless Pit, who, because he extirpates error and releases others from it, is said to become one with the Mighty Angel (see Revelation 9:1, and cf. 1:18 and 20:1). Having completed his descent, then, and having delivered Redcrosse "from bands," Arthur is now in relation to Redcrosse like Christ in relation to John: however the roles of Arthur and Redcrosse are quickly reversed, Redcrosse giving a book to Arthur just as Christ gives one to John—a book "writ with gold letters . . . / A worke of wondrous grace, and able souls to save" (I.ix.19; cf. Revelation 10:8–10). The importance Spenser assigns to *books* is underscored by the reference in the next canto to "A booke . . . sealed . . . / Wherein dark things were writ, hard to be understood" (the reference here is to the Book of Revelation, to the passage proclaiming that "I saw in the right hand of him . . . a book . . . sealed . . . and no man . . . was able to open the book, . . . to read the book" [5:1–4]). Those dark things in both Spenser's poem and John's Apocalypse relate to "God . . . grace . . . justice . . . free will" (I.x.13, 19; I.x.1, 60–62); in both works, those dark things convey the theme of spiritual warfare (the great subject of John's Apocalypse). *Books* also figure prominently in Book II of *The Faerie Queene*, where it is said that "records from auncient times" are preserved, "Some . . . in books, some in long parchment scrolles" (ix.57). That is, as in the Bible, some history is chronicled and some is set down prophetically, in scrolls. Here, in Spenser's poem and in the Bible, there are two kinds of books, historical ones and prophetic ones: both are concerned with history—the first with history recounted in a straight-forward fashion, the second with history mythologized. This same sort of distinction between books is drawn by Spenser in his epigraph to Canto x: one book is "A *chronicle* of British Kings," the other (read by Guyon) is *"rolles* of Elfin Emperours" (my italics); the chronicle details the history of the world, and the scrolls deal with history mythologized, with the spiritual history of man in the world.

[88] See Stanley Fish, *Surprised by Sin: The Reader in Paradise Lost* (London and Melbourne: Macmillan, and New York: St. Martin's Press, 1967); and compare his "modern" conception with that advanced by Hartlib *et al.*, *The Revelation Reveled*, p. 135. For other expressions of the idea, see Broughton, *A Revelation of the Holy Apocalyps*, p. 144; Bernard, *A Key of Knowledge*, pp. 25, 80; John Melton, *Astrologaster; or, the Figure-Caster* (London: Printed for Edward Blackmore, 1620), sig. A2; Henry Burton, *The Seven Vials or a Briefe and Plaine Exposition upon the 15: and 16: Chapters of the Revelation* (London: William Jones, 1628), unpaginated dedicatory epistle; Bayley, *The Shepheard's Starre*, p. 2; David Pareus, *A Commentary upon the Divine Revelation of the Apostle and Evangelist John*, tr. Elias Arnold (Amsterdam: C. P., 1644), preface p. 20, commentary, p. 99 (Pareus' commentary was first published in 1618 and was probably read by Milton in *Operum Theologicorum* [Frankfurt, 1628]); Isaac Newton, "Fragments from a Treatise on Revelation," in Manuel's *The Religion of Isaac Newton*, pp. 107, 123, 124; Thomas Newton, *Dissertations on the Prophecies*, 3:438;

and Lowth, *Lectures on the Sacred Poetry of the Hebre*ws, p. 339. This idea of literature as mental exercise is, of course, traceable to St. Augustine (see fn. 9 above); and, related to Milton by Stanley Fish, it has also been applied to Spenser by Paul J. Alpers, *The Poetry of The Faerie Queene* (Princeton Univ. Press: Princeton, 1967).

[89] See the propositions advanced by Waldock in *Paradise Lost and Its Critics* (1947; rpt. Cambridge: University Press, 1966) and then Fish's subversion of them in *Surprised by Sin.*

[90] *Apocalypsis Apocalypseos; or the Revelation of St. John the Divine Unveiled* (London: Printed for J. Martin and William Kettilby, 1680), pp. 332–33.

[91] See Brocard, *The Reveled Revelation,* sig. B2; Bullinger, *A Hundred Sermons,* p. 16ᵛ; and Burton, *The Seven Vials,* p. 11; and also see Cowper, who describes the Book of Revelation as a "most comely order" whose parts possess proportion and correspondence so as to answer one to another (*Pathmos,* unpaginated dedicatory epistle).

[92] Albert J. LaValley, *Carlyle and the Idea of the Modern: Studies in Carlyle's Prophetic Literature and Its Relation to Blake, Nietzsche, Marx, and Others* (New Haven: Yale Univ. Press, 1968), p. 186.

[93] For Fulke's structural analysis, see *Prælections upon the Sacred and Holy Revelation of S. John,* trans. George Gifford (London: Thomas Purfoote, 1573); and for Bullinger's, see *A Hundred Sermons.* For other rhetorical analyses of Revelation's structure, see fn. 95 below. And for the extent to which these Renaissance understandings of Revelation's structure are indebted to medieval thinking, see Nolan, *The Gothic Visionary Perspective,* pp. 3–34.

[94] *A Hundred Sermons,* pp. 6, 15ᵛ.

[95] For Brightman's observations, see *The Revelation of S. John,* sigs. A4, A6, pp. 264, 267, 310. George Gifford had already analyzed the "particular prophecy" in similar fashion: there are, he says, seven epistles, each of those epistles possessing three parts—an exordium, a narration, and a peroration (see *Sermons upon the Whole Booke,* p. 39). And for Bernard's comments, see *A Key of Knowledge,* pp. 4, 113, 130. Cowper provides a handy summary of the various structural analyses of the Apocalypse (see *Pathmos,* pp. 14–29). For a modern discussion of the Book of Revelation as "the most exquisitely and artistically constructed of all the apocalypses," along with a summary of different structural analyses, see J. Massyngberde Ford, *The Anchor Bible: Revelation,* esp. pp. 46–50.

[96] *Shakespeare's Living Art,* p. 244, also pp. 252, 262.

[97] Paz, *The Bow and the Lyre,* p. 184.

[98] *The Religion of Isaac Newton,* pp. 90–91.

[99] See both E. F. Siegman, "Book of Apocalypse," in *New Catholic Encyclopedia,* ed. William J. McDonald *et al.* (16 vols.; New York: McGraw-Hill, 1967–74), 1:658, and Isaac Newton, "Fragments from a Treatise on Revelation," in Manuel's *The Religion of Isaac Newton,* p. 121. George Stanley Faber, for example, singled out Mede as the "great father of apocalyptic interpretation" (*The Sacred Calendar of Prophecy,* pp. xii–xiii).

[100] *The Key of the Revelation,* unpaginated translator's note and pt. I, 1–2, 12–13, 16, 29, 122; and cf. Smith, "Of Prophecy," in *A Collection of Theological Tracts,* ed. Watson, 4:319, 328. For further comment by Mede on "the Order and connection" of these visions and on the "knitting and jointing" in the eleventh chapter of John's prophecy, see *Remaines on Some Passages,* esp. pp. 3, 11. If Mede calls attention to the eleventh chapter of the Apocalypse, John Alsted emphasizes the twentieth chapter as "the summe of all the foregoing visions, and a succinct and brief iteration of the whole prophesie" (*The Beloved City or, the Saints Reign on Earth a Thousand Yeares* [London: n. p., 1643], p. 74). Like Mede, Paul Grebnar refers to the Book of Revelation as "an intricate labyrinth" (*Europe's Wonder: Or, the Turks Overthrow* [Hague: Printed by John Owen, 1661], sig. A1ᵛ and p. 2). This labyrinthine design of prophecy, often reflected in "imagery of infolding and unfolding," implies a state of vision (see Snare, "The Poetics of Vision," in *Renaissance Papers,* eds. Donovan and Deneef, p. 1). The best discussion of labyrinthine design in Milton's poetry appears in Donald F. Bouchard's *Milton: A Structural Reading* (Montreal: McGill-Queen's Univ. Press, 1974), pp. 4, 118–19; but Angus Fletcher's *The Prophetic Moment* and Donald Howard's *The Idea of The Canterbury Tales* (Berkeley and Los Angeles: Univ. of California Press, 1975) provide important historical and literary perspectives on labyrinthine design. Of course, Rudolph B. Gottfried, pointing out that the word "labyrinth" occurs only three times in the whole of *The Faerie Queene,* argues that all this is irrelevant to the poem—is simply "stamped on it" ("Spenser Recovered: The Poet and Historical Scholarship," in *Contemporary Thought on Edmund Spenser,* ed. Frushell and Vandersmith, p. 77). Gottfried might raise the same objection to applying this conception to Milton's poetry; for Milton, too, uses the word "labyrinth" only three times in all his poetry. And Donald Howard allows that Chaucer uses the word "labyrinth" only once and the word "maze" just twice (*The Idea of The Canterbury Tales,* p. 330). Yet Howard also offers the appropriate rejoinder: " 'models' are only comparisons—we are using them to try to grasp the nature of an art-form, to get the feel of an esthetic" (*ibid.,* p. 325). Furthermore, though it may be claimed, justly, that each of these poets uses the word labyrinth infrequently, it should also be allowed that each of them uses the word "wandering" with considerable frequency.

Like both Mede and Smith, Hezekial Holland keeps the idea of the Apocalypse as "a Theatre" in the forefront of his commentary (see *An Exposition or, a Short, but Full, Plaine, and Perfect Epitome of the Most Choice Commentaries upon the Revelation of Saint John* [London: Printed for George Calvert, 1650], esp. p. 31, and cf. Heschel, *The Prophets,* pp. 46, 48, 52). According to Mede and to the tradition he represents, then, the Apocalypse possesses a structure deliberately obscure, not one (as D. H. Lawrence would have it) that "the christian scribes smashed up" in order to make the prophecy "safe" (see *Apocalypse,* p. 136). That structure is designed to test the reader's perceptual faculties and, because it is within the prophecy, is meant to shape the reader's experience of it. In this regard, the prophetic paradigm I am here describing should be associated with Vinaver's romance-structure (he himself notes the correspondence; see *The Rise of Romance,* pp. 111, 116)—and should be distinguished sharply from Stanley Fish's version of affective criticism, most recently presented in "Interpreting the Variorum," *Critical Inquiry,* 2 (1976), 465–85. In this essay, Fish counters "the assumption that there *is* a sense, that it is embedded or encoded in the text, and that it can be taken in at a single glance" (p. 473). Here, there are really three assumptions, and the last does not necessarily follow the others. That is, in a text like the Book of Revelation there is a sense, encoded within the prophecy's structure, that is released only when its structure has been apprehended. Prophecy defies Fish's contention that "formal units . . . are not 'in' the text," that they are to be hazarded by readers (p. 478). So long as the reader of prophecy is committed to a proposition like Fish's, that the structure of the reader's experience rather than any structures available on the page should be the object of concern and description, what he reads will remain sealed to him, though the reader of prophecy must of course remember that its outer structure remains an obstacle to him and to his apprehension of inner form.

[101] *The Key of the Revelation,* pt. I, pp. 30–68, 92, 98.

[102] *The Exposition of the Revelation,* 3:1, 7, 17, 18, 30, 207, 209.

[103] MacCaffrey, *Spenser's Allegory,* pp. 6–7.

[104] Pareus, *A Commentary upon the Divine Revelation,* preface, pp. 20, 26.

[105] *An Exposition of the Seven Epistles,* p. 179.

[106] *A Commentary upon the Divine Revelation,* preface, pp. 19–20. See also Holland, who contends that "though the Revelation may seeme to be one continued Vision, . . . it is not one . . . but seven" (*An Exposition,* unpaginated epistle).

[107] Beverley, *The Prophetical History of the Reformation,* p. 20.

[108] *The Idea of The Canterbury Tales,* p. 194.

[109] Jerald Zaslove, "Fiction Extended: The Genre of Apocalypse and Dead Ends," *Genre,* 3 (1970), 19–20.

[110] *Lectures on the Sacred Poetry of the Hebrews,* pp. 240, 280, 433.

[111] *Ibid.,* pp. 15, 64, 240, 274, 289, 412, 474.

[112] See the anonymous commentary, *Prophetic Conjectures on the French Revolution,* pp. 4, 39–40; Newton, *Dissertations on the Prophecies,* 3:3, 8; the anonymous commentary, *A Key to the Mystery of the Revelation,* pp. ii, 96, 209, 305; and see also King, *A Supplement to the Remarks on the Signs of the Times,* sig. A2. Norman Cohn devotes an entire book to the exploration of Revelation's radicalism, describing John's Apocalypse as a "world-shattering, world-transforming drama" (*The Pursuit of the Millennium: Revolutionary Millenarians and Mystical Anarchists of the Middle Ages,* rev. ed. [New York: Oxford Univ. Press, 1970], p. 136). Christopher Hill's *Antichrist in Seventeenth-Century England* (London: Oxford Univ. Press, 1971) is also pertinent here; and see by the same author, *The World Turned Upside Down: Radical Ideas During the English Revolution* (New York: Viking Press, 1972), esp. pp. 76, 259.

[113] Bengel, *Bengelius's Introduction,* pp. 104, 111, 115, 234.

[114] See Winthrop, *An Attempt to Translate the Prophetic Part of the Apocalypse,* pp. 4, 5, and Bicheno, *The Signs of the Times,* p. 10. See also Newton, *Dissertations on the Prophecies,* 3:201–02; and for an opposing view, see Moses Lowman who, believing that Revelation's seven prophecies are part of a "natural order" and thus "successive to each other," dismisses the idea of synchronism (*A Paraphrase and Notes on the Revelation of St. John,* 4th ed. [London: Printed for W. Baynes, 1807], pp. xx).

[115] Langdon, *Observations on the Revelation,* pp. 28–29, 85. Just as epic, in the seventeenth century, was likened to a five-act drama, prophecy, in Lowman's commentary, is viewed as a play in five parts (see *A Paraphrase and Notes on the Revelation of St. John,* p. ix). Shaffer would have us believe that, making "a radical break with the past," the Romantic poets create prophecy as one of their "new forms." The summary she provides of Johann Gottfried Eichhorn's *Commentarius in Apocalypsin Joannis* (1791) is useful; but her conclusion, that the Romantic understanding of prophecy is a German invention, is misguided; and her imputation of newness to such terms as "the celestial theatre," "the visionary theatre," "a dramatic poem," and a "grand prophetic drama" (the last phrase is Coleridge's) is simply mistaken (see *Kubla Khan and the Fall of Jerusalem,* pp. 12, 17, 98, 292–95). Milton, of course, subtitles *Samson Agonistes* "A Dramatic Poem" and, in his Preface to that play, recalls the Book of Revelation as a model for high and stately tragedy. Prophecy is Milton's gift to the Romantic poets, not, as Shaffer argues, the Germans' gift to them; and as M. H. Abrams shows, the tradition of prophecy comes to the Romantics out of a radical English tradition (see *Natural Supernaturalism,* esp. pp. 19–70).

[116] Thomas Sherlock, *The Use and Intent of Prophecy, in the Several Ages of the World* (London: Printed for John Whiston, 1740), pp. 78, 100.

[117] *The Sacred Calendar of Prophecy,* p. 351, and also by Faber, *A General and Connected View of the Prophecies* (Boston: William Andrews, 1809), p. xi.

[118] Hartlib *et al., The Revelation Reveled,* sig. [4ᵛ].

[119] See Augustin Marlorat, *A Catholike Exposition upon the Revelation of Sainct John* (London: Printed by H. Binneman, 1574), p. 101ᵛ.

[120] See Winthrop, *An Attempt to Translate the Prophetic Part of the Apocalypse,* p. 35, and Bullinger, *A Hundred Sermons,* p. 46. For discussion of Christ as most perfect hero (an idea that figures in Milton's poetry from *The Passion* to *Paradise Regained*), see Marlorat, *A Catholike Exposition,* pp. 11, 25; Richard Coppin, *Antichrist in Man Opposeth Emmannuel or God in Us* (London: Printed for Giles Calvert, 1649), p. 45; More, *An Explanation of the Grand Mystery,* pp. 411–12; and the anonymous commentary, *A Short Survey of the Kingdom of Christ Here on Earth with His Saints* (London: Printed by M. Fabian, 1699), p. 11.

[121] See the anonymous tract, *Strange and Remarkable Prophesies and Predictions of . . . James Usher* (1678), in *The Old Book Collector's Miscellany,* ed. Charles Hindley (London: Reeves and Turner, 1873), pp. 7–8.

[122] Bicheno, *The Signs of the Times,* sig. A3.

[123] Bray, *A Dissertation on the Sixth Vial* (Hartford: Hudson and Goodwin, 1780), p. 102.

[124] See the anonymous tract, *The Coppie of a Letter Sent from One of the Queenes Servants* (London: Printed for I. T., 1642), sig. A3.

[125] See epigraph for H. Niclas's *The Prophecy of the Spirit of Love* (n. p.: n.p., 1574).

[126] Edmund Chishull, *The Great Danger and Mistake of All New Uninspir'd Prophecies, Relating to the End of the World* (London: Printed by H. Hills, 1707), p. 12; see also Taylor, *The Political Prophecy in England,* pp. 105–06.

[127] See the anonymous tract, *Clavis Prophetica; or, a Key to the Prophecies of Mons. Marion* (London: Printed by J. Morphew, 1707), unpaginated preface.

[128] Goodwin, *The Exposition of the Revelation,* 3:186. On Revelation's iconography, see my book, *Angel of Apocalypse,* esp. pp. 262–68; and see also Gifford, *Sermons upon the Whole Booke,* p. 166; Guild, *The Sealed Book Opened,* p. 293; and Dent, *The Ruine of Rome,* p. 272.

[129] See Hartlib *et al., The Revelation Reveled,* p. 135. The revolutionary ideology, here associated with prophecy, is by Stanley Fish associated with his "self-consuming artifact." The reader of such artifacts, says Fish, is "forced to reexamine and discredit . . . assumptions" commonly held (see *Self-Consuming Artifacts,* p. 10). Fish's artist, like Heschel's prophet, is characterized by a deep distrust of both the reigning systems of value and the usual modes of perception; such an artist, in Heschel's words, is "an iconoclast, challenging the apparently holy, revered, and awesome. Beliefs cherished as certainties, institutions endowed with supreme sanctity, he exposes as scandalous pretensions"; he "challenge[s] the whole country: kings, priests, false prophets, and the entire nation" (see *The Prophets,* pp. 10, 14); the prophet, in other words, turns the world up side down in an act of seeming perversity, which is his way of ridding the world of its own perversities. This iconoclastic spirit is much in evidence in Milton's poetry and prose. Coincidently, in the same year that Milton's *Eikonoklastes* is published a contemporary of Milton observes that the breaking of icons—especially of the king's image—signals man's individual redemption and hence the deliverance of his nation (see the anonymous tract, *Strange and Wonderfull Prophesies* [London: Printed for Robert Ibbitson, 1649], p. 7). Also noteworthy is the fact that the prophetic Milton is portrayed as an iconoclast, a revolutionary, in plate 18 of Blake's *Milton* (see fig. 6).

[130] Sacvan Bercovitch, "Emerson the Prophet: Romanticism, Puritanism, and Auto-American-Biography," in *Emerson: Prophecy, Metamorphosis, and Influence,* ed. David Levin (New York: Columbia Univ. Press, 1975), p. 3.

[131] See both More, *An Exposition of the Seven Epistles,* unpaginated preface, and Newton, *Dissertations on the Prophecies,* 3:439. Newton also observes that "prophecies are the only species of writing, which is designed more for the instruction of future ages than of the times wherein they are written" (3:438).

[132] As a commentator on the Book of Revelation, William Blake opposed himself to the mode of interpretation practiced in the sixteenth century by many Revelation commentators and set in the eighteenth century by Isaac Newton, a mode that reduced John's visionary drama to a rigid historical allegory. Blake thereby sets limits on the efficacy of the kind of interpretation that has been placed on his poetry by David V. Erdman in *Blake, Prophet Against Empire: A Poet's Interpretation of the History of His Own Times*, rev. ed. (Princeton: Princeton Univ. Press, 1969); *he sets limits,* I emphasize, but he does not wholly deny its utility. There is a message here for interpreters of Spenser and Milton. Blake returns us to the dictum, formulated by Hartlib *et al.* in *The Revelation Reveled: we must not read prophecies in a private,* that is, in a purely literal sense; "we must not analyze and interpret them so, as if the Prophecies thereof did relate onely to the particular occasions, and circumstances of times, of places, and of persons, in, by, and to whom, they were first uttered" (p. 22). Such a proposition establishes the limitations of any criticism which would divine only historical allegory in prophecy; and it inspires the distinction Blake draws between allegory and vision in *A Vision of the Last Judgment,* a distinction traceable to Revelation commentary like that of Henry Bullinger: "how great a difference there is between . . . Allegories, and visions," says Bullinger; "parables taken of earthly thinges, differ very much from heavenly visions," which lift up "mindes . . . to heavenly thinges"; allegory sets forth matters in a "deade picture," whereas vision sets matters forth in "a livyng & talkyng image" (*A Hundred Sermons,* sig. Biii and pp. 1–2). I do not deny that there is historical allegory in *The Faerie Queene,* but believe it is a mistake to think that at this level the allegory is as continuous as it is in Dante's poem. Milton moves as far away from systematized historical allegory in relation to Spenser as Spenser does in relation to Dante. The best discussion of history in relation to prophecy is provided by Marjorie Reeves, *The Influence of Prophecy in the Later Middle Ages.* E. König also comments importantly when he observes that prophecy runs parallel to history but then cautions that history is not the source of prophecy (see *Encyclopedia of Religion and Ethics,* ed. James Hastings [New York: Charles Scribner's Sons, and Edinburgh: T. and T. Clark, 1925], 10:391).

[133] Reeves, *The Influence of Prophecy in the Later Middle Ages,* p. 291.

[134] I mark this distinction with terms borrowed from Barthes, *Mythologies,* p. 149, and would underscore the prophet's mission with a passage from Christopher Caudwell's *Illusion and Reality: A Study of the Sources of Poetry.* The revolutionary artist's experience, says Caudwell, "is so opposed to the existing consciousness that it requires a wholesale change, a complete revision of existing categories"; it requires "constant revolution . . . constant sweeping away of venerable prejudices and opinions" (New York: International Publishers, 1967, pp. 57, 202). For my purposes, it is noteworthy that Caudwell directs considerable attention to revolutionary art in the Renaissance (see, esp., pp. 81, 202). Moreover, the conservative character I have here ascribed to epic is a commonplace of its criticism; see, e.g.,

E. M. W. Tillyard, *The English Epic and Its Background* (1954; rpt. New York: Oxford Univ. Press, 1966), pp. 444–46, and also by Tillyard, *The Epic Strain in the English Novel* (London: Chatto and Windus, 1958), esp. pp. 15–17; Robert M. Durling, *The Figure of the Poet in Renaissance Epic* (Cambridge, Mass.: Harvard Univ. Press, 1965); Murrin, *The Veil of Allegory,* esp. p. 209; and J. B. Broadbent, *Paradise Lost: Introduction* (Cambridge: University Press, 1972), p. 28.

[135] *A Rebirth of Images,* pp. 6, 313.

[136] Gombrich, *Norm and Form,* p. 76.

[137] Smith, "Of Prophecy," in *A Collection of Theological Tracts,* ed. Watson, 4:347.

[138] *Norm and Form,* p. 78. Spenser shows Milton what Milton, according to Leslie Brisman, shows the Romantics, "how the old footsteps point the way to open spaces rather than traumatic intimidation" (*Milton's Poetry of Choice and Its Romantic Heirs* [Ithaca: Cornell Univ. Press, 1973], p. 301). Moreover, Milton surely saw in *The Faerie Queene* what Harry Berger, Jr., has seen: a poem swinging on its axis from the form of Dante's *Commedia* (in Book I) toward the symbolic mode of *Paradise Lost* (in Book VI and the Mutabilitie Cantos); see "A Secret Discipline: *The Faerie Queene,* Book VI," in *Form and Convention in the Poetry of Edmund Spenser,* ed. William Nelson (New York and London: Columbia Univ. Press, 1961), p. 73. The first serious study of the Spenser-Milton relationship, Edwin Greenlaw's " 'A Better Teacher Than Aquinas'," *Studies in Philology,* 14 (1917), 196–217, remains the starting point for all other studies. As Greenlaw observes, "the relationship between Chaucer and Spenser is curiously analogous to that between Spenser and Milton in that it is . . . a relationship manifested in . . . [a] relationship of the spirit" (p. 197); it is, Greenlaw concludes, "a sense of something far more deeply interfused that caused Milton to recognize in Spenser his 'original' " (p. 217); and see Guillén, who suggests that "the surge of popularity of the model, the pattern, the genre" often is sustained "not singly but conjointly" (*Literature as System,* p. 143).

[139] I quote from the broadside, *A Vision, Which One Mr. Brayne . . . Had in September, 1647* (London: Printed for John Playford, 1649).

[140] Fletcher's views are advanced in a paper, "Standing, Waiting, and Travelling Light: Some Thoughts on the Context of Milton's Narrative," delivered in April, 1975, at the Princeton University symposium on Renaissance narrative and narrative theory; but see also *The Transcendental Masque,* pp. 135, 143.

[141] "Standing, Waiting, and Travelling Light" (Princeton lecture).

[142] Bloom's conception of likeness between Spenser and Milton is never made clear, though I presume that he would read Milton's theological individualism, which he acknowledges above, back into Spenser's poetry, thus ignoring Virgil Whitaker's conclusion (one accepted by Kathleen Williams) that Spenser is "a conservative Anglican." That conclusion seems to me, as it does to Williams, "clearly right" (see Whitaker, *The Religious Basis of Spenser's Thought* [Stanford: Stanford Univ. Press, 1950], p. 31, and Wil-

liams, *Spenser's Faerie Queene,* p. 27). For Bloom's view of the Spenser-Milton relationship, see *A Map of Misreading* (New York: Oxford Univ. Press, 1975), esp. pp. 125–27; and see, too, my rejoinder to Bloom's views in "Cartographies: Reading and Misreading Milton and the Romantics," *Milton and the Romantics,* 1 (1975), 1–3. For altogether different approaches to the Spenser-Milton relationship, see Patrick Cullen, *Infernal Triad: The Flesh, the World, and the Devil in Spenser and Milton* (Princeton: Princeton Univ. Press, 1974), and A. Kent Hieatt, *Chaucer, Spenser, Milton: Mythopoeic Continuities and Transformations* (Montreal: McGill-Queen's Univ. Press, 1975). These various studies, however disparate their premises and aims, agree on one point: "Source study in the usual sense is not involved,—it is this misconception of the problem that has so long led us astray"; rather, what is involved is "a sort of spiritual transmigration" (Greenlaw, "'A Better Teacher Than Aquinas'," p. 197).

[143] *A Dissertation on Prophecy,* p. 35.

[144] *Essays and Introductions* (New York: Macmillan, 1961), p. 369. Yeats' observation echoes Leigh Hunt's earlier claim, that Spenser's morals are those of his age, and that his aristocratic politics are being daily refuted. On Spenser's criticism of radical Protestantism, see Cullen, *Infernal Triad,* p. 36.

[145] Quoted by Kerrigan in *The Prophetic Milton,* p. 57.

[146] *A Plaine Discovery of the Whole Revelation,* sig. A2. For other commentators who would defuse the Book of Revelation (and prophecy generally) of its political radicalism, see William Lilly's two books: *A Collection of Ancient and Moderne Prophesies* (London: Printed for John Partridge and Humphrey Blunden, 1645), esp. pp. 26, 39, and *Englands Propheticall Merline, Foretelling to All Nations of Europe until 1663* (London: Printed for John Partridge, 1644), sig. [A4ᵛ]. And see also the anonymous commentary, *Catastrophe Mundi,* sigs. A2–A2ᵛ; and Lowman, *A Paraphrase and Notes,* pp. xxff.

[147] Gifford, *Sermons upon the Whole Booke,* sig. A3 and p. 339.

[148] *Ibid.,* p. 39. See also Symonds who, in his dedicatory epistle, praises the Queen and who, in his formal commentary, describes her as "the mirrour of true Christian nobilitie and chevalrie" (*Pisgah Evangelica,* p. 260).

[149] *A Discursive Probleme Concerning Prophesies* (London: John Jackson, 1588), pp. 2, 58, 62.

[150] John Cotton, *An Exposition upon the Thirteenth Chapter of the Revelation* (London: Printed for Livewel Chapman, 1655), p. 101.

[151] Bullinger, *A Hundred Sermons,* pp. 277–79.

[152] Josephine Waters Bennett notes that "the part played by Christ in the Revelation has been divided between Arthur and Redcrosse, Arthur functioning as 'heavenly grace' and Redcrosse performing the human mission of the Savior" (*The Evolution of The Faerie Queene,* p. 113). This division between the two characters is, of course, marked by Spenser's association of Arthur with the great victory of the Apocalypse; thus, through knight and prince respectively, Spenser figures the first and second resurrections. Yet, having noted these separations of character by roles assigned to each, we

should also observe that Redcrosse and Arthur, like so many other characters in *The Faerie Queene,* merge into one another, to become one character as it were. This impression of melding is created throughout *The Faerie Queene* by a complicated system of typology in which first this character, then another, is identified with the Christ of the Apocalypse. Moreover, the fact that all the dragon combats are related to the first resurrection (see Revelation 20:5) turns Spenser's vision back into this world. These various combats may pave the way for the establishment of the New Jerusalem. It may be Spenser's final goal and his reader's ultimate destination, but its establishment is also dependent upon man's awakening in this world to a new spiritual life. Such is the concern of Spenser's poetry, and later of Milton's and Blake's, of Wordsworth's and Shelley's. See n. 87 above.

[153] *Ibid.,* p. 110.

[154] See *ibid.,* esp. pp. 108–16; Hankins, "Spenser and the Revelation of St. John," in *Essential Articles for the Study of Edmund Spenser,* ed. A. C. Hamilton (Hamden, Conn.: Archon Books, 1972), pp. 40–57; and More, *An Explanation of the Grand Mystery,* pp. 169–70 (More cites *The Faerie Queene* I.vi.12–19). In the eighteenth century, of course, Thomas Warton, following More, observed that Book I of *The Faerie Queene* is "perpetually interwoven with the mysteries contained in the BOOK of REVELATIONS" (*Observations on the Fairy Queen of Spenser,* 2nd ed. [2 vols.; London: Printed for R. and J. Dodsley, 1762], 2:98).

[155] I quote from Hankins, "Spenser and the Revelation of St. John," in *Essential Articles for the Study of Edmund Spenser,* p. 41, who follows Bennett, *The Evolution of The Faerie Queene,* p. 109, in circumscribing Spenser's debt to the Apocalypse to "the last half" and in limiting his discussion of that debt to Book I. Setting those boundaries on their respective discussions, neither critic perceives the analogy between the Angel of the Bottomless Pit and Arthur in his descent into Orgoglio's dungeon; nor is either critic aware of the correspondences between the aesthetic of John's Apocalypse and the one governing Spenser's poem (Bennett, for example, accounts for Arthur's descent and Spenser's narrative technique by turning from John as model to Virgil as model; see pp. 115, 116). For a critic who does find echoes of the Book of Revelation in *The Faerie Queene* I.vii, see Heninger, "The Orgoglio Episode in *The Faerie Queene,*" in *Essential Articles for the Study of Edmund Spenser,* pp. 125–38; and see, too, the remarks by Kermode who, describing Book I of *The Faerie Queene* as "a Tudor Apocalypse," notes both the profusion of references to Revelation in Spenser's text and the profoundly apocalyptic and protestant nature of Spenser's poem (*Shakespeare, Spenser, Donne,* pp. 14, 40, 49). Kermode's interest here, as he explains, is with structural resemblances, not minor allusions (p. 15). In *Natural Supernaturalism,* Abrams also remarks on the indebtedness of *The Faerie Queene* to the Book of Revelation (p. 49). Not only is the argument that Spenser's interest is restricted to the last half of the Apocalypse untenable, but so too is the proposition that, unlike Book I, Book II contains no significant reference either to the Apocalypse or, for that matter, to the Bible

as a whole. On the contrary, Una of Book I and Gloriana of Book II are yoked together through the same allusion to the Book of Revelation (2:28, 22:16). Una appears "as bright as doth the morning starre . . . / with flaming lockes bedight, / To tell that dawning day is drawing neare" (I.xii.21; the morning star of course is Christ, the Mighty Angel of the Apocalypse, and here, as in both the books of Daniel and of Revelation, it symbolizes man's resurrection into a new life [see Bullinger, *A Hundred Sermons*, p. 47^v]). The same equation, made through simile, occurs in Book II, where Gloriana, "the mighty Queene of *Faerie*," is, like the Mighty Angel, "the flowre of . . . chastitie," and like him too in that her "glory shineth as the morning starre" and her "mercies" reach far, through all the world (xi.4; cf. Revelation 1:16). In this same canto, moreover, Alma is garbed in white, like the heroes of the Apocalypse who stand before the throne of God (18–19; cf. Revelation 3:4–5, 6:11, 7:9, 13, 15:6, 19:4); and in the corresponding canto of Book I, the phrase, "they knockt" (x.5), recalls the verse from the Apocalypse, "I stand at the door, and knock" (3:20), along with its various implications—especially the entry of Christ into man's heart and man's subsequent resurrection and triumph in this life. It may be that Spenser's borrowings from the Apocalypse are not so conspicuous or so various in Book II; nevertheless, the themes of Book II— divine providence, the unmasking of evil, spiritual versus carnal warfare, and fainting / falling-awakening / rising—all, in their separate developments, owe a substantial debt to John's Apocalypse. Furthermore, as successive but interrelated books that mutually illuminate one another, Books I and II both mirror the design and marshal the strategies of John's prophecy.

[156] I quote from Røstvig, "Structure as Prophecy," in *Silent Poetry*, p. 164. Such a view, of course, stands behind the elaborate structural analyses of Mede and More (see figs. 2 and 3), both commentators insisting that the apprehension of structure provides the basis for interpreting visionary work. Very early, Isaac Newton adopted the same view: "consider . . . the designe of the Apocalypse" ("Fragments from a Treatise on Revelation," in Manuel's *The Religion of Isaac Newton*, p. 111). All these commentators, as Manuel observes, "would have been at home with modern structuralists"; and like Newton, they felt that "To decipher . . . prophecy, the structure had to be re-created with meticulous accuracy, its ground-plan and equipment laid out, because every detail was a prefiguration" (*ibid.*, p. 92). For literature, Heninger makes the same point in *Touches of Sweet Harmony:* "In such a poetics . . . the form of a poem is its essence. Its structure is the core of its meaning" (p. 296). Heninger does not specifically associate this aesthetic with prophecy, but prophecy is one of its sources and its finest example.

[157] For the distinction, see Bicheno, *The Signs of the Times*, p. 73; but see also Bernard, *A Key of Knowledge*, pp. 95–96, and More, *Apocalypsis Apocalypseos*, p. 333.

[158] I borrow this descriptive phrase from S. K. Heninger's headnote to the Mutabilitie cantos in *Selections from the Poetical Works of Edmund*

Spenser, ed. Heninger (Boston: Houghton Mifflin, 1970), p. 787. Of these cantos, Heninger says that they are an independent poem, fully developed and autonomous (p. 786).

[159] *Samson Agonistes* is a particularly interesting example here. Usually the respondent is delivered a purely visionary experience which he alone must interpret; but in *Samson,* almost perversely, Milton substitutes for the very reliable narrator-commentator of his epics a notoriously unreliable chorus that at every turn misinterprets the action to which it is a witness. In this final poem, the reader is doubly taxed, both by the complications of the drama itself and by the distorted interpretations of it devised by the Chorus. Here, the technique of reader harassment is taken even further than it had been in Milton's epics.

[160] At this point in either book, one cannot, of course, speak unreservedly about either Redcrosse's or Guyon's victory: both heroes are saved by the agency of grace, yet neither is in any ordinary sense victorious. Guyon's fainting, for example, attests to this last point. In *Sermons upon the Whole Booke,* Gifford writes that true Christians do not faint: ". . . faint not: thou art one of those which get the victory in the great battaile, even over the dragon, and over his angels." Gifford's point is that we overcome not by our own strength but "by the bloud of the Lambe"—that is, by grace from which we should never be separated because, if we are, we will faint (p. 234). Similarly, William Perkins (like Spenser throughout Book I) associates fainting with the temptation process, explaining that to faint is to succumb: "The fall is, whereby the souldier through infirmitie fainteth, being subdued by the power of the enemie" (*A Golden Chain,* in *The Works of Perkins* [London: Printed by John Legate, 1608–09], I, 87). Guyon's frailty here and, later, his intemperance in destroying the Bower of Bliss suggest that Spenser, in Books I and II, is exploring the Christian paradox that while the humble are exalted (Book I) the exalted are humbled (Book II). I do not find compelling the argument that Guyon's action here is like Christ's outburst in *Paradise Regained:* Guyon uses physical might, while Christ displays the power of the Word. Guyon is rather one with Samson; and both "heroes" stand self-condemned.

[161] "Eterne in Mutabilitie: The Unified World of *The Faerie Queene,*" in *Critical Essays on Spenser from ELH* (Baltimore and London: Johns Hopkins Press, 1970), p. 59. See also Heninger, *Touches of Sweet Harmony,* pp. 351–57, 372–77, 390–93. But for an opposing view, see A. C. Hamilton who, while denying this kind of structure to *The Faerie Queene,* attributes it to *Piers Plowman.* For all the similarities between these two poems, which have their common source in the Bible, they remain structurally different, says Hamilton: Spenser's poem is "clearly rhetorical . . . radically rhetorical" in contrast to Langland's cumulative structure, which Hamilton describes as a "slow gathering of significance . . . suddenly precipitat[ing] into the clarity of vision" ("The Visions of *Piers Plowman* and *The Faerie Queene,*" in *Form and Convention in the Poetry of Edmund Spenser,* pp. 20–21). In this regard, it is noteworthy that the Book of Revelation was discussed as both a visionary and a rhetorical structure; and Spenser would doubtless have

realized that a poem modelled after Revelation should possess both kinds of structure. Nevertheless, I follow Williams and Heninger in emphasizing the visionary design of *The Faerie Queene* and thus would observe similarity between Spenser's poem and Langland's where Hamilton sees only difference. His description of the structure of *Piers Plowman* is, of course, like that provided by Williams and Heninger for *The Faerie Queene* and like that offered by Renaissance commentators for the Apocalypse.

More recently, Austin Farrer has attributed the same cumulative pattern to the Apocalypse and, so doing, has gathered into focus a related feature of Revelation's design: "The Apocalypse wears the superficial likeness of a prophetic narrative, the description of an order of events about to be enrolled. We look more closely, and find it almost impossible to make sense of the continuous story as it stands"; instead, says Farrer, we begin to comprehend John's prophecy when we come to realize that each of its sections "mirrors in little the form of the whole," that each is "a small-scale Apocalypse in its own account" (*A Rebirth of Images*, pp. 185, 299). Both *The Faerie Queene* and *Paradise Lost* have been described in virtually the same way. *The Faerie Queene* is an epic, according to Graham Hough, containing within itself the "miniature epic" of Book I; or, as Hough's title to his last chapter suggests, Spenser's poem embodies "the whole in the part"; that is, each book is, as it were, an epic within a larger epic (see *A Preface to The Faerie Queene* [New York: Norton, 1963], pp. 84, 223). Similarly, according to Northrop Frye, the last two books of *Paradise Lost* are a brief epic within the diffuse epic or, more exactly, a small prophecy within a larger one (*Anatomy of Criticism: Four Essays* [Princeton: Princeton Univ. Press, 1957], p. 324). Thus a principal characteristic of the epic-prophecy (especially of these poetic examples of it) is what Joan Webber calls "the incipient existence of everything in everything else" (*Milton and the Western Tradition of Literary Epic*, forthcoming). And the best epitome of this characteristic is provided by Milton himself—in his phrase from *Paradise Lost*, "Cycle and Epicycle, Orb in Orb" (VIII.84). That phrase is also an accurate poetic description of two diagrams (figs. 2 and 3). Models for epic-in-epic, prophecy-in-prophecy, were available to Renaissance authors, of course, both through Virgil's *Aeneid* and the Bible. By collapsing the patterns of the *Iliad* and the *Odyssey* into his poem, Virgil in effect embraces two epics within his own poem—one of wayfaring (Books I–VI) and one of warfaring (Books VII–XII). By turning each of his books into an epic, Spenser outdoes his Virgilian model, and lays claim to doing so, one might add, by presenting each of his books in *twelve* cantos. The more precise analogy for Spenser's achievement, however, is provided by the Bible: within this panoramic epic are the not-so-brief epic of the Pentateuch and the much briefer epics of both the Book of Job and the Book of Revelation, as well as the miniature epic of St. Paul's Epistle to the Hebrews. During the Renaissance, as Lewalski observes, writers became increasingly conscious of the poetic dimension of scripture, and some "consciously proposed the Bible to themselves as literary model" (*Donne's Anniversaries*, p. 147).

[162] Langdon, *Observations on the Revelation*, p. 126. Spenserians have

generally recognized synchronization in *The Faerie Queene* but usually have not identified it with the aesthetic of prophecy. Rosalie L. Colie, for example, suggests that "every single thing [is] referred finally to *one* thing, *one* form, *one* idea, and *one* Being" (*Paradoxia Epidemica: The Renaissance Tradition of Paradox* [Princeton: Princeton Univ. Press, 1966], p. 352; cf. Donald Cheney, "Plowman and Knight: The Hero's Dual Identity," in *Spenser: A Collection of Critical Essays,* ed. Harry Berger, Jr. [Englewood Cliffs, N. J.: Prentice-Hall, 1968], p. 64). Similarly, Joanne Field Holland notes that the effect of such convergences in *The Faerie Queene* is to reduce time to a moment; making everything happen at once, she says, Spenser creates the sense of cyclical reenactment ("The Cantos of Mutabilitie and the Form of *The Faerie Queene,"* in *Critical Essays on Spenser from ELH,* pp. 253–55).

[163] More, *A Plaine and Continued Exposition of the Several Prophecies or Divine Visions of the Prophet Daniel* (London: Printed for Walter Kettilby, 1681), p. 269.

[164] *Spenser's Faerie Queene,* pp. xii–xiii, xviii, xix.

[165] Nodding again, Dr. Johnson says of Milton's *L'Allegro* and *Il Penseroso* that "No mirth can . . . be found in his melancholy; but I am afraid that I always meet some melancholy in his mirth!" (*Lives of the English Poets,* ed. George Birkbeck Hill [3 vols.; Oxford: Clarendon Press, 1905], 1:167). For the second part of Johnson's statement, the Orpheus myth provides corroboration (in *L'Allegro* Milton injects the tragic version of this myth). For the first part of his statement, "No mirth can . . . be found in his melancholy," the Orpheus myth also provides the rejoinder (in *Il Penseroso* Milton introduces the comedic version of the myth).

The alternative perspectives of *L'Allegro* and *Il Penseroso* provide one analogue to the later companion poems, *Paradise Regained* and *Samson Agonistes,* but so, too, do the alternative perspectives of *Lycidas,* where the Old Testament theology of the first two movements is replaced, in the vision of the marriage feast, by the Christocentric theology of the Apocalypse. Just as *Paradise Regained* and *Samson Agonistes* reverse the perspectives of Milton's twin lyrics, those poems also reverse the progression implied by the perspectives within *Lycidas.*

[166] As Leslie Brisman demonstrates—in *Milton's Poetry of Choice.* Milton's tactics, however, are more involved than Brisman allows. All Milton's poetry, from the Nativity Ode to *Paradise Lost,* mixes the genres; in these poems one may talk about the preeminence of one generic perspective over another (of prophecy over epic, for example), but one cannot deny the multiplying of perspectives, or ignore the pressure created by composite forms, without greatly distorting Milton's intention and achievement in these poems. The process of purification to chaster forms that Brisman sees in *Paradise Lost,* as well as in the poems preceding it, is more relevant to Milton's brief epic and tragedy (Ralph Condee brilliantly elucidates this process in *Paradise Regained,* in *Structure in Milton's Poetry: From the Foundation to the Pinnacle* [University Park: Pennsylvania State Univ. Press, 1974], the chapter entitled *"Paradise Regained* as the Transcendence over Epic,"

pp. 153–73; and through his Preface to *Samson Agonistes* Milton himself directs attention to that process in his dramatic poem). In *Paradise Lost* and before, Milton is deliberately complicating the matter of choice; in *Paradise Regained* and *Samson Agonistes* he sharply dichotomizes alternatives. Those final two poems, as Kerrigan observes, "complement each other almost as profoundly as 'L'Allegro' and 'Il Penseroso' " (*The Prophetic Milton*, p. 288).

[167] I am aware of Patrick Cullen's argument that pastoral is "a mode for the juxtaposition of contending values and perspectives" and that Spenser employs the genre in *The Shepheardes Calender* in order to create "a confrontation of conflicting perspectives." I am aware, too, that such an observation may be extended to *The Faerie Queene*. Yet in both poems, as Cullen says of the *Calender*, from such confrontation "emerges an ambivalence in which neither perspective can claim to the whole truth" (see *Spenser, Marvell, and Renaissance Pastoral* [Cambridge, Mass.: Harvard Univ. Press, 1970], pp. 1, 26, 31). Therein lies the essential difference between Spenser's poetry, and Milton's, Milton presenting time after time the "either-or" alternatives that Spenser avoids. In this regard, Spenser may be said to violate the prophetic tradition that Milton assiduously observes. The various perspectives on a common predicament, represented by Milton's last three poems, have analogues within the poems themselves: in *Paradise Lost,* Milton distinguishes infernal, heavenly, Edenic, and fallen perspectives; in *Paradise Regained,* Milton provides multiple perspectives on Christ's baptism; and in *Samson Agonistes,* Milton's perspectivism becomes more complicated still— some perspectives are developed within the tragedy, but one prominent perspective, that of New Testament Christianity, is located outside the poem, in Milton's audience, who brings to *Samson* the perspective of *Paradise Regained* and must judge the play, both its action and its hero, accordingly.

[168] Fulke, *Prælections,* unpaginated Preface.

[169] *Spenser's Allegory,* pp. 195, 205, 206.

[170] See Heschel, *The Prophets,* p. 160. It is to such a tradition of commentary that Spenser and Milton adhere, both rejecting (Milton, after the failure of the Puritan Revolution) the idea of Holy Wars and Crusades as a part of God's plan, both believing with Napier that such wars represent the way of Rome and of Antichrist (see *A Plaine Discovery of the Whole Revelation,* p. 195; and cf. Francis Ellington, *Christian Information Concerning These Last Times* [London: n. p., 1664], pp. 7–8). On the other hand, there are commentators, some Revelation commentators, who assume attitudes toward warfare which both poets would resist. Patrick Forbes, for instance, argues that God's justice "commeth forth, in bloudy warres" (*An Learned Commentarie upon the Revelation of Saint John* [Middelburg: Printed by Richard Schilders, 1614], p. 40); and, correspondingly, Gifford contends that the Book of Revelation "doth give both speciall instruction and direction, and also incouragement unto these warres," though he acknowledges, too (as Milton does in his Defenses), that while some must use the material sword to defend God's word, others who are the masters of truth employ the spiritual sword against Antichrist (*Sermons upon the Whole*

Booke, sigs. A3ᵛ; cf. Milton's *Sonnet XVI* and *Defensio Secunda,* in *Yale Milton,* 4:i, 552). In their epics, Spenser and Milton would clearly place themselves among those who extract from the Apocalypse the message that man must learn "to War no more" (Ellington, *Christian Information Concerning These Last Times,* p. 8; cf. Milton's *Sonnet XV,* 10–11) and against those who would say, "Gird on your swords . . . , and prepare for the bloody fray" (see the anonymous tract, *The Prophet of Prophets, or Wonderful Prophecies* [n. p.: n. p., 1791], p. 2).

[171] Allen Grossman, "Milton's Sonnet 'On the Late Massacre in Piedmont': A Note on the Vulnerability of Persons in a Revolutionary Situation," in *Literature in Revolution,* p. 299. I have been focusing on the contributions of Spenser and Milton to the Christian epic, but Tasso's contribution, as Judith Kates observes, deserves attention as well. Like Milton, Tasso assumes "a highly ambivalent relationship to the classical epic," says Kates; and thus "while imitating the conventional martial setting for heroic action, shifts the weight of emphasis to the interior conflicts of its grand, idealized figures." Kates concludes, therefore, that *Gerusalemme Liberata* provides a precedent for Milton's "radical critique of the conventional idea of the heroic," creating along with *Paradise Lost* "a new vision of what constitutes the heroic in human life" (see "The Revaluation of the Classical Heroic in Tasso and Milton," *Comparative Literature,* 26 [1974], 300–01, 302, 307–08, 317). For the major statement on Milton's reassessment of heroic ideals, see John M. Steadman, *Milton and the Renaissance Hero* (Oxford: Clarendon Press, 1967).

[172] *Piers Plowman,* ed. Goodridge, p. 53.

[173] See, e.g., Lewis Thomas, "Sermon IV," in *Seauen Sermons, or the Exercises of Seauen Sabbaths* (London: Printed for John Wright, 1615), no pagination. On spiritual warfare as a Revelation theme, see Napier, *A Plaine Discovery of the Whole Revelation,* p. 143; Gifford, *Sermons upon the Whole Booke,* p. 149; Dent, *The Ruine of Rome,* pp. 83, 183–84; Taylor, *Christs Victorie over the Dragon: or Satans Downfall* (London: Printed for R. Dawlman, 1633), pp. 89, 333–35, 338, 823; Pareus, *A Commentary upon the Divine Revelation,* p. 491; More, *Apocalypsis Apocalypseos,* pp. 119, 129. As John Mayer observes, "No man doth hold that this [battle in the Book of Revelation is] to bee understood according to the letter"—its scene is thus the church, the world, the human mind (see *Ecclesiastica Interpretatio,* p. 393). So Spenser understands and portrays the battle, and so too does Milton. On the interiority of this battle, see esp. Taylor, *Christs Victorie over the Dragon,* pp. 468, 599, 622; Richard Coppin, *The Exaltation of All Things in Christ, or of Christ in All Things* (London: Printed for Giles Calvert, 1649), pp. 35–36; Hartlib *et al., Revelation Reveled,* pp. 67, 69; More, *An Explanation of the Grand Mystery,* p. 390, and also by More, *Apocalypsis Apocalypseos,* pp. 66–69.

[174] Paz, *The Bow and the Lyre,* pp. 234–35.

[175] *Five Essays on Milton's Epics* (London: Routledge and Kegan Paul, 1965), pp. 95–98.

[176] See Shepherd's remarks in *The Interpreter's Dictionary of the Bible,* ed. Buttrick *et al.,* 3:918.

[177] *Spenser's Allegory,* p. 92.

[178] See Reeves, *The Influence of Prophecy in the Later Middle Ages,* and Cohn, *The Pursuit of the Millennium.* Also helpful is Patrick Collinson's discussion of prophecy in *The Elizabethan Puritan Movement* (Berkeley and Los Angeles: Univ. of California Press, 1967), pp. 168–90.

[179] *The Resources of Kind,* p. 116.

[180] "The Road of Excess," in *The Stubborn Structure,* p. 167.

[181] *Essays and Introductions,* p. 289.

[182] *Preludes to Vision: The Epic Adventure in Blake, Wordsworth, Keats, and Hart Crane* (Berkeley, Los Angeles, and London: Univ. of California Press, 1971), p. 6.

[183] The phrase is Colie's; see *The Resources of Kind,* p. 67.

[184] *Literature as System,* p. 147, also pp. 133, 155.

[185] Lowth, *Lectures on the Sacred Poetry of the Hebrews,* p. 355. Michael Lieb's discussion of Milton's philosophy of form emphasizes the poet's commitment to the perfection of form, while exploring the significance of that commitment in terms of a distinction drawn by Milton himself between external and internal form ("Milton and the Metaphysics of Form," *Studies in Philology,* 71 [1974], 214). Such a distinction, I am arguing, is involved in the different attitudes Milton assumes toward epic and prophecy.

[186] *Illusion and Reality,* p. 139; cf. Mao-Tse Tung, *On Literature and Art* (Peking: Foreign Languages Press, 1967), p. 30.

[187] "Milton's Brief Epic," p. 210.

Chapter II   [Page 80]

[1] "Introduction," *Ode on the Morning of Christ's Nativity* (San Francisco and New York: Paul Elder, 1907), p. i. So unequally are those elements mixed, from Herbert J. C. Grierson's point of view, that he denies *Comus* any "prophetic burden": Milton's masque, he says, is "didactic . . . , but not prophetic." In *Lycidas,* Grierson finds the same mixture of the poet and the critic of life that he discovers in what is for him Milton's most prophetic poem, *Samson Agonistes;* yet *Lycidas* itself, Grierson concludes, is not prophetic: it is but "a splendid experiment in a traditional form, the pastoral elegy" (*Milton and Wordsworth, Poets and Prophets: A Study of Their Reactions to Political Events* [London: Chatto and Windus, 1950], pp. 84, 91, 136).

[2] "Who Is Lycidas?", *Yale French Studies,* 47 (1972), 170–88. See also Joanne M. Riley, "Milton's 'Lycidas': New Light on the Title," *Notes and Queries,* N.S. 24 (1977), 545.

[3] John Alsted, *Templum Musicum,* tr. John Birchensha (London: Printed for Peter Dring, 1664), p. 78; and see also Isabel G. MacCaffrey, who suggests that the word *monody* offers a clue to the poem's meaning ("*Lycidas:*

The Poet in a Landscape," in *The Lyric and Dramatic Milton,* ed. Joseph H. Summers [New York: Columbia Univ. Press, 1965], p. 67), as does Gretchen Finney, *Musical Backgrounds for English Literature: 1500–1650* (New Brunswick, N. J.: Rutgers Univ. Press, 1962), pp. 218–19.

⁴ See both J. B. Leishman, *Milton's Minor Poems,* ed. Geoffrey Tillotson (Pittsburgh: Univ. of Pittsburgh Press, 1969), p. 269, and Morton W. Bloomfield (quoting Maimonides), *Piers Plowman as a Fourteenth-century Apocalypse* (New Brunswick, N. J.: Rutgers Univ. Press, 1962), p. 174. On Maimonides' idea of the prophet, see Harold Fisch, *Jerusalem and Albion: The Hebraic Factor in Seventeenth-Century Literature* (London: Routledge and Kegan Paul, 1964), p. 191, and also Menachem Marc Kellner, "Maimonides and Gersonides on Mosaic Prophecy," *Speculum,* 52 (1977), 62–79.

⁵ I borrow the phrase from Don Cameron Allen, *The Harmonious Vision: Studies in Milton's Poetry,* rev. ed. (Baltimore: Johns Hopkins Press, 1970), p. 4.

⁶ *Ibid.,* pp. 6, 7, 9.

⁷ *Milton: A Biography* (2 vols.; Oxford: Clarendon Press, 1968), 1:157.

⁸ Allen, *The Harmonious Vision,* p. 22.

⁹ See Stanley E. Fish, "What It's Like to Read *L'Allegro* and *Il Penseroso*," *Milton Studies,* 7 (1975), 94; Rosemond Tuve, "Theme, Pattern, and Imagery in *Lycidas,*" in *Milton's Lycidas: The Tradition and the Poem,* ed. C. A. Patrides (New York: Holt, Rinehart, and Winston, 1961), p. 167; and David Shelley Berkeley, *Inwrought with Figures Dim: A Reading of Milton's Lycidas* (The Hague and Paris: Mouton, 1974), pp. 81, 148. Though Michael Fixler argues that Milton "was not yet thinking prophetically" when he wrote *Lycidas* he nevertheless acknowledges that St. Peter's invective constitutes an apocalyptic moment in the poem (*Milton and the Kingdoms of God* [London: Faber and Faber, 1964], pp. 56, 61).

¹⁰ See both Mr. Scott's note in *The Poetical Works of John Milton,* ed. Henry John Todd, 3rd ed. (6 vols.; London: Printed for C. and J. Rivington, 1826), 5:57, and Smith's remarks, "Of Prophecy," in *A Collection of Theological Tracts,* ed. Richard Watson (6 vols.; London: J. Nichols, 1785), 4:362.

¹¹ *Oration on the Dignity of Man,* trans. Elizabeth Livermore Forbes (Lexington, Ky.: Anvil Press, 1953), pp. 4–5, 9, 19. As A. B. Van Os observes, birds are a common visionary symbol and as such, it would appear, are here employed by Milton, almost as a signature of vision (see *Religious Visions: The Development of the Eschatological Elements in Mediaeval English Religious Literature* [Amsterdam: J. J. Paris, 1932], p. 40). For a discussion of Milton's twin lyrics, which makes specific reference to Pico, see Michael Fixler, "The Orphic Technique of 'L'Allegro' and 'Il Penseroso',' *English Literary Renaissance,* 1 (1971), 165–77.

¹² A. E. Dyson, "The Interpretation of *Comus,*" *Essays and Studies,* ed. D. M. Low (London: John Murray, 1955), p. 95.

[13] Alice Parmelee, *A Guidebook to the Bible* (1948; rpt. New York: Harper and Row, 1965), pp. 40, 43.

[14] William Kerrigan, *The Prophetic Milton* (Charlottesville; Univ. Press of Virginia, 1974), p. 189.

[15] Christopher Hill, *Antichrist in Seventeenth-Century England* (New York and London: Oxford Univ. Press, 1971), p. 68.

[16] Frank Kermode, *Shakespeare, Spenser, Donne: Renaissance Essays* (London: Routledge and Kegan Paul, 1971), p. 40. See also Jason P. Rosenblatt, "The Mosaic Voice in *Paradise Lost*," *Milton Studies*, 7 (1975), 207–32. On Amos as the archetype of the shepherd-prophet, see Cornelia Steketee Hulst, *Homer and the Prophets* (Chicago and London: Open Court, 1925), pp. 74, 86. The Old Testament association of shepherds and poets is, of course, reinforced in the New Testament by Luke's reference to shepherds returning and then, through song, glorifying God (see J. F. Goodridge's note to his edition of *Piers Plowman* [Middlesex, Eng.: Penguin, 1959], p. 292).

[17] *Shakespeare, Spenser, Donne*, p. 40.

[18] *The Key of the Revelation*, trans. Richard More (London: Printed for Phil. Stephens, 1643), unpaginated preface.

[19] *The Romance and Prophecies of Thomas of Erceldoune*, ed. James A. H. Murray, Early English Text Society, 61 (London: N. Trübner, 1875), p. 63. There were editions of this prophecy in 1603 and 1615, and in it St. George is apostrophized as "my owne knight" and two knights receive visions both of the Queen of Heaven and of St. Michael (p. 49).

[20] *The Bow and the Lyre*, trans. Ruth L. C. Simms (1973; rpt. New York: McGraw-Hill, 1975), p. 273.

[21] George Gifford, *Sermons upon the Whole Booke of the Revelation* (London: Printed by Richard Field and Felix Kingston, 1599), p. 29.

[22] Charles W. Hieatt, "The Integrity of Pastoral: A Basis for Definition," *Genre*, 5 (1972), 24.

[23] I borrow the phrase from Rupert Taylor, *The Political Prophecy in England* (New York: Columbia Univ. Press, 1911), p. 3.

[24] John Alsted, *The Beloved City or, The Saints Reign on Earth a Thousand Yeares* (London: n. p., 1643), p. 4.

[25] Stewart A. Baker, "Milton's Uncouth Swain," *Milton Studies*, 3 (1971), 51; and in the same volume, see Donald M. Friedman, "*Lycidas*: The Swain's Paideia," p. 32. If John Spencer Hill sees in *Lycidas* no indication that Milton had come to think of himself as a mature poet and even argues, rather oddly, that until 1640 Milton would have regarded his poetic ambitions as quite compatible with his role as church defender, John T. Shawcross applies the corrective. Dating Milton's decision to become a poet in the early autumn of 1637 and describing *Lycidas* (which Shawcross would date in late November) as a farewell to the past and a heralding of the future, Shawcross proposes that not just isolated passages in *Lycidas,* but "the whole poem," may be read "as a metaphor of Milton's life, ambitions, and thought" (see Hill's "Poet-Priest: Vocational Tension in Milton's Early Development," *Milton*

Studies, 8 [1975], 41–69, and Shawcross's "Milton's Decision to Become a Poet," *Modern Language Quarterly,* 24 [1963], 23, 25, 29, 30). See also George W. Nitchie, "Milton and His Muses," *ELH,* 44 (1977), 75–84.

[26] "Literature as Context: Milton's *Lycidas,*" in *Milton's Lycidas,* ed. Patrides, p. 209.

[27] Harry A. Beers, *Milton's Tercentenary* (New Haven: Yale Univ. Press, 1910), p. 10.

[28] See Northrop Frye, "The Road of Excess," in *The Stubborn Structure: Essays on Criticism and Society* (Ithaca, N. Y.: Cornell Univ. Press, 1970), p. 170. On the importance of allusion and context in prophecy, see especially Richard Bernard who argues that, since "allusion will make plaine the truth, and cleere the interpretation from the obscurity," one must know inside out the works to which allusions are made (*A Key of Knowledge for the Opening of the Secret Mysteries of St. Johns Mysticall Revelation* [London: Felix Kyngston, 1617], pp. 136–40).

[29] See John M. Steadman, "The Epic as Pseudomorph: Methodology in Milton Studies," *Milton Studies,* 7 (1975), 5.

[30] E. F. Siegman, "Book of Apocalypse," in *New Catholic Encyclopedia,* ed. William J. McDonald *et al.* (16 vols.; New York: McGraw-Hill, 1967–74), 1:658. Observing that the Book of Revelation is "a contemplation on some of the most arresting Old Testament citations," J. Massyngberde Ford emphasizes that, full of allusion and citation, this Book has no real quotation—a feature which testifies to the fact that the prophetic spirit *creates* (*The Anchor Bible: Revelation* [Garden City, N. Y.: Doubleday, 1975], p. 27).

[31] *Prophecy, Viewed in Respect to Its Distinctive Nature, Its Special Function, and Proper Interpretation* (Edinburgh: T. and T. Clark, 1856), pp. 193–94.

[32] "Milton's Early Poems: A General Introduction," in *John Milton: Introduction,* ed. J. B. Broadbent (Cambridge: University Press, 1973), p. 284.

[33] Christopher Grose, *Milton's Epic Process: Paradise Lost and Its Miltonic Background* (New Haven: Yale Univ. Press, 1973), p. 108. For all the poems in this section of *Justa Edovardo King Naufrago,* see Appendix B.

[34] See Michael Lloyd, "Justa Edouardo King," *Notes and Queries,* N. S. 5 (1958), 432–34, and Leishman, *Milton's Minor Poems,* pp. 247–55. Lloyd is right to emphasize that *Lycidas* is responding chiefly to the poems in the English section of the volume; yet it should be noted that, because of its conventional appearance, *Lycidas* also looks most like the poems, Latin and Greek, in the first section of the volume. Generically, at least, *Lycidas* finds its only analogue in that section of the volume, where the last poem (in a position corresponding with that of *Lycidas*) is a pastoral elegy. But then *Lycidas* is not, finally, a conventional poem, pushing as it does beyond all these efforts at lamentation—beyond elegy, beyond even pastoral, into prophecy.

It has been proposed that "Lloyd hardly allows enough for what he recognizes as the inevitable and central themes of Christian elegists" (*A Variorum Commentary on the Poems of John Milton,* ed. A. S. P. Woodhouse and

Douglas Bush [6 vols.; London: Routledge and Kegan Paul, 1970], 2:ii, 547). A more ample and thus more persuasive discussion of *Justa Edovardo King Naufrago* is provided by Leishman, who notices that "rivalry may have been at work" here and who suggests that Milton probably "saw copies of some, or perhaps of all, of the other contributions," which "inspired him to go and do otherwise" (*Milton's Minor Poems*, pp. 249, 255). For discussions of the text and printing of *Lycidas*, see the two essays by John T. Shawcross: "Establishment of a Text of Milton's Poems through a Study of *Lycidas*," *The Papers of the Bibliographical Society of America*, 56 (1962), 317–31, and "Division of Labor in *Justa Edovardo King Naufrago*," *The Library Chronicle*, 27 (1961), 176–79.

[35] Lloyd, "Justa Edouardo King," p. 434.

[36] " 'To Shepherd's ear': The Form of Milton's *Lycidas*," in *Silent Poetry: Essays in Numerological Analysis,* ed. Alastair Fowler (New York: Barnes and Noble, 1970), p. 181.

[37] Austin Farrer, *A Rebirth of Images: The Making of St. John's Apocalypse* (1949; rpt. Boston: Beacon Press, 1963), p. 24 (my italics).

[38] I borrow the phrase from D. H. Lawrence's *Apocalypse* (Florence: G. Orioli, 1931), p. 213.

[39] Lloyd, "Justa Edouardo King," p. 433.

[40] See both Thomas Belsham, *A Summary View of the Evidence and Practical Importance of the Christian Revelation* (London: Printed by R. Taylor, 1807), p. 200, and George Puttenham, *The Arte of English Poesie,* ed. Edward Arber (1589; rpt. London: English Reprints, 1869), p. 62.

[41] Bartholomew Traheron, *An Exposition on the Fourth Chapter of St. Johns Revelation* (London: Printed for Edward Aggas, 1577), sig. Di.

[42] Hulst, *Homer and the Prophets,* p. 73.

[43] *The Transcendental Masque: An Essay on Milton's Comus* (Ithaca, N. Y.: Cornell Univ. Press, 1971), p. 7.

[44] Thomas Taylor, *Christs Victorie Over the Dragon: or Satans Downfall* (London: Printed for R. Dawlman, 1633), p. 652.

[45] By underplaying the narrative component of the conventional elegy, Milton avoids the trite hyberboles that appear in some of these poems. When he adds the epigraph to his poem for its 1645 printing, however, Milton indulges in his own hyperbole; for funeral songs called "Monodia," he surely knew, were used specifically for honoring kings and princes (see Puttenham, *The Arte of English Poesie,* p. 63). But of course the generic label is wittily apt: Milton is commemorating a "King" and in the process is honoring the King of Kings.

[46] See Thyer's note in *The Poetical Works of John Milton,* ed. Todd, 5:54.

[47] Leslie Brisman, *Milton's Poetry of Choice and Its Romantic Heirs* (Ithaca, N. Y.: Cornell Univ. Press, 1973), pp. 60, 218.

[48] See both Paz, *The Bow and the Lyre,* p. 249, and Kathleen M. Swaim, "Retributive Justice in *Lycidas:* The Two-Handed Engine," *Milton Studies,* 2 (1970), 121.

[49] Pico della Mirandola, *Oration on the Dignity of Man,* p. 11.

[50] *Poetry and Repression: Revisionism from Blake to Stevens* (New Haven: Yale Univ. Press, 1975), p. 3.

[51] Harold Bloom, *Kabbalah and Criticism* (New York: Seabury Press, 1975), p. 66.

[52] The concept is Harold Bloom's, *ibid.*, p. 68, which I here relate to *Lycidas*.

[53] *Lycidas*, ed. Oliver Elton (Oxford: Clarendon Press, 1893), p. 4.

[54] This conceit is analogous to the one employed by John Donne in his *Anniversary* poems, where an equation is made involving Elizabeth Drury, Queen Elizabeth, and the Queen of Heaven. The association of Edward King with Christ is best understood in terms of the tradition charted by Barbara K. Lewalski wherein persons are related to Christ or to other biblical personages "on the basis of Christian typology, a mode of historical symbolism whereby a real historical person or event figures forth, foreshadows, or recapitulates Christ" (see *Donne's Anniversaries and the Poetry of Praise: The Creation of a Symbolic Mode* [Princeton: Princeton Univ. Press, 1973], p. 27, and also pp. 65, 160–61, 167, 170, 197).

[55] The feast day of yet another Edward, St. Edmund of Abingdon, falls on November 16; and it is noteworthy that he is remembered especially as an opponent of corruption in the church and as a regular disputant with the state on religious matters. The liturgical readings for this feast day—Ecclesiasticus 43, John 8, Ecclesiasticus 44, and 1 Timothy 5—seem less closely related to Milton's poem than those for November 20th; yet they are not wholly irrelevant to it. Ecclesiasticus 43, developing the image of a rising sun sending forth its beams and speaking of the dangers of the sea, is complemented in chapter 44 by a glorification of heroic men—of prophets who are the leaders of their people and the makers of social harmony. Milton's use of another liturgy does not prevent him from reflecting upon this one. But Milton is understandably silent about Edward the Confessor—a subject for British tragedy, noted for "his slacknesse to redresse the corrupt clergie" (*Columbia Milton*, 18:244).

[56] See, e.g., A. B. Chambers, "Christmas: The Liturgy of the Church and English Verse of the Renaissance," in *Literary Monographs: Medieval and Renaissance Literature*, ed. Eric Rothstein and Joseph Anthony Wittreich, Jr. (Madison: Univ. of Wisconsin Press, 1975), 6:142–53; James G. Taaffe, "Michaelmas, The 'Lawless Hour,' and the Occasion of Milton's *Comus*," *English Language Notes*, 6 (1969), 257–62; and in the same journal, see William B. Hunter, Jr., "The Liturgical Context of *Comus*," 10 (1972), 11–15; and finally A. B. Chambers, "The Double Time Scheme in *Paradise Regained*," *Milton Studies*, 7 (1975), 189–205. A very general study by Thomas B. Stroup proposes that throughout his poetry Milton christianizes secular forms by grafting on to them liturgical elements; and specifically Stroup suggests that *Lycidas*—"a complex of meditation-sermon and ritual" —invokes "several passages from the burial services in the several versions of the Book of Common Prayer" (*Religious Rite and Ceremony in Milton's Poetry* [Lexington: Univ. of Kentucky Press, 1968], pp. 11, 12).

[57] See Archer's *Comfort for Believers about Their Sinnes and Troubles* (London: Printed for Benjamin Allen, 1645), p. 11.

[58] See both Augustin Marlorat, *A Catholike Exposition upon the Revelation of Sainct John* (London: Printed by H. Binneman, 1574), p. 10, and Alsted, *The Beloved City,* p. 81.

[59] Alsted, *The Beloved City,* p. 68.

[60] See both John Calvin, *A Commentarie on the Whole Epistle to the Hebrewes* (London: Felix Kingston, 1605), pp. 1, 333, and David Dickson, *A Short Explanation of the Epistle of Paul to the Hebrews* (Aberdene: Edward Raban, 1635), pp. 327–28. Also pertinent here are the observations of William Gouge, *An Learned and Very Useful Commentary On the Whole of the Epistle to the Hebrewes* (2 vols.; London: Printed for Joshua Kirton, 1655), II, 354.

[61] Dickson, *A Short Explanation,* pp. 301–02.

[62] *Ibid.,* p. 281, and Calvin, *A Commentary on the Whole of the Epistle,* pp. 318, 333.

[63] I quote from John Bale on providence and the Book of Revelation; see *The Image of Both Churches* (1548; rpt. London: Thomas East, 1570), sig. Aiii, but see also Traheron, *An Exposition on the Fourth Chapter,* sigs. Aiiii^v, Av, Bvii^v, Cv^v, as well as Milton's *De Doctrina Christiana* (*Yale Milton,* 6:326–42). See also fn. 135. For Fixler's comment inspired by Kermode's book, see "The Apocalypse within *Paradise Lost,*" in *New Essays on Paradise Lost,* ed. Thomas Kranidas (Berkeley and Los Angeles: Univ. of California Press, 1969), p. 133, and also Kermode's *The Sense of an Ending: Studies in the Theory of Fiction* (New York: Oxford Univ. Press, 1967). This pressing toward the Book of Revelation, evident in both Spenser's and Milton's poetry, takes on added significance when we recall that the church liturgy provided for a reading through of the New Testament three times a year, except for the Apocalypse which was read only selectively (just three passages were assigned for the entire year): chapters 1, 19 through "I saw an angel stand," and 22. Spenser and Milton thus place an accent on the Book from which the Church had lifted one; they impose a meditation that the Church itself would discourage (see *The Book of Common Prayer 1559: The Elizabethan Prayer Book,* ed. John E. Booty [Charlottesville: Univ. Press of Virginia for the Folger Shakespeare Library, 1976], p. 25).

[64] "Allegory and Pastoral in *The Shepheardes Calender,*" *ELH,* 36 (1969), 104–05.

[65] Sacvan Bercovitch recognizes that, according to the poetics of influence advanced by scriptural exegetes, "the sons . . . improve upon the fathers" who are exemplars but who also assume at times "the role formerly held by the tenacious natural self" ("Emerson the Prophet: Romanticism, Puritanism, and Auto-American-Biography," in *Emerson: Prophecy, Metamorphosis, and Influence,* ed. David Levin [New York: Columbia Univ. Press, 1975], pp. 4–5, 7). Harold Bloom, however, says that "what the New Testament lacks in regard to the Old is a transumptive stance, which is why the New Testament is a weak poem": "Poets," Bloom concludes, "no more fulfill one an-

other than the New Testament fulfills the Old. It is the carry-over from the tradition of figural interpretation of Scripture to secular literature that has allowed a curious overspiritualization of texts" (*Poetry and Repression,* pp. 89, 95). Bloom unwittingly locates the source of the poetics of influence to which Spenser, Milton, and their Romantic successors subscribe, but at the same time eradicates the paradox of fulfillment of tradition and of subversion of tradition that these poets observed and maintained. For Bloom's views, see *Poetry and Repression,* p. 96; for my own, see *Angel of Apocalypse: Blake's Idea of Milton* (Madison: Univ. of Wisconsin Press, 1975), esp. pp. 221–50; and for others' views, see *Milton and the Line of Vision,* ed. Joseph Anthony Wittreich, Jr. (Madison: Univ. of Wisconsin Press, 1975).

⁶⁶ "The Argument of Spenser's *Shepheardes Calender,*" in *Spenser: A Collection of Critical Essays,* ed. Harry Berger, Jr. (Englewood Cliffs, N. J.: Prentice-Hall, 1968), p. 31. For Milton's remarks, see *Yale Milton,* 1:722–23. John Harvey's remarks on prophecy, in *A Discoursive Probleme Concerning Prophesies* (London: John Jackson, 1588), esp. p. 98, suggest that some of Spenser's contemporaries, certainly, were aware of the prophetic purpose of his poetry.

⁶⁷ *John Skelton's Poetry* (New Haven and London: Yale Univ. Press, 1965), p. 178. On Colin Clout as a descendant of Piers, see A. R. Heiserman, *Skelton and Satire* (Chicago: Univ. of Chicago Press, 1961), p. 238. Heiserman also comments on Skelton's indebtedness, both structural and thematic, to the Book of Revelation, calling *Colin Clout,* finally, a little drama (pp. 238, 242). For a discussion of this poem as a pastoral, see H. L. R. Edwards, *Skelton: The Life and Times of an Early Tudor Poet* (London: Jonathan Cape, 1949), pp. 210–11. Like the later poems by Spenser and Milton, *Colin Clout's* target is wicked priests and prelates; its objective, the revelation of the beast. All these poems help to sharpen the difference between pastoral and prophecy: the former is an image of a moment in history; the latter, a vehicle for transforming history, for reconstituting it. That Spenser sees a disjunction between Colin and Piers in Skelton's poem—or at the very least, that he wishes to insist on such a disjunction in his own poem—finds confirmation in the fact that Piers and Colin are separate, contrasting figures in the *Calender.*

⁶⁸ *Spensers's Shepheardes Calender: A Study in Elizabethan Allegory* (Notre Dame: Univ. of Notre Dame Press, 1961), p. 301; see also pp. 47–60.

⁶⁹ William Nelson, *The Poetry of Edmund Spenser: A Study* (New York: Columbia Univ. Press, 1963), p. 32. In his lament for Dido (Queen Elizabeth) which prefigures the death of Colin (the English people), Spenser adopts both the voice and tactic of Jeremiah who, as Barbara Lewalski explains, "contrived a series of personae in the Lamentations for King Josiah, whose death portends the destruction of Israel" (*"Is There in Truth No Beauty?": Protestant Poetics and the Seventeenth-Century Religious Lyric,* forthcoming from Princeton Univ. Press, 1979).

It is enlightening to read Spenser's implied criticism of Elizabeth in the context of one of the Queen's own prayers where she acknowledges herself as "chosen . . . to feed thy people":

> O Lord, . . . my flesh is frail and weak. . . . If I swell against thee, pluck me down in my own conceit. . . . Create . . . in me . . . a new heart and . . . renew my spirit. . . .

(See *The Book of Common Prayer,* ed. Booty, p. 333). It is also tempting to believe that Spenser wrote the November eclogue against the background of two different liturgies: the one set for November 5, the feast day of St. Elizabeth; and the other, for November 17, the day designated by the New Calendar of 1561 for celebrating the Accession of Queen Elizabeth (see *ibid.,* p. viii). The liturgy prescribed for November 5 includes Psalms 24–29, Ecclesiasticus 20–21, Luke 21, and 1 Thessalonians 1. One of these psalms contains the prayer, "let not mine enemies triumph over me"; another, the exhortation that rulers give glory to God by protecting their subjects. Given the critical posture Spenser must assume toward the Queen, he probably hoped she would remember the counsel of Ecclesiasticus: that it is better to offer reproof than to be angry secretly, that those who are objects of reproof should be grateful for the reproval, particularly in this time of general betrayal that Luke speaks of. The readings for November 17 include Psalms 86–89, Ecclesiasticus 36–37, John 9 and 1 Timothy 6. Especially noteworthy here are Timothy's reminder that men under the yoke should recall that there is but one prince, one king, who promises eternal life; John's assurance that the eyes of the blind will be opened; and in Ecclesiasticus "the praise of a good woman."

[70] Hamilton, "The Argument of Spenser's *Shepheardes Calender,*" in *Spenser,* ed. Berger, p. 33.

[71] MacCaffrey, "Allegory and Pastoral in *The Shepheardes Calender,*" p. 104.

[72] *Ibid.,* pp. 88–109.

[73] *Ibid.,* p. 93.

[74] Michael Murrin, *The Veil of Allegory: Some Notes Toward a Theory of Allegorical Rhetoric in the English Renaissance* (Chicago: Univ. of Chicago Press, 1969), p. 160.

[75] MacCaffrey, "Allegory and Pastoral in *The Shepheardes Calender,*" p. 109. See also S. K. Heninger, Jr., "The Renaissance Perversion of Pastoral," *Journal of the History of Ideas,* 22 (1961), 254–62.

[76] "*Lycidas:* The Poet in a Landscape," in *The Lyric and Dramatic Milton,* p. 78.

[77] E. De Selincourt, "Introduction," *The Poetical Works of Edmund Spenser,* ed. J. C. Smith and E. De Selincourt (London: Oxford Univ. Press, 1924), p. xxxv. Sam Meyer argues similarly, that *Colin Clouts Come Home Againe* is a kind of sequel to the *Calender;* but he also denies, as I am unprepared to do, that there is point to calling *Colin Clouts Come Home Againe* a pure pastoral and, furthermore, that any "organic connection exists . . . between the title poem and the seven memorials on Sidney published with it"

(*An Interpretation of Edmund Spenser's Colin Clout* [Notre Dame, Ind.: Univ. of Notre Dame Press, 1969], pp. 2–3, 19). See also Nancy Jo Hoffman, *Spenser's Pastorals: The Shepheardes Calender and Colin Clout* (Baltimore: Johns Hopkins Univ. Press, 1977).

[78] Paz, *The Bow and the Lyre,* p. 133.

[79] MacCaffrey, "*Lycidas:* The Poet in a Landscape," in *The Lyric and Dramatic Milton,* pp. 83, 89.

[80] Paz, *The Bow and the Lyre,* p. 137.

[81] *Lives of the English Poets,* ed. George Birkbeck Hill (3 vols.; Oxford: Clarendon Press, 1905), 1:163.

[82] "The Scandal of Literary Scholarship," *Harper's Magazine,* 235 (December, 1967), 90–91.

[83] See Puttenham, *The Arte of English Poesie,* p. 53; Erwin Panofsky, "*Et in Arcadia Ego:* Poussin and the Elegiac Tradition," in *Meaning in the Visual Arts* (Garden City, N. Y.: Doubleday, 1955), pp. 295–320; and Peter V. Marinelli, *Pastoral* (London: Methuen, 1971), pp. 47, 51.

[84] *Milton: The Critical Heritage,* ed. John T. Shawcross (London: Routledge and Kegan Paul, 1970), p. 98.

[85] *A Full Enquiry into the True Nature of Pastoral* (London: H. P., 1717), pp. 9, 28, 57.

[86] "*Lycidas* Yet Once More," *Huntington Library Quarterly,* 41 (1978), 103–117.

[87] See both E. K. Chambers, *English Pastorals* (London: Blackie and Son, 1895), p. xv, and Honig, *Dark Conceit: The Making of Allegory* (Cambridge: Walker-DeBerry, 1960), p. 164.

[88] I borrow the phrase from Tuve, "Theme, Pattern, and Imagery in *Lycidas,*" in *Milton's Lycidas,* ed. Patrides, p. 179.

[89] See both "Preface," *Milton's Lycidas,* ed. Scott Elledge (New York and London: Harper and Row, 1966), p. xii, and *Literature as System: Essays Toward the Theory of Literary History* (Princeton: Princeton Univ. Press, 1971), p. 51. Within this context, Balachandra Rajan observes that every point on the surface of *Lycidas* inherits a long tradition to which the poem "is competitively and creatively responsive" (*The Lofty Rhyme: A Study of Milton's Major Poetry* [Coral Gables, Fla.: Univ. of Miami Press, 1970], p. 55). The classic essay on *Lycidas* and the pastoral tradition is James Holly Hanford's "The Pastoral Elegy and Milton's *Lycidas,*" in *Milton's Lycidas,* ed. Patrides, pp. 27–55; but see also Edward W. Tayler, *Nature and Art in Renaissance Literature* (New York: Columbia Univ. Press, 1964); Renato Poggioli, *The Oaten Flute: Essays on Pastoral Poetry and the Pastoral Ideal* (Cambridge, Mass.: Harvard Univ. Press, 1975); and Ellen Zetzel Lambert, *Placing Sorrow: A Study of the Pastoral Elegy Convention from Theocritus to Milton* (Chapel Hill: Univ. of North Carolina Press, 1976). Lambert's book takes literary history and literary understanding far beyond Thomas Perrin Harrison's edition, *The Pastoral Elegy: An Anthology* (Austin: Univ. of Texas Press, 1939).

[90] *Literature as System,* p. 130.

[91] *The Green Cabinet: Theocritus and the European Pastoral Lyric* (Berkeley and Los Angeles: Univ. of California Press, 1969), pp. 4, 5, 30.

[92] Chambers, *English Pastorals*, p. xix. Maurice Evans comments similarly, that *The Shepheardes Calender* "epitomizes all that the pastoral had done and heralds what it was to do during the next three decades. It is the first and also the last expression in English of the full range of the Renaissance pastoral, with the exception of *Lycidas* which crushes all the main pastoral themes into a single poem" (*English Poetry in the Sixteenth Century*, 2nd ed. [New York: W. W. Norton, 1967], p. 93).

[93] "Milton, Greatest Spenserian," in *Milton and the Line of Vision*, ed. Wittreich, p. 28. Previous to Williams, John Crowe Ransom had observed that "the enterprising Spenser prepared the way for the daring Milton" ("A Poem Nearly Anonymous," in *Milton's Lycidas*, ed. Patrides, p. 69); and Douglas Bush has acknowledged that "Spenser occupies a conspicuous place in the background of *Lycidas*" (*A Variorum Commentary*, 2:ii, 560).

[94] *Cursory Remarks on Some of the Ancient English Poets, Particularly Milton* (London: Privately Printed, 1789), p. 112; and see also *Lycidas*, ed. Elton, p. 22.

[95] See Tolliver's *Pastoral Forms and Attitudes* (Berkeley and Los Angeles: Univ. of California Press, 1971), p. vii, and Fletcher's *The Transcendental Masque*, p. 115. For other important discussions of pastoral, see Hallett Smith, *Elizabethan Poetry: A Study of Conventions, Meaning, and Expression* (Cambridge, Mass.: Harvard Univ. Press, 1952), pp. 1–63, and Thomas McFarland, *Shakespeare's Pastoral Comedy* (Chapel Hill: Univ. of North Carolina Press, 1972), pp. 3–48; and for discussions of pastoral that emphasize its mixed nature, see Chambers, *English Pastorals*, p. xxviii; Marinelli, *Pastoral*, pp. 7, 17–18; and Rosalie L. Colie, *Shakespeare's Living Art* (Princeton: Princeton Univ. Press, 1974), pp. 243–316. S. K. Heninger, Jr., also notes the mixed nature of pastoral, particularly in Renaissance literature; but rather than seeing the mixing with other genres as a source of pastoral's strength, Heninger argues that the Renaissance "violently perverted both its purpose and method, both its content and form" and thus concludes that by being "perverted to satire, moral allegory, and sentimental narrative," pastoral "assumed modish, superficial forms. Unlike tragedy, pastoral never realized its potentiality" ("The Renaissance Perversion of Pastoral," pp. 254, 261). Rosalie Colie offers another perspective: "By the end of the sixteenth century, the pastoral mode embraced many particular options to writers interested in literary experimentation, particularly in mixed genres"; by this time, Colie explains, the tradition of Christian pastoral had found an "unabashed model" in Spenser who "enrich[ed] the imaginative possibilities for . . . [his] successors" (*Shakespeare's Living Art*, p. 243). Also relevant to any discussion of Milton's revision of pastoral is Shakespeare's achievement within the genre, a subject explored by Colie in her last chapter, "The Limits of the Pastoral Pattern." The process of assimilation and development that involves pastoral is ongoing in English poetry. The next great example of the form is Shelley's *Adonais*, which "but for *Lycidas*, and the hints that

Lycidas suggested, . . . could not have been what it is" (Leishman, *Milton's Minor Poems,* p. 270). In some cases, it may be, as Harold Bloom would have it, that to be a fulfillment is "the later poet's self-idealization" (*Poetry and Repression,* p. 88); but it may be argued that in the case of Milton and Shelley to be a fulfillment is the poet's realization, not his delusion. *Lycidas* and *Adonais* are the testimony.

[96] "An Answer to Davenant's Preface to *Gondibert,"* in *Critical Essays of the Seventeenth Century,* ed. J. E. Spingarn (3 vols.; Oxford: Clarendon Press, 1908), 2:55–56.

[97] See E. S. Shaffer, *Kubla Khan and the Fall of Jerusalem: The Mythological School in Biblical Criticism and Secular Literature 1770–1800* (Cambridge: University Press, 1975), pp. 144, 183.

[98] MacCaffrey, *"Lycidas:* The Poet in a Landscape," in *The Lyric and Dramatic Milton,* p. 91.

[99] *European Literature and the Latin Middle Ages,* trans. Willard R. Trask (New York: Pantheon Books, 1953), p. 260.

[100] Purney, *A Full Enquiry into the True Nature of Pastoral,* p. 35.

[101] *Ibid.* On pastoral and perspectivism, see Colie, *Shakespeare's Living Art,* pp. 256, 266, as well as her remark that "perspectivism insists . . . upon the convergence of all views at its central and controlling point" (p. 261).

[102] *Of Sacred Poetry and Music* (Boston: Printed by Green and Russell, 1764), p. 16.

[103] I am here extending to Milton the argument that John B. Bender makes for Spenser; see *Spenser and Literary Pictorialism* (Princeton: Princeton Univ. Press, 1972).

[104] *Vision and Resonance: Two Senses of Poetic Form* (New York: Oxford Univ. Press, 1975), pp. 27–28.

[105] Leishman, *Milton's Minor Poems,* p. 315; but see also Berkeley's book, *Inwrought with Figures Dim.*

[106] "Spenser: Some Uses of the Sea and the Storm-tossed Ship," *Research Opportunities in Renaissance Drama,* 13–14 (1970–71), 136.

[107] *Spenser and Literary Pictorialism,* pp. 108–09, 119, 120.

[108] *A Full Enquiry into the True Nature of Pastoral,* p. 4.

[109] "Milton's Uncouth Swain," p. 45.

[110] I quote from Paz, *The Bow and the Lyre,* p. 251. For an elaborate description of the aesthetic to which Paz here alludes, see S. K. Heninger, Jr., *Touches of Sweet Harmony: Pythagorean Cosmology and Renaissance Poetics* (San Marino, Calif.: Huntington Library, 1974).

[111] See *Attitudes toward History* (2 vols.; New York: Editorial Publications, 1937).

[112] *The Poetical Works of John Milton,* ed. David Masson, 2nd. ed. (3 vols.; London: Macmillan, 1890), 1:193.

[113] MacCaffrey, *"Lycidas:* The Poet in a Landscape," in *The Lyric and Dramatic Milton,* ed. Summers, p. 81. Speaking of *Lycidas,* Douglas Bush reminds us of several pertinent facts: first, that the pastoral elegy is "a distinct division of pastoral poetry"; second, that the histories of the two forms are

interconnected; and third, that before *Lycidas* there are "relatively few pastoral elegies" (*A Variorum Commentary,* 2:ii, 550, 561). Bush's point is elaborated by Leishman who says that the *Lament for Bion* is "the only classical poem . . . that can be correctly described as a pastoral elegy" and that "the first English pastoral elegy before *Lycidas* . . . is Spenser's lament for Dido." Milton, Leishman concludes, "has enlarged the scope of the pastoral elegy in a manner analogous to that in which various Renaissance poets, and chiefly Spenser in *The Shepheardes Calender,* had enlarged the scope of the ordinary pastoral" (*Milton's Minor Poems,* p. 269).

[114] "The Rising Poet, 1645," in *The Lyric and Dramatic Milton,* p. 4.

[115] *Ibid.,* pp. 9, 12. For further discussion of the design of this volume, see Nitchie, "Milton and His Muses," pp. 75–84.

[116] Harold Bloom, of course, thinks otherwise; see *A Map of Misreading* (New York: Oxford Univ. Press, 1975), p. 126; and for a rejoinder to his theory, see Northrop Frye, "Expanding Eyes," *Critical Inquiry,* 2 (1975), 199–216.

[117] *John Milton: Poet and Humanist,* ed. John S. Diekhoff (Cleveland: Press of Western Reserve Univ., 1966), p. 62.

[118] On the indebtedness of *Comus* to the Book of Revelation, see Alice-Lyle Scoufos, "The Mysteries in Milton's *Masque,*" *Milton Studies,* 6 (1974), 113–42; and for an introduction to the subject of the indebtedness of *Lycidas* to the Book of Revelation, see my own essay, " 'A Poet Amongst Poets': Milton and the Tradition of Prophecy," in *Milton and the Line of Vision,* esp. pp. 111–29.

[119] See both Tayler's *"Lycidas* Yet Once More," pp. 105–10; and Martz's "Who Is Lycidas?", p. 187. *Lycidas* "is only intermittently 'pastoral' ": the opening lines present an "incompletely realized pastoral landscape," alerting us to the fact, says Isabel MacCaffrey, that Milton could have, but did not, "take his bearings in the tradition of pastoral elegy" (*"Lycidas:* The Poet in a Landscape," in *The Lyric and Dramatic Milton,* pp. 67, 69, 71). Balachandra Rajan describes Lycidas as a poem of "mergings," noting specifically its conflation of various kinds of pastoral (*The Lofty Rhyme,* p. 54).

[120] "Milton's Uncouth Swain," pp. 43, 49, 50.

[121] For Warton's note, and Todd's, see *The Poetical Works of John Milton,* ed. Todd, 5:9. For the tradition of St. Michael and the Mount of Vision, see Os, *Religious Visions,* pp. 80–81.

[122] "Who Is Lycidas?", p. 184.

[123] *Some Versions of Pastoral,* p. 6.

[124] Shaffer, *Kubla Khan and the Fall of Jerusalem,* p. 155.

[125] Marinelli, *Pastoral,* p. 9.

[126] Poggioli, *The Oaten Flute,* pp. 88, 95, 101, 103.

[127] *The Pursuit of the Millennium: Revolutionary Millenarians and Mystical Anarchists of the Middle Ages,* rev. ed. (New York: Oxford Univ. Press, 1970), pp. 254–55. It should be noted that when Theodore Bathurst translated Spenser's May eclogue (ca. 1608) "Piers" became "Lycidas." Milton, moreover, quotes twenty-nine lines from this eclogue in *Animadversions.* See

The Shepherds Calendar, trans. Bathurst (Printed for M. M. T. C. and Ga-briell Bedell, 1653), pp. 44–64, and *Yale Milton,* 1:723. On Milton's in-debtedness to Dante, who is "an ally in his protest against a church greedy for earthly realms and power," see Irene Samuel, *Dante and Milton: The Com-media and Paradise Lost* (Ithaca, N. Y.: Cornell Univ. Press, 1968), pp. 36–38.

[128] Marlorat, *A Catholike Exposition,* pp. 11ᵛ, 25, but see also Henry More, *An Explanation of the Grand Mystery of Godliness* (London: Printed for W. Morden, 1660), pp. 411–12.

[129] Hill, *Antichrist in Seventeenth-Century England,* pp. 73, 77.

[130] See *Milton's Lycidas,* ed. Elledge, pp. 241–42.

[131] *The Necessity of Divine Revelation, or the Truth of the Christian Reve-lation, Asserted* (London: Printed for W. Innys and R. Manby, 1740), p. xxxviii.

[132] *Milton's Lycidas,* ed. Elledge, p. 243.

[133] "A Poem Nearly Anonymous," in *Milton's Lycidas,* ed. Patrides, p. 74 (my italics). I am aware of Hanford's contention that Milton did not have "to resort to a particular model" but, in this instance, must offer a demurral (*John Milton: Poet and Humanist,* p. 14).

[134] *Literature as System,* p. 129.

[135] Henry More, *Apocalypsis Apocalypseos* (London: Printed for J. Martyn and W. Kettilby, 1680), p. 356. Prophecy was thought, during the Renais-sance, to be the great emblem of God's providence in the world and the Book of Revelation, to be the great example of providence in the Bible. Offering the most exhaustive testimony to providence, John's Apocalypse was said to be its farthest extension in the Bible (see, e.g., the headnote to the Book of Revelation in the Geneva Bible). "Gods providence," says Bullinger, is John's master-theme (*A Hundred Sermons upon the Apocalipse of Jesu Christ* [London: John Daye, 1573], p. 6). See also William Fulke, *Prælections upon the Sacred and Holy Revelation of S. John,* trans. George Gifford (London: Thomas Purfoote, 1573), p. 21; William Cowper, *Pathmos: or, A Commen-tary on the Revelation of Saint John* (London: Printed by George Purslow, 1619), unpaginated dedicatory epistle; Taylor, *Christs Victorie over the Dragon,* p. 811; John Trapp, *Gods Love-Tokens, and the Afflicted Mans Les-sons* (London: Richard Badger, 1637), pp. 5–6; More, both *An Explanation of the Grand Mystery,* pp. 7, 201–05, and *Apocalypsis Apocalypseos,* p. 351; the anonymous commentary, *A New Systeme of the Apocalypse* (London: n. p., 1688), p. 6; Rogers, *The Necessity of Divine Revelation,* p. xxxviii; Thomas Wells Bray, *A Dissertation on the Sixth Vial* (Hartford: Hudson and Goodwin, 1780), pp. 10–11; and Henry Hunter, *A Sermon* (London: Printed for Henry Hunter, 1793), p. 109.

[136] More, *An Explanation of the Grand Mystery,* p. 202.

[137] See both *The Wonderfull Works of God Declared by a Strange Proph-ecie of a Maid* (London: Printed for John Thomas, 1641), p. 8, and More, *An Explanation of the Grand Mystery,* p. 206.

[138] Thomas Brightman, *The Revelation of S. John* (Leyden: Printed by John Class, 1616), sig. A5ᵛ.

[139] Shaffer, *Kubla Khan and the Fall of Jerusalem,* p. 177.

[140] *The Bow and the Lyre,* p. 40.

[141] Dickson, *A Short Explanation,* p. 307. It even has been proposed that "Yet once more" refers to Milton's recently published masque; but if so, it is curious that in both the 1645 and 1673 editions of Milton's poems *Comus* is printed after, rather than before, the poem that is supposed to look backward to it (see John Spencer Hill, "Poet-Priest: Vocational Tension in Milton's Early Development," p. 60).

[142] George Wesley Buchanan, *The Anchor Bible: To the Hebrews* (Garden City, N. Y.: Doubleday, 1972), p. 225. A remark made by Wordsworth on the language of "The Thorn" serves well as a gloss to the "Yet once more" phrase in *Lycidas:* in the course of the poem, the mind is made "to attach interest to words, not only as symbols of the passion . . . but as . . . themselves part of the passion." See also Michael Lieb, " 'Yet Once More': The Formulaic Opening of *Lycidas,*" *Milton Quarterly,* 12 (1978), 23–28.

[143] See James Peirce, *A Paraphrase and Notes on the Epistles of St. Paul to the Colossians, Philippians, and Hebrews* (London: Printed for J. Noon and J. Chandler, 1727), p. 191; Gouge, *An Learned and Very Useful Commentary,* 2:354; and Theodore Haak, *The Dutch Annotations upon the New Testament* (London: Printed by Henry Hills, 1657), sig. Oo.

[144] John Foxe, *Christ Jesus Triumphant,* trans. Richard Daye (London: Printed for John Daye, 1579), p. 5; and see also William Perkins, *A Declaration of the True Manner of Knowing Christ Crucified* (London: Printed by John Legate, 1611), pp. 53–54, and Milton, *De Doctrina Christiana* (*Yale Milton,* 6:394, 461–65).

[145] *Annotations upon All the Books of the Old and New Testament* (London: Printed by John Legatt and John Raworth, 1645), sig. NN3^{v}.

[146] See Isaac Newton, *Observations upon the Prophecies of Holy Writ, Particularly the Prophecies of Daniel, and the Apocalypse of St. John,* in *Opera* (5 vols.; London: John Nichols, 1785), 5:442; and "Appendix B" in Frank Manuel's *The Religion of Isaac Newton* (Oxford: Clarendon Press, 1974), p. 126.

[147] *Apocalypsis Apocalypseos,* pp. 69, 216, and see also Hugh Broughton, *A Revelation of the Holy Apocalyps* (n. p.: n. p., 1610), p. 290.

[148] Abraham Woodhead, *The Apocalyps Paraphrased* (n. p.: n. p. [1682]), p. 32; see also Samuel Hartlib *et al., The Revelation Reveled by Two Apocalyptical Treatises* (London: Printed by William Du-Gard, 1651), pp. 75–76.

[149] *The Exposition of the Revelation,* in *The Works of Thomas Goodwin* (12 vols.; London: James Nisbet, 1861–66), 3:142.

[150] *The Oaten Flute,* pp. 111, 118–19.

[151] Marjorie Reeves, *The Influence of Prophecy in the Later Middle Ages: A Study of Joachimism* (Oxford: Clarendon Press, 1969), p. 154. See, too, James G. Taaffe, "*Lycidas*—Line 192," *Milton Quarterly,* 6 (1972), 36–38, and in the same journal, James F. Forrest, "The Significance of Milton's 'Blue Mantle'," 8 (1974), 41–48. Hallett Smith, quoting Lomazzo, associates blue garments with the aspiring mind, concluding that "the central meaning of pastoral is the rejection of the aspiring mind"; that "the shepherd's denial of

ambition . . . [is] the central pastoral philosophy of life" (*Elizabethan Poetry*, pp. 10, 38). If so, *Lycidas* forces a radical revision of this pastoral idea: everywhere, but no where more emphatically than here, showing the poet to be an ambitious, aspiring mind.

[152] " 'To Shepherd's ear': The Form of Milton's *Lycidas,*" in *Silent Poetry,* ed. Fowler, p. 174. Remarking upon a reference to Elijah in Andrew Marvell's *The First Anniversary,* John M. Wallace observes that "the ascent of Elijah . . . [is] one of the favourite texts for funeral sermons in the seventeenth century" (*Destiny His Choice: The Loyalism of Andrew Marvell* [Cambridge: University Press, 1968], p. 127; see also pp. 129–30). Here, it appears, a sermon convention obtrudes upon *Lycidas;* but so too does another convention noted by Wallace: that of Adam watching the first sunset and wondering whether there will be another dawn. The posture of the first Adam, so prominent in all the other poems of *Justa Edovardo King Naufrago,* is here reversed by Milton as he assumes the posture of the second Adam: there will be a *tomorrow,* another dawn. This convention, as Milton employs it, reinforces the idea that the poet is a second Adam, a type of the new spiritual man.

[153] Gifford, *Sermons upon the Whole Booke,* p. 394.

[154] Martz, "Who is Lycidas?", p. 77.

[155] *The Green Cabinet,* p. 16.

[156] *Some Versions of Pastoral,* pp. 180–81.

[157] *The Bow and the Lyre,* p. 28.

[158] I borrow the phrase from Harold Bloom who applies it to the Romantic lyric (*A Map of Misreading,* p. 173); but for an application of the phrase to *Lycidas,* see my essay, "Cartographies: Reading and Misreading Milton and the Romantics," *Milton and the Romantics,* 1 (1975), 3.

[159] *Milton: A Structural Reading* (Montreal: McGill-Queen's Univ. Press, 1974), p. 33.

[160] "*Lycidas:* The Poet in a Landscape," in *The Lyric and Dramatic Milton,* pp. 65–67. In contrast, Rosemond Tuve urges that "it is necessary to get into the poem by some consideration of its first fourteen lines" ("Theme, Pattern, and Imagery in *Lycidas,*" in *Milton's Lycidas,* ed. Patrides, p. 179).

[161] See both Lodge's "Defence of Poetry," in *Elizabethan Critical Essays,* ed. G. Gregory Smith (2 vols.; Oxford: Clarendon Press, 1904), 1:71, and More's *Apocalypsis Apocalypseos,* p. 43.

[162] Pareus, *A Commentary upon the Divine Revelation of the Apostle and Evangelist John,* trans. Elias Arnold (Amsterdam: C. P., 1644), commentary, p. 553.

[163] Gifford, *Sermons upon the Whole Booke,* p. 155.

[164] Archer, *Comfort for Believers,* p. 48. Broughton says that "the first resurrection is by faith, to be risen with Christ" (*A Revelation of the Holy Apocalyps,* p. 278). On the first resurrection, see also Bernard, *A Key of Knowledge,* pp. 317–18, and the anonymous commentary, *An Explanation of the Whole Revelation of Saint John* (London: Printed for Nathaniel Newberry, 1622), p. 123, as well as Pareus, *A Commentary upon the Divine*

Revelation, commentary, pp. 519–20, and More, *An Explanation of the Grand Mystery,* p. 179.

[165] *Christs Victorie over the Dragon,* p. 343.

[166] See both Trapp, *Gods Love-Tokens,* p. 64, also pp. 157–58, and Pareus, *A Commentary upon the Divine Revelation,* commentary, p. 41.

[167] *Disciplinary, Moral, and Ascetical Works,* trans. Rudolph Arbesmann (New York: Fathers of the Church, 1959), p. 213.

[168] *Sermons upon the Whole Booke,* p. 155.

[169] Puttenham, *The Arte of English Poesie,* p. 23. See also Joan Webber, "Walking on Water: Milton, Stevens, and Contemporary American Poetry," in *Milton and the Line of Vision,* esp. pp. 263–65.

[170] Cf.: "Most criticism of *Lycidas* is off the mark, because it fails to distinguish between the nominal and the real subject, what the poem professes to be about and what it is about. It assumes that Edward King is the real, whereas he is but the nominal subject. Fundamentally *Lycidas* concerns Milton himself; King is but the excuse for one of Milton's most personal poems" (E. M. W. Tillyard, *Milton* [London: Chatto and Windus, 1930], p. 80).

[171] MacCaffrey, *"Lycidas:* The Poet in a Landscape," in *The Lyric and Dramatic Milton,* p. 71.

[172] See Traheron, *An Exposition on the Fourth Chapter,* sig. Cviii^v.

[173] *Annotations upon All the Books,* sig. NN3^v.

[174] *The Beloved City,* pp. 4–5.

[175] I quote from Thomas R. Edwards, *Imagination and Power: A Study of Poetry on Public Themes* (London: Chatto and Windus, 1971), p. 140. Edwards mistakenly regards this "equivalence" as a distinctive phenomenon of Romantic poetry.

[176] Traheron, *An Exposition on the Fourth Chapter,* sig. Bvii.

[177] Quoting Gorki, in *Some Versions of Pastoral,* p. 18.

[178] *Kubla Khan and the Fall of Jerusalem,* p. 178.

[179] See Gifford, *Sermons upon the Whole Booke,* p. 85, and also Arthur Dent, *The Ruine of Rome, or an Exposition upon the Whole Revelation* (London: Printed for Simon Waterson, 1633), p. 36.

[180] Trapp, *Gods Love-Tokens,* p. 216.

[181] "How to Read *Lycidas,*" in *Milton's Lycidas,* ed. Patrides, p. 95.

[182] For a discussion of the emotion generated by the phrase, see Edward S. LeComte, *Yet Once More: Verbal and Psychological Pattern in Milton* (New York: Liberal Arts Press, 1953), p. 25.

[183] *Pious Annotations upon the Holy Bible* (London: Printed for Nicolas Fussell, 1643), p. 72.

[184] See Farrer, *A Rebirth of Images,* p. 56.

[185] *The Personall Reign of Christ upon Earth* (London: Printed by Benjamen Allen, 1642), pp. 14, 58.

[186] "Of Prophecy," in *A Collection of Theological Tracts,* ed. Watson, 4:362 (my italics).

[187] *A Commentary on the Whole of the Epistle,* p. 31.

[188] *The Personall Reign of Christ,* pp. 2, 12, 14–15, 26.

[189] See both James Peirce, *A Paraphrase and Notes,* pp. 192–93, and John Owen, *A Continuation of the Exposition of the Epistle of Paul the Apostle to the Hebrewes* (London: Printed for Nathaniel Ponder, 1684), p. 280.

[190] *Other Prophecies Which Add Some Confirmation to R. Ingram's View of the Great Events of the Seventh Plague or Period* ([Colchester]: n. p. [1785]), pp. 7–8, 14. See also Hunter, *A Sermon,* pp. 17–18.

[191] *The Lord of Hosts* (London: Printed by Thomas Newcomb, 1648), pp. 3–4.

[192] *Mercurius Teutonicus; or a Christian Information Concerning the Last Times* (London: Printed by M. Simmons, 1649), p. 3.

[193] *A Rebirth of Images,* p. 305.

[194] *The Prophetic Faith* (1949; rpt. New York: Harper and Row, 1960), p. 35.

[195] I borrow the phrase from Farrer, *A Rebirth of Images,* p. 85. See also Leslie Brisman who, borrowing a phrase from Sartre, speaks of the "melodic organization" of *Lycidas* (*Milton's Poetry of Choice,* p. 81).

[196] "On Milton's *Lycidas,*" in *The Romantics on Milton: Formal Essays and Critical Asides,* ed. Joseph Anthony Wittreich, Jr. (Cleveland: Press of Case Western Reserve Univ., 1970), p. 366.

[197] *The Age of Reason* (1795; rpt. London: J. Watson, 1845), p. 13. Betty Leigh Merrell has suggested to me the apt analogy: "*Lycidas* is rather like the last movement of Beethoven's 9th Symphony, which begins by reviewing the themes of the first three movements, turning them aside as unsatisfactory, and then goes on to make its own joyous statement."

[198] *Milton's Knowledge of Music: Its Sources and Its Significance in His Works* (Princeton: Princeton Univ. Press, 1913), pp. 47–48. See also Farrer, *A Rebirth of Images,* pp. 7–8; John Hollander, *The Untuning of the Sky: Ideas of Music in English Poetry, 1500–1700* (Princeton: Princeton Univ. Press, 1961), pp. 315–31; and Gretchen Finney, *Musical Backgrounds for English Literature,* pp. 195–219. Finney argues that *Lycidas* "shows definite structural parallels with sung poetry . . . and . . . suggests a definite manner of musical setting"; then Finney turns to musical drama as offering the best analogy for the musical character of Milton's poem (pp. 198, 210). In 1767 *Lycidas* was set to music by William Jackson.

[199] *Templum Musicum,* pp. 61–62. See also Scaliger's *Poetics,* where it is argued that a monody "must be understood in a quite different sense than is accepted by the learned"; that is, a monody is not a poem in one voice but one in a sequence of voices with musical accompaniment (*Milton's Lycidas,* ed. Elledge, p. 109). Both Milton's father and Henry Lawes were musicologists.

[200] See both Farrer, *A Rebirth of Images,* pp. 15–17, and Richard Daye's unpaginated preface to John Foxe's *Christ Jesus Triumphant.*

[201] *Vision and Resonance,* p. ix.

[202] *Templum Musicum,* pp. 3–4.

[203] *A Plain and Continued Exposition of the Several Prophecies or the*

Divine Visions of the Prophet Daniel (London: Printed by Walter Kettilby, 1681), p. 271.

[204] *The Arte of English Poesie,* p. 253.

[205] *Spenser's Allegory: The Anatomy of Imagination* (Princeton: Princeton Univ. Press, 1976), p. 191.

[206] *Nature and Art in Renaissance Literature,* p. 109.

[207] MacCaffrey, "The Meditative Paradigm," *ELH,* 32 (1965), 392.

[208] MacCaffrey, *"Lycidas:* The Poet in a Landscape," in *The Lyric and Dramatic Milton,* p. 90.

[209] *Milton and the Kingdoms of God,* p. 72.

[210] "The Pattern of Milton's Nativity Ode," *University of Toronto Quarterly,* 10 (1941), 171–72.

[211] See Farrer, *A Rebirth of Images,* pp. 80, 313.

[212] It is noteworthy that Ransom speaks of eleven separate topics of discourse in the pastoral elegy, all of which Milton utilizes in his poem ("A Poem Nearly Anonymous," in *Milton's Lycidas,* ed. Patrides, p. 74).

[213] See A. L. Bennett, "The Principal Rhetorical Conventions in the Renaissance Personal Elegy," *Studies in Philology,* 51 (1954), 107–26.

[214] *The Bow and the Lyre,* p. 4.

[215] *The Arte of English Poesie,* pp. 98–102.

[216] See Maren-Sofie Røstvig, "Structure as Prophecy: The Influence of Biblical Exegesis upon Theories of Literary Structure," in *Silent Poetry,* p. 39, and Howard, *The Idea of The Canterbury Tales* (Berkeley and Los Angeles: Univ. of California Press, 1975), p. 329.

[217] Dent, *The Ruine of Rome,* p. 202.

[218] *A Commentary upon the Divine Revelation,* commentary, pp. 60, 545; and see also Trapp, *Gods Love-Tokens,* sig. B3. A similar point had already been made by Richard Daye: we are not "saved by workes, . . . we are saved by Fayth whiche is the fruite of our workes" (see the unpaginated preface to John Foxe's *Christ Jesus Triumphant*).

[219] Trapp, *Gods Love-Tokens,* sig. B4.

[220] *A Commentary upon the Divine Revelation,* commentary, p. 369.

[221] *Kubla Khan and the Fall of Jerusalem,* pp. 65–66; and see also Cowper, *Pathmos,* p. 33.

[222] *Paradise Lost and the Genesis Tradition* (Oxford: Clarendon Press, 1968), p. 99.

[223] On the time structure in *Lycidas,* see Lowry Nelson, Jr., *Baroque Lyric Poetry* (New Haven: Yale Univ. Press, 1961), pp. 41–52, 67–76, 138–52; and on the poem's numerical structure, see both John T. Shawcross, "Some Literary Uses of Numerology," *Hartford Studies in Literature,* 1 (1969), 59–62, and Alastair Fowler, " 'To Shepherd's ear': The Form of Milton's *Lycidas,*" in *Silent Poetry,* pp. 170–84.

[224] See both Marlorat, *A Catholike Exposition,* p. 29ᵛ, and Bernard, *A Key of Knowledge,* p. 122.

[225] Fairbairne, *Prophecy,* p. 183.

[226] *Christs Victorie over the Dragon,* p. 329.

[227] Shaffer, *Kubla Khan and the Fall of Jerusalem*, p. 138.

[228] *An Essay on Man: An Introduction to the Philosophy of Human Culture* (New Haven: Yale Univ. Press, and London: Oxford Univ. Press, 1944), pp. 54–55. I am grateful to S. K. Heninger, Jr., for calling this passage to my attention.

[229] Fowler, " 'To Shepherd's ear': The Form of Milton's *Lycidas*," in *Silent Poetry*, p. 171.

[230] *An Explanation of the Grand Mystery*, p. 197.

[231] *A Key of Knowledge*, p. 325.

[232] Leishman, *Milton's Minor Poems*, p. 314. The pattern of revision, especially as it affects the rhyme scheme of *Lycidas*, does not corroborate Ransom's contention that Milton, having "read the formal poem he had written, . . . deformed it": "*Lycidas* . . . was written smooth," says Ransom, "and rewritten rough" ("A Poem Nearly Anonymous," in *Milton's Lycidas*, ed. Patrides, pp. 71, 73).

[233] "The Dry and Rugged Verse," in *The Lyric and Dramatic Milton*, p. 151.

[234] *The Arte of English Poesie*, pp. 96, 99–100.

[235] Catherine Ing, *Elizabethan Lyrics: A Study in the Development of English Metres and Their Relation to Poetic Effect* (London: Chatto and Windus, 1951), p. 90.

[236] *Ibid.*, p. 165.

[237] *Milton: A Structural Reading*, pp. 107–08.

[238] For Warton's note, and Hurd's, see *The Poetical Works of John Milton*, ed. Todd, 5:5, 54.

[239] See Robert Beum, "So Much Gravity and Ease," in *Language and Style in Milton*, ed. Ronald David Emma and John T. Shawcross (New York: Frederick Ungar, 1967), p. 350. See also the exchange between Anthony Low and Joseph Anthony Wittreich, Jr., "Circular Rhymes in *Lycidas?*", *PMLA*, 86 (1971), 1032–35, along with the more recent essay by Alberta Turner, "The Sound of Grief: A Reconsideration of the Nature and Function of the Unrhymed Lines in *Lycidas*," *Milton Quarterly*, 10 (1976), 67–73.

[240] See Hughes's Introduction to *Lycidas* in *John Milton: Complete Poems and Major Prose*, ed. Merritt Y. Hughes (New York: Odyssey Press, 1957), p. 119; and for Ransom's argument, see "A Poem Nearly Anonymous," in *Milton's Lycidas*, ed. Patrides, pp. 64–81.

[241] Each paragraph seems to grow out of the one that precedes it with the "inevitability and logic of a mathematical progression" (Ans Oras, "Milton's Early Rhyme Schemes and the Structure of *Lycidas*," *Modern Philology*, 52 [1954], 12–22). Oras details an important aspect of this progression as he draws attention to the rhyme schemes with which paragraphs seven, nine, and ten begin (*ababcc, ababbcc, ababbacc*). Clearly, Milton is moving confidently toward the *ottava rima* stanza with which the poem closes. Each of these paragraphs adds another line until, in the penultimate verse paragraph, the *ottava rima* stanza is all but achieved, were it not for the inversion of one set of rhymes.

[242] *Vision and Resonance*, p. 285.

[243] *New Memoirs of the Life and Poetical Works of Mr. John Milton* (London: n. p., 1740), p. 32. It should not be thought that Peck's perception is unique to him: for example, William Shenstone notices that in *Lycidas* the rhyme "is very frequently placed at such a distance . . . that it is often dropt by the memory . . . before it be brought to join its partner"; and John Scott concludes that this "irregularity of . . . rhyme is obviously the effect of design, not of carelessness" (both commentators are cited in *Milton 1732–1801: The Critical Heritage,* ed. John T. Shawcross [London and Boston: Routledge and Kegan Paul, 1972], pp. 231, 327).

[244] Phillips, "Preface to *Theatrum Poetarum,*" in *Critical Essays of the Seventeenth Century,* ed. Spingarn, 2:257.

[245] *Touches of Sweet Harmony,* pp. 7, 383.

[246] *The Italian Element in Milton's Verse* (Oxford: Clarendon Press, 1954), pp. 71–88.

[247] "Spenser and the Epithalamic Convention," in *The Prince of Poets: Essays on Edmund Spenser,* ed. John R. Elliott, Jr. (New York: New York Univ. Press, and London: Univ. of London Press, 1968), p. 163.

[248] I borrow the phrase from Greene; see *ibid.*

[249] See *The Collected Works of Thomas DeQuincey,* ed. David Masson (14 vols.; London: A. and C. Black, 1896–97), 5:215.

[250] The first of these unrhymed words is *Lycidas,* which looks back to the poem's title and which recalls the ten separate invocations of the name within the poem (title, plus lines 8, 9, 10, 49, 51, 151, 166, 173, 182; in line 151, *Lycidas* is clipped to *Lycid*).

[251] *The Art of English Poetry* (London: R. Knaplock, E. Castle, and B. Tooke, 1702), p. 11.

[252] Ransom argues to the contrary (see "A Poem Nearly Anonymous," in *Milton's Lycidas,* ed. Patrides, pp. 69–70). The following rhymes appear with exceptional frequency (the number in parentheses indicates the number of times the rhyme appears in the poem): *-ore* (11), *-ead* (9), *-ear* (8), *-use* (7), *-ays* (6).

[253] "Some Notes on Organic Form," *Poetry,* 106 (1965), 422.

[254] *Literary Remains,* ed. Henry Nelson Coleridge (London: W. Pickering, 1836), 2:34–35.

[255] See the dedicatory page of Marjorie Hope Nicolson's *The Breaking of the Circle: Studies in the Effect of the "New Science" on Seventeenth-Century Poetry,* rev. ed. (New York: Columbia Univ. Press, 1962).

[256] John T. Shawcross, "The Balanced Structure of *Paradise Lost,*" *Studies in Philology,* 62 (1965), 708.

[257] *Prælections,* p. 14.

[258] *Milton's Epic Voice: The Narrator in Paradise Lost* (Cambridge, Mass.: Harvard Univ. Press, 1963), p. 150.

[259] M. H. Abrams (quoting Proclus), *Natural Supernaturalism: Tradition and Revolution in Romantic Literature* (New York: W. and W. Norton, 1971), p. 150.

[260] *Ibid.,* p. 184.

[261] See A. H. Bullen's Preface to *Cobbes Prophecies, His Signs and Tokens,*

His Madrigalls, ed. Charles Praetorius (London: Private Circulation, 1890), pp. v–vi, and also Cobbes's own Preface, sig. A3.

[262] See Fleming, *A Discouse on the Rise and Fall of the Papacy,* p. 109, and the anonymous tract, *Prophetic Conjectures on the French Revolution,* pp. 61–62.

[263] Puttenham, *The Arte of English Poesie,* pp. 110–11.

[264] Traheron, *An Exposition on the Fourth Chapter,* sig. Ciiii.

[265] "Lycidas: The Poet in a Landscape," in *The Lyric and Dramatic Milton,* p. 86. Northrop Frye comments similarly: "The prophecy of Michael in *Paradise Lost* presents the whole Bible as a miniature contrast-epic, with one pole at the apocalypse and the other at the flood" (*Anatomy of Criticism: Four Essays* [Princeton: Princeton Univ. Press, 1957], p. 324).

[266] H. R. MacCallum, "Milton and Sacred History: Books XI and XII of *Paradise Lost,*" in *Essays in English Literature from the Renaissance to the Victorian Age,* ed. Millar MacLure and F. W. Watt (Toronto: Univ. of Toronto Press, 1964), p. 150.

[267] "The Death of Adam: Vision and Voice in Books XI and XII of *Paradise Lost,*" *Modern Philology,* 70 (1972), 10.

[268] *The Exaltation of All Things in Christ, and of Christ in All Things* (London: Printed for Giles Calvert, 1649), pp. 6–7. See also *Antichrist in Man Opposeth Emmanuell or God in Us* (London: Printed for Giles Calvert, 1649), pp. 35–36, 68.

[269] *Mercurius Teutonicus,* p. 24.

[270] See "The Apocalypse within *Paradise Lost,*" in *New Essays on Paradise Lost,* pp. 131–78.

[271] C. S. Lewis, *A Preface to Paradise Lost* (London and New York: Oxford Univ. Press, 1942), p. 125.

[272] Fixler writes, "The seven visions are really the important things," both in the Apocalypse and in *Paradise Lost;* and Milton's epic clearly "preserves something of that . . . idea" ("The Apocalypse within *Paradise Lost,*" in *New Essays on Paradise Lost,* pp. 142, 146). Burton Jasper Weber makes clear that the same sevenfold pattern pervades *Paradise Regained;* and beyond this, he emphasizes that "the same structural principle by which Milton incorporates the other two days' temptations with each day's trial is present also within each episode: each of Satan's tests," he concludes, "mirrors the three days' series" (*Wedges and Wings: The Patterning of Paradise Regained,* [Carbondale and Edwardsville: Southern Illinois Univ. Press, and London and Amsterdam: Feffer and Simons, 1975], pp. 3, 13). In other words, each temptation contains all the others; and each new temptation, usually in expanded form, repeats the one preceding it.

[273] C. A. Patrides (quoting John Gaule), *Milton and the Christian Tradition* (Oxford: Clarendon Press, 1966), p. 129.

[274] "The Death of Adam," p. 9.

[275] *A Preface to Paradise Lost,* p. 125.

[276] H. R. MacCallum, "Milton and the Figurative Interpretation of the Bible," *University of Toronto Quarterly,* 31 (1962), 402.

[277] Goodwin, *An Exposition of the Revelation,* in *Works,* 3:113.

[278] "Calm Regained through Passion Spent: The Conclusion of the Miltonic Effort," in *The Prison and the Pinnacle: Papers to Commemorate the Tercentenary of Paradise Regained and Samson Agonistes 1671–1971*, ed. Balachandra Rajan (London: Routledge and Kegan Paul, 1973), pp. 14, 15, 16.

[279] " 'To Which Is Added *Samson Agonistes*—'," in *The Prison and the Pinnacle*, pp. 95–96.

[280] *Anatomy of Criticism*, p. 318.

[281] *Lectures on the History of Literature*, ed. Henry G. Bohn (London: H. G. Bohn, 1873), p. 277. See also Arnold Stein, who writes, "Milton's whole poetic vision is to be found in the three major poems, with some minor additions in the minor poems; but no one major poem, though *Paradise Lost* comes closest, contains the whole vision" (*Heroic Knowledge* [Minneapolis: Univ. of Minnesota Press, 1957], p. 205).

[282] Northrop Frye describes the relationship between *Samson Agonistes* and the Book of Revelation somewhat differently: "Nothing could be less like the Book of Revelation than *Samson Agonistes*, and yet, with its seven great choral odes (it has seven characters also, counting the Chorus as one) its subject is a prototype of the underside, so to speak, of the vision of that book, the aspect of it that comes to a climax in the elegy over the fall of Babylon" ("Agon and Logos: Revolution and Revelation," in *The Prison and the Pinnacle*, pp. 150–51). See also Barbara K. Lewalski, "*Samson Agonistes* and the 'Tragedy' of the Apocalypse," *PMLA*, 85 (1970), 1050–60.

[283] See, e.g., William Riley Parker, *Milton's Debt to Greek Tragedy in Samson Agonistes* (Baltimore: Johns Hopkins Press, 1937); F. Michael Krouse, *Milton's Samson and the Christian Tradition* (Princeton: Princeton Univ. Press, 1949); Jackie DiSalvo, " 'The Lord's Battells': *Samson Agonistes* and the Puritan Revolution," *Milton Studies*, 4 (1972), 39–62; and Raymond B. Waddington, "The Politics of Metaphor in *Samson Agonistes*" (a lecture delivered at the Modern Language Association Meeting, San Francisco, December, 1975).

[284] *The Heavenly Muse: A Preface to Milton*, ed. Hugh MacCallum (Toronto: Univ. of Toronto Press, 1972), p. 296. For opposing views, see John Carey, *Milton* (London: Evans Brothers, 1969), pp. 138–46, and esp. Irene Samuel, "*Samson Agonistes* as Tragedy," in *Calm of Mind: Tercentenary Essays on Paradise Regained and Samson Agonistes*, ed. Joseph Anthony Wittreich, Jr. (Cleveland: Press of Case Western Reserve Univ., 1971), pp. 235–57. Also relevant here are the iconographic traditions alluded to by E. H. Gombrich, *Norm and Form: Studies in the Art of the Renaissance*, 2nd ed. (London and New York: Phaidon, 1971), p. 48, and the historical ones cited by John T. Shawcross, "A Survey of Milton's Prose Works," in *Achievements of the Left Hand*, p. 337.

[285] See Samuel's essay, "*Samson Agonistes* as Tragedy," in *Calm of Mind*, pp. 235–57; Frye's essay, "Agon and Logos," in *The Prison and the Pinnacle*, pp. 135–63; and Hill, *The World Turned Upside Down*, p. 326.

[286] Anon., *Reflections on Sir Richard Bulkeley's Answer to Several Treatises, Lately Published, on the Subject of the Prophets* (London: Printed for J. Morphew, 1708), p. 53.

[287] See, e. g., the anonymous commentary, *A Plaine Explanation on the Whole Revelation*, p. 25, where Samson is likened to the soldiers who, in turn, are likened to the apocalyptic angels with vials—the angels who do nothing until they are so commanded:

> . . . though a man have excellent graces given him, yet he is not to execute any function, especially publiquely, before he receive a particular warrant and calling from God thereunto *Sampson,* though he had strength given him that he was able to have defended the *Israelites,* and revenged them of their enemies, yet he could not take upon him the governement of the people, before the Lord called him unto it: In a like manner, the Ministers of the Word . . . are not . . . to intrude themselves . . . unlesse they have a particular calling from the Lord.

John Lilburne is one of Milton's contemporaries who resolved to follow Samson even unto death, for either Lilburne would be delivered "from his causelesse and illegall imprisonment" or he would "by his death . . . do them [his oppressors] (Samson like) more mischeife, then he did them all his life" (*The Resolved Mans Resolution* [London: n. p., 1647], p. 1).

[288] *Paradise Lost: Introduction* (Cambridge: University Press, 1972), p. 94.

[289] *An Alarme Beat up in Sion, to War against Babylon* (London: Printed for Christopher Meredith, 1644), p. 16.

[290] *Ibid.*

[291] Mrs. West's poem (1799) is reprinted in *The Works of the English Poets from Chaucer to Cowper* (21 vols.; London: J. Johnson, 1810), 7:347.

[292] Abraham Heschel, *The Prophets: An Introduction* (1962; rpt. New York: Harper and Row, 1969), pp. 162, 166.

[293] Hill (quoting Williams), *Antichrist in Seventeenth-Century England,* pp. 126–27.

[294] *Ibid.,* pp. 142, 144.

[295] Irene Samuel contends that to read *Paradise Regained* "as a 'Who am I?' poem is to limit it . . . ; to read it as a 'How am I to live?' poem is to see its availability as the mimesis of a universal action, a program for every man" ("The Regaining of Paradise," in *The Prison and the Pinnacle,* p. 186). If, as I have argued, *Paradise Regained* and *Samson Agonistes* are companion poems, then Samuel's argument may be extended to Milton's tragedy—with the proviso that instead of a progress it represents a warning, a negative example. I am, of course, challenging Arnold Stein's supposition, which has become a *topos* of Milton criticism, that the hero of each poem, Christ and Samson, "presents a human and individual way to the same truth" (*Heroic Knowledge,* p. 205 [my italics]).

[296] Christopher Caudwell, *Illusion and Reality: A Study of the Sources of Poetry* (1937; rpt. New York: International Publishers, 1967), p. 81. In the eighteenth century, Thomas Hollis anticipated such a reading of Milton's play but then rejected it:

> Let us consider his tragedy in this allegorical view. Samson imprisoned and blind, and the captive of Israel, lively represents our blind poet, with the republican party after the Restoration, afflicted and persecuted. But these revelling

idolaters will soon pull an old house on their heads, and GOD will send his people a deliverer. How would it have rejoiced the heart of the blind seer, had he lived to have seen with his mind's eye the accomplishment of his prophetic predictions! when a deliverer came and rescued us from the Philistine oppressors.

Entertaining this view, Hollis adds a final note: "these mystical and allegorical reveries have more amusement in them, than solid truth, and savour but little of cool criticism, where the head is required to be . . . rather sceptical than dogmatical" (*Memoirs of Thomas Hollis,* comp. Francis Blackburne [London: Privately printed, 1780], p. 642).

[297] Frye, "Agon and Logos," in *The Prison and the Pinnacle,* p. 163.

[298] *The Works of Perkins* (2 vols.; London: Printed by John Legate, 1608–09), 1:86.

[299] *Christs Victorie over the Dragon,* pp. 279, 461–62.

[300] See the first sermon (unpaginated) by Lewis Thomas, *Seauen Sermons, or the Exercises of Seauen Sabbaths* (London: Printed for John Wright, 1615).

[301] *The Image of Both Churches,* p. 28.

[302] See both Hartlib *et al., The Revelation Reveled,* p. 52, and Marlorat, *A Catholike Exposition,* p. 35ᵛ.

[303] See Foxe, *Christ Jesus Triumphant,* p. 15ᵛ.

[304] Taylor, *Christs Victorie over the Dragon,* p. 89.

[305] *Lectures upon the Three First Chapters of the Revelation* (London: Printed by Cuthbert Burbie, 1604), p. 272.

[306] *Apocalypsis Apocalypseos,* p. xxvii.

[307] See *A Key of Knowledge,* pp. 34–36.

[308] *Christs Victorie over the Dragon,* p. 622.

[309] *Gods Love-Tokens,* pp. 42, 63, 113–14, 141.

[310] Goodwin, "The Folly of Relapsing After Peace Spoken" and *Of Christ the Mediator,* in *Works,* 3:419; 5:152–53, also p. 158. See, too, Hezekial Holland, *An Exposition or, a Short, but Full, Plaine, and Perfect Epitome of the Most Choice Commentaries upon the Revelation of Saint John* (London: Printed for George Calvert, 1650), p. 91.

[311] See the anonymous *Song of the Prophets* (London: Orr and Smith, 1835), pp. 91–92.

[312] *The Prophetic Faith,* p. 171.

[313] Bouchard, *Milton: A Structural Reading,* pp. 145, 147, 154. Bouchard also remarks that "Samson's violence, a violence which undermines the aspirations and convictions of others, is grounded in the violence of his speech" (p. 149–50).

[314] *Ibid.,* pp. 139, 141.

[315] "Calm Regained through Passion Spent," in *The Prison and the Pinnacle,* p. 40.

[316] *Milton: A Structural Reading,* p. 145.

[317] Reeves, *The Influence of Prophecy in the Later Middle Ages,* p. 292 (my italics).

[318] For the passages, here quoted, from Farmer's commentary, see *An Appendix to an Inquiry into the Nature and Design of Christ's Temptation in the Wilderness* (London: Printed for J. Buckland and J. Waugh, 1765), pp. 13, 22, 25, 31, 35, 41. Farmer's interpretation was first published in 1761 under the title, *An Inquiry into the Nature and Design of Christ's Temptation in the Wilderness*. A third, enlarged edition of Farmer's commentary appeared in 1775, and in the next century Farmer's views are happily reinforced by H. Cates, *Lent Sermons; or, An Inquiry into the Nature and Design of Christ's Temptation in the Wilderness* (London: Printed for C. Cradock and W. Joy, 1813). Cates repeatedly invokes *Paradise Regained* as an authority supporting his and Farmer's interpretation. More recently, J. Massyngberde Ford, invoking the authority of tradition, has pointed to the story of Christ's temptations in the wilderness as representing one of only four visionary moments in the Gospels (*The Anchor Bible: Revelation*, p. 5).

[319] Belsham, *A Summary View of the Evidence*, p. 85. Both Stuart Curran and Joan Webber have advanced interpretations of *Paradise Regained* that resemble this historical interpretation of the wilderness story and that are authenticated by it (see, respectively, "The Mental Pinnacle: *Paradise Regained* and the Romantic Four-Book Epic," in *Calm of Mind*, pp. 133–60, and *Milton and the Western Tradition of Literary Epic*, forthcoming).

[320] *Leviathan*, ed. C. B. MacPherson (Middlesex, Eng.: Pelican, 1968), p. 662 (IV. 45).

[321] *The Personall Reign of Christ*, p. 18.

[322] *Milton: A Structural Reading*, p. 10.

[323] *Ibid.*, pp. 2, 10.

[324] See both Frye, *The Stubborn Structure*, p. 160, and Bouchard (quoting Levi-Strauss), *Milton: A Structural Reading*, p. 10.

[325] "Foreword," *The Prison and the Pinnacle*, p. x. Elsewhere Rajan speaks of the wholeness of Milton's canon, of "the collective design" of Milton's poems (see *The Lofty Rhyme*, pp. 1, 10).

[326] See *Mythologies*, trans. Annette Lavers (1970; rpt. New York: Hill and Wang, 1972), pp. 121–36.

[327] See Ira Clark, "*Paradise Regained* and the Gospel according to John," *Modern Philology*, 71 (1973), 1–15.

[328] Kermode, *The Sense of an Ending*, pp. 18, 30.

[329] *The Stubborn Structure*, p. 172.

[330] *The Matter of Britain: Essays in a Living Culture* (London: Lawrence and Wishart, 1966), p. 201.

[331] I borrow the phrase from John F. Huntley, "The Images of Poet and Poetry in Milton's *The Reason of Church-Government*," in *Achievements of the Left Hand*, p. 113; but see also Barker's "Calm Regained through Passion Spent" and Rajan's " 'To Which Is Added *Samson Agonistes*—'," in *The Prison and the Pinnacle*, pp. 3–48, 82–110.

[332] *Mythologies*, pp. 130, 133, 136.

[333] *Milton: A Structural Reading*, p. 171.

[334] *The Prophets*, p. xv.

[335] Rajan, " 'To Which Is Added *Samson Agonistes*—'," in *The Prison and the Pinnacle,* p. 97.

[336] *The Heavenly Muse,* p. 290.

[337] Manuel, *The Religion of Isaac Newton,* p. 89.

[338] Mede, *The Key of the Revelation,* p. 82; and see also Reeves, *The Influence of Prophecy in the Later Middle Ages,* pp. 416, 423, 443.

Christopher Hill's *Milton and the English Revolution* (New York: Viking, 1977)—certain to become a landmark in Milton studies—arrived only after my own book had gone to the printer. I have not, therefore, been able to incorporate his many valuable insights or to let his own arguments augment my own. It should be noted, though, that despite many shared assumptions and procedures we reach decidedly different conclusions about *Samson Agonistes.* On the other hand, our discussions of *Lycidas* are happily complementary. Exactly the same point may be made about Mary Ann Radzinowicz's *Toward Samson Agonistes: The Growth of Milton's Mind* (Princeton: Princeton Univ. Press, 1978): we differ in our reading of *Samson* both in terms of what the relevant contexts are and of how those contexts are to be read; but we agree, certainly, on the "embedded political force" of *Lycidas* (p. xxi). With regard to that poem, these critics have called my attention to certain elements that are germane to my own reading of *Lycidas* and that I wish I had had the opportunity to integrate within my own discussion of that poem. Hill draws attention, for example, to the Latin quotation on the title-page for *Justa Edovardo King Naufrago* which he translates: "If you estimate it correctly, there is shipwreck everywhere" (p. 11). That epigraph generalizes King's fate as *Lycidas* will do; it epitomizes the process that will control Milton's own presentation of his subject matter. Radzinowicz, on the other hand, draws attention to Milton's own thoughts on consolation (p. 214) and, later, presents a brilliant analysis of Psalms 103 and 104 which, as it happens, along with Psalm 102, begin the liturgy for November 20 (p. 223). Their bearing on *Lycidas* should now be explored.

Appendix A:

Henry More's Explanation of His Own, and of Joseph Mede's, Table of Synchronisms

---

Reproduced in facsimile from *Apocalypsis Apocalypseos; or the Revelation of St. John the Divine Unveiled* [London: Printed for J. Martyn and W. Kettilby, 1680], pp. 256–60).

V. In the Table therefore prefented to thy fight, let *The Authors* there be noted that principal Line of the whole Apo-*Table of Synchro-* calyptick Scheme A D. divided into three parts A B. *nifms pro-* B C. C D. and let the whole Semicircle A Z D. con-*pofed and explained.* tain the *Prophecy* of the *Sealed Book*, but the Semicircle A N D. the *Prophecy* of the *Opened Book.* But of thofe two particular Semicircles A L B. and B R D. the former contains the firft fix Seals, the latter the feventh, which comprehends the feven Trumpets. The fix firft of which Trumpets the Semicircle B M C. includes, and the Semicircle C N D. the feventh, diftributed into feven Thunders, orderly diftinguifhed by numbers I. II. III. IV, *&c.* as is done in the Seals and Trumpets. And to this Line, or row of *Seals, Trumpets,* and *Thunders* all the reft of the Vifions, not only of the *Opened Book*, but of the *Seven Churches* may fome way be annected and applyed by *Syn-*

273

Synchronifmes either *proper* and *perfect*, or by *imperfect* and *partial*, as we fhall advertife as we go through them.

We fhall begin with the *Antimedial* Vifions, where A E B. is the Woman in travail, cloathed with the Sun, and Crowned with twelve Stars, *Rev. Chap.* 12. *verf.* 1. A F B. the Court of the Temple and Altar Commenfurate, or Symmetral, *Chap.* 11. *verf.* 1. A G B. the fight of *Michael* with the Dragon, about the Woman in travail, *Chap.* 12. *verf.* 4, 7, 8. A I R. the Church of *Ephefus*, or the *Ephefine* Interval contemporizing in part with the firft Seal, *Chap.* 2. *v.* 1. R H K. the *Smyrnean* Interval, which contemporizes with the latter part of the firft Seal, and with the fecond, third, fourth and fifth Seal, and with the forepart of the fixth, *Chap.* 2. *verf.* 8.

The *Medial* Vifions now follow, where B C. is the company of the 144000. Servants of God, fealed with the Seal of the living God in their foreheads, *Chap.* 7. *verf.* 3. B D C. the outward Court incommenfurate, or *afymmetral*, troden down of the Gentiles for forty two months, *Chap.* 11. B E C. the two witneffes clad in Sackcloth, and mournfully prophefying for 1260. days, *Chap.* 11. B e C. the fame witneffes flain, and lying in the ftreet of the great City for three days and an half. B F C. the Woman in the Wildernefs there to be nourifhed for 126ͺ. days, or for a time and times and half a time, *Chap.* 12. *verf.* 6, and 14. B G C. the feven-headed Beafts with ten Horns, whofe deadly wound is healed, *Chap.* 13. *verf.* 3. B H C. the two-horned Beaft, or falfe Prophet, the reftorer or healer of the Beaft, *Chap.* 13. *verf.* 11. B I C. the Virgin Company of the 144000. Sealed of the Lamb, *Chap.* 14. *verf.* 1. B K C. that

L l   great

great City, the Whore of *Babylon* fitting upon the feven-headed Beaft, with ten Horns, which was, and is not, and yet is, *Chap.* 17. *verf.* 3. 8. K P R. the *Pergamenian* Interval, contemporizing with the latter part of the fixth Seal, and with the five firft Trumpets. R Q C. the *Thyatirian* Interval, Synchronizing with fome fmall part of the fifth and with the whole fixth Trumpet. As for L N C and M C. in thefe Vifions, and C E H. and g H. in the following, they refpecting the voices of the three Angels, and *Anaplerofes* of them, I fhall take no notice of them here ; nor is their placing, nor *Anaplerofis* fo found as what I have intimated in this my *prefent Expofition* of the *Apocalypfe*, where thefe three Angels, *Chap.* 14. the firft is affigned to the times of the *Turks* taking *Conftantinople*, the fecond to the appearing of the Reformation, and the third to about the times of the fourth Vial, which being a more fimple way, to me feems more affured. But we proceed to the *Poftmedial* Vifions.

Where C A H. H Y P. P Z Q. Qq R. Rr S. Sp T. and T o D. are the feven *Antifynchronals* of the feven Thunders. C A H. the Interval of the feven Vials, *Chap.* 16. C F H. the compendium of the Vials, *Chap.* 11. *verf.* 16. to the end of the Chapter. C B O. the Interval of the *Sardian* Church, contemporizing with the Interval of the fix firft Vials, *Chap.* 3. *verf.* 1. G H. comprehends three Combinations of Synchronal Vifions, the Vifion of the *Harveft* and the *Wineprefs*, *Chap.* 14. *verf.* 15, 18. The Vifion of the *fixth* and *feventh Vial*, *Chap.* 16. *verf.* 12. and the Vifion of the *preparation* of the *Bride*, and of the *Battle* of the *Rider of the white horfe*, *Chap.* 19 *verf.* 7, 11.

H Y P. is the *New Jerufalem* defcending from Heaven,

ven. H i P. the laying hold of Satan. P Z Q. the thousand years Reign of Christ upon Earth. P L Q. the imprisoning of Satan in the bottomless Pit, and Sealing of him up there, contemporizing with the Raign of Christ upon Earth, *Rev. Chap.* 20. H M Q. the *Palm-bearing* Company, *Chap.* 7. *verf.* 9. O W Q. the Interval of the *Philadelphian* Church, *Chap.* 3. *verf.* 7. beginning with the seventh Vial, and ending at the Commencement of the fourth Antisynchronal. Q q R. which is the loosing of Satan, *Chap.* 20. *verf.* 3. R r S. the besieging of the Holy City by *Gog* and *Magog, Chap.* 20. *verf.* 7. S p T. the coming of Christ to Judgment, *Chap.* 20. *verf.* 11. P V T. a continuance of the New Jerusalem, or Holy City, contemporizing with the third, fourth, fifth and sixth Antisynchronals. P N T. the wicked Rabble (contemporizing with the same Antisynchronals) excluded out of the Holy City, *Chap.* 22. *verf.* 15. Q X T. the Interval of the Church of *Laodicea, Chap.* 3. *verf.* 14. T o D. the Conflagration of the Earth, *Chap.* 20. *verf.* 14. T e D. the Consummate happiness of the Saints.

This is the description of all my Synchronisms belonging to the Apocalyptick Visions, which differ from the Synchronisms of Mr *Mede* only in this, that I place all the Vials after the middle Synchronals under the first Thunder of the seventh Trumpet, he six of them before the seventh Trumpet, and that he does not distinguish the seventh Trumpet into seven Thunders in his Table as I have done, and therefore makes the binding of Satan and Millennial Reign of Christ, *&c.* to commence immediately (and consequently the Raign of the Beast quite to expire) at the beginning of that Trumpet; when as in truth the Entireness of his Kingdom only then expires. But being that else the

VI. The main difference betwixt Mr Mede's Table of Synchronisms and the Authors.

the main of the Synchronisms of Mr *Mede* so far as he has gone (for he never medled with the seven Churches, nor was aware that the three days and an half the Witnesses lye slain, are the same with 1260 days of their Prophesying) agree with this description I have proposed; I will vindicate the truth of his Synchronisms so far as they agree with the said description, against the cavils of a late writer *R. H.* of *Salisbury:* Because some men phansie though his Interpretations of the Apocalypse are so absurd, that as he boasts himself the sole Inventor of them, so he is like to prove the sole Assertor to them; yet that he has said something material against Mr *Mede's* Synchronisms, which how little it is we shall now see, but with all possible briefness, alledging only the main stress of Mr *Medes* Arguments, and taking notice only of the main stress of *R. H.* his Answers unto them.

THE

Appendix B:

*The English Poems
From Justa Edovardo King Naufrago*

(Reproduced in facsimile from *Justa Edovardo King naufrago, ab Amicis mœrentibus, amoris* [Cambridge: Printed by Thomas Buck and Roger Daniel, 1638].)

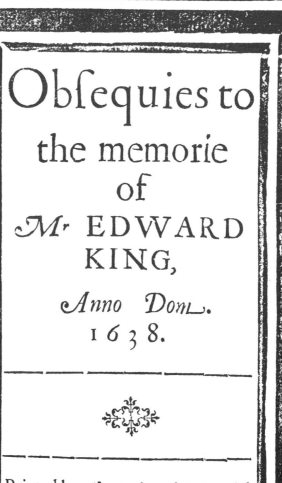

Obsequies to the memorie of Mr EDWARD KING,

Anno Dom.
1638.

Printed by *Th. Buck*, and *R. Daniel*,
printers to the *Universitie* of
Cambridge. 1638.

¶ Obsequies to the memorie of
Mr *Edward King.*

NO Death! I'le not examine Gods decree,
Nor question providence, in chiding thee:
Discreet Religion binds us to admire
The wayes of providence, and not enquire.
My grief is sober, and my faith knows thee
To b' executioner to destinie;
Brought in by sinne, which still maintains thee here,
As famines, earthquakes, and diseases were,
Poore mans tormentours, with this mischief more,
More grievous farre, his losse whom we deplore;
His, whose perfections had that Atheist seen,
That held souls mortall, he would straight have been
In t'other extreme, and thought his body had
Been as immortall, as his soul was made.
Whose active spirit so swift and clearly wrought
Free from all dregs of earth, that you'd have thought
His body were assum'd, and did disguise
Some one of the celestiall Hierarchies.
Whose reason quite outstript our faith, and knew
What we are bound but to beleeve is true;
Religion was but the position
Of his own judgement, truth to him alone
Stood nak'd; he strung th' arts chain, and knit the ends,
And made divine and humane learning friends;
Of which he was the best edition,
Not stuft with doubts, but all decision;
Conjecture, wonder, probabilitie,
Were terms of weaknesse; nothing bound his eye

With

With fold or knot, but the earths globe did seem
Full as transparent as the aire to him.
He drest the Muses in the brav'st attire
That e're they wore, and taught them a strain higher,
And farre beyond their winged horses flight.
But oh! the charming tempest, and his might
Of eloquence, able to Christianize
India, or reconcile Antipathies!
He--- but his flight is past my reach, and I
May wrong his worth with too much pietie:
I will not lessen then each single part
Of goodnesse, by commending; (for the art
Of severall pens would soon be at a losse)
But take him whole, and praise him in the grosse,
And say that goodnesse, learning, vertue, all
Strove to recover him from the first great fall;
Had not that sad irrevocable breath
Resisted them, which curst us all to death.

    Spare me suspicion: what though once I shin'd
In a relation? duty sure does bind
Me as much now to praise him, as before
To love his worth: but I will praise no more.
To count and say what vertues lov'd him most,
Were but to vex my fancy with his ghost.
You then whose pious unconfounded wit
Truly can apprehend this grief, and yet
Not be struck silent; here, take up this theme,
And sing the world his Epicedium.
Pattern a grief, may serve us all to mourn
For future losses, like the actours urn:
That all that reade your well-spunne lines with tears,
May envy you, and wish your grief were theirs.

    Mean while let me poore, senselesse, dead, alone
Sit and expect my resurrection,
To follow him; two sorrows sure will do,
That he is dead, that I am not dead too.

                                    Yet

Yet dead I'm once already: for in him
I loſt my beſt life, which I did eſteem
Farre beyond nature's, reputation
And credit, which the mere reflection
Of his worth, like a twilight, caſt on me,
And fix'd me as it were i'th Galaxie:
But now my ſtock is ſhipwrack't all, and loſt,
Quite bankrupt, all my hopes and fortunes croſt.
    Yet as thoſe wretches that in dungeons lie,
Sorrow the leſſe, 'cauſe they have company:
So I me thinks do feel my grief abate,
When I conſider that both Church and State
Joyn in this loſſe, and many thouſands more
Owe tributarie tears (for 'tis a ſcore
And generall debt of pietie) though we
Small ſprigs or branches of the ſelf-ſame tree
Suffer the worſt, ſince He the faireſt arm
Is torn away by an unluckie ſtorm.
    'Tis nothing for mens houſes to reprieve
Themſelves by iſſue, that may keep alive
Their ancient names and titles: but 'tis rare
To find one in the largeſt rank, whoſe bare
Merits and ample fame gilds all the line,
And makes the whole ſtemme in his brightneſſe ſhine.
And ſuch was he, by whoſe relation
We had a tincture, and were better known,
Then by our ſelves; for he had worth to ſpare,
And to diſpenſe to all of his a ſhare.
But oh! his fatall love did prove too kind,
To truſt the treacherous waves and careleſſe wind,
Which did conſpire to intercept this prize
Aiming t' undo the land by Piracies.
    Curſt element, whoſe nature ever vies
With fire in miſchiefs, as in qualities!
Thou ſav'dſt but little more in the whole ark,
Then thou haſt ſwallow'd now in this ſmall bark;

As

As if it strove the last fire to outrunne,
And antedate the worlds destruction.
  But we have sinn'd, and now must bear the curse,
  Even that is our worst plague, which is our nurse:
(Though drowning but a second baptisme was,
T' admit him to the other Churches place)
My griefs eternall hate) hence I'le not own
One drop on't in my composition,
But throw't away in tears. And sad sea, thou,
Thou, whose black crime, though the dry sun should now
Drink all thy waters into clouds, and rain
Them on the deserts down in tears again,
Yet could not expiate; may the memorie
Of this be thy perpetuall infamie;
May that hid cause that rocks thee, now be still;
And may thy guilty waters turn as ill
As the dead sea, that it may ne're be said
That any thing lives there, where he lies dead.
Who though he want an Epitaph, yet they
That henceforth crosse those seas, shall use to say,

  Here lyes one buried in a heap of sand,
  Whom this sea drown'd, whose death hath drown'd the land.

Hen. King.

———————————————————————————————

When first this news, rough as the sea
  From whence it came, began to be
Sigh'd out by fame, and generall tears
Drown'd him again, my stupid fears
Would not awake; but fostering still
The calm opinions of my will,
I said,The sea, though with disdain
It proudly fomes, does still remain

A flave to him, who never wrought
This piece fo fair to waſh it out.
I check't that fame, and told her how
I knew her trade, and her; nay, though
Her honeſt tongue had given before
A faithfull Echo, yet his ſtore
Of grand deſerts, which did prepare
For envies tooth ſuch dainty fare,
Would tempt her now to fain his fate
And then her lie for truth relate.

    But when mature relation grew
Too ſtrong for doubts, and ſtill the new
Spake in the fame difaſterous grone
With all the old; my hopes alone
Could not fuſtain the double ſhock
Of theſe reports and of the rock :
And when the truth, the firſt (alas!)
That e're to me deformed was,
Eſcap'd the ſea, and ougly-fair
Did ſhine in our beloved aire,
At length too ſoon my loſſe I found,
Him and my hopes together drown'd.
Oh! why was He (be quiet tears)
Complete in all things, but in yeares?
Why did his proper goodneſſe grace
The generous luſtre of his race?
Why were his budding times ſo ſwell'd
With many fruits, which parallel'd
Their mutuall beauteous ſelves alone,
In vertues beſt reflection?
As when th' Heſperian living gold
With priviledg'd power it ſelf did mould
Into the apples, whoſe divine
And wealthy beams could onely ſhine
With equall ſplendour in the graces
Of their brethrens anſwering faces.

                                    Why

Why did his youth it self allot
To purchase that it needed not?
Why did perfection seek for parts?
Why did his nature grace the Arts?
Why strove he both the worlds to know,
Yet alwayes scorn'd the world below?
Why would his brain a centre be
To learnings circularitie,
Which though the vastest arts did fill
Would like a point seem little still!

Why did discretions constant hand
Direct both his? why did he stand
Fixt in himself, and those intents
Deliberate reasons help presents?
Why did his well-immured mind
Such strength in resolution find,
That still his pure and loyall heart
Did in its panting bear no part
Of trembling fear; but having wrought
Eternall peace with every thought,
Could with the shipwrack-losse abide
The splitting of the world beside?
The universall axle so
Still boldly stands, and lets not go
The hold it fastens on the pole,
Though all the heavens about it roll.

Why would his true-discerning eye
His neighbours excellencies spie,
And love those shadows his own worth
Had upon others darted forth?
Whom he with double love intends,
First to make good, and then his friends.
Why did he with his hony bring
The med'cine of a faithfull sting,
And to his friend when need did move
Would cease his praise but not his love ?

Why made his life confession,
That he more mothers had then one?
Why did his duty tread their way
His generall Parent to obey,
Whil'st in a meek and cheerfull fear,
His whole subjection he did square
With those pure rules, whose load so light
Confesse a mother did them write?
Why did his whole self now begin
With vertuous violence to win
Admiring eyes? Why pleased he
All but his own sweet modestie?
Why gave his noble worth such ground
Whereon our proudest hopes might found
Their choicest promises, and he
Be Expectations treasurie?
O why was justice made so blind?
O why was heaven it self so kind,
And rocks so fierce? O why were we
Thus partly blest? O why was he?
　　Whil'st thus this senselesse murmure broke
From grieving lips, which would have spoke
Some longer grones, a sudden noise
Surpriz'd my soul; which by that voice
Hath learn'd to quiet her self, and all
Her questions into question call.
She saw his soul too mighty grow,
To be imprison'd thus below;
And his intelligence fitted here,
As if intended for a sphere.
His spirits which meekly soar'd so high,
Grew good betimes, betimes to die.
And when in heaven there did befall
Some speciall businesse which did call
For present counsel, he with speed
Was sent for up. When heaven has need,

G　　　　　　　　Let

Let our relenting wills give way,
And teach our comfort thus to say;

Our earth hath bred celestiall flowers:
What heaven did covet, once was ours.

J. Beaumont.

WHiles *Phebus shines within our Hemisphere,*
There are no starres, or at least none appear:
Did not the sunne go hence, we should not know
Whether there were a night and starres, or no.
Till thou ly'dst down upon thy western bed,
Not one Poetick starre durst shew his head;
Athenian owls fear'd to come forth in verse,
Untill thy fall darkned the Universe:
Thy death makes Poets: Mine eyes flow for thee,
And every tear speaks a dumbe elegie.
Now the proud sea grown richer then the land,
Doth strive for place, and claim the upper hand:
And yet an equall losse the sea sustains,
If it lose alwayes so much as it gains.
Yet we who had the happinesse to know
Thee what thou wast, (oh were it with us so!)
Enjoy thee still, and use thy precious name
As a perfume to sweeten our own fame.
And lest thy body should corrupt by death,
To Thetis we our brinish tears bequeath.
As night, close-mourner for the setting sunne,
Bedews her cheeks with tears when he is gone
To th' other world: so we lament and weep
Thy sad untimely fall who by the deep
Didst climbe to th' highest heav'ns: Where being crown'd
A King, in after-times 'twill scarce be found,

Whether

Whether (thy life and death being without taint)
Thou wert Edward the Confeſſour, or the Saint.

I *Like not tears in tune; nor will I priſe*
His artificiall grief, that ſcannes his eyes:
Mine weep down pious beads: but why ſhould I
Confine them to the Muſes Roſarie?
I am no Poet here; my penne's the ſpout
Where the rain-water of my eyes run out
In pitie of that name, whoſe fate we ſee
Thus copi'd out in griefs Hydrographie.
The Muſes are not Mayr-maids; though upon
His death the Ocean might turn Helicon.
The ſea's too rough for verſe ; who rhymes upon't.
With Xerxes ſtrives to fetter th' Helleſpont.
My tears will keep no chanell, know no laws
To guide their ſtreams; but like the waves, their cauſe,
Run with diſturbance, till they ſwallow me
As a deſcription of his miſerie.
But can his ſpacious vertue find a grave
Within th' impoſtum'd bubble of a wave?
Whoſe learning if we ſound, we muſt confeſſe
The ſea but ſhallow, and him bottomleſſe.
Could not the winds to countermand thy death,
With their whole card of lungs redeem thy breath?
Or ſome new Iland in thy reſcue peep,
To heave thy reſurrection from the deep ?
That ſo the world might ſee thy ſafety wrought
With no leſſe miracle then thy ſelf was thought.
The famous Stagirite, who in his life
Had Nature as familiar as his wife,
Bequeath'd his widow to ſurvive with thee
Queen Dowager of all Philoſophie.

An

An ominous legacie, that did portend
Thy fate, and Predeceffours fecond end!
Some have affirm'd, that what on earth we find,
The fea can parallel for fhape and kind:
Books, arts, and tongues were wanting; but in thee
Neptune hath got an Univerfitie.
*   We'll dive no more for pearls. The hope to fee*
Thy facred reliques of mortalitie
Shall welcome ftorms, and make the fea-man prize
His fhipwrack now more then his merchandife.
He fhall embrace the waves, and to thy tombe
(As to a Royaller Exchange) fhall come.
What can we now expect? Water and Fire
Both elements our ruine do confpire;
And that diffolves us, which doth us compound:
One Vatican was burnt, another drown'd.
We of the Gown our libraries muft toffe,
To underftand the greatneffe of our loffe,
Be Pupills to our grief, and fo much grow
In learning, as our forrows overflow.
When we have fill'd the rundlets of our eyes,
We'll iffue 't forth, and vent fuch elegies,
As that our tears fhall feem the Irifh feas,
We floating Ilands, living Hebrides.

J. Cleveland.

I do not come like one affrighted, from
The fhades infernall, or fome troubled tombe;
Nor like the firft fad meffenger, to wound
Your hearts, by telling how and who was drown'd.
I have no ftartled hairs; nor their eyes, who
See all things double, and report them fo.
My grief is great, but fober; thought upon
Long fince; And Reafon now, not Paffion.

Nor

Nor do I like their pietie, who to sound
His depth of learning, where they feel no ground,
Strain till they lose their own ; then think to ease
The losse of both, by cursing guiltlesse seas.
I never yet could so farre dote upon
His rare prodigious lifes perfection,
As not to think his best Philosophie
Was this, his skill in knowing how to die.
No, no, they wrong his memorie, that tell
His life alone, who liv'd and di'd so well.
I have compar'd them both, and think heavens were
No more unjust in this, then partiall there.
Canst thou believe their paradox, that say
The way to purchase is to give away?
This was that Merchants faith, who took the seas
At all adventures with such hopes as these.
Which makes me think his thoughts diviner, and
That he was bound for heaven, not Ireland.

Tell me no more of Stoicks : Canst thou tell
Who'twas, that when the waves began to swell,
The ship to sink, sad passengers to call,
Master we perish, *slept secure of all?*
Remember this, and him that waking kept
A mind as constant, as he did that slept.
Canst thou give credit to his zeal and love,
That went to heav'n and to those fires above
Rapt in a fierie chariot? Since I heard
Who'twas that on his knees the vessel steer'd
With hands bolt up to heaven, and since I see
As yet no signe of his mortalitie;
Pardon me, Reader, if I say he's gone
The self-same journey in a watry one.

W. More.

Pardon

Pardon, blest soul, the slow-pac'd Elegies
Of sad survivers: they have pregnant eyes
For vulgar griefs. Our sorrows find a tongue,
Where verse may not the losse or merit wrong:
But an amazed silence might become
Thy obsequies, as fate deni'd a tombe.
Poetick measures have not learn'd to bound
Unruly sorrows: shallow streams may sound,
And with their forward murmures chide the sea,
While deepest griefs a silent tribute pay.
Scarce can the widow'd Sisters let thee have
An Epitaph, as thou dost want a Grave.
All fun'rall rite earth can afford thee, is
Not to attend, but weep: and even of this
The too officious seas the earth prevent,
And yeeld thee tears, as they a tombe have lent.
Who doth for thee with his eyes issue grieve,
Seems but salt water to the seas to give.
But those ambitious waves which were thy grave,
Since they have thee, shall our sad tribute have.
They have usurp'd a new dominion o're
Us, who did pride our selves their Lords before;
And are enrich'd more by this single spoil,
Then had they pass'd their shore t' invade our soil.
Securely did our Iland-Muses sleep,
And envi'd not the treasures of the deep:
Unblamed might it re-intombe that ore
Which once lay buried in the deep before;
It doth but change gola's grave, or re-assume
Those pearls which from its watry issue come :
But now is made the mistresse of a prize,
Which nor her own, nor earths wealth equalize.
Heav'n would (it seems) no common grave intrust,
Nor bury such a Jewel in the dust.
The fatall barks dark cabbin must inshrine
That precious dust, which fate would not confine

To vulgar coffins. Marble is not fit
T' inclose rich jewels, but a cabinet.
Corruption there shall slowly seise its prize,
Which thus embalm'd in brinie casket lies.
The saucy worm which doth inhabit here
In earthy graves, and quickly domineer
In stateliest marbles, shall not there assail
The treasure hidden in that watry vale.
'Twas to secure thee from th' insulting power
Of these two hasty Tyrants, which devoure
Our common clay, that heav'n intomb'd thee there
(Dead friend) where these shall no dominion share.
Or did for us foreseeing heav'n desire
To quench in waters thy celestiall fire,
Lest we adore his ashes in an urn
Who dazzled all while vitall fire did burn?
Should some enriched earthly tombe inherit
The empty casket of that parted spirit,
The easie world would idolize that shrine,
Or hast to mix their dust with that of thine.
Grieving survivers, did they know thy grave,
Would there dissolve, and death a labour save
By voluntarie melting into tears:
To spare them, fate to interre thee forbears.
Thus doth the setting sunne his evening light
Hide in the Ocean, when he makes it night;
The world benighted knows not where he lies,
Till with new beams from seas he seems to rise:
So did thy light, fair soul, it self withdraw
To no dark tombe by natures common law,
But set in waves, when yet we thought it noon,
And thence shall rise more glorious then the sunne.

W. Hall.

When

WHen common souls break from their courſer clay,
 Nature ſeems not diſturb'd: they paſſe away
As ſtrangers meet i'th' rode, and bid farewell :
No clap of thunder 's heard to ring their knell;
Day ſtrikes not in; nor comet at their fall
Appears torch-bearer to the funerall.
But when as noble earth refin'd from droſſe
Returns to duſt, the whole world feels the loſſe.
Nature 's afraid to ſee ſuch brave men die,
And travails then with ſome ſtrange prodigie.
So dy'd our King, a man of men, whoſe praiſe
Detraction her ſelf durſt not but blaze;
One whom the Muſes courted: rigg'd and fraught
With Arts and Tongues too fully, when he ſought
To croſſe the ſeas, was overwhelm'd; each wave
Swell'd up, as coveting to be his grave;
The winds in ſighs did languiſh; Phebus ſtood
Like a cloſe-mourner, in a ſable hood
Compos'd of darkeſt clouds; the pitying ſkies
Melted and dropt in funerall elegies.
Such generall diſturbance did proclaim,
'Twas no ſlight hurt to Nature, but a maym:
Nor did it ſeem one private man to die,
But a well order'd Univerſitie.

 And is he dead? Alas! too true he 's gone:
Yet I ſcarce find belief to think it done.
For when becauſe of ſinne God opened all
Heavens cataracts, to let his vengeance fall,
And call'd the deeps up to perform his will,
Making them climbe above the higheſt hill;
After his anger was appeas'd, he bound
Himſelf, never again the world to drown:
How can my faith but ſtartle now, that we
Are yet reſerv'd another floud to ſee,
To drown this little World! Could God forget
His covenant which in the clouds he ſet?

            Where

Where was the bow?
                    But back my Muse, from hence;
'Tis not for thee to question Providence ;
Rather live sober still: such hot disputes
Riddle us into atheisme. It ill sutes
With men thus to expostulate with God;
Who seeing his hand, should rather aw the rod,
    Which as it strook this vertuous King, if thus
    We murmure, may more justly fall on us.

              Samson Briggs.

WHat water now *shall vertue have again*
    (*As once*) *to purge? The Ocean't self's a stain:*
And at this mourning, weeping eyes do fear
They sinne against thee, when a pious tear
Steals from our cheeks. Go, go you waters back
So foully tainted: all the Muses black
Came from your surges. Had the Thebane Swan
Who lov'd his Dirce (while it proudly ran
Swell'd by his lyre) now liv'd, he would repent
The solemn praises he on Water spent.
Why did not some officious dolphine hie
To be his ship and pilot through the frie
Of wondring Nymphs; and having passed o're,
Would have given more then Tagus to his shore?
Be this excuse; Since first the waters gave
A blessing to him which the soul could save,
They lov'd the holy body still too much,
And would regain some vertue from a touch:
They clung too fast; great Amphitrite so
Embraces th' earth, and will not let it go.
So seem'd his soul the struggling surge to greet,
 As when two mighty seas encountring meet:
              H   *For*

For what a sea of arts in him was spent,
Mightier then that above the firmament?
As Achelous with his silver fleet
Runnes through salt Doris purely, so to meet
His *Arethusa;* the Sicanian maid
Admires his sweetnesse by no wave decai'd:
So should he, so have cut the Irish strand,
And like a lustie bridegroom leapt to land;
Or else (like Peter) trode the waves: but he
Then stood most upright, when he bent his knee.

Isaac Olivier.

To the deceased's vertuous sister
the Ladie *Margaret Loder.*

Madame, I should have feared that this crosse
Would have disturb'd your patience, and the losse
Of such a noble father, such a brother,
Coming upon the neck of one another,
Would have disorder'd you, but that I knew
Your godly breast prepared well enough
With antidotes of grace against such haps
As Divine providence casts in our laps.
The early *Mattens* which you daily said,
And *Vespers,* when you dwelt next doore * saint *Chad,*
And home-devotion when the closet-doore
Was shut, did me this augurie afford,
That when such blustring storms as these should start,
They should not break the calmnesse of your heart.
With joy I recollect and think upon
Your reverent Church-like devotion;
Who by your fair example did excite
Church-men and clerks to do their duty right,

*The Ca-
thedrall
Church in
Lichfield.*

And

And by frequenting that most sacred quire,
Taught many how to heav'n they should aspire.
For our Cathedralls to a beamlesse eye
Are quires of angels in epitomie,
Mangre the blatant beast, who cries them down
As savouring of superstition.
Misguided people! But for your sweet self,
Madame, you never dash'd against that shelf
Of stubbornnesse against the Church; but you
(Pauls virgin and saint Peters matrone too)
Though I confesse you did most rarely * paint,
Yet were no hypocrite, but a true saint:
Nature hath given you beauty of the skin,
And grace hath made you beautifull within,
* Like a Kings daughter; Nature, Grace and Name,
Concurring all to raise your vertuous fame:
  Which may you long enjoy below, till Jove
  Call you to your bless'd Pedegree above.

My verse and tears would gladly sympathize,
And be both without number; but my eyes
Are the best Poet, for they shed great store
Of elegies, when I have not one verse more.

J. H.

An excellent
Limner.

*Psal. 45.
14.

To his vertuous sister.

T Ears, whither do you make such haste,
  And keep on your way so fast ?
Whither throng those waters forth,
Fairest image of his worth?
In staying them, your love make shown;
He has too many of his own.

H 2   *Alas!*

Alas! you can have no good plea
For adding waters to the sea.

Ours is that grief, those tears we ow:
To us he's dead, he lives in you;
All his vertues in your breast
Have regain'd their place and rest;
And to these, his true counterfeit,
You adde life, and make't complete.
Who sees, would say you are no other,
But your sex-transformed brother.

In you he lives, yet lives withall
Where you must once expect a call:
When y' have enricht our earth a while
Heav'n will have you, and beguile
The world, your ever-losing mother;
And we once more shall misse your brother.
Deigne yet a while to stay with us,
Before that universall losse.

C. B.

BUt must we say he's drown'd? May't not be said,
That as the gold, which cannot be betray'd
To fires corruption, Chymists cast i'th' fire,
Not there to be demolisht, but retire
A more refined metall, and more pure;
Or as the Ocean often doth endure
   The absence of his Nymphs, when they enwombe
   Their streams into the earth, but after come
   With a more copious current to their home:

May't not be said, the sea shall thus restore
Our treasure greater, purer then before,

Repolisht

Repolisht with a soul whose surer eyes
May both descry it self, and mysteries
Such as the Gods and Nature will'd to keep
Hid in the lowest region of the deep?
  Yes, with a soul refin'd he must revive;
  But what's our vantage, if ensphear'd be live,
  Where none but starres can their applauses give?

Weep then, ye sonnes of Phebus, ye that know
The burden of this losse, let your tears flow;
Let not one briny drop shroud in your head:
Water enclos'd with banks may swell and spread
Into a Lethe, and more treacherously
Drown all that's left of him, his memory.
  Weep forth your tears then, poure out all your tide?
  All waters are pernicious since King dy'd.

                              R. Brown.

---

*T*Hen quit thine own, thou western *Moore,*
  And haste thee to the northern shore;
I'th' Irish sea one jewel lies,
Which thy whole cabinet outvies.
Poets, then leave your wonted strain;
For now you may no longer feigne
Apollo, when he goes to bed,
O'th' western billows layes his head:
I'th' Irish sea, there set our Sun;
And since he's set, the day's undone.
Perpetuall night, sad, black, and grim,
Puts on her mourning-weeds for him.
What man hath sense, or dare avouch
H' ath reason, and yet hath no touch?

                  H 3   *Reason*

Reason not limits them that weep,
But bids them lanch into the deep;
Tells us they not exceed, that drain
In tears the mighty Ocean;
Nor all that in these tears are found
As in a generall deluge drown'd.

T. Norton.

Lycidas.

YEt once more, O ye laurels, and once more,
Ye myrtles brown, with ivy never-sere,
I come to pluck your berries harsh and crude,
And with forc'd fingers rude
Shatter your leaves before the mellowing yeare.
Bitter constraint, and sad occasion deare
Compells me to disturb your season due:
For Lycidas is dead, dead ere his prime,
(Young Lycidas!) and hath not left his peere.
Who would not sing for Lycidas? he knew
Himself to sing, and build the lofty rhyme.
He must not flote upon his watry biere
Unwept, and welter to the parching wind
Without the meed of some melodious tear.
   Begin then, Sisters of the sacred well
That from beneath the seat of Jove doth spring;
Begin, and somewhat loudly sweep the string:
Hence with deniall vain, and coy excuse.
So may some gentle Muse
With lucky words favour my destin'd urn,
And as he passes, turn
And bid fair peace be to my sable shroud.

For

For we were nurst upon the self-same hill,
Fed the same flock, by fountain, shade, and rill;
Together both, ere the high lawns appear'd
Under the glimmering eye-lids of the morn,
We drove a-field, and both together heard
What time the gray-fly winds her sultry horn,
Batt'ning our flocks with the fresh dews of night,
Oft till the ev'n-starre bright
Toward heav'ns descent had slop'd his burnisht wheel.
Mean while the rurall ditties were not mute
Temper'd to th' oaten flute:
Rough Satyres danc'd, and Fauns with cloven heel
From the glad sound would not be absent long,
And old Dametas lov'd to heare our song.
　　But oh the heavy change, now thou art gone,
Now thou art gone, and never must return!
Thee shepherds, thee the woods, and desert caves
With wild thyme and the gadding vine oregrown,
And all their echoes mourn.
The willows and the hasil-copses green
Shall now no more be seen
Fanning their joyous leaves to thy soft layes.
As killing as the canker to the rose,
Or taint-worm to the weanling herds that graze,
Or frost to flowers that their gay wardrobe wear,
When first the white-thorn blowes;
Such, Lycidas, thy losse to shepherds eare.
Where were ye Nimphs, when the remorselesse deep
Clos'd ore the head of your lord Lycidas?
For neither were ye playing on the steep,
Where the old Bards the famous Druids lie,
Nor on the shaggie top of Mona high,
Nor yet where Deva spreads her wisard stream:
Ah me, I fondly dream!
Had ye been there——for what could that have done?
What could the Muse her self that Orpheus bore,

The *Muse* her self, for her inchanting sonne?
Whom universall nature did lament,
When by the rout that made the hideous rore
His goary visage down the stream was sent,
Down the swift *Hebrus* to the *Lesbian* shore.
Alas! what boots it with uncessant care
To tend the homely slighted shepherds trade,
And stridly meditate the thanklesse *Muse*?
Were it not better done as others do,
To sport with *Amaryllis* in the shade,
Hid in the tangles of *Neera's* hair?
Fame is the spurre that the clear spirit doth raise,
(That last infirmitie of noble mind)
To scorn delights, and live laborious dayes;
But the fair guerdon where we hope to find,
And think to burst out into sudden blaze,
Comes the blind *Furie* with th' abhorred shears,
And slits the thin-spun life; But not the praise,
Phebus repli'd, and touch'd my trembling eares.
Fame is no plant that growes on mortall soil,
Nor in the glistring foil
Set off to th' world, nor in broad rumour lies;
But lives, and spreads aloft by those pure eyes
And perfect witnesse of all-judging *Jove*:
As he pronounces lastly on each deed,
Of so much fame in heav'n expect thy meed.
Oh fountain *Arethuse*, and thou honour'd floud,
Smooth-sliding *Mincius*, crown'd with vocall reeds;
That strain I heard was of a higher mood.
But now my oat proceeds,
And listens to the herald of the sea
That came in *Neptunes* plea.
He ask'd the waves, and ask'd the felon winds,
What hard mishap hath doom'd this gentle swain?
And question'd every gust of rugged wings,
That blowes from off each beaked *Promontorie*:

                                        They

They knew not of his storie;
And sage Hippotades their answer brings,
That not a blast was from his dungeon stray'd;
The aire was calm, and on the level brine
Sleek Panope with all her sisters play'd:
It was that fatall and perfidious bark,
Built in th' eclipse, and rigg'd with curses dark,
That sunk so low that sacred head of thine.
Next Chamus (reverend sire) went footing slow,
His mantle hairie, and his bonnet sedge,
Inwrought with figures dim, and on the edge
Like to that sanguine flower inscrib'd with wo;
Ah! who hath reft (quoth he) my dearest pledge?
Last came, and last did go,
The Pilot of the Galilean lake,
Two massie keyes he bore of metalls twain,
(The golden opes, the iron shuts amain)
He shook his mitred locks, and stern bespake,
How well could I have spar'd for thee, young swain,
Enough of such as for their bellies sake
Creep and intrude and climbe into the fold?
Of other care they little reckoning make,
Then how to scramble at the shearers feast,
And shove away the worthy bidden guest.
Blind mouthes! that scarce themselves know how to hold
A sheephook, or have learn'd ought else the least
That to the faithfull herdmans art belongs!
What recks it them? what need they? they are sped;
And when they list their lean and flashie songs
Grate on their scrannel pipes of wretched straw,
The hungry sheep look up, and are not fed,
But swoln with wind, and the rank mist they draw,
Rot inwardly, and foul contagion spread:
Besides what the grimme wolf with privy paw
Daily devoures apace, and little said.
But that two-handed engine at the doore,

I   Stands

Stands ready to smite once, and smites no more.
    Return, Alpheus, the dread voice is past
That shrunk thy streams; return, Sicilian Muse,
And call the vales, and bid them hither cast
Their bells, and flowrets of a thousand hues.
Ye valleys low, where the mild whispers use
Of shades and wanton winds and gushing brooks,
On whose fresh lap the swart starre sparely looks,
Throw hither all your quaint enammell'd eyes,
That on the green turf suck the honied showres,
And purple all the ground with vernall flowers.
Bring the rathe primerose that forsaken dies,
The tufted crow-toe, and pale gessamine,
The white pink, and the pansie freakt with jeat,
The glowing violet,
The musk-rose, and the well-attir'd wood-bine,
With cowslips wan that hang the pensive head,
And every flower that sad embroidery wears :
Bid Amaranthus all his beauty shed,
And daffadillies fill their cups with tears,
To strew the laureat herse where Lycid lies.
For so to interpose a little ease,
Let our frail thoughts dally with false surmise;
Ay me ! whil'st thee the shores and sounding seas
Wash farre away, where ere thy bones are hurl'd,
Whether beyond the stormy Hebrides,
Where thou perhaps under the humming tide
Visit'st the bottom of the monstrous world;
Or whether thou to our moist vowes deni'd,
Sleep'st by the fable of Bellerus old,
Where the great vision of the guarded mount
Looks toward Namancos and Bayona's hold;
Look homeward Angel now, and melt with ruth,
And, O ye dolphins, waft the haplesse youth.   -
    Weep no more, wofull shepherds, weep no more;
For Lycidas your sorrow is not dead,

Sunk

Sunk though he be beneath the watry floore:
So sinks the day-starre in the Ocean bed,
And yet anon repairs his drooping head,
And tricks his beams, and with new spangled ore
Flames in the forehead of the morning skie:
So Lycidas sunk low, but mounted high
Through the dear might of him that walk'd the waves;
Where other groves, and other streams along,
With Nectar pure his oazie locks he laves,
And heares the unexpressive nuptiall song;
There entertain him all the Saints above
In solemn troups and sweet societies,
That sing, and singing in their glory move,
And wipe the tears for ever from his eyes.
Now, Lycidas, the shepherds weep no more;
Henceforth thou art the Genius of the shore
In thy large recompense, and shalt be good
To all that wander in that perillous floud.

Thus sang the uncouth swain to th' oaks and rills,
While the still morn went out with sandals gray;
He touch'd the tender stops of various quills,
With eager thought warbling his Dorick lay:
And now the sunne had stretch'd out all the hills,
And now was dropt into the western bay;
At last he rose, and twitch'd his mantle blew,
To morrow to fresh woods and pastures new.

J. M.

Index

Index

Bible, xiii, xvi–xvii, xvii–xviii, 18, 98, 99, 119, 122–23, 126, 128, 139, 154, 156, 159, 162–63, 166, 208, 209–11, 240; aesthetics of, 219, 221; as epic, 12, 266; as a garden, 28; history in, 229; imagination in, 29; as a literary model, xvi, xx, 6, 8, 241; as mixed form, 12, 224, 241; mythology in, 209; prophetic spirit in, 223; reason in, 28–29; Renaissance commentators on, 12; structures of, 160, 210; views of, 99
—examples of: Geneva Bible, 138, 139, 209, 223, 258; Kitto Bible, 23, 56, 71; September Bible, 58; *Souldiers Pocket Bible, The,* 200
—individual books of: Acts, 99–100; Baruch, 103–04; Corinthians, 155; Daniel, 14, 18, 215, 224, 239; Deuteronomy, 194; Ecclesiasticus, 103, 250, 253; Ephesians, 68, 70, 155; Ezekiel, 14, 134; Genesis, xiii, 156, 157, 179, 206, 208; Hebrews, 15, 99, 100–01, 138–39, 140–41, 150, 156, 241; Hosea, 197; Isaiah, 14, 134, 138, 145, 155, 223, 224; Jeremiah, 99–100, 134, 141, 149; Job, xiii, 224, 241; John, 103–04, 204, 210, 250, 253; Judges, 195; Lamentations, 252; Luke, 247, 253; Mark, 132; Psalms, 7, 107, 153, 271; Thessalonians, 253; Timothy, 103–04, 250, 253
—parts of: Epistles, 3; Gospels, 3, 26, 102, 141, 156, 201, 204–05, 206, 210, 270; New Testament, xviii, 14, 18, 20, 102, 119, 128, 191, 197, 209, 210, 223, 224, 243, 247, 251; Old Testament, xviii, 6, 7, 14, 18, 20, 31, 88, 102, 119, 128, 132, 191, 197, 210, 215, 223, 224, 242, 247, 251; Pentateuch, 12, 241
—Revelation, xiii, 3–78, 89, 94, 104, 128, 136–53, 155, 179, 206, 209, 210, 239, 241, 266, 267; aesthetics of, 4, 7, 9, 14, 18, 24, 28, 38, 39, 44, 73, 75, 155, 166–67, 238; allegory in, 26, 46, 60, 235; allusion in, 88; as analogical universe, 18, 31, 159; angels in, 47, 48, 50, 62, 123, 124, 136, 138, 207, 214, 229, 238, 268, 275; attitudes toward, 3–9, 58, 75, 215–16, 220, 225–26; beast in, 274–75; books in, 186, 229; bottomless pit in, 50, 62; bride in, 275; chaos in, 44; Christ in, 7, 20, 21, 27, 28, 35, 46, 147, 151, 163, 189, 209, 229, 237, 239, 276; church in, 15, 28, 41, 135, 159, 162–63, 164, 179; and church liturgy, 251; clarity of, 32–33; as comedy, 37, 193; as commentary, 64; commentary on, 6–7, 8, 10, 15, 21–22, 36, 37–38, 40, 46, 59, 60, 61, 65, 66, 68–69, 71, 74–75, 147, 151–52, 192, 209, 219, 227, 230, 235, 243, 277; composition of, 39, 88, 224, 231; continuity in, 41, 231, 232, 241; and Daniel, 31, 88, 224, 228; Death in, 139; design of, 6, 7, 16, 23, 41, 43, 47, 153, 159, 162, 239; as drama, 34, 37, 38, 40–41, 46, 47, 55, 61, 224, 232, 233; drowning in, 135; eating the book in, 31; as epic, 14–16, 18, 216, 241; as epic-prophecy, 15, 57; epilogue to, 37; epistolary form of, 41; as an epitome, 15, 231; exercise in, 229; and Genesis, 156–57; genres of, 4, 7, 9, 18, 216; God in, 27, 66, 163; Gog and Magog in, 276; good and evil in, 46–51; and Hebrews, 141; heroes of, 50, 62, 239; hieroglyphs in, 22, 24; and history, 18, 46, 60, 235; hymns in, 41; ideology of, 4, 7, 14, 48–54, 57,

—characters in: Alma, 239; Arthur,
29–30, 35, 60, 62, 64, 228–29,
237–38; Calidore, 61; Duessa,
29–30, 61, 65; Error, 65; Fidelia,
64; Gloriana, 74, 239; Guyon,
61, 65, 71, 229, 240; Merlin, 35;
Ministering Angels, 65; Orgoglio,
62; Palmer, 65; Redcrosse, 35,
60, 61, 62, 64, 65, 68, 74, 229,
237–38, 240; Sansfoy, 65; Sans-
joy, 61; Una, 29–30, 62–63, 239
Fairbairn, Patrick, 88
Fairy tale. *See* Genres
Farmer, Hugh, 270
Farmer, Norman F., 222
Farrer, Austin, 3, 53, 153, 215, 241,
262
Fatal bark. *See* Symbolism
Ferry, Anne Davidson, 182
Field, Walter Taylor, 80
Finney, Gretchen, 246, 262
Fisch, Harold, 246
Fish, Stanley, xx, xxi, 31, 35, 106–
07, 228, 229, 230, 232, 234
Fixler, Michael, xiii, 8, 104, 157,
218, 220, 246, 251, 266
Fletcher, Angus, xx, xxi, 54–55, 95,
121, 216, 218, 221, 231, 236
Flowers. *See* Symbolism
Forbes, Patrick, 243
Ford, J. Massynberde, 248
Forms: of acceptance and rejection,
126; biblical, xix; classical, xviii–
xix, 7; composite, 9, 10; and
content, 77; internal and external,
44, 232, 245; mechanical and
living, 43; perfect, 9, 12, 14, 19;
philosophy of, 245; total, 78,
221; transcendental, 9, 221. *See
also* Genres
Fowler, Alastair, xx, xxi, 90
Frye, Northrop, xiii, xxi, 72–73, 87,
186, 195, 210, 226, 241, 257,
266, 267
Frye, Roland Mushat, 226
Fugue, 154

Fulke, William, 37, 182, 230
Fuseli, Henry, 4, 221

Garland. *See* Symbolism
Garments. *See* Symbolism
Genera Mista. See Genres and titles
of individual works
Genres, xv, xvii, 5, 10, 11, 44–45,
47, 76, 77, 89–90, 104, 121–
22, 126, 142, 157–58, 213, 224,
236; hierarchy of, 76, 79; mixed,
9, 10, 12, 18, 30, 37, 75, 122,
221–22, 225, 255. *See also*
Countergenres
—comedy, 10, 11, 18, 79, 115,
121, 122, 126, 193–94
—elegy, 96, 115, 120, 121, 122,
126, 141, 142, 155, 248, 249, 260
—epic, 7, 11–12, 14–15, 18, 51,
73–76, 77, 79, 83, 118, 121,
126, 138, 143–44, 187, 193, 206,
213, 221, 222, 224, 233, 242,
244; brief, 187, 212; classical and
Christian, 12, 14, 69, 223, 244;
consciousness in, 25–26; con-
servatism of, 26, 53, 235–36; and
history, 34, 51–52; ideology of,
50–51, 57; miniature, 241; as
mixed form, 9, 10; and prophecy,
9, 14, 15, 18, 26, 34–35, 42, 50–
51, 53, 57, 60, 76, 77, 78, 216;
as pseudomorph, 12–14; scope of,
10, 18, 76; theology of, 10;
transcendence in, 76; warfare in,
69–70
—pastoral, 10, 11, 79, 80, 81, 83,
86, 88, 89, 104, 105–06, 111,
112, 114, 115, 117–37, 142, 155,
156, 157–58, 180, 243, 248, 252,
253, 255; aesthetics of, 119;
classical and Christian, 87, 118–
19, 120, 128, 131; as collaborative effort, 89; conventions of,
157–58; elegy, 109–10, 128, 248,
256, 257, 263; history of, 120–
21; as mixed form, 30, 120–21;

modes of, 125, 128; perspectives in, 256; and prophecy, 119, 130–31, 149–50, 156, 157, 252; as pure form, 120; as symbol, 131; theories of, 130
—prophecy, xvii, xviii, 3–78, 79–80, 89, 104, 105, 108, 112, 115, 117–37, 213, 216, 219, 222, 224, 225, 242, 245, 248, 252, 255; aesthetics of, 8, 9, 32, 47, 153, 239, 242; and allegory, 235; allusion in, 30, 32, 38, 79, 88, 248; as analogical universe, 25, 31, 63; and apocalypse, 5, 26, 29, 157; clarity in, 32–33; as commentary, 33; as composite art form, 19–20; composition of, 223; consciousness in, 25–26, 41, 43, 183, 227; contexts for, 32, 248; deception in, 29–30; as drama, 34, 36, 55, 233; emblem of, 183; and the future, 34, 51–52, 142, 157, 163–64, 165–66, 234; and history, 19, 26, 34, 36, 51–52, 73–74, 164, 235; history of, 3, 4, 189, 213, 216–17, 233; as ideal form, 25; ideology of, 26, 36, 47, 48–54, 57, 58, 234; imagery in, 231; and imagination, 29; interconnectedness of, 31, 88, 105, 224, 228; interiority of, 34, 40, 44, 188; kinds of, 18, 19, 215; and knowledge, 27, 30, 31, 32; as mental exercise, 28–29, 30, 32, 35; Milton's idea of, 27; as mixed form, 9, 10, 18, 37, 40, 121–22, 225; and music, 153–54, 217–18; objectives of, 24–25, 26, 27, 31, 33, 34, 36, 48–49, 52, 59, 103, 228; obscurity of, 30, 32, 33, 35, 219, 248; in the Old and New Testaments, 14, 18, 31, 132, 142; and orthodoxy, 28, 43, 49, 75; outlawing of, 106, 108–09; perspectives in, 225, 226–27; pictorialism in, 19, 22,

123, 189, 229; and politics, 19, 48–49, 52, 58; progression in, 32, 33, 66, 163–64, 207–08; providence in, 26, 258; reader in, 28–29, 30, 32, 33–35, 232; reader of, 30, 36, 192, 235; and reason, 28–29; Romantic understanding of, 233; and revolution, 26, 46, 49, 51–52, 53, 58, 75, 78, 132, 235; as self-consuming artifact, 31–32, 33–34; signatures of, 52–53, 55, 186; strategies of, 26–36, 44, 47, 57, 188, 189–90, 228, 231, 239; structures of, 26, 33, 34, 36–47, 63, 88, 232, 239; styles of, 27; surface of, 29–30; synchronism in, 242; as system, 228; thematic content of, 26; transcendence in, 76; and truth, 31, 32; typology in, 163–64; and vision, 33, 235; as warning, 123; writing of, 192. *See also* Bible, Revelation; Poetry; Prophets
—romance, 10, 55, 79, 120, 231–32
—tragedy, 11, 18, 41, 67, 76, 115, 118, 120, 122, 126, 193–94, 204, 206, 210, 213, 233, 250, 255, 268
—other: ballad, 12; canzone, 122, 174–75; fairy tale, 121; hymn, 18; lay, 80, 154, 169; madrigal, 122, 167, 168–69, 183; masque, 79, 121, 128; monody, 110, 154, 169, 249, 262; novel, 121; ode, 121; satire, 120, 121, 122, 126, 255; sonnet, 175

Gifford, George, 59, 145, 147, 230, 240, 243
God, 59, 91, 94, 102, 191, 209, 211; as creator, 9, 11–12, 18–19, 63, 137, 180–81, 225, 227; justice of, 137–38, 200, 205; mercy of, 102, 103, 104, 137–38, 200; wrath of, 99–100, 102, 104, 137–38, 200, 205
Goethe, Johann Wolfgang von, 99